Acclaim for Charles A. Kupchan's

The End of the American Era

"With his expansive knowledge of history, Kupchan places contemporary trends in perspective. . . . Offers revealing insights into contemporary policy matters with a spectacular eye for detail."
—*The Christian Science Monitor*

"Elegantly explores the benefits and dangers of U.S. primacy and the system of globalization that has come with it. His call for a rethinking of America's role in the world could not be more timely. . . . Well worth reading."
—George Soros

"An important and provocative reassessment of American power and foreign policy."
—Lee H. Hamilton, Director,
Woodrow Wilson International Center

"This original and informative work challenges our conventional wisdom and offers useful strategic guidance. Agree with it or not, Kupchan will make you think and reexamine your assumptions as you enjoy the clarity of his writing and thought."
—Anthony Lake,
National Security Adviser
in the first Clinton administration

"Provocatively embedding his argument in examinations of historical power shifts . . . Kupchan argues that American preeminence is dangerous to sustain, because it is in fact unsustainable."
—*Booklist*

"Compelling analysis, rich in the lessons of history, that will shatter the illusions of a perpetual Pax Americana. . . . As controversial as it is insightful."
—Ronald Steel, author of
Walter Lippmann and the American Century

"An ambitious enterprise. . . . Kupchan should be congratulated for bravely tackling broad issues in an age of specialization."
—*The Times Literary Supplement*

CHARLES A. KUPCHAN
The End of the American Era

Charles A. Kupchan is professor of international relations at Georgetown University and senior fellow at the Council on Foreign Relations. He served on the National Security Council during the first Clinton administration. He lives in Washington, D.C.

The End of the American Era

U.S. Foreign Policy and the Geopolitics
of the Twenty-first Century

CHARLES A. KUPCHAN

VINTAGE BOOKS

A DIVISION OF RANDOM HOUSE, INC.

NEW YORK

To my family

FIRST VINTAGE BOOKS EDITION, NOVEMBER 2003

Copyright © 2002 by Charles A. Kupchan

The Library of Congress has cataloged the Knopf edition as follows:
Kupchan, Charles.
The end of the American era : U.S. foreign policy and the geopolitics
of the twenty-first century / Charles A. Kupchan.—1st ed.
p. cm.
Includes bibliographical references and index.
ISBN 0-375-41215-8 (alk. paper)
1. United States—Foreign relations. 2. United States—
Foreign relations—1989– I. Title.
JZ1480 .K87 2002
327.73—dc21
2002018443

Vintage ISBN: 0-375-72659-4

Author photograph © Kaveh Sardari
Book design by Robert C. Olsson

www.vintagebooks.com

Contents

Contents

Acknowledgments

I am indebted to numerous institutions and individuals for the contributions they made to this book. Georgetown University and the Council on Foreign Relations have been my dual intellectual homes for the better part of a decade. Together they offered an ideal environment in which to write a book that attempts to bridge the growing divide between the academic and policy communities. The Council on Foreign Relations provided the primary financial support for this project, appointing me as the Whitney H. Shepardson Fellow for 2000–2002. Georgetown contributed additional funding and granted me a sabbatical leave to carry out the research and writing. I would also like to acknowledge the financial support of the United States Institute of Peace.

Two individuals played a special role in encouraging me to undertake this book—James Chace and Leslie Gelb. I first met James Chace in the late 1980s. Over the course of the following decade, as we became fast friends and intellectual kin, he steered me toward this project and then was a trusted guide from start to finish. For his good cheer, tireless spirit, and steady advice, I am deeply grateful.

Les Gelb, the president of the Council on Foreign Relations, began prodding me along well before I had even conceived of this book. During long walks in Central Park, he repeatedly exhorted me to think bigger and push harder, insisting, between puffs on his cigar, that it was time for the "great foreign-policy novel" of the day. Whether or not I have succeeded in meeting his expectations, his friendship and insight are much appreciated.

When this book was in draft form, I presented it in a series of seminars at the Council on Foreign Relations in both New York and Washington, D.C. James Chace did an excellent job of chairing the seminars in New York. I am indebted to Stephen Walt for chairing the Washington meetings and steering the discussion in just the right direction. The participants in these seminars were Robert Art, Warren Bass, Max Boot, Lael Brainard, Ralph Buultjens, Fraser Cameron, Kurt Campbell, Steven Clemons, Jean-Marc Coicaud, Ivo Daalder, Terry Deibel, I. M. Destler, Frances FitzGerald, David Fromkin, Alton Frye, Michael Getler, James Goldgeier, Paul Golob, Stephanie Golob, Rose Gottemoeller, John Ikenberry, Robert Jervis, Lawrence Korb, Steven Kull, James Lindsay, Robert Manning, Jessica Mathews, Charles William Maynes, Michael McFaul, Karl Meyer, Henry Nau, John Newhouse, Suzanne Nossel, Joseph Nye, Jr., Nouriel Roubini, Allison Silver, Jack Snyder, Fritz Stern, Daniel Tarullo, Cynthia Tindell, Richard Ullman, Enzo Viscusi, Joris Vos, Martin Walker, Jacob Weisberg, and Melvin Williams. A meeting of the Council's national program in Dallas, chaired by Rena Pederson, also provided excellent feedback. I am grateful to all the participants in these seminars for their time and effort. It is an author's dream to benefit from such a talented group of critics.

I would also like to thank the following individuals for commenting on the manuscript in draft form: Caroline Atkinson, Dick Barnebey, Jonathan Davidson, Jeff Legro, Joseph Lepgold, John McNeill, David Painter, Nicholas Rizopoulos, Howard Rosen, Don Rosenthal, Debra Singer, and Peter Trubowitz. In addition, I am grateful to my colleagues and students at Georgetown and the Council on Foreign Relations, who were always ready to let me try out new ideas as they were taking shape.

David Stevens, my research assistant at the Council, was a true partner in this enterprise. He constantly fed me fresh material and explored new arguments, anticipating where the unfolding plot was likely to head. When I ran up against a historical or conceptual obstacle, I turned first to David—and more often than not he had a solution. He regularly had the pleasure of arriving at his desk in the morning to find at least a dozen voice messages from me, left the evening before as I sought in vain to trace down a fact or resolve a puzzle. I am grateful to David for his assistance and commitment. He, in turn, seems not to have suffered excessively, as he has now gone off to do a doctorate in international relations. I would also like to thank

Jason Davidson and Mira Sucharov, former graduate students at Georgetown; Shane Smith, my former assistant at the Council; and Jamie Fly, my new assistant at the Council, for help with research.

It was a pleasure to work with Ash Green, my editor at Knopf. From our initial encounter to go over the book proposal to his final edits on the manuscript, his counsel was as gracious as it was wise. The book benefited enormously from his experience and skill. Knopf's Jonathan Fasman, Ellen Feldman, and Luba Ostashevsky did a superb job of smoothly guiding the manuscript through the publication process. I would also like to thank my literary agents, Suzanne Gluck, Kris Dahl, and Liz Farrell.

Final thanks go to my family. My mother, Nancy Kupchan Sonis, my brother, Clifford Kupchan, and my stepfather, Richard Sonis, were there for me throughout, providing unlimited and unconditional support and encouragement—what an author most needs amid writing's more trying moments. My father, S. Morris Kupchan, although no longer with us, was always by my side in spirit.

Charles A. Kupchan
Washington, D.C.
July 2002

Preface to the 2003 Vintage Edition

America's successful war to topple Saddam Hussein appears to have opened a new American century. The United States demonstrated the stunning effectiveness of a military establishment that is second to none. Washington also made clear that it is prepared to act as it sees fit, launching the war against Iraq even though it failed to attain the approval of the UN Security Council. The lessons seem to be clear. The countries that opposed America, such as France, Germany, and Russia, had better think twice before they again cross the world's only superpower. Rogue nations, too, had better change their ways—or prepare for the worst. America under George W. Bush appears to be the new Rome.

There is, however, an alternative view of the long-term consequences of the U.S. war against Iraq, one that puts the future of American primacy in a different light. Far from opening a new American century, Washington has embarked on a course that is precipitating the end of the American era. America's military might may be unsurpassed and its resolve unwavering, but by acting against the court of world opinion, the United States has compromised perhaps its most precious asset—its international legitimacy. In the eyes of the world, America's benign hegemony is no longer so benign. As a result, nations are more likely to resent rather than respect U.S. power and to resist rather than rally behind U.S. leadership.

This second vision is the more accurate one. The diplomatic standoff over the war against Iraq was a symptom, not a cause, of the wider rift that has divided America from much of Europe—indeed, from much of the world. American unilateralism, strengthened by the vulnerability and anger left behind by September 11, has been tearing away at the fabric of the international community. Even before the UN debate over Iraq was under way, many members of the Security Council agreed on the need to restrain a defiant America. Containing U.S. power was one of the main reasons that France, Germany, and Russia sought to block the war, despite their awareness that doing so would put the Atlantic Alliance at risk. Even smaller members of the Security Council—Mexico, Chile, Guinea, and Cameroon among them—were prepared to say no to America. All roads used to lead through Washington. Now a second road is opening up, one that runs primarily through Europe.

The principal cause of the intensifying estrangement between America and its traditional allies is Washington's approach to global leadership. Indeed, the three guiding principles of the Bush administration's foreign policy have put the United States on a collision course with Europe. First, Washington has operated under the assumption that the more powerful America is and the more uncompromising its leadership, the more readily the rest of the world will get in line. But exactly the opposite has transpired. Bush's swagger may come off as determination at home, but in Europe and the rest of the world it smacks of arrogance. Far from evoking deference, America's policy of preemption and preeminence has invited European resentment and resistance.

Second, the Bush administration presumes that a country as strong as the United States does not need international institutions to manage the global landscape; they are tools of the weak and only constrain America's room for maneuver. Bush is right that institutions contain American power, but that is precisely why they are so integral to international stability. By obligating Washington to adhere to common rules, they level the playing field and increase confidence in the purpose and predictability of American power. When Washington walks away from international institutions, Europe and the rest of the world run for cover.

The third assumption that has imperiled America's key international partnerships is Bush's vast overestimation of the autonomy that comes with military supremacy. The administration has been dismissive of allies because it feels it does not need them. But Washington should look again. The war on terrorism requires extensive international cooperation. Afghanistan is being held together by a broad multinational coalition. Although France, Germany, and Russia could not stop the war against Iraq, they ultimately denied Washington the legitimacy of UN backing, making the war an especially risky gamble. Turkey refused to permit U.S. ground forces access to its territory, leaving America unable to open a northern front.

Despite these obstacles, America's military prowess enabled coalition forces to win the Iraq war handily. But the legacy of the conflict is a deeply divided diplomatic landscape, not one in which a dominant America leads and the rest of the world dutifully follows. Europe, in particular, has made clear its discontentment with America's heavy hand. Indeed, the transatlantic link is one of the main casualties of the war, with the United States and its principal continental allies parting company on fundamental questions of war and peace. Now that American and European security are no longer indivisible, the Atlantic Alliance, even if it survives in name, is coming undone in spirit.

To be sure, the war over Iraq proved to be as divisive within Europe as it was across the Atlantic. Europe's internal divide stemmed primarily from contrasting visions of the future of the European Union (EU). One camp was led by France and Germany, which staunchly resisted the war and cast themselves as counterweights to U.S. hegemony. In the other camp were the smaller countries that stood by Washington, viewing the United States as a hedge against Europe's major powers and a continued protective presence in the region. Far from edging toward unity and serving as a counterpoise to America, EU members were unable to find common ground.

The divide across the Atlantic, however, promises to prove far more permanent and intractable than the one that opened up within Europe. On Iraq, there was more unity within the EU than met the eye; European governments might have disagreed, but their electorates were almost uniformly opposed to military action. The EU is also in the midst of reforms that will strengthen its governing institutions, including those responsible for forging a common foreign policy.

Perhaps most importantly, those European countries that sided with Washington may well have no choice but to alter course in the years ahead. Most of them backed the Bush administration because they did not want to let the Iraq conflict scuttle the transatlantic link, not because they sincerely supported the war. But even if countries like Poland and Italy remain committed to the transatlantic alliance for years to come, they are unlikely to find a welcoming partner on the other side of the Atlantic. With Europe wealthy, at peace, and no longer as willing to follow Washington's lead, America is losing interest in remaining its protector. Meanwhile, pressing threats in the Middle East and East Asia are already diverting U.S. resources to those regions. Whether they like it or not, Europeans are increasingly on their own.

France and Germany have realized as much, one of the main reasons they have been taking steps to deepen defense cooperation. Britain has continued to cling to its role as a bridge between America and Europe. But the British will soon realize that they can wield far more influence by becoming a leading member of the EU than by chasing after the American goliath. The Poles have yet to give up hope of a strong Atlantic Alliance, but they can ignore reality for only so long; Warsaw and other like-minded capitals will soon realize that their only option is to settle for a strong EU. As current and prospective EU members face the fact that America is in the midst of decamping from Europe for good, the more readily they will throw their weight behind a more effective and collective union.

The EU's efforts to acquire greater military capacity are admittedly moving slowly. But there are signs of life—France is increasing its defense spending by twenty percent and Germany appears ready to end conscription in favor of a more capable professional force. At a summit in April 2003, France, Germany, Belgium, and Luxembourg announced plans to establish a joint command headquarters. Even under the most optimistic of scenarios, the EU will not challenge America's military primacy anytime soon—if ever. But Europe will become far less reliant on the United States for its security and will take its place alongside America as one of the globe's two main centers of power.

A final source of skepticism toward pronouncements of a new American century stems from the likely consequences of the Iraq war for American foreign policy. The success of the military operation and the speed with which Saddam Hussein's regime crumbled have unquestionably strengthened the hands of the neoconservative hawks within the Bush administration. That U.S. forces suffered relatively few casualties should also help consolidate broader public support for determined U.S. leadership around the globe.

It would be illusory, however, to presume that the political consensus that formed in favor of war against Iraq will be sustainable over the long term—even amid President Bush's closest advisers. They may have closed ranks on the question of war, but deep splits reemerged soon after the fighting was over. Neoconservatives like Deputy Secretary of Defense Paul Wolfowitz envisaged America's foothold in Iraq as a lever for fostering broader political change throughout the Middle East—and accordingly favored a long stay. Conservative pragmatists like Secretary of Defense Donald Rumsfeld held a more circumscribed view of America's objectives in the region and planned on a shorter stay in Iraq—even as he sought to maintain the Pentagon's tight control over postwar reconstruction. Secretary of State Colin Powell favored civilian control of Iraq as well as efforts to mend fences with the United Nations and America's allies. These differences played out in testy confrontations over postwar policy.

Domestic support for America's new ambition also appears uncertain. The U.S. public, although behind the war, is unlikely to remain enthusiastic about a long-term occupation of Iraq; even in the heartland—where George W. Bush's main constituency resides—there is little appetite for maintaining a colonial outpost in the Middle East. It is true that since the Cold War Americans have accepted a broad range of international commitments, with U.S. troops on permanent station in many quarters of the globe. But America's forces have generally stayed only where they are welcome. With anti-American sentiment running strong in Iraq and gaining steam even among traditional allies such as Germany, Japan, and South Korea, U.S. citizens may well begin to wonder whether their country should continue to play the role of global guardian. Americans believe that their troops abroad are bringing good to the world—and will take umbrage if host countries disagree, ultimately fueling calls for U.S. forces to come home. America's isolationist instincts have been quiet since September 11, but they are by no means gone for good.

In the pages that follow, I describe how and why the rise of Europe and the return of unilateralism and isolationism to the United States are combining to divide the West, set Europe and America against each other, and expedite the transition to a world of multiple centers of power. When I wrote the first edition of this book—before the war in Iraq—I expected these developments to take the better part of this decade, if not longer. The Bush administration has not changed the course of history, but it has speeded it up considerably. As the war over Iraq made clear, the West is already divided against itself, shaking the foundations of the political community that have anchored the international system since the 1940s. In this sense, the Iraq war served primarily to accelerate powerful geopolitical forces that were already in the process of changing the world in which we live. With history moving at such a fast clip—and the global landscape changing in step—America, Europe, and the broader international community must confront with a new urgency how to prepare for the end of the American era and the epoch that will follow.

Preface to the 2002 Knopf Edition

On September 11, 2001, terrorists turned hijacked airliners into guided missiles, destroying the twin towers of New York's World Trade Center as well as a sizable section of the Pentagon. The attacks killed thousands and dealt a deft blow to prime symbols of America's economic and military might. The searing images of destruction left Americans with a new, and perhaps inescapable, sense of vulnerability that will permanently affect how the United States interacts with the rest of the world.

The tragic events of September 2001 served as a wake-up call to America. From the end of the Cold War until terror struck the heart of New York and Washington, the United States had been steadily losing interest in foreign affairs. Elected officials and the public alike had tuned out, lulled into complacency by American primacy and the presumed inviolability of the homeland. The media had all but stopped covering foreign news. Congress rarely found time to debate foreign policy, with crucial issues of the day—controlling the proliferation of nuclear weapons, bringing peace to the Balkans, protecting the environment—regularly subjected to partisan infighting rather than sound deliberation. America's allies watched with a mix of consternation and dismay as the world's only superpower appeared to have lost its way.

Not so after September 11. Defending the homeland and combating terrorism became top national priorities. Newspapers were filled with foreign reporting, and many television channels devoted around-the-clock coverage to America's "new war." Democrats and Republicans closed ranks, providing a bipartisan spirit long absent from

Washington. And America reached out to others, apparently forsaking its increasingly unilateralist bent in favor of rejuvenating fraying alliances and striking new partnerships. One commentator after another invoked Pearl Harbor as the appropriate analogy. September 11, 2001, like December 7, 1941, was a historical turning point, driving home to Americans that they live in a perilous world requiring engagement, vigilance, and sacrifice.

It is, however, an illusion to assume that America's new sense of vulnerability has put its foreign policy back on course. On the contrary, by riveting the country's attention and resources on combating terrorism and defending the homeland, the events of September 11 and the bioterrorism that followed make it even less likely that the United States will bring into focus more profound, even if more distant, threats to America's well-being. Bolstering homeland security is certainly a must. Despite numerous warnings, the United States failed to take adequate steps to prevent terrorist attacks against its territory—and it paid a heavy price for the complacency. The Bush administration has justifiably been working hard to find adequate remedy. But this task should not be allowed to stand in the way of efforts to address the central and much more dangerous challenge that lies ahead—the return of rivalry among the world's main centers of power.

America's lack of concern with great-power rivalry is understandable. The opening of the twenty-first century marks the triumph of the democratic ideals upon which the United States was founded and for which it spilled much blood. Some 120 of the almost 200 countries in the world now have democratic governments. Communism, the main rival to liberal democracy during the twentieth century, has been turned back, its adherents struggling to maintain their grip in a few holdouts such as China, North Korea, and Cuba. And the United States itself is in a position of unchallenged dominance. America's military and its national economy are second to none; no other country even comes close. In combination with its seemingly unlimited capacity for technological innovation and its cultural appeal, these assets provide the United States an unprecedented level of global primacy.

As they survey this landscape, most of America's strategists remain convinced not only that U.S. primacy is here to stay, but also that a lasting era of great-power peace has finally arrived. The ongoing spread of liberal democracy and capitalism are leading to the "end of history," the obsolescence of major war, and a world in which satisfied nations will learn to live happily alongside each other. Disaffected individuals and the fringe groups to which they gravitate may well continue efforts to do harm to America and its partners. But assuming that the world's democracies can contain, if not eliminate, terrorism, they will be headed for a peaceful and prosperous future.

Such confidence about the longevity of the American era is not only misplaced, but also dangerous. America appears to be committing the same error as most other great nations that have come before it—mistaking for a more permanent peace the temporary quiescence that usually follows resolution of a major geopolitical divide. The decade that followed the Cold War's end was admittedly one of bounty and peace for America. The world's major players have been at rest, contemplating their next moves. And the current dominance of the United States is no illusion; by any measure, America is in a class by itself.

But the international system is fickle and fragile, and can come apart with remarkable speed. In 1910, Europeans were confident of the peace-causing benefits of economic interdependence and the irrationality of armed conflict. By the late summer of 1914, Europe's great powers were at war. The United States enjoyed prosperity and optimism during the second half of the 1920s. By 1933, the world was well into a painful depression, Hitler was in control of Germany, and the century was fast headed toward its darkest moments. In early 1945, the United States was busy building a postwar partnership with the Soviet Union, U.S. forces were rapidly demobilizing, and the American people were looking to the United Nations to preserve world peace. Within a few short years, the Cold War was under way and the United States and Soviet Union were threatening each other with nuclear annihilation.

The reemergence of rivalry and conflict among the world's major states is by no means foreordained. But there is no better way to ensure its return than for America to set its sights on terrorism and presume that great-power peace is here to stay. Instead, America should realize that its preponderance and the stability it breeds are already beginning to slip away. Europe is in the midst of a revolutionary process of political and economic integration that is gradually eliminating the importance of its internal borders and centralizing authority in Brussels. The European Union's collective wealth will soon rival that of the United States. Russia will ultimately rebound and may well take its place in an integrating Europe. Asia is not far behind. China is already a regional presence and its economy is growing apace. And Japan, the world's second-largest economy, will eventually climb out of recession and gradually expand its political and military influence.

At the same time that challengers to its dominance are on the rise, the United States is fast losing interest in playing the role of global protector of last resort. The U.S. did pursue a remarkably activist foreign policy during the 1990s; America was busy stopping ethnic slaughter in the Balkans, hemming in Saddam Hussein, keeping the peace in East Asia, working hard to resolve festering conflicts in the Middle East and Northern Ireland, all the while managing a globalized international economy. But American internationalism was at a high-water mark during the last decade and is already on the wane.

During his first few months in office, President George W. Bush made amply clear that he intended to rein in the country's commitments and focus on matters closer to home. It was no accident that his first foreign trip was to visit President Vicente Fox of Mexico and that Bush held his first state dinner in honor of Fox. Bush also revealed his unilateralist proclivities, early on announcing his intention to back away from many of the institutions and pacts that America itself had helped establish to preserve international order. Moreover, the internationalism of the 1990s was sustained by a remarkably strong and durable economic expansion. An economy suffering through leaner times means a foreign policy that loses its outward-looking activism.

For many, the events of September 2001 arrested this trend, convincing the Bush administration and the American public of the need for global engagement. As Andrew Sullivan, the former editor of *The New Republic*, wrote only a few days after the attack, "We have been put on notice that every major Western city is now vulnerable." "For the United States itself," Sullivan continued, "this means one central thing. Isolationism is dead."[1] Others were confident that the threat of terrorism would reawaken not just U.S. internationalism, but a liberal brand—one committed to multilateral action and reliance on international institutions. Terrorism poses a collective threat and thus should elicit a collective response.

It is by no means clear, however, that terrorism inoculates the United States against the allure of either isolationism or unilateralism. In the long run, America's leaders may well find the country's security better served by reducing its overseas commitments and raising protective barriers than by chasing terrorists through the mountains of Afghanistan. The United States has a strong tradition dating back to the founding fathers of seeking to cordon itself off from foreign troubles, an impulse that could well be reawakened by the rising costs of global engagement. America's initial response to the attacks of September 11, after all, was to close its borders with Mexico and Canada, ground the nation's air traffic, and patrol the country's coasts with warships and jet fighters. Americans also have a long-standing aversion to multilateral institutions, stemming from an unwillingness to compromise the freedom of unilateral initiative. Accordingly, when the United States does act, it may well lash out on its own, alienating the partners that it will need to help tame an increasingly divided global system. The liberal internationalism that has sustained America's global leadership since World War II is under siege from both isolationist and unilateralist extremes.

The American era is alive and well, but the rise of alternative centers of power and a declining and unilateralist U.S. internationalism will ensure that it comes undone as this new century progresses— with profound geopolitical consequences. The stability and order that devolve from American preponderance will gradually be replaced by renewed competition for primacy. The unstoppable locomotive of globalization will run off its tracks as soon as Washington is no longer at the controls. Pax Americana is poised to give way to a much more unpredictable and dangerous global environment. And the chief threat will come not from the likes of Osama bin Laden, but from the return of traditional geopolitical rivalry.

As a matter of urgency, America needs to begin to prepare itself and the rest of the world for this uncertain future. To wait until American dominance is already gone would be to squander the enormous opportunity that comes with primacy. America must devise a grand strategy for the transition to a world of multiple power centers now, while it still has the luxury of doing so. This is the central challenge of *The End of the American Era*.

Although this book is primarily about where America and the global system erected under its watch are headed, much of it focuses on the past. I develop each of the book's main arguments by first exploring those historical periods that can best shed light on the nature of our contemporary predicament. This reliance on the past may seem odd for a book that is about the future. But the indeterminacy of the current moment provides no other option. Unless put in historical context, the present offers only a snapshot of a world in the midst of profound transition. Unless anchored in the past, analysis of the present is likely to be of only fleeting relevance and risks overlooking the potent sources of change that run beneath the surface and become apparent only in historical relief.

Using the past as a guide to the future admittedly entails its own analytic dangers. The spread of democracy has unquestionably altered the character of life both within and among nations. Digital technology and its impact on everything from weaponry to communications to commerce surely make it hard to compare the travails of the Roman Empire during the fourth century with the challenges facing America today. The aim is therefore to sift and weigh, to use the past selectively, and to be on the watch for historical lessons that might mislead rather than illuminate. Furthermore, there are certain lasting truths about world affairs that endure because they are rooted in the human condition. It is these truths that provide a sober warning of the need to be on guard against the return of great-power rivalry and the bloodshed that accompanies it. But it is also these truths that provide cause for optimism about our ability to learn from history and avoid repeating the costly mistakes that have come before.

The central challenge of the future, I contend, will be the same as in the past—managing relations among contending centers of power. This claim runs counter to prevailing wisdom, which identifies terrorism, overpopulation and disease in the developing world, ethnic conflict, international crime, and environmental degradation as the purported security challenges of the twenty-first century. By focusing on a more traditional threat, I by no means intend to dismiss or trivialize this new security agenda. On the contrary, I devote significant attention to terrorism, collapsing states, and poverty in the pages that follow. However, these concerns may well pale in comparison to the dangers that will reemerge if America embraces the illusion that its primacy is here to stay and that more traditional geopolitical challenges are gone for good.

This book is thus meant to be a corrective to a national debate that has gone seriously off course. The costs will be high should the United States fail to adjust its foreign policy to a changing international system. The benefits of getting it right are equally substantial. Only if America and the rest of the world start imagining life after Pax Americana now will they have the time and foresight to manage peacefully the turbulent years that lie ahead. Perhaps then the United States can bequeath the best of the American era to the world that comes next.

The End of the American Era

CHAPTER ONE

Grand Strategy and the Paradox of American Power

G REAT POWERS are the main actors in international life. They extend their influence well beyond their borders, seeking to craft a global environment conducive to their interests. To do so effectively, great powers need a conceptual map of the world and a grand strategy that follows from it aimed at keeping the international ends they pursue in balance with the means available to attain those ends. It is by maintaining this equilibrium between commitments and resources that they are able to protect their security while also pursuing the ambition that comes with wealth and military might.

Preponderant power alone can do a nation much more harm than good. When unchecked, primacy often invites enemies and provokes the formation of hostile, countervailing coalitions. When wielded with prudence, however, dominance handsomely rewards the nation that possesses it, securing not only its well-being, but extending through the international system a stable order crafted in its image. The Roman Empire, Pax Britannica, Pax Americana—it was not just the strength of Rome, Great Britain, and the United States that gave rise to these epochs, but also the innovative and farsighted grand strategies that each devised to manage and preserve its primacy.

A look at how Britain dealt with the rise of Germany during the early twentieth century makes amply clear how important an appropriate grand strategy is to the well-being of a great power and to the overall stability of the international system. Despite having focused for centuries on its distant imperial possessions, British elites responded with alacrity to Germany's decision in 1898 to build a major battle fleet. Sensing that growing German ambition was about to overturn the European balance of power, London recalled the Royal Navy from imperial posts and prepared the British army for continental warfare. These moves set the stage for the successful efforts of Britain, France, and Russia to block the German advance in 1914 and ultimately defeat Berlin's bid for European dominance. In short, Britain got it right. During the 1930s, Britain took the opposite course. Germany again embarked on an ambitious military buildup and made another bid for European primacy. This time, however, the British failed to prepare for war against Germany, instead choosing to appease Hitler and focus on the defense of colonial possessions. Britain, and Europe along with it, suffered grievously for letting its grand strategy go so woefully awry.

THE PAST

THE MALTA SQUADRON, Winston Churchill insisted on June 22, 1912, "certainly will not operate in the Mediterranean till a decisive and victorious general action has been fought in the North Sea." "Then, and not till then," Churchill continued, "can it go to the Mediterranean."[1] With this decision, Churchill was completing the recall of the Royal Navy from its sprawling network of overseas stations. London did cushion the impact of this momentous strategic shift by striking a deal with Paris whereby the French fleet patrolled the Mediterranean in return for the Royal Navy's protection of France's Atlantic coast. Nonetheless, the consequences of withdrawal from the Mediterranean were potentially devastating; Britain was effectively abandoning the vital link between the home islands and the eastern empire. By the summer of 1912, however, Churchill saw no choice. The unmistakable menace from a Germany that was arming and declaring its right to "a place in the sun" was denying Britain the luxury of focusing on its overseas possessions.

Churchill, who had risen to the position of first lord of the admiralty only the previous year, stated his case with such vehemence precisely because he knew he faced committed opponents. After all, by arguing that the Royal Navy should be withdrawn from its imperial outposts and concentrated in home waters, Churchill was striking at the heart of the grand strategy that had brought Britain to the pinnacle of global power. It was by developing a lucrative seaborne empire while avoiding entanglement on the European continent—a strategy affectionately dubbed "splendid isolation"—that the British had attained a position of primacy.

By Churchill's time, Britain had established impeccable credentials as a seafaring nation. As early as 1511, Henry VIII's advisers were urging him to turn to seapower to promote England's wealth and security. "Let us in God's name leave off our attempts against the *terra firma,*" the king's councilors recommended. "The natural situation of islands seems not to consort with conquests of that kind. England alone is a just Empire. Or, when we would enlarge ourselves, let it be that way we can, and to which it seems the eternal Providence hath destined us, which is by the sea."[2]

Queen Elizabeth I refined this emerging naval strategy during the second half of the sixteenth century. She agreed that England's calling was at sea, but she insisted that the country also had to keep an eye on the Continent to ensure that no single power came to dominate the European landmass. A European behemoth, Elizabeth argued, would ultimately endanger England. Even as the country developed as a sea power, it therefore had to intervene on the Continent as necessary to preserve a stable balance of power on land. It was by following this simple yet elegant strategy that Great Britain found itself by the nineteenth century with complete mastery of the seas, continental neighbors that checked each other's ambitions, and unprecedented global influence.

Encouraged by the success of splendid isolation, most Britons had become ardent champions of empire and naval mastery. It is no wonder, then, that the Admiralty met staunch opposition when it began in 1904–1905 to recall the Royal Navy to home waters at the expense of fleet strength at overseas stations. The Foreign Office and the Colonial Office were particularly vehement in arguing against this redistribution. The Foreign Office complained to the Admiralty that "the navy will be unable to give the foreign policy of this country such support in the future as the Foreign Office have felt entitled to expect, and have received in the past.... The exigencies of British world-wide policy and interests, in the present and immediate future, are being sacrificed."[3] India, Singapore, Australia, Egypt, and Britain's other possessions in the Middle East might end up dangerously exposed. Britain would suffer an incalculable blow to its economy and prestige should the empire be dismantled.

The Admiralty was not about to be swayed. During the first decade of the twentieth century, a quiet revolution in the European balance of power was taking place. And as Queen Elizabeth had wisely admonished, England had to watch the balance of power on the Continent even as it constructed a great seaborne empire.

Germany, a unified country only since 1871, had embarked at the turn of the century on a naval program aimed at building a battleship fleet that would rival Britain's, giving London little choice but to accord Berlin the influence it sought. The imperious and impetuous Kaiser Wilhelm II, a self-styled naval buff and avid student of the Royal Navy, had decided that Germany should rank among the world's great powers and enjoy a political status equal to its growing economic might. The kaiser enlisted Admiral Alfred von Tirpitz, renowned for his ruthless destruction of personal and professional rivals alike, to draw up the plans and convince the Reichstag to finance the fleet. By buying off the landed gentry with grain tariffs and invoking nationalist passions to disarm political opponents, the kaiser and Tirpitz readily accomplished their objectives. The First Navy Law of 1898 envisaged nineteen battleships; the Second Law of 1900 raised the fleet strength to thirty-eight.

The British did not react immediately to Germany's gambit. At the turn of the century, Britain's "official mind" was still focused on the defense of empire. The Boer War broke out in South Africa in 1899 and proved to be a much greater drain on resources than expected. And other great powers posed threats primarily to British possessions, not to the home islands. As one high-ranking official put it in 1899, "There are two Powers, and two only, of whom I am afraid, *viz.* the United States and Russia."[4] Growing American power threatened Canada and British naval supremacy in the western Atlantic. And Russia menaced India, the "jewel in the crown." A firm consensus existed within the cabinet that "the main purpose for which the army exists is not the defence of these shores but the protection of the outlying portions of the Empire, and notably India."[5]

By 1906–1907, however, Britain's map of the world was in the midst of dramatic change. A consensus was taking shape around the proposition that the threat posed by Germany had to take top priority; other commitments could be attended to only after this primary danger had been adequately addressed. A Foreign Office memorandum by Sir Eyre Crowe helped consolidate this line of thinking. The Crowe Memorandum accepted that German intentions were still unclear but maintained that even if Germany did not embark on an aggressive path, its ascent to a position of dominance would nonetheless "constitute as formidable a menace to the rest of the world as would be presented by any deliberate conquest of a similar position by 'malice aforethought.'"[6]

In response to the threat posed by the Germans, Britain, France, and Russia formed an informal coalition, the so-called Triple Entente. London also overturned its aversion to intervention on the Continent and began building an expeditionary force to be dispatched across the Channel to join Britain's partners in blunting a German advance. The Committee of Imperial Defence would then confirm that the main mission of the British army was in Europe, not India. And First Sea Lord Sir John Fisher began the painful process of withdrawing the Royal Navy from imperial waters. This task was facilitated by London's successful effort to orchestrate a lasting rapprochement with the United States, a move that made easier the reduction of Britain's naval presence in the western Atlantic. Churchill then picked up where Fisher left off, striking the naval bargain with Paris and completing the recall of the battle fleet to home waters. To critics still arguing for the defense of empire, Churchill retorted that "if we win the big battle in the decisive theater we can put everything straight afterwards" in other theaters. "It would be very foolish to lose England," Churchill added, "in safeguarding Egypt."[7]

When Churchill in 1912 ordered the Malta squadron to return to the North Sea, he was putting the finishing touches on a swift and thorough overhaul of British grand strategy. This rethinking of priorities and interests is all the more impressive in light of how deeply Britain was invested—both economically and psychologically—in empire and the centuries-old policy of splendid isolation that put it atop the world. Britain's admirable preparations did not spare the country immense sacrifice in the great conflict that broke out in August 1914. But its withdrawal from empire and its new grand strategy for stopping Germany from overrunning Europe were essential in securing the ultimate victory of the Allies.

ON JUNE 9, 1920, Sir Henry Wilson, chief of the Imperial General Staff, felt compelled to express to the cabinet his grave concern about the growing mismatch between Britain's military capabilities and its strategic commitments. "I would respectfully urge that the earnest attention of His Majesty's Government," Wilson pleaded, "may be given to this question with a view to our policy being brought into some relation with military forces available to it. At present this is far from the case. . . . I cannot too strongly press on the Government the danger, the extreme danger, of his Majesty's Army being spread all over the world, strong nowhere, weak everywhere, and with no reserve to save a dangerous situation or avert a coming danger."[8]

Wilson's anxieties stemmed principally from the severe constraints placed on the conduct of foreign policy by a lagging economy. Throughout most of the interwar period, economic considerations trumped all others in shaping British grand strategy. Despite the eventual Allied victory in World War I, the lengthy conflict drained Britain's manpower and financial resources and exposed underlying weaknesses in its economy. Getting the country back on its feet and redressing the public discontent arising from hardship necessitated that defense expenditure be kept to a minimum. The collapse of Wall Street and the global depression of the early 1930s only intensified the preoccupation with economic vulnerability.

With Britain facing these austere conditions, the chancellor of the exchequer understandably played a crucial role in shaping grand strategy throughout the interwar years. The results were self-evident. Between 1920 and 1922, defense spending fell from 896 million to 111 million pounds. The dwindling size of the military was justified through the adoption of the Ten-Year Rule—a planning assumption, regularly renewed, positing that the country would not have to fight a major war for at least ten years. Britain struck agreements in Washington in 1921–1922 and London in 1930 to prevent a naval race with other powers, thereby obviating the need for major expenditure on new ships. The size of the army was kept to a minimum, its mission focused, with the help of colonial recruits, on defense of imperial possessions. Developing international trade, preserving the stability of the pound sterling, and restoring the health of the economy were the top priorities of British grand strategy.

The problem was that developments in Germany soon called these priorities into question. After Hitler became chancellor in 1933, Germany rearmed and proceeded to cast aside the restrictions put in place to preserve a stable balance of power on the Continent. Hitler began by rebuilding the Wehrmacht, violating the troop ceiling of 100,000 soldiers stipulated in the Versailles Treaty. By 1935, he was amassing an army of more than 500,000 men. Hitler soon put his troops to use. In 1936, he unilaterally militarized the Rhineland, embarking on a policy of territorial expansion that was to culminate in Nazi Germany's occupation of Austria in 1938, its invasion of Czechoslovakia in the spring of 1939, the sweep into Poland that fall, the thrust north in the spring of 1940, and the attack on France in May. Just over a week after General Heinz Guderian's panzer corps crossed the Meuse at Sedan, German tanks had reached the Channel coast, effectively cutting off France from the Allied armies in Belgium. The fall of the Third Republic was imminent.

The rise of a menacing Germany during the 1930s should have prompted a reorientation of British grand strategy, as during the century's first decade. It did not. When both Japan and Germany started to show signs of hostile intent during the early 1930s, efforts to commence British rearmament were quickly snuffed out by the Treasury: "The fact is that in present circumstances we are no more in a position financially and economically to engage in a major war . . . than we are militarily. . . . The Treasury submit that at the present time financial risks are greater than any other we can estimate." Prime Minister Ramsey MacDonald concurred that "it must clearly be understood that there would be no big extension of expenditure because this would be out of the question."[9]

In 1932, the Committee of Imperial Defence did cancel the Ten-Year Rule, recognizing that major war was no longer a remote possibility. But the cabinet still refused to authorize funds for rearmament. In 1935, Britain's Mediterranean fleet had enough antiaircraft ammunition to last only one week. In 1936, Britain was spending 4 percent of its gross national product on defense, compared with 13 percent in Germany. The superiority of the Nazi war machine—and the intensity of its perverse nationalism—was growing by the day.

The distribution of Britain's ships and soldiers made as little sense as its complacent levels of spending. To its credit, the Treasury, even as it argued against full-scale rearmament, did counsel that Britain focus its limited defense expenditures on preparing for war with Germany. In 1934, the chancellor of the exchequer, Neville Chamberlain, insisted that "during the ensuing five years our efforts must be chiefly concentrated upon measures designed for the defence of these islands."[10]

Chamberlain's voice, however, was lost in a ministerial consensus in favor of focusing Britain's defense efforts almost exclusively on imperial outposts. The Admiralty, in particular, would not countenance withdrawal from the Far East and the exposure of the naval base in Singapore, arguing it was "the principal link which holds the

Empire together."[11] During the late 1930s, even as Hitler's troops were occupying Austria and Czechoslovakia, the Royal Navy was building capital ships to send to Singapore to take on the Japanese fleet rather than acquiring the smaller vessels needed for antiaircraft and antisubmarine operations in the European theater. As Russell Grenfell, an influential British commentator on naval matters, observed in 1938, planners at the Admiralty "seem to have been committing the grave error of preparing for ambitious operations in a far distant theater without first taking the steps to ensure the safety of the home base."[12]

British preparations for stopping Germany on land were even more inadequate. Although hard to believe, it was not until Germany's invasion of Czechoslovakia in 1939 that Britain began to build an army capable of intervention on the Continent. During the 1920s, the War Office admitted that the expeditionary force intended for use on the Continent "consisted merely of the spare parts of our oversea military machine" and its size "had no relation whatever to the strategical problem of a Franco-German conflict."[13] Despite the steady pace of German rearmament from 1933 onward, Britain took little action. Reviewing a study of the state of British rearmament in the middle of the decade, General William Edmund Ironside commented, "The paper on our rearmament . . . is truly the most appalling reading. How we can have come to this is beyond believing. . . . No foreign nation would believe it."[14] In 1937, the Chiefs of Staff reaffirmed that the "Regular Army is being maintained at the strength necessary for its duties in garrisoning and policing overseas possessions."[15] Even after Germany's occupation of Austria and the incorporation of 100,000 Austrian troops into the Wehrmacht, the cabinet confirmed that the British army still had no continental role and instructed the War Office to continue outfitting it with equipment and supplies for only colonial missions.

After the fall of Czechoslovakia in March 1939, the cabinet finally convinced Neville Chamberlain, who had by then become prime minister, to begin full preparations for the dispatch of troops to France. But it was so late and its forces were in such a state of disrepair that Britain could do little to prevent Hitler's army from overrunning Western Europe in a matter of months in 1940.

Constrained by preoccupation with the health of the British economy and haunted by memories of the bloody trenches of World War I, the British deluded themselves into thinking that they could avoid confrontation with Nazi Germany. Britain tried to escape into empire and to keep Hitler at bay by repeatedly accommodating his appetite for aggression and intimidation. Chamberlain was perhaps right to give in to the Nazi leader at their fateful meeting in Munich in September 1938, but only because Britain was so militarily weak that it had no chance of standing up to Germany's forces. As the Chiefs of Staff warned the cabinet while its members were considering Hitler's demands for the Sudetenland, taking offensive action against Germany "would be to place ourselves in the position of a man who tries to show how brave he is by twisting the tail of a tiger which is preparing to spring before he has loaded his gun."[16] Britain's leaders fully deserve the dishonor that history has bequeathed them, not because they capitulated to Hitler, but because they devised and tolerated a grand strategy that left them with no other choice. As the historian Martin Gilbert has commented, "Munich was not appeasement's finest hour, but its most perverted."[17]

Britain got off relatively easy. Thanks to Hitler's reluctance to invade the British Isles and to Franklin Roosevelt's eventual decision to come to Europe's rescue, the British suffered only German bombs, not German occupation. Others were less fortunate, with Germany's armored divisions easily overcoming the outmoded defenses devised by France's high command. Coupled with poor leadership in France, Britain's deluded and dysfunctional grand strategy played a crucial role in enabling Hitler's troops to conquer much of Europe, plunging the Continent into war and unleashing the Nazi death machine that was to leave an indelible blight upon the course of history.

THE PRESENT

THESE HISTORICAL reflections contain a lesson that Americans ignore at their peril. It is that great powers like the United States need a sound grand strategy if they are to protect themselves and preserve the international order that they have labored hard to construct. Get the pieces of the puzzle right, and even grave threats can be turned back. Get the pieces of the puzzle wrong—or worse, fail to recognize that there is a puzzle—and those same threats can bring great nations to their knees. Before World War I, Britain enjoyed a level of naval supremacy and economic dominance that could have left it feeling invincible and invulnerable. Nonetheless, the British reacted swiftly to the rise of Germany, adjusting their grand strategy accordingly.

During the interwar period, misled by the priority assigned to economic stability and still reeling from the death and economic destruction wrought by World War I, Britain clung to an outmoded grand strategy that grew increasingly divorced from reality as the 1930s proceeded—with disastrous results.

America today arguably has greater ability to shape the future of world politics than any other power in history. The United States enjoys overwhelming military, economic, technological, and cultural dominance. America's military has unquestioned superiority against all potential challengers. The strength of the dollar and the size of its economy give the United States decisive weight on matters of trade and finance. Globalization enables America's multinational corporations to penetrate virtually every market. The information revolution, born and bred in Silicon Valley and the country's other high-tech centers, gives U.S. companies, media, and culture unprecedented reach. In every quarter of the globe, governments as well as ordinary citizens hang on the decisions that emanate from Washington.

The opportunity that America has before it also stems from the geopolitical opening afforded by the Cold War's end. Postwar periods are moments of extraordinary prospect, usually accompanied by searching debate and institutional innovation. It is no accident that the Concert of Europe was erected after the end of the Napoleonic Wars, that the League of Nations came into being at the close of World War I, and that the founding of the United Nations followed the end of World War II. None of these institutions brought war to an end. But all of them were born of courageous and creative efforts to fashion a new order and avert yet another round of geopolitical rivalry and bloodshed.

Despite the opportunities at hand, America is squandering the moment. From the fall of the Berlin Wall until September 11, 2001, the United States had no grand strategy, no design to guide the ship of state. Since September 11, the United States has had a grand strategy—one based on principles of preeminence and preemption—but it has succeeded primarily in alienating much of the world and compromising America's key partnerships. America has thus been a great power adrift, as made clear by its erratic behavior.

In the early 1990s, the Pentagon announced that it would brook no challenge to U.S. supremacy, pledging to "prevent the reemergence of a new rival."[18] The Cold War was over, but America would remain the keeper of global order. This objective quickly proved to be easier said than done. The first Bush administration backed off when faced with the prospect of military intervention in the Balkans, preferring to leave matters to the Europeans. Absent American help, however, the Europeans could do little to stop Slobodan Milosevic from proceeding with the vivisection of Bosnia. As a presidential candidate, Bill Clinton pledged to do more to bring the ethnic slaughter to an end. But he too had second thoughts once in office. Colin Powell, the chairman of the Joint Chiefs of Staff, wanted nothing to do with the dispatch of U.S. forces to the Balkans. The bloodshed continued throughout 1993 and 1994. President Clinton was disquieted but only looked on.

After Powell left the scene, a more confident Clinton eventually rose to the occasion and the U.S. military succeeded in bringing peace to both Bosnia and Kosovo. But by stressing the humanitarian rather than the strategic motivations behind intervention, Clinton created confusion about the circumstances under which America would use force. He came close to offering up a new doctrine, asserting that "there's an important principle here that I hope will be now upheld in the future—and not just by the United States, not just by NATO, but also by the leading countries of the world, through the United Nations. And that is that while there may well be a great deal of ethnic and religious conflict in the world . . . if the world community has the power to stop it, we ought to stop genocide and ethnic cleansing."[19] The problem was that the Balkans were a clear exception, with the United States passing on intervention in Rwanda—where in 1994 at least 500,000 Tutsis were killed—East Timor, the Sudan, Sierra Leone, and many other sites where ethnic and religious conflict occurred during the 1990s. Secretary of State Madeleine Albright, seemingly aware of the double standard, attempted to reinterpret Clinton's message, noting, "Some hope, and others fear, that Kosovo will be a precedent for similar interventions around the globe. I would caution against any such sweeping conclusions."[20]

The Balkan wars led to a further inconsistency in U.S. policy. Congress resented Europe's dependence upon the U.S. military to bring peace to the region, making clear that it expected the members of the European Union to redress the imbalance within the Atlantic Alliance. After the fighting stopped and the peacekeeping began, voices on Capitol Hill urged that the United States hand over the mission to the Europeans and withdraw from the Balkans. The Europeans heard these messages and responded by embarking on efforts to build a military force capable of operating without the help of U.S. troops.

Washington reacted with affront, warning the European Union not to become too assertive and self-reliant lest it undermine the Atlantic link. America asked Europe to carry more of the defense burden, and then grew resentful when the EU did as asked.

American policy toward Russia, ostensibly one of the Clinton administration's top priorities, fared little better. Clinton regularly pronounced that one of his chief goals was to encourage the development of a democratic Russia and to integrate America's former enemy into the West. But the centerpiece of Clinton's European policy was the expansion of the North Atlantic Treaty Organization (NATO) into Central Europe, a move that put the most impressive military alliance in history that much closer to Russia's borders. Moscow was justifiably apoplectic, with President Boris Yeltsin warning that the United States risked building a new dividing line across Europe. Clinton repeatedly reassured the Russians that America meant no harm. But the United States would hardly sit by idly if Russia formed an alliance with Mexico and Canada and started building military installations along the U.S. border.

Incoherence also plagued Clinton's approach to China. At times, China was America's strategic partner, fully deserving of membership in the World Trade Organization (WTO) and the broader community of nations. Clinton even held a town meeting in China, live on national television, a sure sign that China was one of us. At other times, however, the Chinese government was intent only on trampling the human rights of its citizens and threatening to invade Taiwan. And rather than taking steady steps to build a strategic partnership with Beijing, the Clinton team regularly veered off in favor of confrontational measures, such as sending U.S. warships toward Taiwan or planning deployment of a national missile defense system, a policy that risked pushing the Chinese to expand their limited arsenal of nuclear weapons.

The principles were as confused as the policies. According to the rhetoric, the Clinton administration was deeply committed to liberal internationalism, insisting that it would lead through multilateral institutions and shape international order by consensus, not fiat. The United States was "the indispensable nation" because of its ability to build coalitions of the willing and organize joint action.

But the record belies the rhetoric. On a regular basis, the United States opted out of multilateral efforts. In Kyoto in 1997, the international community reached agreement on new measures to protect the environment. Washington was a party to the negotiations, but then dragged its feet on implementation. A broadly successful effort to ban landmines won the 1997 Nobel Peace Prize for Jody Williams and the organization she headed, the International Campaign to Ban Landmines. The United States did not sign on. Washington preferred to play by its own rules. And Clinton withheld support for the International Criminal Court (ICC) for years, changing his mind only at the end of his second term.

This unilateralist inclination only intensified after George W. Bush took over from Clinton. His aides reassured worried allies that America was a team player and would practice "à la carte multilateralism."[21] But within six months of taking office, Bush had pulled out of the Kyoto Protocol on global warming, made clear his intention to withdraw from the Antiballistic Missile (ABM) Treaty, stated his opposition to the Comprehensive Test Ban Treaty and the pact establishing the International Criminal Court (both signed by Clinton but not ratified by the Senate), backed away from establishing a body to verify the 1972 Biological Weapons Convention, and watered down a U.N. agreement aimed at controlling the proliferation of small arms. Friends and foes alike were quick to express their chagrin, vowing to take steps to restrain a wayward America.

The Bush administration exhibited isolationist as well as unilateralist instincts. Bush early on promised to scale back America's overseas commitments and focus more attention on the Western Hemisphere. He also reduced the U.S. role in mediating peace efforts in the Middle East and Northern Ireland. Secretary of State Colin Powell followed suit by dropping from the State Department's roster more than one-third of the fifty-five special envoys that the Clinton administration had appointed to deal with trouble spots around the world. The *Washington Post* summed up the thrust of these moves in its headline, "Bush Retreats from U.S. Role as Peace Broker."[22]

Incoherence and inconsistency also became almost daily fare. Following through on his pledge to place new emphasis on Latin America, Bush took his first foreign trip to Mexico to meet President Vicente Fox on his ranch. Both clad in cowboy boots, the leaders were to demonstrate a new partnership and an America that would meet Mexico on its own terms. But just before the gathering, U.S. aircraft bombed Iraq. The Mexicans were stunned. The attack stole the limelight, riveting the attention of the press on American unilateralism and putting Fox in a difficult and embarrassing position. Rather than serving as an opportunity for Bush to reach out to Mexico, the visit stoked resentment and set back America's relationship with its southern neighbor.

South Korea was the next victim of the Bush administration's strategic incoherence. Prior to President Kim Dae Jung's March 2001 meeting with Bush, Powell had indicated that the United States intended to continue Clinton's policy of supporting rapprochement between the Koreas in return for North Korea's willingness to halt export of missile technology and stop production and deployment of long-range missiles. Bush took the opposite tack, telling a surprised Kim that he would not pursue a missile deal with the North Koreans because "we're not certain as to whether or not they're keeping all terms of all agreements." After the meeting, the White House admitted that the United States had entered into only one deal with North Korea, a 1994 agreement shutting down nuclear energy plants that were producing materials usable in nuclear weapons, with which Pyongyang had been in compliance. When asked what Bush meant by his remarks in the Oval Office, an aide replied, "That's how the president speaks."[23] In the summer of 2001, the Bush administration reversed course yet again, announcing that it would engage in a diplomatic dialogue with North Korea after all.

America's failure to avert the terror attacks of September 2001 was a further sign of strategic drift. Neither the Clinton nor the Bush administration responded effectively to repeated warnings that the country had to do more to counter "asymmetric" threats. As the Hart-Rudman Commission warned in a report released in 1999, "America will become increasingly vulnerable to hostile attack on our homeland, and our military superiority will not entirely protect us." The report went on to predict that during the early twenty-first century "Americans will likely die on American soil, possibly in large numbers."[24] Despite similar admonitions from other groups, America's leaders did little to improve coordination among the dozens of agencies responsible for domestic security. And they failed to take adequate steps to shut down terrorist networks operating abroad. With its guard down, America was blindsided by a terrorist attack disarming in its simplicity. The most sophisticated surveillance satellites and eavesdropping technologies were no match for hijackers armed with knives and box-cutters.

The attacks of September 11 served as a conceptual anchor for the Bush administration, which proceeded to focus with single-minded determination on the fight against terrorism. Although successful in striking back at terrorist groups and their sponsors, the Bush administration has overreached, exaggerating the extent to which the threat of terror defines a new international system. By identifying the struggle against terrorism as its guiding priority and laying out a new doctrine of preeminence and preemption, Washington has embraced a grand strategy opposed by many of the world's nations. The United States may well eliminate Al-Qaeda, but at the expense of the partnerships and institutions that remain the bedrock of international peace and prosperity.

To be sure, America has been hard at work trying to maintain international stability and ensure its citizens security and prosperity. Clinton traveled abroad more than any other U.S. president, making almost as many overseas trips as Ronald Reagan and the elder George Bush combined. He repeatedly sent U.S. forces into combat over Iraq, in Haiti, and in the Balkans, generally with positive results. And George W. Bush followed suit, assembling an impressive team of experts who quickly started working around the clock to manage Pax Americana. But the United States is spinning its wheels. It does not know where to head, so it certainly does not know how to get there. Without the right set of guiding principles—a grand strategy—even well-intentioned efforts are going nowhere.

US: on the road w/no Map

EVEN MORE DISTURBING than the incoherence of U.S. policy has been the fact that few seem to care. The intellectual initiative and institutional creativity of 1815, 1919, and 1945 have been entirely missing from Washington. During the 1990s, America simply tinkered with the status quo. NATO certainly did a good job of keeping the peace in Europe during the Cold War. And it was resilient enough to survive the disappearance of the Soviet Union, the enemy that prompted its formation. So America went ahead and added a few new members. The G-7 worked reasonably well as a forum in which the world's wealthiest nations could coordinate their policies. After the demise of the Soviet Union, the United States gave Russia a seat at the table and called it the G-8. America, at the height of its power, has been running on the fumes of the Cold War.

As the political class grew disinterested in America's engagement abroad, the broader public essentially tuned out. Coverage of foreign affairs on television and in newspapers and magazines dropped precipitously. The time allocated to international news by the main television networks fell by more than 65 percent between 1989 and 2000.[25] Between 1985 and 1995 the space devoted to international stories declined from 24 to 14 percent in *Time* and from 22 to 12 percent in *Newsweek*.[26]

Even when Bill Clinton tried to focus the public's attention on foreign affairs, he had little success. He attempted to ignite a searching national debate about the enlargement of NATO; after all, the proposal to add new members to the alliance had to pass muster among two-thirds of the Senate. Top members of the administration, including Clinton himself, fanned out across the country to rally the flag. Javier Solana, then secretary-general of NATO, came across the Atlantic to help out.

But few Americans paid attention. Solana sat glumly in various motel rooms, unable to get bookings even on radio talk shows. Senators would schedule town meetings on NATO enlargement in their home states, only to find the audience populated primarily by their staff. The debate in the Senate began haphazardly one afternoon in late March 1998, when Majority Leader Trent Lott tired of the topic under discussion on the floor and casually decided to turn to NATO. The bill passed the following month by a vote of 80 to 19, after an intermittent debate that barely scratched the surface. Despite the fanfare, only 10 percent of the American public could name even one of the three countries (Poland, Hungary, the Czech Republic) granted a U.S. nuclear guarantee via their admission to NATO on March 12, 1999.[27]

With the public much more concerned about the travails of Elián Gonzáles, the young Cuban refugee whose story dominated the news for weeks, than the scope and nature of America's broader engagement in world affairs, the disinterest of elected officials intensified into outright irresponsibility. Congress regularly treated the foreign policy agenda as little more than a playpen for partisan politics. Consider the battle over Kosovo. A month into a war that had not produced a single U.S. casualty, the House nevertheless expressed grave misgivings, voting 249 to 180 to refuse funding for sending ground troops to Yugoslavia without congressional approval. The House could not even muster the wherewithal to pass a resolution endorsing the bombing campaign. What better way to send a message to Slobodan Milosevic—in the middle of the war—that his opponent might crack.

Congress's next blunder was the Senate's rejection of the Comprehensive Test Ban Treaty, a pact aimed at eliminating the testing of nuclear weapons. When it became clear that the treaty would fall short of the votes needed for passage, the Clinton administration was prepared to withdraw it from consideration and avoid the outright rejection of an important treaty already ratified in fifty-two countries of the world (and soon thereafter ratified by many more). The Senate proceeded nonetheless, voting 51 to 48 to kill the pact. The Republicans preferred dealing Clinton a deft political blow to upholding America's credibility abroad. America's allies were astonished. As two British commentators put it in the *Financial Times,* the rejection of the treaty was "the clearest indication yet of the radical change in U.S. politics and the country's view of its role in the world. Thumbing its nose at the rest of the world was not an option open to the U.S. during its struggle with communism."[28] It is a sad day when the deliberative bodies meant to guide the world's strongest country hold foreign policy hostage to partisan rancor.

The terror attacks of September 2001 were widely interpreted as an antidote to these worrisome trends. And they were, at least in the short run. Instead of acting unilaterally, the Bush administration went out of its way to enlist the support of not just NATO allies, but also Russia, China, and moderate Arab regimes. Rather than reining in America's commitments, Bush declared a war on terrorism, sending ground troops, aircraft, and warships into battle. And Congress and the American people were fully engaged, with the Senate, the House, and the public overwhelmingly behind Bush's decision to use military force to combat the Al-Qaeda network and its supporters.[29]

In the long run, however, the struggle against terror is unlikely to serve as a solid basis for ensuring either multilateral engagement or a durable brand of American internationalism. Despite the statements of support from abroad, U.S. forces were accompanied only by the British when the bombing campaign against Afghanistan began. Other countries offered logistical and intelligence support, but Americans did almost all the fighting. And that is exactly how the United States, along with many of its allies, wanted it.

America was loath to give up the autonomy that would have been compromised by a broader coalition. Other states were happy to let America take the lead, thereby distancing themselves from the operation. Some countries in the theater of conflict, Saudi Arabia among them, were jittery about letting U.S. forces operate from their bases, justifiably fearful that they might suffer a domestic backlash for supporting attacks against a Muslim neighbor. And America's NATO allies were cautioning restraint, concerned that they too could face retribution from a radicalized Islamic world. After all, although terrorists pose a collective threat, they are careful to single out their actual targets. That is why the apparent solidarity did not run deep. That is why terrorism is unlikely to make of America an avowed multilateralist.

It is also by no means clear that terrorism will eradicate, rather than fuel, isolationist strains within American society. The United States responded resolutely to the attacks on New York and Washington. But the call for engagement in the global battle against terror was accompanied by an alternative logic, one that is likely to gain currency over time. A basic dictum of the country's founding fathers was that America should stay out of the affairs of other countries so that they stay out of America's affairs. The United States is a formidable adversary and is unlikely to let any attack on its own go unpunished. But should the burdens of hegemony mount and Americans come to believe that their commitments abroad are compromising their security at home, they will legitimately question whether the benefits of global engagement are worth the price.

The potential allure of the founding fathers' admonition against foreign entanglement explains why, as one scholar put it, the attacks made "Israelis worry that Americans may now think that supporting Israel is too costly."[30] This logic also explains why François Heisbourg, one of France's leading analysts, commented in Le Monde the day after the attacks that "it is to be feared that the same temptation [that led America to withdraw from the world after World War I] could again shape the conduct of the United States once the barbarians of September 11 have been punished. In this respect, the Pearl Harbor of 2001 could come to close the era opened by the Pearl Harbor of 1941."[31]

The long-term consequences of the events of September 2001 could thus be an America that devotes much more attention and energy to the security of its homeland and much less attention to resolving problems far from its borders. The Bush administration admittedly showed no lack of enthusiasm for waging war against terrorism. But prior to the events of September 2001, the initial instincts of Bush and his advisers were to scale back, not to deepen, America's involvement in distant lands. In combination with the new focus on homeland defense and the political appeal of seeking to cordon off the country from foreign dangers, these instincts are a better indication of long-term trends than are actions taken amid shock and anger.

It is equally doubtful that the threat of terror will over the long run ensure a more responsible Congress and a more engaged and attentive public. Bipartisan rancor did disappear instantly on September 11, 2001, and the U.S. public stood firmly behind military retaliation. But these were temporary phenomena arising from the grief of the moment; after a few months, partisan wrangling returned to Capitol Hill and the public mind again began to wander. As one reporter commented on December 2, "The post–Sept. 11 Congress has now almost fully abandoned its briefly adopted pose of high-minded bipartisanship."[32]

The relatively rapid return to business as usual stemmed from the fact that the United States proceeded to embark on a long march, not a war. After Pearl Harbor, American leaders had in Imperial Japan and Nazi Germany dangerous and identifiable enemies against which to mobilize the nation and evoke continued sacrifice. The threat posed by the Soviet Union similarly kept the country focused and determined during the long decades of the Cold War, underwriting the liberal internationalism that sustained America's global engagement. In contrast, terrorism represents a much more elusive enemy. Instead of facing a tangible adversary with armored columns and aircraft carriers, America confronts an enemy schooled in guerrilla tactics—a type of warfare that, as the Vietnam War demonstrated, plays to the strengths of neither America's armed forces nor its citizens. The United States handily defeated its foes in Afghanistan, but many members of Al-Qaeda escaped, melding into village life or fleeing to the tribal lands of Pakistan. In this kind of war, patience and tact are more useful weapons than military power.

With much of the struggle against terrorism occurring quietly beyond the public eye—through intelligence, surveillance, and covert operations—this new challenge will not be accompanied by the evocative images that help rally the country around the flag. Rather than inducing Americans to join the army or the production line to contribute to the war effort, terrorism's main impact on the average citizen is to induce him to stay at home. In the wake of the attacks on New York and Washington and the anthrax scare that followed, President Bush asked of Americans not that they make a special sacrifice, but that they return to normal life by shopping in malls and traveling by air. Even as American soldiers were fighting and dying in Afghanistan, ABC was trying to woo David Letterman to its late-night slot to replace *Nightline*—one of the few network programs providing in-depth analysis of foreign news. As before September 2001, keeping the U.S. public engaged in international affairs promises to be an uphill battle.

WHY HAS AMERICA thus far offered such a flat-footed response to the historic opening afforded by the end of the Cold War? Why, when the opportunities are so apparent and the stakes so high, has an otherwise vigorous America failed to rise to the occasion?

The Cold War's unassuming end provides a partial answer. At about 10:30 P.M. on November 9, 1989, Berliners began climbing over and tearing down the wall that had separated their city for decades. To the great surprise of Russians, Americans, and virtually everyone in between, the great ideological schism of the twentieth century was fading away—and with remarkably little bloodshed. There was no war between the Warsaw Pact and NATO. Moscow willingly let its client states leave the fold, presiding, albeit ruefully, over the dismantling of the Soviet bloc. The Soviet Union was perhaps the first empire in history to bow out without a bloody fight. Soviet communism died quietly, to the benefit of all.

The unusual manner in which the Soviet Union fell apart, although fortunate in most respects, did have a downside. There was no wake-up call, no equivalent to the blood-filled trenches of the Somme or the flattened, smoking remains of Hiroshima, to drive home the point that something bold had to be done to interrupt the recurring cycles of great-power rivalry and war. On the contrary, the West's bloodless victory was a vindication of its values and institutions. The United States therefore plodded ahead with little change of course. The foreign policy of George Bush (the elder) was aptly dubbed "status quo plus." Bill Clinton, try as he might to leave a distinctive mark, fell back upon the same basic logic.

America was also left with too much strength for its own good. The commanding position afforded the United States by the collapse of the Soviet Union reinforced a complacent triumphalism. The Soviet Union did not just give up the fight; it utterly collapsed. The Russian economy shrank by more than 50 percent between 1990 and 1998. Ukraine saw its economy essentially self-destruct. By 1995, companies could not even pay their employees. Along the highway heading south from Kiev, impoverished factory workers lined the shoulders selling the shoes and tires they had just manufactured—their single source of hard currency. Add to that picture a chronic recession in Japan and a financial crisis that swept much of East Asia, and the United States was left with a stark preponderance of power. The inability of other major nations to challenge American supremacy itself produced stability; others followed because they had no choice. America, by virtue of its dominance, was able to create order without even trying.

This surfeit of power also provided America a large margin for error. The United States was able to take successive missteps without confronting adverse consequences. Washington expanded NATO's borders eastward against the vociferous objections of the Russians. Moscow, however, had no option but to acquiesce and to keep currying America's favor. If Russia wanted loans and entry into the Atlantic community's markets and institutions, it needed America's blessing. During NATO's war over Kosovo, U.S. planes accidentally bombed China's embassy in Belgrade. But after a few months of strain, relations with China were back on track. Beijing knew that entry into the World Trade Organization and other coveted goals depended on U.S. approval. Even when the United States, whether deliberately or accidentally, crossed other major nations, they still came calling.

America, of course, did suffer the consequences of its complacency about terror attacks against its territory. And the Bush administration responded sensibly, destroying terrorist cells abroad and taking steps to increase security at home. But America's new preoccupation with targeting terrorists and rogue nations makes it all the more likely that other matters of grand strategy will fail to receive the attention they deserve.

Consider the case of national missile defense. On September 10, 2001, Senator Joseph Biden, chairman of the Senate Foreign Relations Committee, delivered a major speech in which he outlined why America should worry much more about low-technology threats from terrorists than about incoming nuclear missiles from rogue states. He also laid out why withdrawal from the ABM Treaty and deployment of a missile defense system could lead to a new arms race. Biden's intention, at least in part, was to explain why the Democrats had refused to provide the Bush administration the full $8.3 billion it had requested to fund missile defense. Although the attacks on September 11 fully confirmed Biden's analysis—terrorists were able to do grievous damage with alarming ease—political debate about missile defense came to an abrupt halt. On September 21, the Democrats announced that they had decided to back away from their objections and provide Bush his full funding request. Considered discussion of the issue became impossible amid the political preoccupation with homeland defense. In December, the Bush administration formally gave notice that the United States was withdrawing from the ABM Treaty.

Not only has there been little demand for Americans to think about broad questions of grand strategy, there has also been little supply. The Cold War generation continues to debate matters of geopolitics, at least in the pages of academic journals. But there is little in the way of a rising generation of strategists. The professional and institutional structure of the U.S. research community is biased against just the type of broad inquiry needed to stimulate new thinking about grand strategy. On the one hand, scholars of international relations at universities tend to produce work that is highly abstract and, for the most part, of little use to the policy community. The field is preoccupied with mathematical modeling and is growing more distant from the real world. Policy-makers could not even read the main political science journals if they wanted to (which they don't); they contain too much jargon and too many mathematical equations.

On the other hand, most think tanks have been moving to the other extreme. To contribute to a fast-moving policy debate driven by the explosion of twenty-four-hour-per-day news channels (CNN, FOX News, CNBC, MSNBC, C-SPAN, and counting), policy analysts write op-eds and issue briefs. The sound bite has triumphed over sound analysis. Think tanks thus turn out work whose shelf life is measured in days or weeks, while universities generate scholarship of little relevance to policy. The result is an arid intellectual landscape, a hollowed-out foreign policy community, and the neglect of the sustained deliberation needed to fashion a new American grand strategy.

The dot-com revolution only made matters worse, attracting America's best and brightest to Internet start-ups, venture capital firms, and business consultancies. The country's best public policy schools—Harvard, Princeton, Georgetown, Johns Hopkins—have not been putting sufficient emphasis on training their graduates to be diplomats or public servants. Instead, they tend to turn out technocrats capable of competing on the job market with their business school counterparts. These students graduate with enviable facility in Microsoft Excel and PowerPoint. They have mastered the art of drafting memos. But most sorely lack the historical grounding and interdisciplinary training needed to become America's new strategists.

A cursory glance at who called the shots during the Clinton administration underscores the immediacy of the problem. To the extent that the administration had a dominating strategist, it was Robert Rubin, the secretary of the Treasury. Rubin left his job as the head of Goldman Sachs, one of the world's premier investment banks, to take the helm of America's—and the world's—economy. He brought with him a handful of the country's top economists. Rubin started off as head of the newly created National Economic Council, quietly establishing himself as the anchor of Clinton's inner circle. He then replaced Lloyd Bentsen at the Treasury in January 1995. When he stepped down in the summer of 1999 to go back to Wall Street, Rubin turned over the reins to his able deputy, Harvard economist Lawrence Summers. The economic side of the house could not have been in better hands. Rubin will go down in history as one of the most distinguished and talented individuals to grace the Treasury since Alexander Hamilton, a leading member of George Washington's cabinet.

Clinton's foreign and defense team had considerable talent but was overshadowed by the priority assigned to the global economy. Furthermore, it contained few individuals schooled in matters of grand strategy. The most influential player over the course of Clinton's eight years was Samuel Berger, deputy national security adviser during the first term, and national security adviser during the second. Drawing on a career as one of the capital's best trade lawyers, he brought to the table admirable judgment and refined political instincts. But Berger had neither the training nor the inclination to fashion a new conceptual foundation for U.S. strategy.

The Bush team has had a different problem. Many of its members have had valuable experience in matters of geopolitics and grand strategy. But from the outset, they were unable to find common ground on the fundamental issues of the day. Secretary of Defense Donald Rumsfeld made clear that he strongly favored a missile defense program and that he thought the efforts of the European Union to build up their own military forces could undermine NATO. Colin Powell, meanwhile, wanted to move slowly and cautiously on missile defense and believed that a stronger European Union could well mean a stronger NATO. Vice President Richard Cheney and Condoleezza Rice, Bush's national security adviser, indicated that the administration intended to withdraw U.S. troops from the Balkans. Powell insisted that U.S. soldiers in Kosovo were not going anywhere anytime soon. Deputy Secretary of Defense Paul Wolfowitz wanted to overthrow Iraqi leader Saddam

Hussein by arming his opposition, while Powell favored easing economic sanctions in order to "relieve the burden on the Iraqi people."[33] After the terror attacks of September 2001, Wolfowitz hoped that America would target Iraq as well as Afghanistan, while others preferred a more restricted campaign. Wolfowitz eventually carried the day.

Furthermore, to the extent that Bush's top advisers share a conceptual map, it is out of date. The Bush team consists of ex–Cold Warriors, seasoned to meet the challenges of the past, not the present or future. Their hard-line stance on missile defense, confrontational approach to China, neglect of issues such as protecting the environment and managing globalization, and unilateral dismissal of the value of numerous international agreements were reminiscent of the blustery days of the Cold War—and ended up alienating European and Asian nations alike. The international solidarity demonstrated in the fight against terrorism masked, but by no means erased, the wide gap existing between the Bush team's approach to foreign policy and that of its foreign counterparts.

THE FUTURE

A NECESSARY starting point for redressing America's strategic drift is clarifying exactly what grand strategy is. Coming up with a grand strategy for the future entails coming down on a particular map of the world. What matters on that map are not so much the geographic features—oceans, mountains, rivers, or even national boundaries. Rather, grand strategy is about identifying geopolitical fault lines, figuring out where and in what manner underlying global forces will come up against each other, producing the fissures that are ultimately responsible for causing major war. The challenge is not just determining where these fault lines lie, but also figuring out how to overcome them—or at least how to mitigate their destructive potential.

Devising grand strategy is thus akin to architectural design. When an architect drafts plans for a building, he relies on the rules of engineering to come up with a design that not only fulfills a function, but is also structurally sound. Certain beams will hold a certain weight. Different materials have different tolerances. The objective is to ensure that the fault lines will withstand the winds, the settling or shaking of the earth on which the building rests, and other forces that will be brought to bear on the structure.

Formulating grand strategy involves a similar enterprise but is considerably more complicated. Unlike engineering, there are no hard and fast laws about loads and tolerances. Changes in communications, weapons, and transportation technology continuously alter the rules of the game. The advent of the railroad, for example, had a revolutionary impact on geopolitics. For centuries, the country that ruled the seas enjoyed unquestioned dominance. Not so after the railroad enabled armies and goods to move quickly and cheaply across land. The relative strategic importance of land power versus sea power has continued to shift with the advent of submarines, airplanes, nuclear weapons, satellites, and fiber optics. The tectonic forces that shape geopolitics are anything but constant.

That a grand strategy suited for good times may not be appropriate for bad times complicates matters further. A house will certainly fare well in a light breeze and on stable soil if it is built to withstand a gale and an earthquake measuring 6.0 on the Richter scale. But a grand strategy designed to preserve economic stability during a period of growth could do more harm than good amid a downturn. Although today's international economy was erected on America's watch and is still run from Washington, it may well serve as a transmission belt for recession in a system under stress.

What should America's new map of the world look like? Where do the emerging geopolitical fault lines lie? Although there has been little debate about grand strategy within the American government since the end of the Cold War, some outside thinkers have done better. A relatively lively debate has gradually emerged among the handful of analysts still interested in thinking about grand strategy.

Is Francis Fukuyama right in his book, *The End of History and the Last Man*, that liberal democracy is taking the world by storm, making the divide between democratic and nondemocratic states the last global fault line? Is Samuel Huntington right in *The Clash of Civilizations and the Remaking of World Order* when he argues that cultural dividing lines now define geopolitics, and that a struggle among Judeo-Christian, Islamic, and Confucian civilizations is in the offing? Or is Thomas Friedman right in *The Lexus and the Olive Tree* that globalization has changed the rules for good, putting the new fault line between those countries that have joined the globalization bandwagon and those that are fighting back?

These analysts and a few others have produced competing visions of America's map of the world for the twenty-first century. Each of the visions has its merits, but all of them are wrong. And most of them are wrong for the same reason.

They represent maps of the world that are ephemeral and will remain relevant only as long as American preponderance persists. According to this book's map of the world, *the* defining element of the global system is the distribution of power, not democracy, culture, globalization, or anything else. We now live in a unipolar world—a world with only one pole of power. And it is America's unipolar world. The fundamental, inescapable geopolitical feature of the moment is American predominance.

The stability of today's global landscape follows directly from its unipolar structure. When one state has much more wealth and military capability than all other states, the system is unipolar. When two states of roughly equal size exist, the world is bipolar. When three or more major players exist, the system is multipolar. In the bipolar world of the Cold War or the multipolar world of the 1930s, rivalry among the great powers was a constant. In a world with only one pole, there is no rivalry among the great powers simply because there is only one great power. No other major state can even think about taking on America. Such marked asymmetry does mean that extremists in the Middle East or elsewhere will vent their wrath against the United States; primacy invites resentment. But even successful efforts to lash out against the world's only superpower do not alter the unipolar nature of the global system.

It should therefore be no surprise that analysts are having so much trouble agreeing upon today's geopolitical fault line. Because there isn't one. If geopolitical fault lines fall between poles of power, and there is today only one such pole, then it follows that there is no fault line. America is the only contestant in the ring. It wins by default.

The problem is that America's unipolar moment and the global stability that comes with it will not last. Europe now has a single market, a single currency, and more frequently speaks with a single, self-confident voice. The aggregate wealth of the European Union's fifteen members already approaches that of the United States, and the coming entry of new members, coupled with growth rates comparable to America's, may eventually tilt the balance in Europe's favor. The EU has embarked on efforts to build a military force capable of operating without U.S. participation. These moves will make Europe more autonomous and less willing to follow America's lead. Along with an integrating Europe, Russia, Japan, and China will gradually emerge as counterweights to American strength.

The waning of U.S. primacy will result not just from the rise of alternative centers of power, but also from an America that is tiring of the burdens of global hegemony. The United States should not and will not pursue a foreign policy as ambitious as that of the Cold War now that it lives in a world in which it faces no major adversary but instead confronts a terrorist threat that is better countered by freezing bank accounts than by dropping bombs. As during earlier periods in American history, the absence of a commanding threat will make the country considerably more reluctant to shoulder strategic commitments abroad. Americans and their elected leaders are justifiably losing interest in playing the role of global guardian. At the same time, the United States is drawing away from multilateral institutions in favor of a unilateralism that risks estranging alternative centers of power, raising the chances that their ascent will lead to a new era of geopolitical rivalry.

The rise of other powers and America's waning and unilateralist internationalism will combine to make America's unipolar moment a fleeting one. As unipolarity gives way to multipolarity, the stability that follows naturally from the presence of an uncontested hegemon will be replaced by global competition for position, influence, and status. As in the past, the world's principal fault lines will fall where they have fallen throughout the ages—between the world's main centers of power. The disorder that comes with rivalry will soon replace the order afforded by Pax Americana.

Whether or not they want to hear it, Americans will have to pay attention when confronted with the new dangers and uncertainties that will accompany the end of U.S. preponderance. The American economy is deeply tied into international markets. The boom of the past decade was pushed along by the greater openness of the global economy, which both fueled a sizable increase in trade and pressured the United States to become more competitive. International trade now represents more than one-quarter of global output. Americans would suffer should economic nationalism and protectionism return.

Other, perhaps more important, determinants of the basic quality of life are also on the line. For more than forty years, Americans awoke to the Cold War and the specter of nuclear war. Close to 100,000 U.S. citizens lost their lives in the battles to contain communism in Korea and Vietnam. And this prolonged struggle came on the heels of the crushing effort needed to defeat Germany, Japan, and Italy, a worldwide war that claimed upward of 50 million lives.

Politicians and scholars alike now regularly proclaim that major war is becoming obsolete, making way for a permanent peace. But this would not be the first time such pronouncements have proved wrong. If history is any guide, the end of American primacy will bring with it a more unpredictable and unpleasant world. Now, while U.S. dominance still provides a relatively stable global environment, is the time to start fashioning a grand strategy for managing the return to a multipolar world.

A similar window of opportunity exists with respect to crafting a new brand of American internationalism. The permissive brand of U.S. internationalism that continues to make possible an activist foreign policy should not be seen as a precedent for the future. The foreign policy of both the Democratic and Republican parties remains heavily influenced by older individuals who bring to the table powerful memories of World War II and the Cold War; they instinctively appreciate the importance of U.S. leadership. Not so the rising generation that came of age after the fall of the Berlin Wall. Its appetite for steady international engagement has yet to be tested.

The internationalism of the 1990s was also sustained by a prolonged economic expansion. The end of that boom will dampen the country's appetite for foreign engagement, producing an America that is more reluctant about expending blood and treasure in the name of international order. This turning inward is particularly likely if the costs of engagement rise. America has of late enjoyed an activist internationalism without suffering high numbers of combat fatalities. Especially in the wake of the battle over Kosovo, the American public has come to expect casualty-free war. Even the campaigns in Afghanistan and Iraq, which required ground troops, produced relatively few casualties. Al-Qaeda was adept at striking against office towers and embassies, but neither its forces nor those of Saddam Hussein constituted a worthy enemy on the battlefield. Public support for overseas missions may dwindle quickly should future missions involve greater loss of American life.

America's war against terrorism notwithstanding, the broader outlines of the George W. Bush presidency confirm that a downward trend in U.S. internationalism has already taken effect. After taking the helm, Bush generally adhered to his promise to pursue a more "humble" foreign policy and be more selective in picking the country's fights. During his first months in office, he drew down U.S. troop levels in Bosnia and kept American soldiers in Kosovo on a tight leash despite the spread of fighting to Serbia and Macedonia. He reduced America's diplomatic involvement in mediating regional conflicts. And the administration stepped away from a series of multilateral commitments, preferring the autonomy that comes with unilateral initiative.

After the events of September 11, Bush reversed course, making foreign policy his top priority. He vowed to take the fight well beyond Afghanistan, eyeing in particular Iraq, Iran, and North Korea. He reengaged in the Middle East peace process, appointing General Anthony Zinni as his special envoy. Nonetheless, the unilateralist and isolationist tones of Bush's first months in office should not be seen as passing idiosyncrasies. They reflected the preferences of not only his foreign policy team, but also his political base. Bush was reaching out to voters in the South and the Mountain West, regions of the United States that have generally been much less enthusiastic about liberal internationalism than urban areas on the coasts. These regions represent Bush's core constituency; he has clear incentives to appeal to the more populist and unilateral brand of internationalism that holds sway in these areas. And the president himself hails from these quarters, having exhibited little interest in foreign affairs prior to occupying the White House.

It is admittedly puzzling that isolationism and unilateralism are making a comeback at the same time. At least on the surface, they represent contradictory impulses, with isolationists calling for disengagement and unilateralists favoring unfettered global leadership. But they are in reality opposite sides of the same coin. They share common ideological origins in America's fear of entanglements that may compromise its liberty and sovereignty. The country should do its best to shun international engagement, but if it does engage, it should do so in a way that preserves national autonomy. They also share origins in the notion of U.S. exceptionalism, providing the nation an impetus to cordon itself off from the international system, but also to remake that system as America sees fit. It is precisely because isolationism and unilateralism are so deeply embedded in the country's political culture that they pose a dual threat to liberal internationalism, inducing the United States to retreat from the global stage even as it seeks to re-create the world in its image.

For better or for worse, this political culture and democracy

American-style have a crucial influence on the conduct of foreign policy. Diplomacy is no longer the preserve of an internationalist Ivy League elite that shuttles between Foggy Bottom, Wall Street, and foreign capitals. What happens "inside the Beltway" still matters, but, more than ever before, so do decisions and attitudes in Atlanta, Dallas, Seattle, Silicon Valley, and Los Angeles, each of which has its unique interests and brand of internationalism. Regional divides hardly evoke the passions that they did during America's early decades. But political, economic, and cultural differences that fall along regional lines are again coming to play an important role in shaping the country's foreign relations.

The demographic makeup of the American population is also changing, complicating the domestic politics of foreign policy. An electorate with ancestral allegiances primarily to Europe is being transformed by the ongoing influx of immigrants from Latin America and Asia and by high birthrates within these communities. By the second half of this century, Caucasians of European background will represent less than 50 percent of the U.S. population. If a coherent foreign policy is to emerge from this ethnic hodgepodge and diversity of regional interest, America's leaders must educate and cajole in the service of laying the political groundwork for a new U.S. grand strategy.

America's engagement in the international economy, although deep and wide, will not prove sufficient to sustain political support for the country's role as the globe's strategic guardian. The United States erected an extensive network of overseas military commitments and international institutions to contain communism, not to protect markets. Although the flag sometimes follows trade, economic interest and strategic commitment often part company. During the era of colonialism, Britain and France certainly extracted wealth from their overseas possessions, but they also expended much time and energy carving up Africa—despite poor prospects of economic gain. And lucrative commercial ties to places like India, the Persian Gulf, and Indochina hardly kept the colonial troops on station when political and strategic considerations dictated otherwise.

Like other great powers that have come before, the United States need not preserve the full range of its global strategic commitments to pursue its global economic interests. America's overseas presence still has important economic implications in some regions. The forward deployment of U.S. troops in East Asia does help keep the peace, thereby contributing to a favorable business environment. And the U.S. military plays an important role in maintaining the flow of oil through the Persian Gulf.

But with the wealthy members of the EU enjoying a lasting peace with each other, a permanent U.S. military presence in Europe is hardly needed to protect the healthy volume of trade and capital that flows across the Atlantic. These flows are the result of the benefits that accrue to both parties, not the product of America's strategic outpost in Europe. Furthermore, the United States can afford to weather an occasional setback in its overseas markets. Although hardly insignificant, exports in 2000 represented only about 11 percent of U.S. domestic product. And roughly 30 percent of those exports went to Canada and Mexico, giving North America a reasonable degree of commercial self-sufficiency even in the age of globalization.[34] Should political and strategic considerations dictate a waning internationalism and a distancing from multilateral institutions, economic interests will not stand in their way. America could over time find itself reverting to a strategy similar to that of the pre–Cold War era, when it on occasion used force abroad to defend its traders and investments, but remained reluctant to take on more permanent overseas commitments or institutional entanglements.

It is understandable and perhaps healthy for America to lighten its load and step back from at least some of the onerous international responsibilities of the last six decades. The world that gave rise to these responsibilities is gone, and U.S. strategy needs to change accordingly. But in light of the isolationist and unilateralist instincts that have played such a central role in American history, today's leaders need to fashion a new political equilibrium, a new, even if reduced, level of American engagement in the world that enjoys the support of the public.

Doing so entails rebuilding a liberal internationalism that guides America toward not just engagement, but multilateral engagement through international institutions. Predicated upon the notion of sharing the rights and responsibilities of managing the international system with others, liberal internationalism offers a stable middle ground between isolationist and unilateralist extremes, providing the political foundations for an America that at once resists the urge to retreat and works with, rather than against, emerging centers of power. Before a precipitous withdrawal from world affairs becomes likely and go-it-alone impulses alienate potential partners, America needs to find this new internationalism.[35]

Americans should certainly not be asked to shoulder more than a fair share of the burden of preserving international order or to muster enthusiasm for each and every international institution. An overly ambitious foreign policy, by provoking a domestic backlash against excessive sacrifice, could be even more dangerous than a gradual drift toward isolationism. The Senate rejected U.S. participation in the League of Nations, after all, because President Woodrow Wilson over-reached, insisting upon a level and form of American commitment for which there was insufficient political support. At the same time, Americans cannot allow themselves to gravitate toward isolationism; the history of the twentieth century makes all too clear the geopolitical and economic chaos that can ensue when the United States retreats into a protective shell. The challenge is therefore to craft a grand strategy that keeps the scope of America's foreign engagement in a comfortable equilibrium with the public's appetite for internationalism. Laying out that vision and building the new internationalism needed to realize it should be at the apex of America's national priorities.

ALTHOUGH THE FUTURE holds in store a competitive world of multiple centers of power, the coming era of multipolarity will likely have its own unique characteristics and may resemble only distantly its historical antecedents. Much has changed in the recent past to provide optimism that the era that is opening will be less bloody than the one that is closing. Nations no longer have the same incentives to engage in predatory conquest. They now accumulate wealth through developing information technology and expanding financial services, not conquering and annexing land and labor. Nuclear weapons also increase the costs of war. And democratic states may well be less aggressive than their authoritarian ancestors; democracies seem not to go to war with each other. Perhaps future poles of power, as long as they are democratic, will live comfortably alongside each other.

In this sense, the end of the American era does not represent a turning back to the traditional balance-of-power system of, say, Europe before World War I. Rather it signifies a turning forward to a new and uncharted historical era that will be guided by a new set of underlying forces and new rules of the game. Francis Fukuyama is therefore right to assert that the collapse of the Soviet Union and the triumph of liberal democracy constitute a historical end point. The closing of the current era will mark not just the end of American primacy, but also the end of a particular historical epoch—that of industrial capitalism, liberal democracy, and the nation-state. America has in many respects been at the forefront of each of these defining characteristics of the contemporary era. And it has admirably succeeded in completing or at least bringing to their most elevated form each of these grand historical projects.

Fukuyama is wrong, however, to assert that history itself is coming to a close. It is only a particular historical era that is ending, not history's longer march. One cycle of history is finishing, and a new cycle is beginning. That is why the end of the American era represents the close of one epoch but also the opening of another. That is why a book about the end of the American era must also address the rebirth of history.

Looking ahead to the next historical era is admittedly a treacherous undertaking; its essential building blocks are still uncertain and inchoate. But nascent trends are visible. Industrial capitalism has begun to give way to digital capitalism. Liberal democracy is still going strong, but civic disengagement and social inequalities are already providing mounting challenges. And the nation-state is under attack from below by demographic change and regional fragmentation and from above by globalization and transnational integration. From these basic starting points will come the outlines of the era that will accompany a new cycle of history.

CHAPTER TWO

America's New Map of the World

I F AMERICA is to have a new grand strategy, it first has to come up with a new map of the world. The task of constructing this map must begin with first principles and the identification of the fundamental geopolitical forces that will shape the emerging global system. The conceptual taproot for this book's map of the world is realism—the logic of realpolitik and the balance of power. The tendency for nations to compete with each other is intrinsic to the human condition. It stems from basic human drives—the search for security, wealth, and dignity. Humans form nation-states and other types of communities to pursue these goals, and these communities then manifest the same essential drives in relations with each other.

Realism explains why competition among poles is the most persistent and pervasive feature of international life. It clarifies why today's unipolar system is a relatively stable one—America has no equal capable of challenging its primacy. It explains why a Europe that grows more collective in character and stronger in economic and military terms will as a matter of course acquire new geopolitical ambition. And realism provides the rationale for this book's claim that the return of a world of multiple centers of power will inevitably produce new fault lines among contending poles.

The weight of history provides the main reason for relying on realism as the organizing principle for a new map of the world. States have throughout the ages gone after each other so persistently and with such vehemence that realism's logic appears irrefutable. The contemporary era has admittedly given rise to trends that provide at least some room for optimism; democratization and globalization may well help counter geopolitical rivalry. Nonetheless, that humans have time and again forsaken the comforts of peace for the horrors of war makes it difficult to accept that realism and the competition for primacy arising from its logic have finally run their course.

This book does, however, depart from its realist roots in a crucial respect. Competition in the international arena may be endemic, but the right grand strategy can counter the system's competitive instincts. The default position is one of rivalry, driven by the search for security, wealth, and prestige. But by recognizing the system's tendency to gravitate to conflict and by identifying and seeking to repair fault lines before they erupt, leadership and planning can mitigate, and in some cases override, the logic of realism and the rivalry that derives from it. Realism can and must be tempered by idealism—belief in the potential for reason, law, values, and institutions to tame material power—if the future is to be less bloody than the past.

Contemporary Europe is a case in point. Through a steady process of political and economic integration, the EU is erasing the fault lines among Europe's nation-states, holding out the prospect of banishing war from the Continent. Although Europe's success in this respect is rare and has required great effort and leaders to match, its experience provides a way forward. In the aftermath of World War II, Europeans saw the challenge before them, designed their geopolitical map of the future, and set out to make that map a reality. They did so by blending realism and idealism, according Europe's major states the privileges that come with wealth and military strength, but also binding those states to each other in a manner that replaced the logic of rivalry with that of cooperation and mutual gain. My main agenda is the same—to generate an accurate map of the emerging world, to design a grand strategy for overcoming the fault lines on that map by blending realism with idealism, and to lay out the discrete steps needed to realize that grand strategy and establish a new and peaceful international system.

Before embarking on this task and laying out the geopolitical map that follows from this conceptual foundation, we first look at America's last map of the world—the one that emerged amid the onset of the Cold War. During the course of 1946, Soviet intransigence was gradually extinguishing Roosevelt's dream of turning wartime alliance into peacetime partnership. Moscow was installing puppet regimes in Eastern Europe, making a bid for control of the Dardanelles, and leaving Soviet troops in northern Iran past the agreed deadline of March 2, 1946—all signs of trouble to come.

What guiding vision did American strategists generate to respond to Soviet behavior? If much of the world was to be incorporated into two hostile blocs, which parts of the globe would side with the Soviets, and which with the West? Should the United States rely on military strength to contain communism, or would economic recovery in Western Europe and Japan, nationalism in the Third World, and divisions within the communist camp do the job? What, in short, was America's last map of the world to look like? The answers to these questions will help illuminate the task at hand today.

THE PAST

ON FEBRUARY 22, 1946, George Kennan sent back to Washington Moscow Embassy Telegram #511. The so-called long telegram, coupled with an article Kennan published the following year in *Foreign Affairs* under the pseudonym "X," laid the foundation for a new U.S. grand strategy focused on one primary objective—containment of the Soviet Union.[1] Kennan soon left Moscow to become a lecturer at the National War College. In 1947, Secretary of State George Marshall then appointed him as the first director of the State Department's Policy Planning Staff, an office explicitly created to help formulate the core principles that would guide policy over the long term.

Kennan took the lead in forging the new template that gradually took shape during the course of 1947. It consisted of the following principles. The threat posed by the Soviet Union was primarily political in nature. The United States therefore could most effectively contain communism by restoring economic health and political self-confidence to the world's main power centers—Britain, France, Germany, and Japan. Prevailing against the Soviets, Kennan wrote, would ultimately turn on the "degree of cohesion, firmness and vigor which [the] Western world can muster."

Kennan did not argue in favor of ignoring other parts of the world. On the contrary, the spread of communist government to China and other countries in East Asia was to be resisted. The United States should, he believed, avoid military intervention on the Asian mainland and other less industrialized areas, instead ensuring access to islands and other strategic points needed to launch long-range bombers and protect the sea-lanes on a global basis—such as the Philippines, the Dardanelles, the Suez Canal, the Strait of Gibraltar, and the Strait of Hormuz. Military and economic aid would at times be needed to shore up defenses against Soviet expansionism. But surrounding the Soviet Union with superior military capability would require excessive expenditure and fuel the "traditional and instinctive Russian sense of insecurity," which was at the root of the "Kremlin's neurotic view of world affairs."[2]

Kennan's map of the world was thus multifaceted. The central fault line was between the Soviet bloc and the industrialized democracies. Inoculating Western Europe and Japan against communism through economic growth and political confidence, while maintaining control over strategic strong points, would enable the West to stay the course. Meanwhile, it would be along other, more subtle fault lines, that communism would eventually come undone. Contradictions within the Soviet system, divisions within the broader communist bloc, and the natural forces of resistance afforded by nationalism would ultimately enable the West to prevail.

America's grand strategy was guided by Kennan's map of the world only until the end of 1949. Three principal events—the Soviet atomic test in August 1949, the communist victory in China and proclamation of the Chinese People's Republic in October, and the outbreak of the Korean War in June 1950—induced the Truman administration to gravitate to a new and more alarmist strategic vision. Paul Nitze, who followed Kennan as the director of the Policy Planning Staff in 1950, was the chief architect of this new map. He oversaw the drafting of NSC-68, a planning paper that was to replace the "long telegram" as the defining document in America's conceptual arsenal.

Nitze's map of the world was black and white. There was the free world and the communist world, and only one fault line where the two met. Rather than wait out the communist bloc and buy time for it to erode from within, the United States had to take the initiative and surround the Soviets with superior military strength. The U.S. government had no choice but to allocate the resources necessary to sustain a major increase in conventional armaments. As NSC-68 put it, "a build-up of the military capabilities of the United States and the free world is a precondition . . . to the protection of the United States against disaster."[3] Rather than working against each other, Moscow and Beijing were joining forces: "Developments in Asia confirm that there is a comprehensive program, in which the Soviet and Chinese communists are cooperating, designed as a present phase to eliminate all Western influence from the Asiatic mainland."[4] And instead of nationalism acting as a constraint on the expansion of communist

influence, the states of Southeast Asia were poised to fall like domi-
noes: the "loss of any one of the countries to the enemy would almost
certainly result in the loss of all the other countries."[5] John Foster
Dulles, who was to become secretary of state in 1953, ventured that
"the repercussions will not be limited to Asia, but will extend to Western Europe and the British Commonwealth."[6]

The grand strategy that emerged from Nitze's map of the world
was to guide U.S. policy for most of the Cold War. The United States
took the fight to the Soviets. America beefed up its conventional capability while amassing an overkill nuclear arsenal, organized alliances
along the perimeter of the Soviet Union, found client states in all
quarters of the globe, and fought costly wars in Korea and Vietnam.
Washington temporarily backed off during the 1970s, pursuing a
decade of détente with the Soviet Union and adhering to a vision
more reminiscent of Kennan's era. President Jimmy Carter then
reversed course after the 1979 Soviet invasion of Afghanistan. And
President Ronald Reagan followed with a level of diplomatic and military pressure against the "evil empire" that quickly brought the Cold
War back to a fever pitch. Not until the fall of the Berlin Wall did the
United States begin to contemplate an alternative vision of international order.

Throughout the long years of the Cold War, successive administrations ensured that the American people were prepared to make the
necessary sacrifices by whipping up anticommunist sentiment—at
times, to excess. But well armed with a clear map of the world and a
compelling enemy in the Soviet Union, America's leaders had little
trouble engaging the public in the battle against communism.

The end of the Cold War has not settled the debate as to whether
Kennan's or Nitze's map of the world was the right one. On the one
hand, the hard-line strategy emerging from Nitze's vision may well
have prolonged the Cold War by escalating tensions on both sides.
Perhaps Kennan's strategy would have much sooner exposed the
cracks in the Soviet system. On the other hand, the rigid application of
the tenets of NSC-68 may well have helped convince the Soviets to
give up the fight, suggesting that Kennan's approach was not sufficiently tough to do the job.

The central point here is not whether Kennan or Nitze was right,
but that each offered a clear and compelling map that served both to
guide grand strategy and to garner the domestic support needed to
bring that strategy to fruition. At times, America was probably too

compliant with the Soviet Union. At other times, it was probably blinded by anticommunism, missing opportunities to exploit rifts within the communist bloc. But in the end, the United States prevailed because it knew where it wanted to head, mapped out a plan for getting there, and set out on the journey.

NEW FAULT LINES

DURING THE Cold War, the task of formulating grand strategy was admittedly easier than it is today. The mere existence of the Soviet Union concentrated the mind. The immediacy of the threat posed by communism made the development of a strategic vision an urgent matter. And this threat gave natural definition to America's map of the world. The world's principal fault line lay at the inter-German border. The Atlantic democracies were to the west, the enemy to the east. Much of the world automatically fell into one of these two blocs. The main challenges for the strategists of the day were to figure out what part of the periphery mattered and to identify the geopolitical trends that would ultimately undermine the Soviet empire.

Today, no major adversary or commanding threat provides a ready starting point for America's new map of the world. Americans justifiably remain concerned about terrorism. But this threat is evasive and shadowy, and therefore does more to blur than to clarify the strategic landscape. The perpetrators of terrorism are criminal gangs, not states; law enforcement is a more effective weapon than military strength. Sweeping changes in technology and the transition from the industrial to the digital era also make it difficult to get a conceptual handle on which geopolitical forces are now the dominant ones. During the Cold War, the balance of power between East and West was a function primarily of industrial output and the size of conventional and nuclear arsenals. At present, a computer virus may be a much more potent weapon than an F-16 jet fighter.

The same conditions that make a coherent grand strategy so difficult to construct, however, also obligate America to overcome the obstacles and make progress toward identifying the world's new fault lines. The United States did not have great latitude in shaping the world during the Cold War. The Soviets occupied most of Eurasia. The liberal democracies held North America, Western Europe, and Japan. The West could do little more than chip away at the margins. Now the global system is fluid and malleable. The decisions made in

Washington in the coming decade have the potential to chart a course for the next century, if not longer.

The same goes for the whirlwind pace of technological and economic change. They make the world hard to map out. But they also give the United States unprecedented influence and novel tools of management. Whether through leading NATO into battle, disseminating information on the Internet, managing the international flow of capital, or controlling entry to the world's main international institutions, America generally calls the shots. This reach brings great opportunity but also weighty responsibility.

We begin the task of constructing a new map of the world by examining the alternatives that have already been offered up by others. Although neither the U.S. government nor the public has been paying much attention, several of America's strategists have been attempting to map out the new global environment. Surveying these competing visions and exposing their strengths and weaknesses offers an appropriate starting point for an inquiry into U.S. grand strategy and where we go from here.

America's intellectuals have thus far offered up five alternative maps of the world. Francis Fukuyama, now a professor at the Johns Hopkins School of Advanced International Studies, began the debate in 1989, just as the Cold War was winding down. In "The End of History?" an article published in *The National Interest*, and his subsequent book, *The End of History and the Last Man*, Fukuyama pronounced that the demise of the Soviet Union and the triumph of democracy were bringing history to an end.[7] He contended that the world is arriving at an end state in which like-minded and mild-mannered democratic states will together construct a stable and peaceful global order. In the meantime, the main fault line will fall along the border between democratic and nondemocratic states. Fukuyama suggested that the United States should focus its foreign policy on promoting democracy worldwide while avoiding conflict along this fault line.

John Mearsheimer, a professor at the University of Chicago, was the next to stake out a position on the order that would emerge after the Cold War's end. In "Why We Will Soon Miss the Cold War" (*Atlantic Monthly*) and "Back to the Future: Instability in Europe After the Cold War" (*International Security*), both published in 1990, Mearsheimer offered a much gloomier prognosis than Fukuyama's.[8] He lamented the passing of the East-West conflict, arguing that the bipolar distribution of power it engendered played a central role in preserving peace for decades. The withdrawal of Soviet troops from Eastern Europe, the unraveling of the Warsaw Pact, and the consequent reduction of America's strategic role in Europe will lead to renewed rivalry across the Continent. With the return of multipolarity, Europe's future will come to resemble its unfortunate past, with fault lines reemerging among its nation-states. The best hope for stability lies in enhancing deterrence against aggression through the controlled proliferation of nuclear weapons. Mearsheimer's prognosis for East Asia was similarly pessimistic.

In "The Clash of Civilizations?"—a much acclaimed article published in *Foreign Affairs* in 1993—and in a subsequent book titled *The Clash of Civilizations and the Remaking of World Order,* Harvard professor Samuel Huntington proclaimed that the main fault lines of the future would emerge at the intersection of the world's major civilizations.[9] Different cultures hold competing views of both domestic and international order—and thus are destined to clash. According to Huntington's map of the world, four blocs (Judeo-Christian, Eastern Orthodox, Islamic, and Confucian) will compete for dominance. He counseled that America and Europe together gird their loins for battle against other cultures.

Paul Kennedy and Robert Kaplan, although working separately, came up with a fourth take on the key fault line of the future. Kennedy most succinctly stated his case in "Must It Be the Rest Against the West?" an article coauthored with Matthew Connelly in the *Atlantic Monthly* in 1994.[10] Kaplan also published his first statement on the issue, "The Coming Anarchy," in the *Atlantic Monthly* in 1994, and later brought out a book with the same title.[11] According to Kennedy's and Kaplan's map of the world, the globe will be divided along socioeconomic lines. The wealthy and healthy industrialized nations will constitute one bloc. The impoverished developing nations will constitute another. The main fault line will fall between them. Try as they might, the prosperous nations of the North will be unable to cordon themselves off from troubles in the South. Refugees, environmental disaster, the transmission of epidemics, crime and corruption, and collapsing states will ultimately pose threats to even the most advanced countries in the world. The wealthy nations must try to head off this nightmare at the pass, or they will be overrun by chaos.

New York Times journalist Thomas Friedman, in his newspaper columns and his 1999 book, *The Lexus and the Olive Tree,* identified globalization as the dominating geopolitical feature of the new century.[12] The expansion of a global market for goods, capital, and production has transformed the world, Friedman contended, compelling all states to play by the same rules. The market will reward countries that liberalize their economies and democratize. In contrast, it will treat harshly countries that seek to maintain centralized control of economic and political life, punishing their stock markets, their currencies, and their societies. According to Friedman's map of the world, the principal fault line of the future will emerge between those countries that adhere to the rules of a globalized, digital economy, and those that fight back. PCs per household, not the number of tanks or aircraft in the national arsenal, will determine where countries fit into the emerging geopolitical system.

Let us now take a closer look at these competing maps of the world.

HISTORY, according to Francis Fukuyama, has been marching steadily forward. There have been moments of backsliding and the occasional twist and turn, but each new era tends to build on the achievements of the last, improving the quality of life. Science and technological discovery are the main sources of economic growth and social advance. The steam engine, penicillin, the computer chip, the Internet—these innovations have all made possible significant improvement in the material well-being of mankind.

Humans, however, seek not just physical comfort, but also psychological comfort. This psychic well-being comes in the form of dignity or recognition of one's self-worth—what Aristotle called *thymos.* Even as scientific progress leads to greater wealth and comfort, man continues to struggle for recognition and dignity. This drive for *thymos,* according to Fukuyama, is the major cause of history's bloody trail. The search for prestige and status has time and again pitted states against each other in awful contests for superiority. And inside states, slaves and serfs for centuries fought against the rigid social hierarchies that denied them their dignity and autonomy.

Liberal democracy represents a political end state for Fukuyama because it by design accords the individual the self-worth that he has been seeking throughout history. The right to vote, equality under the law, codified freedoms—these are the characteristics of liberal democracy that make it "the end point of mankind's ideological evolution" and "the final form of human government."[13] Man no longer needs to struggle for dignity because reciprocal recognition is at the heart of liberal and democratic order.

In pronouncing that the collapse of Soviet communism and the triumph of democracy signify the end of history, Fukuyama draws on the writings of Friedrich Hegel, the nineteenth-century German philosopher. Hegel had foreseen the end of history in the American and French revolutions. With these twin revolutions and the new political systems they produced, "Hegel asserted that history comes to an end because the longing that had driven the historical process—the struggle for recognition—has now been satisfied in a society characterized by universal and reciprocal recognition. No other arrangement of human social institutions is better able to satisfy this longing, and hence no further progressive historical change is possible."[14] If the American and French revolutions began the ending of history, the contemporary era represents the completion of the process. The main competitors to liberal democracy—fascism, socialism, and communism—have all been defeated. A handful of states are still stuck in history and clinging to the past. But they will eventually acquiesce and go the way of free markets and liberal democracy.

To get from the end of history to America's new map of the world, Fukuyama again turns to a renowned German intellectual from the past—Immanuel Kant. Kant proposed that the rise of republican government held out the promise of building a lasting peace among the nations of the world. Representative government and popular opposition to war would act as a check on aggressive behavior. Kant also believed that democracies, almost like family members, would develop a natural affinity for one another.

Contemporary scholars, Fukuyama among them, have picked up on the idea that democracies may well be able to coexist peacefully with each other. The logic of the so-called democratic peace is similar to that of the end of history.[15] Just as a liberal democratic state naturally satisfies the yearning of its citizens for dignity, so too will liberal democratic states automatically accord each other the recognition and mutual respect that are the foundation of a lasting peace. Wars for prestige and status will be relegated to the history books. In Fukuyama's words, "Liberal democracy replaces the irrational desire to be recognized as greater than others with a rational desire to be recognized as equal. A world made up of liberal democracies, then, should have much less incentive for war, since all nations would reciprocally recognize one another's legitimacy."[16]

Fukuyama thus divides the world into two groupings of states. One is composed of the liberal democracies, the states that have made it to the end of history and no longer engage in strategic competition with each other. In this posthistorical part of the world, "the chief axis of interaction between states would be economic, and the old rules of *realpolitik* would have decreasing relevance. . . . The post-historical world would still be divided into nation-states, but its separate nationalisms would have made peace with liberalism and would express themselves increasingly in the sphere of private life alone."[17] Within the family of democracies, the traditional geopolitics of rivalry and competition are gone for good.

On the other side of the geopolitical divide will be the nondemocracies. In their dealings with each other and with liberal democracies, these states will be stuck in the past, still driven by the search for prestige and status, and therefore still mean, nasty, and beholden to the rules of traditional power politics. The world's new fault line, Fukuyama claims, thus lies at the intersection of the posthistorical (democratic) and historical (nondemocratic) worlds. Even as liberal democracy and the zone of democratic peace expand, "this does not by any means imply the end of international conflict *per se*. For the world at that point would be divided between a part that was historical and a part that was post-historical. Conflict between states still in history, and between those states and those at the end of history, would still be possible."[18]

The top priority of U.S. grand strategy, according to Fukuyama, should be to enlarge democracy, thereby erasing the world's only remaining fault line and completing the process of bringing history to an end. Expanding global markets and using economic liberalization to promote political liberalization hold out the most promise for achieving this task. In the meantime, the United States and its democratic brethren, even as they enjoy life in the posthistorical age, should remain on guard against potential threats from states still stuck in history.

Fukuyama suggests that two developments have the potential to alter his map of the world and get history going again. Citizens in liberal democracies may ultimately find the end of history boring and homogeneous, impelling them to seek new challenges. The search for dignity and self-worth could be insatiable and elemental to the human experience. The satisfaction of completing history aside, life without struggle may simply grow stale. Alternatively, the onward march of science and the development of biotechnological means of altering genetic codes may change man and the drives that shape his behavior.[19] If science changes human nature, all bets will be off. Barring these rather radical developments, Fukuyama believes, democracy will continue to spread, the end of history will draw nearer, and all geopolitical maps of the world will belong in the ash heap left behind.

MEARSHEIMER IS a hard-core realist, steadfastly standing by the claim that "the distribution and character of military power are the root causes of war and peace."[20] The distribution of power resulting from the end of the Cold War, he argues, will ultimately result in the return of a multipolar world. Without a major adversary around to invite America's global engagement, the United States will eventually withdraw from Europe and East Asia, producing rivalry in both regions.[21] Germany will again emerge as Europe's dominant state, disquieting its neighbors as it seeks to fill the vacuum left to its east by a retreating Russia. Disputes over borders and minorities will erupt in Central Europe, with affected states looking for outside help and therefore having "strong incentives to drag the major powers into their local conflicts." Nationalist passions are likely to be reawakened, Mearsheimer contends, quickening Europe's return "to a state system that created powerful incentives for aggression in the past."[22] He foresees a similar return of national rivalries to East Asia.

Mearsheimer laments the end of the Cold War on the grounds that the bipolarity produced by the East-West standoff is inherently more stable than the multipolar world that will come next. He offers three main reasons for preferring bipolarity. A two-bloc world has only one fault line, whereas a multibloc world has several. Bipolarity tends to produce a rough equilibrium of strength between fixed alliances while multipolarity gives rise to imbalances among shifting alliances. And bipolar systems are less complicated and unpredictable than multipolar ones, reducing the likelihood of miscalculation and unintended conflict.

The wars that frequented the international system prior to 1945 were primarily the product of "multipolarity and the imbalances of power that often occurred among the major states in that multipolar system."[23] The end of the East-West divide and the return of multipolarity thus do not constitute good news from Mearsheimer's perspective, explaining why he warns that "we will soon miss the Cold War." His map of the future thus looks much like a map of the pre–Cold War era, with fault lines falling between the world's major nation-states and the international system becoming much more conflict-prone.

Mearsheimer chides Fukuyama and others "who think that armed conflicts among the European states are now out of the question" for "projecting unwarranted optimism onto the future."[24] He contends that there is insufficient historical evidence to support the claim that democracies will not go to war with each other and he challenges on theoretical grounds the alleged link between representative government and pacific behavior: "Mass publics, whether in a democracy or not, can become deeply imbued with nationalistic or religious fervor, making them prone to support aggression and quite indifferent to costs."[25]

Mearsheimer also dismisses the notion that the EU will preserve accord among Europe's major nation-states, integration having been made possible by the Soviet threat and by America's pacifying effect on Western Europe. "Without a common Soviet threat or an American night watchman, Western European states will do what they did for centuries before the onset of the Cold War—look upon one another with abiding suspicion."[26] Far from coming together as a response to America's waning interest in Europe, the EU will come apart and "Germany, France, Britain, and perhaps Italy will assume major-power status."[27]

Faced with the prospect of this unwelcome future, Mearsheimer urges that the United States seek to maintain the Cold War confrontation—even if at lower levels of antagonism—as a means of extending bipolarity. Aware that this recommendation would likely win over few policy-makers, he advocates the controlled proliferation of nuclear weapons in order to stabilize multipolarity by enhancing deterrence against aggression. "Proliferation should ideally stop with Germany," Mearsheimer counsels, because "Germany would no doubt feel insecure without nuclear weapons, and if it felt insecure its impressive conventional strength would give it a significant capacity to disturb the tranquillity of Europe."[28] If unable to restrict proliferation, however, the U.S. and other nuclear states should provide technical assistance to countries that seek to develop a secure nuclear capability. Mearsheimer also urges that the United States and Britain should maintain conventional forces at the ready to intervene on the European continent as necessary "to counter any emerging aggressor actively and efficiently."[29]

ALTHOUGH Samuel Huntington does not foresee the return of rivalry among traditional nation-states, he does share Mearsheimer's pessimism about the future. Like Fukuyama, Huntington is a champion of liberal democracy American-style and thinks it is here to stay. But he parts company with Fukuyama when it comes to the appeal elsewhere of the West's values and politics. Rather than seeing the allure of liberal democracy as universal, Huntington believes that non-Western cultures will chart their own path and progressively resent America's efforts to re-create the world in its image. Instead of joining the stampede toward liberal democracy and enlarging the zone of democratic peace, these states will band together against the West. Cultural dividing lines will become geopolitical fault lines. The "clash of civilizations," not the "end of history," awaits.

A civilization, according to Huntington, is "the highest cultural grouping of people and the broadest level of cultural identity people have short of that which distinguishes humans from other species."[30] Civilization and culture both refer to the overall way of life of a people. Individuals who are part of the same civilization share common values, norms, and modes of thinking. Although they change over time, civilizations have impressive stamina and are "the most enduring of human associations."[31] Today, the world's peoples fall into eight main cultural groupings: Western, Confucian, Japanese, Islamic, Hindu, Slavic-Orthodox, Latin American, and African. "The most important conflicts of the future," Huntington warns, "will occur along the cultural fault lines separating these civilizations from one another."[32]

Huntington contends that civilizations are of rising geopolitical importance for two reasons. First, the ideological differences of the Cold War have all but disappeared, exposing more basic cultural differences that had been obscured by the division of the world into two rival blocs. The "Velvet Curtain of culture," in Huntington's words, is replacing the "Iron Curtain of ideology."[33] As the ideological strictures of the Cold War recede into the past, states and their peoples are guided by the values and modes of thinking embedded in their cultures. And these cultural templates vary widely across civilizations. The underlying values cherished by the West—freedom, individualism, constitutional protections, human rights—do not find fertile ground in most of the world's other civilizations. Peoples from different cultures are just plain different.

Second, global trends are setting civilizations against each other, not bringing them together. Economic modernization, the Internet, and the global market may be improving living standards in many parts of the world. But globalization and the pace of change it engenders are also disorienting and dislocating. As the world gets smaller and faster, people feel threatened by their unfamiliar surroundings. To find their bearings, they turn to traditions that are close to home, resulting in the resurgence of religion and a return to roots. The appeal of Islamic fundamentalism in the Muslim world, the discovery of the "Asian way" in Southeast Asia, and the cultivation of Russia's "Eurasian" identity are all signs of this ongoing revival of the link between culture and politics. Globalization promises to intensify this return to culture and religion in the years ahead, ensuring that "the clash of civilizations will dominate politics." According to Huntington's map of the world, "the fault lines between civilizations will be the battle lines of the future."[34]

Huntington's underlying pessimism is accentuated by his judgment that different civilizations are not just destined to clash, but to clash with the West in particular. The West is not only the most powerful civilization, but also the one that is attempting to foist its culture and values on everybody else. "The efforts of the West to promote its values of democracy and liberalism as universal values, to maintain its military predominance and to advance its economic interests engender countering responses from other civilizations."[35] Huntington is particularly worried about a connection between Confucian and Islamic societies. A rising China allied with anti-Western regimes in the Islamic world would create a potent combination. "A central focus of conflict for the immediate future," Huntington warns, "will be between the West and several Islamic-Confucian states."[36]

The United States, according to Huntington, should develop a grand strategy aimed at protecting the West against all challengers while simultaneously seeking to prevent conflict along the main civilizational fault lines. "The survival of the West depends on Americans reaffirming their Western identity and Westerners accepting their civilization as unique not universal and uniting to renew and preserve it against challenges from non-Western societies."[37] To counter the emerging Confucian-Islamic connection, Huntington urges that the United States seek to limit the military strength of China and Islamic states and to capitalize on opportunities to exploit political and cultural differences between these two civilizations. At the same time, America should do more to understand other cultures, "each of which will have to learn to coexist with the others."[38] Civilizations, after all, are durable and stubborn; the fault lines among them will not go away. The best the United States can hope for, although it is a long way off, is mutual tolerance and peaceful coexistence.

PAUL KENNEDY and Robert Kaplan are unlikely fellow travelers. A renowned scholar at Yale, Kennedy is one of the world's experts on the diplomatic and military history of the British Empire. He is the author of numerous works of scholarship, including a best-seller, *The Rise and Fall of the Great Powers*. While Kennedy graces the seminar rooms of Yale's elegant colleges, Robert Kaplan wanders the squalid shantytowns of the poorest places on earth. Whether reporting from Africa, the Middle East, Europe, or Asia, he chronicles the plight of the dispossessed, the diseased, the desperate. Kaplan's well-known travelogues, such as *Balkan Ghosts* and *The Ends of the Earth*, have met with wide acclaim.[39]

Despite their differences, Kennedy and Kaplan have offered up similar views of what America's new map of the world should look like. Both identify the next fault line as the divide between the wealthy countries of the North and the impoverished countries of the South. According to Kennedy (and his coauthor Matthew Connelly), we are heading into "a world of two 'camps,' North and South, separate and unequal." On one side of the fault line will be "a relatively small number of rich, satiated, demographically stagnant societies." On the other side will be "a large number of poverty-stricken, resource-depleted nations whose populations are doubling every twenty-five years or less.... How those on the two sides of these widening regional or intercontinental fissures are to relate to each other ... dwarfs every other issue in global affairs."[40] And on this paramount issue, Kennedy is anything but optimistic. "A population explosion on one part of the globe and a technology explosion on the other," he warns, "is not a good recipe for a stable international order."[41]

Kaplan also foresees a fault line "between 'North' and 'South'" and "a bifurcated world, divided between societies like ours, producing goods and services that the rest of the world wants, and those mired in various forms of chaos."[42] To help him describe his new map of the world, Kaplan quotes political scientist Thomas Fraser Homer-Dixon: "Think of a stretch limo in the potholed streets of New York City, where homeless beggars live. Inside the limo are the air-conditioned postindustrial regions of North America, Europe, the emerging Pacific Rim, and a few other isolated places, with their trade summitry and computer-information highways. Outside is the rest of mankind, going in a completely different direction."[43]

Although the wealthy nations of the North may think they can turn their backs on the poor nations of the South, Kennedy and Kaplan argue otherwise. Rather than disappearing from the geopolitical map as they spiral downward through famine, disease, and crime to eventual collapse, the states of the South will come to pose the chief strategic threat to the industrialized world. Kennedy and Kaplan offer several arguments as to how what is still a socioeconomic divide will soon become a geopolitical fault line.

Kennedy, at least in his first incarnation in "Must It Be the Rest Against the West?" is worried primarily about massive migration. Populations will continue to swell, quickly overwhelming local resources and degrading the environment. As living conditions in many African countries deteriorate, inhabitants will pick up and leave. And they will head north, where there is food, water, and, at least as far as they can tell, the prospect of a house and car. Whether by raft, bus, cargo hold, or on foot, they will come, and by the millions. Industrialized countries will have only two choices—to be overrun or to use force to repel the waves of migrants. In Kennedy's words, "The rich will have to fight and the poor will have to die if mass migration is not to overwhelm us all."[44]

In Kennedy's second incarnation, he (along with coauthors Robert Chase and Emily Hill) seems less alarmed about the prospect of incoming hordes of refugees. Instead, Kennedy focuses on radiating waves of instability that would accompany the collapse of regional powers—so-called pivotal states. A pivotal state is a large and centrally located country that, if it falls prey to internal turmoil, would become "a hot spot that could not only determine the fate of its region but also affect international stability."[45] The potential causes of domestic turmoil are the familiar ones—overpopulation, migration, environmental degradation, epidemics, and crime. The countries that qualify as pivotal states are Mexico, Brazil, Algeria, Egypt, South Africa, Turkey, India, Pakistan, and Indonesia. The United States and other industrialized nations could not afford to watch passively should one or more of these countries collapse; the strategic consequences would be too grave. Hence the demarcation of the North-South divide as the geopolitical fault line of the future.

Kaplan's coming anarchy will arrive in similar fashion—through massive migration and radiating instability from collapsing states. Kaplan points to rampant crime and environmental scarcity (shortages of water will be particularly acute) as the main culprits. As he puts it, "criminal anarchy" looms on the horizon and the environment is *"the* national-security issue of the early twenty-first century."[46] Add to this mix new and virulent strains of religious and ethnic extremism, and out comes a Third World that is not just descending into chaos, but angry about it and looking for revenge. Kaplan's brand of anarchy thus has Huntingtonian, anti-Western overtones—what might best be called "anarchy with attitude."

As for policy prescriptions, Kennedy argues that if the United States and its main partners act with urgency, they may well be able to reverse the South's descent into chaos. Citizens fortunate enough to live in the North must persuade their leaders "to recognize the colossal, interconnected nature of our global problem and to strain every element of our human ingenuity, resourcefulness, and energy to slow down, or if possible reverse, the buildup of worldwide demographic and environmental pressures."[47] The United States should take the lead in forging a new North-South compact. Its chief elements would include expanding economic assistance to the South, carrying out research on new sources of energy and food production, improving family planning and access to health care throughout the Third World, and making the United Nations a more effective instrument for preventing and stopping conflict.

Kaplan is more skeptical about the benefits of economic assistance. "Development assistance rarely changes history dramatically," he insists. "To think that aid can fundamentally change sub-Saharan Africa . . . is to take a position that few people outside a narrow intellectual elite will accept."[48] Nonetheless, Kaplan does believe aid can on occasion make a difference and that even when it does not it can "help us to reinvent ourselves as a nation in the context of a more interconnected world."[49] He also argues that the United States should put more effort into developing early warning mechanisms in the

Third World; the best time to address a crisis is before it starts. When preventive measures fail, however, America should be very careful about direct involvement. Only in extreme circumstances, when strategic interests are high and likely costs low, should the United States be prepared to intervene militarily. "We must stay engaged," Kaplan counsels, "but within strict limits."[50]

THOMAS FRIEDMAN has been America's prophet of globalization. He has used his position as the foreign affairs columnist for the *New York Times* to pass along one main message to his readers—the digital age, coupled with the expansion of markets, is transforming the international system.

Like Fukuyama, Friedman is basically bullish about the future and the potential for globalization to promote prosperity, democracy, and peace. "The symbol of the Cold War system was a wall, which divided everyone," he explains in *The Lexus and the Olive Tree.* "The symbol of the globalization system is a World Wide Web, which unites everyone." Globalization shapes "the domestic politics and foreign relations of virtually every country" by forcing states to play by the same rules if they want to prosper. Countries that open their markets and clean up their politics will thrive, while the rest will be left behind by the global economy.

Globalization, according to Friedman, is "the inexorable integration of markets, nation-states and technologies to a degree never witnessed before."[51] The global marketplace and the digital technologies that are its infrastructure (the Lexus is the metaphor) are not the only forces shaping the international system; traditional disputes between peoples and states (the olive tree) still matter. But when all is said and done, globalization will be the "One Big Thing," the defining feature of the new era. In Friedman's words, "globalization is not the only thing influencing events in the world today, but to the extent that there is a North Star and a worldwide shaping force, it is this system."[52]

International financiers and corporate executives—the "electronic herd" in Friedman's parlance—are the main agents through which the global marketplace for goods and capital is transforming states and how they interact with each other. The mechanism at work is simple. States need to attract international capital if they are to prosper. In deciding whether to invest in a specific country, all the electronic herd really cares about is "how your country is wired inside, what level of operating system and software it's able to run, and whether your government can protect private property."[53] If a country passes the test, the electronic herd with a single keystroke awards it the capital needed to grow. If a country fails the test, it had better watch out. One day, Malaysia is the darling of emerging market mutual funds. The next, its currency is in a virtual free fall as investors head for the exits. The electronic herd is fast, and it is ruthless.

Friedman contends that globalization is imposing a "golden straitjacket" on all states, encouraging them to adhere to open business practices, to adopt standard accounting procedures, to combat corruption, and to move toward liberal democracy. The electronic herd smiles beneficently on states that don their golden straitjacket and prepare for a snug fit, but it punishes mercilessly those that resist. There is no escape from the inexorable logic of globalization and the golden straitjacket that comes with it. "If your country has not been fitted for one," Friedman warns, "it will be soon."[54]

Friedman's take on globalization has much in common with a broader literature on the ability of international institutions to promote convergence and cooperation. Whereas Friedman sees the market as providing the main impetus behind integration, institutionalists focus more on the capacity of bodies like NATO, the United Nations, and the World Trade Organization to cajole states into following compatible paths. Some scholars concentrate on the ability of institutions to lock in international agreements and punish states that fail to live up to their promises.[55] Others contend that shared participation in international organizations over time engenders common norms and the evolution of transnational coalitions.[56] Still others see institutions as vehicles for exercising "soft power"—that is, expanding their cultural influence.[57] This perspective on the sources of cooperation and peace stresses the globalization of institutions more than of markets. But, as in Friedman's map of the world, the central idea is that global networks have the capacity to embrace states and impose on them strong incentives to adhere to common rules.

The impact of globalization does not stop with its ability to make all states look and behave more or less alike. The golden straitjacket also has potent geopolitical implications. Enter Friedman's "golden arches theory of conflict prevention." After the electronic herd has had its way with a country, that state will have little interest in going to war with others. "When a country reaches the level of economic development where it has a middle class big enough to support a

McDonald's network," Friedman writes, "it becomes a McDonald's country. And people in McDonald's countries don't like to fight wars anymore, they prefer to wait in line for burgers." Whereas Fukuyama foresees a democratic peace, Friedman is banking on a capitalist peace, based on the assumption that globalization "increases the incentives for not making war and increases the costs of going to war in more ways than in any previous era in modern history."[58]

Friedman acknowledges that not all states will go along with this game plan. Despite the prospect of being punished by the electronic herd, a handful of states will resist globalization. Some will find it too threatening to traditional culture and dig in against it. Others will refuse to implement the requisite political and economic reforms because they undermine the authority of corrupt officials and the cronies on whom they rely to govern. At least temporarily, a new geopolitical fault line will emerge between those countries that take advantage of global markets and those that fight against them by refusing to liberalize. "Today, there is no more First World, Second World or Third World," Friedman explains. "There's now just the Fast World—the world of the wide-open plain—and the Slow World—the world of those who either fall by the wayside or choose to live away from the plain in some artificially walled-off valley of their own, because they find the Fast World too fast, too scary, too homogenizing or too demanding."[59]

Friedman is confident, however, that these spoilers will eventually become "road kill" on the information highway. "The free market is the only ideological alternative left. One road. Different speeds. But one road."[60] In the end, globalization will therefore produce a world populated by only fleet-footed, capitalist, Internet-savvy, democratic states, all pursuing common interests.

Friedman also recognizes that globalization can result in a secondary fault line *within* states. Integration into the global economy produces winners and losers, those who ride the Internet to success, and those who only look on and grow ever more resentful. The result could be "civil wars between pro-globalizers and anti-globalizers, between globalists in each society and localists in each society, between those who benefit from change and from this new system and those who feel left behind by it."[61] Furthermore, the "super-empowered angry man" may well take advantage of the very system he resents to bring it down, using the Internet to propagate destructive computer viruses. The terror attacks of September 2001 confirmed

Friedman's worst fears: "Super-empowered angry people . . . turned our most advanced civilian planes into human-directed, precision-guided cruise missiles—a diabolical melding of their fanaticism and our technology."[62]

Friedman is optimistic, however, that good policy can manage these threats. By finding a comfortable balance between the Lexus and the olive tree—creating social safety nets, enabling states to preserve their cultures as they integrate into the global economy, protecting the environment—the international community should be able to reap the benefits of globalization without incurring its potential costs.

THE END OF AMERICA'S UNIPOLAR MOMENT AND A NEW MAP OF THE WORLD

FUKUYAMA, Mearsheimer, Huntington, Kennedy, Kaplan, and Friedman have been thinking hard, wrestling with the big issues of the day in order to help America orient itself in a new and uncertain era. But their maps of the world are misleading—or at least too short-lived to be dependable. Although each captures an important element of the current international system, all of them miss the mark when it comes to identifying the key fault line of the future. Mearsheimer is stuck in the past, offering a vision that overlooks the profound changes taking place in global politics. The others are stuck in the present, advancing visions that provide only a glimpse of a fleeting moment because they fail to understand that their maps are a by-product of a single, fundamental feature of today's world: America's preponderance of power.

According to this book's map of the world, American predominance is the central feature of the current geopolitical environment. The character of the international system is shaped by the distribution of power and how many poles there are to run up against each other; great nations by their nature compete for primacy. The scope and range of U.S. strength mean that there is presently only one pole in the world. It follows that there is no competition for primacy. It is precisely for this reason that unipolarity is more stable and less prone to war than all the alternatives. Unipolarity does not make for a particularly egalitarian world, as many countries often remind the United States—sometimes violently. But it does forestall great-power rivalry, a benefit to all.

History's most destructive wars, after all, occurred when the great nations of the day took to the battlefield to contend for primacy. Consider the bloody record of the last century alone. World War I resulted from Germany's bid for hegemony in a multipolar Europe. World War II emerged from the same dynamic, except the rise of Japan meant that conflict also engulfed East Asia. The Cold War was about two major blocs jockeying for position. Nothing has more consistently bedeviled statesmen throughout history than the challenge of preserving peace among dueling centers of power.

In contrast, unipolar moments correspond with some of the most peaceful periods in history. The superiority of Rome brought long centuries of peace to Europe and the Mediterranean Basin. The Roman legions certainly shed much blood as they expanded the empire's frontiers. But the scope of Rome's dominance then preempted potential contenders. Europe's economy and cultural life burgeoned as a result. British hegemony during the nineteenth century corresponded to a similar period of peace and prosperity. International rivalries were for the most part kept in check, the global economy grew more open and vibrant, science and industry forged ahead.

We are now in America's unipolar moment. The United States spends more on defense than the world's other major nations combined, and more on research and development in the defense sector than the rest of the world combined. The U.S. economy is more than twice the size of that of number two (Japan). The market value of companies like Microsoft and General Electric is larger than the national economies of many countries. Hollywood is so dominant that the French find themselves compelled to legislate protective barriers against U.S. television programs and movies lest America's cultural appeal extinguish their struggling entertainment industry. As a result of these asymmetries, great-power competition is at a minimum and most regions of the world enjoy peace. Disputes over borders, religion, and ethnicity continue, but they tend to remain localized. The global economy has enjoyed a period of remarkable growth. Major breakthroughs in biotechnology and information systems occur on a regular basis.

The relative stability of the current era stems not just from the resources at the disposal of the United States, but also from its willingness to use them. The United States has been either minding the store or putting out fires in virtually every quarter of the globe. American forces preserve the uneasy peace in East Asia, guarding South Korea from the regime to the north, keeping the lid on tensions between

China and Japan, and trying to support Taiwan's de facto independence without inciting Beijing. America still maintains a sizable troop presence in Europe to help ensure stability on the Continent. When the Balkans fell prey to ethnic conflict during the 1990s, it was the United States that eventually came to the rescue. The containment of Iraq throughout the past decade fell principally upon U.S. shoulders. America led the charge against terrorist networks and their sponsors in Afghanistan in 2001. And in the Middle East, Northern Ireland, Cyprus, Eritrea, and many other hot spots, Washington has been a central player in the search for peace.

When not overtly running the show, the United States has been calling the shots and writing the rules of the road from behind the scenes. NATO, the International Monetary Fund (IMF), the World Bank, the Asia-Pacific Economic Cooperation (APEC) forum, and the World Trade Organization are all complex organizations with many members and elaborate decision rules. But the United States quietly exercises a dominating influence over them as well. The Clinton administration thought NATO should expand its membership. A few years later, Washington hosted a welcoming ceremony for Poland, Hungary, and the Czech Republic. China was recently up for membership in the WTO, a body containing well over a hundred countries, all of whom are supposed to have equal voice. But China's prospects for entry were heavily dependent on one issue—whether the U.S. House and Senate would approve permanent trading rights for China (which they both did in 2000). When the Asian financial crisis was unfolding in 1997–1998, Japan proposed the creation of a special Asian bank to help establish monetary stability. Sorry, Washington told Tokyo, the International Monetary Fund—in which the United States has more say than any other nation—will handle matters.

American primacy has also been promoting stability by drawing out the peace-causing effects of other global trends. Unipolarity is the superstructure and determines the primary forces that shape the international system. When the structure itself enhances stability and dampens competition, secondary forces do so as well.

Consider globalization. The global economy, despite its ups and downs, has expanded considerably since the Cold War's end, increasing prosperity among the many countries that have tapped into worldwide flows of trade and capital. Integration into global markets has in turn fostered economic and political liberalization. But the positive effects of globalization are inseparable from American power. That the United States designed, manages, and underwrites the international economy has everything to do with the allure of globalization. The dollar is the dominant reserve currency. More than half of the top one hundred companies in the world are American.[63] The U.S. Treasury has much more impact on the national economies of many countries than their own finance ministries. Virtually all states that can play in the American-led global economy do—it is the only game in town. Globalization *is* Americanization.

The same goes for democracy. Democratic governance is certainly preferable to all the alternatives and has its intrinsic appeal. But democracy is flourishing in much of the world at least in part because the globe's only superpower is a democracy—and a fanatic proselytizer at that. The United States rewards aspiring democracies with loans and coveted membership in international organizations of various stripes. During her tenure as secretary of state, Madeleine Albright declared democracy her "lodestar," and invited all the world's democracies to gather in Warsaw in June 2000.[64] Meanwhile, countries unwilling or unable to make the transition to democratic rule face sanctions, isolation, and in cases like Iraq, Serbia, and Afghanistan, American bombs. Democratization too is inseparable from Americanization.

Another positive spillover effect of unipolarity is humanitarian intervention. The United States and its partners have passed up plenty of opportunities to stop bloodshed and suffering in distant lands. The failure to do anything about the genocide in Rwanda in 1994 was probably the most egregious. But, sad to say, that is business as usual. Except for the Nordic countries, which have made peacekeeping and humanitarian relief into a national cause, most governments put the lives of their citizens on the line only when national security is at stake.

It is for this reason that the record of the past decade stands out. In a reasonable number of instances—Somalia, Haiti, Bosnia, Kosovo, East Timor—the international community did intervene to stop conflict and deliver humanitarian relief. Although these efforts were often tardy and achieved mixed results, at least they were forthcoming. The Clinton administration also did its best to put the AIDS crisis in Africa at the top of America's foreign policy agenda.

This largess was a sign of the times, a product of America's surfeit of power and the global stability that stemmed from it. The world's major states were not distracted by their usual preoccupation—competing with one another. So they had the luxury of paying attention to other matters. Why not focus on bringing peace to East Timor or slowing the spread of AIDS in Africa when the most pressing security threat of the day came from North Korea, a state teetering on the edge of collapse?

The terror attacks on New York and Washington, although they made clear that America's preponderance by no means ensures its invulnerability, were in reality further confirmation of the pervasive reach of the United States. Al-Qaeda directed its wrath toward the U.S. precisely because America's ubiquity and wealth make it the logical scapegoat for any ill that befalls the Islamic world. By virtue of its military presence in Saudi Arabia, America is an infidel treading on holy ground. It is the corrupting spread of American culture that prevents the values and practice of Islam from taking greater hold. So too is America to blame for the plight of the Palestinians and the biting poverty that prevails throughout much of the Islamic world. America's unipolar moment makes it the prime target of the vengeful ideology that emerges from this mix of religious fanaticism and social disaffection. The resulting attacks produce destruction and shock. But they do not alter the underlying structure of the international system.

America's unipolar moment thus continues to define the global landscape. As a consequence, the current geopolitical map of the world has on it no major fault lines. Terrorism will remain a threat even as attempted attacks are foiled and their perpetrators killed, arrested, or starved of the resources they need to operate. But great-power competition—a far more dangerous threat—is for now in abeyance. The United States is reaping considerable benefit from this world, but so too are many other countries. This is good news. But there is bad news as well.

UNIPOLARITY IS HERE, but it will not last long. The numbers deceive. America's economic strength and military might are in a class of their own. Its cultural reach is extraordinary—in the late 1990s, *The Bold and the Beautiful* rivaled *Baywatch* as the most popular show in the world, and Michael Jordan's popularity rating in China stood ahead of Mao's. America is also poised to continue leading the high-tech revolution because of the innovation that springs from a healthy mix of venture capital and entrepreneurial spirit.

But analysts of the future consistently make the same error in fashioning their predictions: they rely too heavily on the present. In the late 1980s, America was in decline. Japan was number one, and its centralized economy was leaving in the dust the undisciplined consumerism of the United States. The Asian century was about to open. By the late 1990s, the American model had not just been exonerated, but beatified. The laissez-faire markets of the Anglo-Saxon world had triumphed over all else. Globalization had eliminated all alternatives to the American way. This new century, like the last, would be an American century.

The problem is that snapshots of the present provide little guidance for the future. Much more useful are historical patterns and long-term trends, which reveal that economic predominance over time shifts from one geographic center to another. The global economy will no doubt experience numerous gyrations in the years ahead; one day, the United States will look invincible, the next, past its prime. But amid these ups and downs, America's economic dominance will gradually slip away.

Two unstoppable trends mean that America's unipolar moment is unlikely to last the decade. The first is the diffusion of power. No dominant country has ever been able to sustain primacy indefinitely. Over time, other states catch up. This diffusion of economic strength will today occur more quickly than in most periods. The near-term challenger to America is not a single country trying to play catch-up—which takes time—but a European Union that is in the process of aggregating the impressive economic resources that its member nations already possess. Taken individually, Britain, France, or Germany could probably never catch the United States; each lacks sufficient population and resources. But amass their collective wealth, add the resources of more than a dozen other European countries—perhaps including before too long a recovered Russia—and an economic behemoth is on the horizon.

The European Union is admittedly not a federal state with a strong central government, and may never become one. Nor does Europe have a military capability commensurate with its economic resources. But after five decades of toiling away at economic and political integration, Europe is arriving on the global stage. Now that its single market has been accompanied by a single currency, Europe has a collective weight on matters of trade and finance comparable to that of the United States. The euro got off to a relatively weak start, losing ground against the dollar. But it has already rebounded and is likely to emerge as one of the world's main reserve currencies. In addition, Europe is forging a common defense policy and acquiring the military wherewithal to carry out operations on its own.

As the EU's resources grow and its governing bodies in Brussels enlarge their authority, influence will become more equally distributed between the two sides of the Atlantic. Europe and America may share democratic traditions. But as Europe grows stronger and more integrated, it will want a voice commensurate with its new station. Whether or not the United States likes it, Europe is becoming a new center of global power. America's sway will shrink accordingly.

East Asian nations are many years away from engaging in the historic process of integration that has brought peace and prosperity to Europe. Nonetheless, the region has great economic potential. Japan already has a highly educated and skilled workforce, an advanced industrial and technological base, and a well-developed market network. Once the necessary reforms are in place, its prolonged economic slowdown will give way to impressive growth. During the last decade, China enjoyed an economic growth rate of about 10 percent per year. The World Bank estimates that by 2020, "China could be the world's second largest exporter and importer. Its consumers may have purchasing power larger than all of Europe's. China's involvement with world financial markets, as a user and supplier of capital, will rival that of most industrialized countries."[65] As this new century progresses, East Asia, like Europe, will emerge as a counterweight to America.

The second trend that will bring the unipolar moment to an end sooner rather than later is the changing character of internationalism in the United States. Unipolarity rests on the existence of a polity that not only enjoys preponderance, but also is prepared to expend its dominant resources to keep everyone in line and to underwrite international order. If the United States were to tire of being the global protector of last resort, unipolarity would still come undone even if American resources were to remain supreme.

America's diminishing appetite for global engagement—and especially for its multilateral form—is a direct product of the changing international environment. For most of its history, America avoided direct involvement in rivalries outside its hemisphere. Its leaders felt that the United States could fulfill the need for expanding commerce without getting embroiled in distant lands. The crucial turning point was World War II, when the prospect of Germany and Japan becoming aggressors with global reach necessitated a new brand of internationalism and compelled America's direct involvement in shaping the balance of power in both Europe and East Asia. The Soviet threat then ensured that the United States would maintain extensive overseas commitments and institutional entanglements for the rest of the twentieth century.

The Cold War is now over and the fault line between two hostile blocs gone. In a world absent a major adversary, the United States will no longer feel compelled to play the role of global guardian. America is blessed with wide oceans to its east and west, and friendly neighbors to its north and south, conditions that afford a natural protection. Under these conditions, many of the same strategic and political considerations that constrained the country's appetite for international engagement from its founding in the eighteenth century until the attack on Pearl Harbor in 1941 are again coming to the fore.

Signs of America's inward turn are only gradually becoming apparent. The leaders of both major political parties have been pretending to continue with business as usual, each trying to best the other in supporting U.S. leadership and defense spending. The attacks of September 11 also put on hold America's retreat from global hegemony. All the while, however, the political center of gravity has been quietly but steadily moving toward a more limited internationalism.

Consider America's strategic presence in Europe, the centerpiece of U.S. security policy for the last five decades. The United States did intervene in Bosnia and Kosovo, suggesting a continuing willingness to remain Europe's peacemaker. But beneath the surface, a different picture is emerging. Americans and their elected representatives are coming to realize that a democratic and wealthy Europe at peace should be able to take care of itself. That is why the U.S. Senate's main reaction to the war over Kosovo was to pass unanimously a resolution bemoaning the "significant shortcomings" in European defense capabilities and urging the European Union to rectify the "overall imbalance" within the Atlantic alliance.[66] That is also why former U.S. Secretary of State Henry Kissinger, hardly an isolationist, argued before the Kosovo bombing campaign began that "the proposed deployment [of U.S. troops] in Kosovo does not deal with any threat to U.S. security as this concept has traditionally been conceived.... If Kosovo presents a security problem, it is to Europe, largely because of the refugees the conflict might generate. Kosovo is no more a threat to

America than Haiti was to Europe."[67] Clinton's air-only, ambivalent conduct of the war for Kosovo and the Bush administration's indications that it would like to withdraw U.S. troops from the Balkans make clear that America's days as Europe's chief protector are fast coming to an end.

America's diminishing internationalism is not the product of political decay. Nor does it mark the return of the dark and illusory brand of isolationism that so sorely misguided the nation in the past. It is the logical consequence of the times, of America's location, and of a strategic environment in which terror attacks against the homeland, not hegemonic wars in Europe or Asia, represent the most immediate threat to the country's well-being. The nation's politics are in the process of catching up with geopolitical realities.

At the same time, a waning internationalism does have the potential to turn into a dangerous isolationism. Especially because of the natural security afforded by America's location, the allure of preserving that security by pulling back from commitments that may compromise it, and the isolationist strains that have influenced U.S. foreign policy since the founding of the republic, a reduction of the country's global role does have the potential to go too far. A reining in of America's overseas commitments is one thing. It is inevitable and can be done gradually and with adequate preparation so as to minimize the attendant risks. An American withdrawal from global affairs is another matter altogether. It would have dire consequences precisely because global stability is at present so dependent on American power and purpose.

Equally worrisome is America's increasing unilateralism. Not only is the United States likely to be less engaged in managing international order in the years ahead, but when it does engage, it is likely to do so in a unilateral fashion. Consider the fate of the Kyoto Protocol on global warming and the Antiballistic Missile Treaty. During his first few months in office, George W. Bush, without first consulting with affected parties, announced that the United States would be withdrawing from both pacts. As to the fate of the Kyoto Protocol, Bush did not even try to hide his go-it-alone rationale: "We will not do anything that harms our economy, because first things first are the people who live in America."[68] As to the fate of the ABM Treaty, the administration did undertake consultations with numerous countries after making known its intention to scrap the arms control pact. But Bush then proceeded to inform the world in August 2001 that "we will withdraw from the ABM treaty on our timetable and at a time convenient to America."[69] In December, Bush made good on his promise.

The Europeans responded to these moves with a mixture of anguish and pique, emotions they did not hesitate to share with the president during his first visit to Europe during the summer of 2001. As one placard put it, "Bush to outer space/Missiles to dust-bin."[70] A public opinion poll conducted later in the summer in France, Germany, Italy, and Great Britain found strong and widespread opposition to Bush's foreign policy. Almost 85 percent of those surveyed disapproved of Bush's decision to withdraw from the Kyoto agreement, while more than 70 percent opposed his intention to rescind the ABM Treaty and develop a missile defense system. Seventy-eight percent believed that Bush made decisions "entirely on U.S. interests" without taking Europe into consideration.[71] The EU is emerging not just as a counterweight to the United States, but an angry one at that.

As in the past, America's unilateralist bent stems from fear that international institutions will encroach upon the nation's sovereignty and room for maneuver. This impulse has been on the rise in part because the restraining effects of the Cold War are gone. Electoral politics is also playing a role; conservative Republicans, especially those hailing from Bush's main constituency in the heartland, are some of the strongest proponents of a unilateral foreign policy. In addition, America will gravitate toward unilateralism out of frustration with its inability to get its way as often as in the past. Accustomed to calling the shots, the United States is likely to go off on its own when others refuse to follow Washington's lead—which the Europeans and others will do with greater frequency as their strength and self-confidence grow.

America did appear to have rediscovered both multilateralism and internationalism after the attacks of September 2001. The battle against terrorism, however, is not the stuff of durable alliance. America cobbled together an impressive coalition, but the United States was virtually alone in the military campaign against the Taliban and Al-Qaeda. A few days into the operation, fifty-six Islamic nations gathered in Qatar, issuing a communiqué stating that "the conference rejected the targeting of any Islamic or Arab state under the pretext of fighting terrorism."[72] The issues that prior to September 11 divided America, Europe, Russia, and China did not disappear; they were only masked by a temporary solidarity, as America's lonely war against Iraq made clear. And even as the long struggle against terror continues, the asymmetric threats posed by rogue regimes and terrorist cells will induce the United States to seek to cordon itself off from distant dangers through missile defenses, coastal patrols, tighter borders, and enhanced domestic security. With homeland defense now a top priority, America is ever more likely to back off from other missions, seek to lighten its load abroad, and expect others to do more.

The combination of unilateralism and isolationism toward which the United States is headed promises to be a dangerous mix. One day, America may well be alienating partners through its stiff-necked, go-it-alone ways. The next, it may be leaving them in the lurch as it backs away from an international system that it finds difficult to control. At the very moment that the United States will need the help of others to address mounting challenges, it may well find the world a lonely place.

It is precisely because of the potential for this scenario to become reality that the United States must prepare itself and the rest of the world for a new and more discriminating brand of American internationalism. For Washington to shape by design a measured and steady internationalism that enjoys the support of the American people is preferable to lurching back and forth between unilateralism and isolationism. In similar fashion, America should give notice to its allies that it expects more of them instead of holding on to the status quo as long as possible, only then to disengage with little warning. If the United States is to find this new brand of liberal internationalism, build the necessary public support at home, fortify the international institutions needed to preserve stability, and prepare itself and its allies abroad for a more equal partnership, Washington must begin laying the groundwork.

Combine the rise of Europe and Asia with a declining and prickly internationalism in the United States and it becomes clear that America's unipolar moment is not long for this world. America's dominance and its political appetite for projecting its power globally have peaked, and both will be dissipating over the course of the coming decade. As unipolarity gives way to multipolarity, the strategic competition now held in abeyance by U.S. primacy will return—and with a vengeance if America's unilateralist impulse prevails. No longer steadied by U.S. hegemony, processes of globalization and democratization are likely to falter, as are the international institutions currently dependent upon Washington's leadership to function effectively. Geopolitical fault lines will reemerge among centers of power in North America, Europe, and East Asia. The central challenge for U.S. grand strategy will be managing and taming the dangers arising from these new fault lines.

THE CHAPTERS that follow build on this map of the world and demonstrate why it is a better guide to the future than the alternatives. The field can be narrowed before proceeding, however, by setting aside at the outset three of the alternative maps—those of Huntington, of Kennedy and Kaplan, and of Mearsheimer.

Huntington's map of the world has several weaknesses. To begin, there is scant evidence to support the claim that other cultures will clash with the West—even though the conditions for anti-American gangs to form have over the past decade been about as good as they could get. With the United States at the peak of its power, and the advanced democracies benefiting from globalization much more than most other parts of the world, resentment toward the West ought to be fueling countering coalitions among non-Western civilizations. That these coalitions are not forming delivers Huntington's vision a potent blow.

Consider what 1999 looked like from an Orthodox, Confucian, or Muslim perspective. America was flexing its military muscle just about everywhere. It expanded NATO despite Moscow's strident objections, intensifying the sting of Orthodox Russia's loss of empire. The United States led NATO into battle against Serbia, another affront to the world of Orthodox Slavs. Furthermore, NATO acted without the approval of the United Nations, contravening the letter of the law, even if not the spirit. In the middle of the conflict, precision-guided bombs from U.S. warplanes turned a wing of the Chinese embassy in Belgrade into rubble, with Washington all the while chastising Beijing because of the regime's repressive ways and its threats against Taiwan. Halfway around the globe, American aircraft were regularly striking Iraqi targets—and had been doing so for most of the decade. And Washington was standing behind, albeit without much enthusiasm, the right-wing Israeli government of Benjamin Netanyahu as it made a mess of the peace process with the Palestinians. This was a veritable recipe for invoking the collective ire of the Orthodox, Confucian, and Muslim peoples.

But did these aggrieved civilizations come together in an angry anti-American alliance? Did the rest sharpen their swords for battle against the West? Nothing of the sort. The Russians barely lifted a finger for their Serb brethren and in the end lent America a helping hand by pressuring Milosevic to withdraw his army from Kosovo. A few short months after the end of the conflict, both Moscow and Beijing were working to put relations with Washington back on a good track. And most Arab countries, far from organizing a jihad against America, kept their distance from Saddam Hussein and did little to help their Palestinian brethren.

If Huntington's map of the world were the right one, this would be the time for cultural gangs to form against America for another reason: developing regions of the world are no longer the object of East-West rivalry. During the Cold War, the United States and the Soviet Union played regional states off one another. Saudi Arabia against Syria. Iraq against Iran. North Korea versus South Korea. Japan versus China. Ethiopia versus Somalia. The Cold War often scuttled any chance for cohesion among neighboring countries with similar cultures. Both Washington and Moscow followed the same dictum—divide and rule.

With the Soviet Union gone, the United States has been using its good offices to resolve regional disputes, not to inflame them. Especially during the Clinton administration, U.S. diplomats were involved in mediating conflicts in almost every quarter of the globe. Nonetheless, many regional disputes continue to fester, the appeal of cultural affinity demonstrating little pacifying or unifying effect. The Korean peninsula remains divided. Political rivalries and ethnic tensions still plague many parts of Africa. The Islamic world shows no signs of greater cohesion, with states in the Middle East frequently at odds with each other. In short, despite the end of the Cold War, there remains much more trouble within civilizations than among them.

The terrorist attacks on New York and Washington, although portrayed by many as a testament to the mounting clash between the West and the Islamic world, only confirm this basic interpretation. Instead of condoning terrorism, most countries in the Middle East were quick to denounce the attacks—including stalwart antagonists of the United States, such as Iran and Libya. The same Islamic conference that raised questions about the legitimacy of the retaliatory campaign against Afghanistan did condemn the terrorist attacks against the United States and insisted they contradicted the teachings of Islam. A group of Muslim clerics, including an authority respected even by militants, issued a *fatwa*—a religious opinion—denouncing the terror attacks and indicating that it was the "duty" of Muslims to help apprehend the perpetrators.[73] Although the government of virtually every Islamic state faces risks when it overtly cooperates with the United States, numerous countries in the Middle East and southwest Asia offered the U.S. access to their bases, military installations, and airspace. Such support helped dispel the notion that in retaliating for the attacks America was taking on Islamic civilization. That U.S. troops took to the field three times during the 1990s to defend Muslim peoples—in Kuwait, Bosnia, and Kosovo—also countered this myth.

Despite the rhetoric of Osama bin Laden and his fellow travelers, the ongoing struggle between the United States and Islamic radicals does not represent a clash of civilizations. On the contrary, the central cleavage fueling the terrorism spawned in the Middle East is within the Islamic world itself, not between the United States and Islam. The illegitimacy of governing regimes, clan and factional rivalries, large income inequalities, pervasive poverty, a sense of having been left behind by history—these are the root causes of the disaffection within Islamic society. Extremist groups and religious zealots then prey upon this discontent, turning it into hatred of the United States and the West. But the underlying source of alienation is homegrown—political and economic stagnation and the social cleavages it produces.

That the Islamic world has no monopoly on anti-American sentiment adds to the strength of this interpretation. Resentment of the United States may run deeper in the Middle East than elsewhere, but anti-American protests are no stranger to France, Russia, China, and many countries in Latin America. The core of the problem is not America's culture, but its power. As with all hegemons throughout history, primacy evokes pique. States at the top are always a popular target of discontent, especially in countries that are poor or in which the hegemon exercises a particularly heavy hand. This resentment, however, rarely proves strong enough to offset the internal cleavages that have consistently kept clashes within civilizations more potent than clashes among them.

The striking absence of reconciliation and cohesion within civilizations has a primary cause—the divisive effects of concern about power and security usually trump the potentially unifying effects of cultural and ideological affinity. Most of the world's disputes tend to take place between neighboring states. The reason is that neighbors, by virtue of their proximity, often threaten each other's well-being, overwhelming the sense of affinity that their shared culture or ethnicity might otherwise engender. Threat is a stronger determinant of how a nation identifies enemies and selects allies than is either culture or ideology.[74]

Potential partnerships among states with cultural similarities have time and again foundered on the shoals of security competition. Pan-Arab aspirations led Syria and Egypt in 1958 to form the United Arab Republic. The Syrian government then backed out in 1961, uneasy with the growing influence of Egyptian President Gamal Abdel Nasser. Islamic unity has similarly been no match for the strategic rivalry between Iran and Iraq. A sense of kinship hardly stopped Saddam Hussein from plundering Kuwait's wealth. Pakistan for years supported the Taliban regime in Afghanistan, but changed course in a matter of days when it faced the prospect of allying itself with America's war on terrorism—and reaping the economic and strategic benefits.

The same logic applies in other regions. Japan and China have cultural ties that go back centuries. But these ties currently do little to ameliorate the political divide between East Asia's two major nations. In similar fashion, the tendency for geopolitical concerns to prove stronger than cultural affinity is precisely why a rising Europe and its American offspring are likely to engage in strategic rivalry. Huntington is right that competition will abound, but such competition will take place among power blocs, not civilizations.

Kennedy's and Kaplan's map also suffers from important flaws. There is no doubt that developing regions of the world, and Africa in particular, are on the verge of a dire crisis. AIDS, famine, environmental degradation, and crime do threaten to turn entire regions into wastelands. The desolate anarchy of the Mad Max film series may ring all too true.

The problem is that the industrialized nations of the North have an almost limitless capacity to cordon themselves off from suffering and conflict in the developing world. The United States has been spending a pittance on foreign aid—about one-tenth of 1 percent of its gross national product. Nonetheless, getting this paltry budget past Congress every year has been a major accomplishment, requiring endless squabbling and horse-trading.

The explanation for this predicament is straightforward. Most developing countries have minimal industrial and financial resources. It follows that their military capabilities are equally primitive. Precisely because they are of little economic and strategic value, the United States and other industrialized countries can, and usually do, ignore their plight. As of 2000, 36 percent of Botswana's citizens between the ages of fifteen and forty-nine had contracted HIV, essentially condemning the country to collapse by devastating its working population. Although a humanitarian nightmare, a ruined Botswana will simply matter less in economic and strategic terms than before. There will be no fault line between Botswana and the West because the country may well disappear.

Some of the states headed toward collapse may well be large ones, creating the potential for regionwide instability and suffering. As they have in the past, however, the industrialized countries will probably turn their backs. Waves of refugees will head north, but the rich nations will block their passage and send them home. The wall between North and South will just reach higher.

It is true that economic and social deterioration in the developing world is likely to make even more fertile the breeding ground for disaffected groups that wish to inflict harm on the North. Terrorists already have the skills to breach the West's protective barriers. The potential proliferation of weapons of mass destruction makes the prospect of future attacks even more serious. And even in the face of the best efforts to eliminate the threat, terrorists are likely to occasionally make their presence felt.

The South thus poses a strategic threat that the North will be unable to ignore, but it is one that comes from a few isolated groups or rogue regimes, not from the developing world as a whole. As a consequence, the United States may on occasion go after terrorist groups and the states that harbor them; Afghanistan is a case in point. But these will be isolated attacks against fringe groups or extremist regimes, not a clash between North and South. And even as the struggle to eliminate terrorism at its source enjoys a measure of success, the uncertain and unpredictable nature of the threat will mean that the barriers between North and South continue to rise. Tighter borders, more restrictive immigration policies, coastal patrols that turn away or sink unidentified vessels—these are not signs of a new geopolitical fault line, but only of the North's redoubled efforts to cordon itself off from potential hazards coming its way from the South.

Furthermore, a self-defeating contradiction would emerge if the

North's interaction with the South becomes defined primarily in terms of a struggle against terrorism. In fighting terror, America will tend to align with conservative regimes that are more comfortable entering into coalition with the West. But many of these regimes—Saudi Arabia is a case in point—play a key role in arresting political and economic development in their regions. Casting America's engagement with the South as a war on terrorism thus risks reinforcing the illiberal governments and economic inequalities that give rise to disaffection and extremism to begin with. In combination with the West's occasional military foray into the developing world, identifying the North-South divide as a geopolitical fault line risks becoming a self-fulfilling prophecy.

The need to prevent fringe groups from inflicting harm on America should be a national priority, but it should not be mistaken as the basis for a new grand strategy or organizing principle. To do so would be to grant the terrorists an effective victory. Osama bin Laden wanted to turn America into a garrison state and to make the country compromise its domestic liberties. He wished to provoke a military retaliation against the Islamic world, one that would in fact succeed in transforming a criminal act into a new fault line and a clash of civilizations. He hoped to frustrate America and cause its retreat by confronting it with an enemy against which overwhelming military superiority would prove of little utility. But America should not play into the hands of the terrorists. The fight against terror requires patience and vigilance, not a new map of the world.

The impending crisis in the South unquestionably warrants the West's attention and resources. But the South as a whole poses to the West a humanitarian emergency, not a strategic threat. In eliciting the West's engagement in this battle, it is better to make the case on moral grounds than to fashion an erroneous geopolitical argument. The North should certainly seek to stamp out terrorist cells wherever and whenever they emerge. The North-South divide will become a geopolitical fault line, however, only if the West turns it into one, viewing developing countries as breeding grounds for terrorism rather than as suffering polities in need of help. Congress is more likely to approve aid for the Middle East and Africa because of a mix of empathy and guilt than because of trumped-up scenarios of a desperate anarchy overrunning America's shores or of superempowered, angry hordes targeting weapons of mass destruction against the United States. The North should undeniably do what it can to avert the suffering that lies ahead. But if so, it should be for humanitarian, not strategic, reasons.

This book's map of the world shares much analytic ground with that of Mearsheimer. Indeed, realism serves as a common intellectual taproot. This fundamental commonality explains why both maps foresee the eventual return of geopolitical competition among the world's power centers. But Mearsheimer's brand of realism is quite different from the one that guides the argument in the chapters that follow. Describing these differences thus serves the dual purpose of outlining where his analysis veers off course and clarifying this book's intellectual foundations.

Mearsheimer's chief analytic flaw is his failure to recognize the ability of political choice to ameliorate, if not overcome, the competitive logic of realism. The only factors shaping his map of the world are the distribution and character of military strength. This starting point gives rise to his assessment of the adverse geopolitical consequences of the return to multipolarity and the policy recommendations that follow—that the United States should seek to preserve the bipolarity of the Cold War and, failing that, encourage the proliferation of nuclear weapons. In Mearsheimer's stark world, the best we can hope for is that the world's major states retreat behind their barricades, aim nuclear weapons at each other, and rely on the threat of mutual destruction to deter war.

While compelling in its simplicity, Mearsheimer's realism is too sparing, and therefore leads to an account of international politics that quickly grows divorced from reality. The more relevant brand of realism that informs this book takes competition among poles to be the default position, the equilibrium to which the international system gravitates when left to its own devices. But history provides irrefutable evidence that we can do much better than let the international arena drift toward this default position. Foresight and leadership have the potential to push the system in a more benign direction and offset the war-causing dynamics that in Mearsheimer's world are inescapable.

Only a few examples are needed to make the case. According to Mearsheimer's brand of realism, the rise of the United States should have led to rivalry and conflict with the reigning hegemon—Great Britain. Instead, the U.S. and Britain traded concessions, agreed to settle disputes through arbitration, and formed strong political bonds. The absence of war between rising challenger and declining hegemon had absolutely nothing to do with mutual deterrence. In similar fashion, Mearsheimer's brand of realism predicts that the EU should have by now unraveled, the victim of the geopolitical rivalry that was to have befallen Europe after the Cold War's end. Exactly the opposite has happened. The EU is thriving and its collective character deepening even as it enlarges eastward. Instead of turning back to self-interested belligerence, Germany is taking the lead in the construction of a Europe that has all but eliminated rivalry among its major states.

Mearsheimer fails to recognize such instances of geopolitical transformation precisely because his intellectual approach does not allow him to do so. The United States and Great Britain at the turn of the last century engaged in an episode of rapprochement that fundamentally altered the identities the parties held of each other, making war between the two virtually unthinkable. The EU was able to resist the logic of realism because of the domestic character of Europe's states, the moderating role of integration and institutions, and the cultivation of a common European identity. These are all forces that lie outside the ambit of Mearsheimer's narrow conceptual framework. Devoid of even a hint of idealism, his version of realism is too stark to capture these profound sources of international change.

Mearsheimer's analytic missteps lead him to policy recommendations that overlook the opportunities at hand. The challenge ahead is not how best to erect the barricades that will separate emerging centers of power, but how best to forestall the drift toward competition that will take effect as unipolarity wanes. Mearsheimer is right that the return of a multipolar world will be fraught with danger. But he is wrong to throw in the towel from the start and deliver a call to nuclear arms. Instead, the prospect of a return to multipolarity should serve as a call to conceptual arms and as a trigger of urgent efforts to tame the competitive instincts that this new landscape will awaken. That the logic of realism is pervasive, but can nonetheless be overcome, is the central insight that both limits the relevance of Mearsheimer's map of the world and serves as the intellectual foundation and motivating purpose of this book.

Fukuyama's and Friedman's arguments are more complex, and their insights about democracy and globalization pose a direct challenge to this book's core claim that the onset of multipolarity will mean the reemergence of geopolitical fault lines and the return of global rivalries. Fukuyama says no need to worry. A world of democracies, even a multipolar world of democracies, will be a kind and stable world. Democracies, after all, don't engage in geopolitical conflict with each other. Friedman agrees that in today's globalized world, multipolarity will not play like it has in the past. The great powers will be too interdependent, too similar, and too busy surfing the World Wide Web to bother with geopolitical competition.

With scholars and policy-makers alike continuing to be confident of the peace-causing effects of both democratization and globalization, these are influential arguments that need to be examined carefully if this book's map of the world and the grand strategy that derives from it are to carry the day. This is the task of the chapter that follows.

CHAPTER THREE

The False Promise of Globalization and Democracy

T HE GREAT DEPRESSION was a defining event for America and the world. In the United States, the confidence and bounty of the 1920s gave way to self-doubt and a level of austerity that most Americans believed could never come their way. The global economy soon transmitted to Europe and Asia the shock waves emanating from the collapse of Wall Street, the downturn moving from one national economy to another. International trade fell sharply. Currencies plunged. The social dislocation that followed played a prominent role in fueling militarism and nationalism in Germany and Japan, the two states whose appetites for aggression would soon lead to a worldwide war.

America may never again experience anything like the stock market collapse of 1929. And today's global economy may well be much more resilient than that of the 1930s, making it better able to weather hard times. Nevertheless, a look back at the Great Depression sheds revealing light on the present. It makes clear just how much the market's extraordinary climb during the 1990s resembled the perilous boom of the 1920s. It shows how quickly economic change can have unpredictable political consequences. It demonstrates that globalization is certainly no panacea, and indeed can serve as a dangerous vehicle for the rapid spread of economic adversity. And it reveals not only the fragility of democracy, but also the dangers that ensue when democracy and nationalism together go awry.

THE PAST

"No Congress of the United States ever assembled, on surveying the state of the Union, has met with a more pleasing prospect than that which appears at the present time. In the domestic field there is tranquillity and contentment . . . and the highest record of years of prosperity. In the foreign field there is peace, the good will which comes from mutual understanding."[1] Although such buoyant optimism would have befitted just about any of President Bill Clinton's eight addresses on the state of the Union, these are not Clinton's words. They were spoken by President Calvin Coolidge on December 4, 1928. Little did Coolidge know that he was delivering his address only months before the crash of the stock market would send America and the world into a deep depression. In the domestic field, prosperity and contentment were soon to give way to impoverishment and despair. In the foreign field, mutual understanding and peace would fall prey to fascism and war.

As of 1928, however, America was in fine shape both at home and abroad, and Coolidge's rosy survey was fully warranted. The U.S. economy had been booming for more than two years, with agricultural and industrial production both reaching new heights. Corporate earnings were rising in step, stimulating unprecedented levels of investment in the stock market. Share prices rose dramatically over the course of 1927 and 1928. The good times continued into 1929. The three summer months of the year were especially kind to shares of America's leading corporations. Westinghouse climbed from $151 to $286, General Electric from $268 to $391, AT&T from $209 to $303.

The rising market fueled, and was fueled by, an inordinate volume of buying on margin. Lured by the prospect of unimaginable profits, investors borrowed heavily to support their speculative inclinations. During the summer of 1929, brokers' loans rose by roughly $400 million per month, reaching a total of $7 billion by the fall, up almost sevenfold from the early 1920s. Demand for money drove up interest rates, attracting so much international capital to New York that credit markets elsewhere grew tight. Loans began to stack up on top of other loans. New York banks were borrowing money from the Federal Reserve Bank at 5 percent so that they could relend it for stock purchases at upward of 12 percent.[2]

As stock prices soared way above their underlying value and buying on margin kept pace, the Federal Reserve Board grew justifiably uneasy. Even before the summer run-up, the Board warned that commercial banks were not to draw on Federal Reserve credit "for the purpose of making speculative loans or for the purpose of maintaining speculative loans."[3] The market grew jittery and paused temporarily in its upward climb during the spring of 1929. But silence from the Board plus banks with brokers' loans at the ready quickly brought this reflective pause to an end. Even academic experts dispensed with their usual caution. Renowned Yale economist Irving Fisher announced in the fall of 1929 that "stock prices have reached what looks like a permanently high plateau."[4] The Harvard Economic Society, a club of economics professors from Harvard, reassured investors that "a severe depression like that of 1920–21 is outside the range of probability. We are not facing protracted liquidation."[5]

The speculative bubble burst in October. It took only a few days for the unbridled confidence to give way to an unchecked panic. The market began to weaken seriously in the trading sessions of Saturday, October 19, and Monday, October 21. The slide was the result of the withdrawal of foreign money, the tightening of the credit market and the initial calling in of brokers' loans, and building talk on Wall Street of the potential for a sharp decline in share prices. The market then stabilized temporarily as the week progressed, due in part to the coordinated efforts of New York's top banks to restore confidence by purchasing stocks.

Uncontrolled selling started up again on Monday morning, October 28. This time, the bankers decided not to intervene. The selling quickened into the next day. Many stocks could not find buyers at any price, their share values plunging to less than $1. The volume and pace of selling were so high that the ticker fell hours behind; investors could only guess how far their stocks had plunged. Even stalwarts like Westinghouse were not spared, ending the day at $126 after trading at $286 in September. The Goldman Sachs Trading Corporation, an investment trust similar to today's mutual funds, had reached $220 before the collapse; it closed at $35. The tiers of loans that had fueled the speculative boom were being called in. The market was coming down like a house of cards.

Although relatively few Americans owned stocks in 1929 (perhaps 1.5 million in a population of 120 million),[6] the effects of the market's collapse were soon felt across the country. Even before the dark days of October, the U.S. economy was suffering from overcapacity and overproduction; wages and prices were not keeping pace with supply. In this environment, the deflationary effects of the plunge on Wall Street quickly spread to the real economy. Credit was tight, and for many, nonexistent. In 1930 alone, 1,352 banks failed. Businesses cut production, spending, and inventory, laying off millions of workers. By 1932, roughly one-quarter of the population was without regular income.[7] Those lucky enough to have a job saw their wages dwindle. The U.S. economy was steadily contracting, with the country's gross national product falling by a third between 1929 and 1933. Not until 1941 did national production return to the value it had reached in the 1920s.

The collapse on Wall Street thus precipitated America's descent into the Great Depression. And America took the rest of the world with it. Credit markets in Europe had eased, but banks and investors still reeling from losses in New York were hard-pressed to find worthy borrowers given the gloomy business environment. Even before the dive of the stock market in New York, the international economy was struggling under the weight of falling agricultural prices, insufficient capital in developing countries, and sluggish growth in Europe. Add to this mix a major contraction in the United States, and international trade began to plunge, falling more than 60 percent between 1929 and 1932.[8] The global economy was in a steady downward spiral.

Matters were made worse by the go-it-alone attitudes that carried the day in national capitals. Rather than working cooperatively to reverse the descent, individual countries tried to cordon themselves off from the international market, only deepening the collective crisis. The United States moved first. Congress passed the Smoot-Hawley tariffs in 1930, leading to a rash of retaliatory tariffs abroad. As the 1930s proceeded, the international economy was carved up into protected—and rival—trading blocs. Protective barriers may have provided temporary relief to politicians, domestic producers, and unions, but they had a devastating impact on an international economy that was already unraveling.

While the United States was the first off the block in undermining the global trading system, it was Britain that took the first step in undoing the monetary system. Britain left the gold standard in September 1931, assuming that it would do so only for a matter of months—long enough to achieve a moderate devaluation of the pound that would serve to promote trade and stimulate economic growth. The pound, however, proceeded to fall 30 percent, wreaking havoc with the global financial system. Japan then left the gold standard later that year, the yen soon losing 40 percent of its value. The consequent appreciation of the dollar and the adverse impact on America's balance of payments helped induce Washington to follow suit; the United States abandoned gold in 1933. With three of the world's major economies off the gold standard, the international economy was effectively without stewardship. A world economic conference was called to sketch the outlines of a new monetary system and work out new exchange rates, but the United States refused to go along with the consensus, again looking out for itself at the expense of international economic stability.

The *sauve qui peut* spirit that fragmented the international economy soon spilled into the political realm. In the trying environment of the times, shortsighted national priorities trumped long-term collective welfare on matters of security as well as economy. As one historian of the period notes, protective tariffs were "the economic counterpart of political isolationism."[9] That individual countries were watching only their own backs proved especially dangerous in light of the frightful toll the Depression was taking on domestic politics—especially in Germany and Japan.

The German economy was in dire straits well before the crash of 1929. The destruction wrought by World War I and the reparations imposed on a defeated Germany at the Versailles peace conference made a speedy recovery all but impossible. Inflation ran rampant during the early 1920s. Between January and November 1923, for example, the mark rose from roughly 18,000 to the dollar to more than 4 trillion to the dollar. Clerks began ensuring that payments were in order by weighing stacks of bank notes rather than counting them. Adolf Hitler, at the time a relatively unknown nationalist politician, prophetically commented on the plight of an average shopkeeper: "Her business is ruined, her livelihood absolutely destroyed. She can go begging. And the same despair is seizing the whole people. We are facing a revolution."[10]

Germany's ailing economy left it particularly vulnerable to the crash on Wall Street and the consequent trailing off of international trade. Unemployment began to mount, quickly outstripping the resources of the country's Unemployment Insurance Fund. The ensuing crisis compelled Chancellor Heinrich Brüning to call elections for September 1930. Support for the National Socialist Party had climbed in step with unemployment. The Nazis, who had previously held only 12 seats in the Reichstag, emerged from the election with 107. Brüning was pressured by the growing power of the Nazi Party to pursue a more nationalistic course, a move that only contributed to further unemployment by causing foreigners to withdraw their investments. As German banks started to fail in significant numbers, the international community considered putting together a collective loan to stabilize the German economy. But the plan foundered on British and American opposition. President Herbert Hoover had little time or concern for the German economy, the U.S. budget deficit climbing to new heights.

Ever more fearful of the rising tide of nationalism in Germany, Britain and France during the summer of 1932 effectively canceled further war reparations owed them by Berlin. But it was too late. Industrial production in Germany had fallen by more than 40 percent since 1929, leaving about a third of the workforce unemployed. The Nazis continued to capitalize on the intensifying economic duress. Through a combination of popular will (the Nazis won 196 parliamentary seats in the November 1932 general elections) and behind-the-scenes maneuvering, Hitler became chancellor in January 1933.

Hitler soon began to rearm. The Versailles Treaty restricted the German army to 100,000 troops in seven infantry divisions. In early 1935, Hitler called for an army of 550,000 men in thirty-six divisions. Germany's growing ambition and might were matched by its rising anti-Semitic fervor. Berlin, one of the world's most cosmopolitan cities and home to nearly 200,000 Jews, became ground zero for the methodical destruction of European Jewry.

Despite the unmistakable warning signs, France, Britain, and the United States all ran for cover. Made fragile and self-absorbed by economic deprivation, the world's major democracies watched passively as Hitler rearmed, remilitarized the Rhineland, invaded and annexed Austria, and conquered Czechoslovakia, gaining access to that country's significant stocks of war matériel and armaments. It was not until Germany invaded Poland in September 1939 that Britain and France faced the reality that they were probably next—and that they had no choice but to declare war. And even then, the United States avoided direct involvement in the conflict for another two years, until its warships were sinking at Pearl Harbor.

The sequence of events in East Asia bore striking resemblance. The interdependent global economy transmitted the Great Depression to Japan. The country's large agricultural sector was hit hard by the sharp fall in farm prices. By 1930, the average income of a rice farmer had already fallen by roughly a third. The decline in world trade coupled with the rise of protectionist barriers—the Smoot-Hawley tariff increased duties on Japanese goods entering the United States by an average of 23 percent—forced many small businesses into bankruptcy. Unemployment soared in urban areas, eventually producing labor unrest. As in Germany, the economic duress had a swift and grave impact on the country's fledgling democratic institutions, discrediting the party system, the ruling elite, and the large cartels (*zaibatsu*) that dominated the economy. The liberal principles embodied in the Meiji constitution fell prey to calls for a return to traditional values, social order, and national strength.

The military established itself as the vanguard of this movement for national renewal. The officer corps, the repository of traditional values of honor and self-sacrifice, was to lead the country out of the disarray brought on by incompetent politicians, corrupt businessmen, and self-serving bureaucrats. The Japanese public joined new nationalist clubs and organizations to contribute to the cause. Under the cover of guiding the nation's new mission, the military proceeded to undermine parliamentary government and wrest control of the country from the parties. A group of army regulars assassinated Prime Minister Tsuyoshi Inukai in May 1932, making way for Admiral Saito Makoto to govern in his stead. From then on, the officer corps was effectively in control of the Japanese state.

Under the leadership of the military, Japan's foreign policy became more aggressive in both tone and substance. The army occupied Manchuria in 1931 and then effectively annexed it, the first step in its effort to establish Japanese dominion over most of East Asia. Military leaders were already acting under their own authority. Although Army Minister Jiro Minami did inform the government of developments in Manchuria, he also made clear to civilian leaders that the army could act "without consulting the cabinet" and that "he was seeking the approval of the cabinet as a matter of form."[11] The navy, equally dismissive of civilian control, was meanwhile laying its plans for a major buildup, preparing for the "southern advance" and a potential confrontation with America's Pacific fleet.

The world's democracies, as they did with Germany after its turn for the worse, watched passively as the Japanese military took over the country and made clear its predatory ambition. The League of Nations did meet to consider a collective response to Japan's occupation of Manchuria. But in the hard times of the early 1930s, the session produced little more than hand-wringing and a rhetorical condemnation of Japan's behavior. Japan responded to its dressing down by withdrawing from the League, promptly turning its attention back to further conquests on the Asian mainland. The League, and the spirit of collective security it embodied, had been mortally wounded. Japanese aggression went virtually unchecked until the second half of 1941, when the advance into Indochina and the preemptive attack on Pearl Harbor left America and its allies little choice but to fight back.

The Great Depression thus lit the fuse at both ends. It set in motion a chain of events in Germany and Japan that transformed fledgling democracies into relentless aggressors. At the same time, it turned the world's stable democracies into passive and preoccupied bystanders, each trying to pass the buck to the other, all unwilling to join arms to avert the looming disaster. Economic chaos became political perversion, not only spawning aggressor states, but clearing the way for them to do evil.

This history provides sobering lessons. It underscores that financial markets can come down even more quickly than they can go up. It illustrates that a globalized economy can transmit impoverishment as easily as prosperity. And it makes unmistakably clear that economic duress can have chilling effects on the character of both domestic and international politics. History may well not repeat itself. But it is worth reflecting on how Charles Kindleberger and John Kenneth Galbraith, two of America's most distinguished economic historians, brought to a close their classic books on the Great Depression.

Kindleberger, writing in 1973, identified several scenarios that caused him most worry about the future. His first concern was that "the United States and the E.E.C. vying for leadership of the world economy" would undermine global economic stability.[12] Now that the European Economic Community has become the European Union, enjoys a single market and a single currency, and is in the midst of acquiring geopolitical ambition, we can only guess that Kindleberger would be anything but complacent about the future stability of the international economy.

Galbraith's main worry was about America itself and the possibility that the country would again fall prey to a vicious cycle of boom and bust. The central challenge, he warned, was to remember the past, to avoid the overconfidence and inordinate optimism that are the sources of speculative booms. As Galbraith wrote in 1954:

A speculative outbreak has a greater or less immunizing effect. The ensuing collapse automatically destroys the very mood speculation requires. It follows that an outbreak of speculation provides a reasonable assurance that another outbreak will not immediately occur. With time and the dimming of memory, the immunity wears off. A recurrence becomes possible. Nothing would have induced Americans to launch a speculative adventure in the stock market in 1935. By 1955 the chances are very much better.[13]

As Galbraith predicted, America's memory did dim with time. During the 1990s, investors bid up the stock market to perilous heights not seen since 1929. This most recent speculative boom has already come to an end. Although millions of Americans saw their savings dwindle, the landing was fortunately softer than the one that followed the boom of the 1920s.

But what recently happened to the American economy could also happen to the international system as a whole. That Americans so easily turned their backs on the lessons of economic history suggests that they may well do so on matters of geopolitics as well. This is especially true during the current era in which globalization blurs the distinction between economics and geopolitics and has given rise to a level of economic interdependence that is purportedly erasing fault lines for good. It is worth keeping in mind, however, that the stock market boom of the 1990s was every bit as irrational and dangerous as that of the 1920s, and that the speed and scope of today's globalized economy could well make it even more ready to transmit shock than the one that extended the Great Depression to every quarter of the world.

GLOBALIZATION: PANACEA OR PERIL?

THOMAS FRIEDMAN tells us in the first chapter of *The Lexus and the Olive Tree* that he is a "tourist with attitude." He is a tourist because he travels widely and reports what he sees. He has attitude because he sees everything through a particular lens—the lens of globalization. After spending the second half of the 1990s traversing the globe, going from corporate boardroom to remote village (mostly the former), Friedman concludes that globalization is "the overarching international system shaping the domestic politics and foreign relations of virtually every country."[14]

In making the case for his claim about globalization, Friedman charges that others who have sought to map out the new global system have been misled by trying "to divine the future too much from the past and the past alone." Friedman, however, commits exactly the opposite error. He tries to divine the future too much from the present and the present alone. He therefore presents a snapshot of a passing moment rather than a template that is likely to withstand the test of time.

Friedman is right that there is much new about globalization and that this novelty warrants a searching evaluation of its geopolitical implications. International flows of trade and capital have reached unprecedented heights; the global economy is more interdependent than ever before. Foreign direct investment in the United States increased by more than 500 percent between 1985 and the end of the century. American exports of goods and services rose more than 200 percent over the past two decades.

Globalization has also changed in qualitative terms. Trade and finance have for centuries enjoyed a global market. Now production itself has gone global. Toyota builds cars in the United States, Ford in Mexico, and Volkswagen in Brazil. While American software developers are getting a good night's rest in Seattle, their colleagues in Bangalore, India, are picking up where they left off, only to e-mail the emerging program back to Seattle in time for the beginning of the workday. The globalization of production sites and intellectual capital raises the stakes of interdependence. A pension fund that has billions of dollars invested in Indonesia can get out overnight. A U.S. corporation that has two manufacturing plants, a research and development lab, and thousands of employees in Indonesia will be much more vested in the long-term welfare of the country.

The Internet and the information revolution have also changed the character of globalization and made it more intrusive. The global market used to operate primarily by linking together entry points that had become national centers of finance and trade. Bankers, shippers, and corporate managers in places like New York, London, Frankfurt, Tokyo, and Hong Kong were integrated into a global network. But most of their countrymen not working in these commercial and financial gateways had little direct contact with foreign markets or their local emissaries.

Not so in the age of CNN, cell phones, and the Internet. As Friedman aptly puts it, new technologies enable "individuals, corporations and nation-states to reach around the world farther, faster, deeper and cheaper than ever before."[15] The average citizen, not just the corporate executive, can now play in global markets. The revolution in information technology is penetrating even societies that would rather resist it. Shanghai is awash with cell phones, advertisements for the Internet, and broadcast towers. It feels more like the set of a futuristic film than a city still under the control, at least nominally, of the Chinese Communist Party. The downfall of Slobodan Milosevic was due in no small part to the opposition's use of cell phones and the Internet to organize and mobilize before the elections of September 2000. Try as he might, Milosevic was unable to monopolize all channels of information. Disarmed by the free flow of ideas, his regime soon crumbled.

New technologies augment not only the information streaming into states, but also the information coming out about them. It is no accident that scandals break almost daily in one country or another; constant scrutiny by the media and by the legion of private firms now publishing newsletters leaves few matters secret. And the size and speed of international financial flows now expose most states to the rigors of the market analyst, inducing countries to play by the rules— or see their bonds downgraded and their interest rates spike. Friedman's notion of the "golden straitjacket" is an appropriate metaphor for the ability of globalization to pressure states to adopt open business practices and good government.

His crucial error is thus not his compelling description of globalization, but his assumption that the "overarching international system" that he describes is the new world of the future—rather than just a momentary and transitional phase along the way to some other, as yet undefined, alternative. Friedman is a newspaper reporter and justifiably writes about what he sees and hears. But if we look beyond the surface of his reportage and place his benign vision of globalization in greater historical relief, his map of the world starts to fall apart.

Friedman is hardly the first to mistake temporary prosperity and its pacifying effects for a more durable peace. In 1792, the essayist Thomas Paine wrote, "If commerce were permitted to act to the universal extent it is capable, it would extirpate the system of war."[16] John Stuart Mill in 1848 ventured that "the great extent and rapid increase of international trade . . . [is] the principal guarantee of the peace of the world."[17] Norman Angell is perhaps the most notorious of the optimists, if only because of his timing. In 1910, Angell published *The Great Illusion*, in which he contended that war among the great powers had become entirely irrational because of the "complete economic futility of conquest." At work, Angell claimed, was economic interdependence "to a greater degree than has ever yet been the case in history," a condition facilitated by "the rapid post, the instantaneous dissemination of financial and commercial information by means of telegraphy, and generally the incredible increase in the rapidity of communication."[18] By the summer of 1914, Europe was in the throes of World War I.

The weight of history is not the only reason for suspecting that Friedman's optimism will prove as illusory as that of Paine, Mill, and Angell. A great deal of evidence already suggests that the global economy is not as stable as it might appear. The U.S. stock market certainly demonstrated impressive strength during the 1990s. Even in the face of the slowdown that began in late 2000, the market's performance over the course of the past decade was unprecedented. But the run-up was more a sign of imbalance and immoderation than of economic health and the prowess and good judgment of policy-makers and the investment community. Despite compelling evidence that share prices had gone well beyond their underlying value, money continued to pour into the market. Despite the lessons of 1929, margin buying was again allowed to feed speculative excess.

Thanks to Alan Greenspan, the chairman of the Federal Reserve Board, and the underlying strength of the U.S. economy, perilous heights gave way to a paced cool-down rather than a panicked flight. Even the major sell-off caused by the terrorist attacks of September 2001 occurred in an orderly fashion. Nonetheless, the heady days of the 1990s, despite the optimism of the moment, put the American economy in a position of considerable vulnerability, exposing it once again to the risk of a stock market collapse. Furthermore, that the Asian financial crisis of 1997–1998 had worldwide effects makes clear that globalization, although at times a source of shared prosperity, can also serve as a transmission belt for economic shock. With the international economy as its conduit, a monetary crisis that started in Malaysia, Thailand, and Indonesia—three countries that are relatively minor economic players and thousands of miles from the world's main markets—made its way around the globe and almost brought about a meltdown of the international financial system.

Even if America avoids a prolonged recession, and good stewardship of the international economy prevents the spread of the financial shocks that will intermittently hit one country or another, globalization is hardly a panacea. The interdependence it breeds is not only no guarantor of peace and prosperity, but it can also be a source of vulnerability and strategic rivalry. After all, Japan embarked on its bid for regional hegemony during the 1930s largely to gain self-sufficiency and end its dependence on imports of foreign steel and oil. Furthermore, globalization might be bringing newfound wealth to many quarters, but it is also widening economic inequality both within countries and between them—a spillover effect that has contributed to anti-American sentiment and played a role in motivating extremist groups to direct violence against U.S. citizens and their territory. So too might the rise of Europe as a new center of economic strength dramatically alter the character of globalization. America continues to design and manage the global economy as it sees fit. But as policy-makers in Washington gradually find their influence slipping away and shifting to their counterparts in Europe and ultimately in Asia, the steadiness that comes with a single captain at the helm may give way to a global economy that goes seriously off course.

A realistic assessment of globalization must thus face up to two scenarios, either of which would render obsolete Friedman's map of the world. The first is that a significant downturn hits the global economy, moving from country to country through exactly the same fiber optics, satellites, and trading floors that made the world economy so vibrant during the 1990s. The second is that the global market ultimately shows resilience and performs in admirable fashion, but that the attendant growth and its political consequences undermine the very conditions that have endowed globalization with its benign effects.

The Dangers of Speculative Excess

Assessments of the health of the U.S. economy are understandably influenced by the country's economic performance. Moods matter. During downturns, analysts seem to find faults around every corner. During upturns, the good news just keeps coming. The sluggish years of the 1980s, for example, produced a preoccupation with America's intractable economic woes, while the impressive growth of the 1990s inspired almost irrepressible confidence in the U.S. economy. Books predicting that the Dow would keep soaring to new heights appeared regularly. Analysts pronounced that the digital age had finally done away with the ups and downs of the business cycle.

Such optimism, combined with year after year of impressive economic growth, fueled a dramatic rise in the U.S. stock market. On December 29, 1989, the Dow closed at 2,753 and the Nasdaq at 454. By December 31, 1999, the Dow had risen more than 300 percent to 11,497, and the Nasdaq had climbed almost 800 percent to 4,069. Lured by the prospect—and reality—of substantial profits, more Americans than ever before invested in stocks. By the end of the decade, about half of U.S. households owned stocks, which accounted for more than 40 percent of the average household's assets. The Federal Reserve estimated that Americans held $13.3 trillion in equities at the end of 1999, a 26 percent increase from the previous year.[19] In the early 1980s, there were about 6 million mutual fund accounts. By 1998, there were about 120 million, roughly two accounts per American family.[20] The proliferation of 401(k) pension plans, and the decision by many employees to invest contributions in stocks rather than fixed-income instruments, contributed to the booming market. A self-perpetuating cycle was in train. Investors bought stocks, driving prices up, encouraging investors to place more confidence and money in the market.

Amid the exuberance, however, the market of the late 1990s began to closely resemble that of the late 1920s. A healthy increase in stock prices was unquestionably warranted by the steady economic expansion of the past decade. Corporate revenues, profits, and productivity had been climbing, justifying rising share prices. But the market rose much faster than the economy as a whole, with the share prices of many companies climbing far more sharply than their earnings. By historical standards, price-earnings ratios were dangerously out of kilter and millions of Americans were buying shares of companies at levels way above their underlying value.

A few voices tried to sound the alarm. Yale economist Robert Shiller in his book *Irrational Exuberance* warned that "the present stock market displays classic features of a *speculative bubble:* a situation in which temporarily high prices are sustained largely by investors' enthusiasm rather than by consistent estimation of real value."[21] Shiller based his claim on striking data revealing just how high stock prices were relative to earnings. Figure 1 shows that stock prices spiked sharply during the 1990s, rising much more rapidly than earnings. Figure 2 tracks the price-to-earnings ratio, again revealing how extraordinary share prices were by historical standards. Only in the late 1920s did prices diverge so sharply from earnings, reaching 32.6 in September 1929 (meaning that shares of companies on the

S&P Composite Index were on average trading at 32.6 times the earnings per share). The real value of the S&P Index then proceeded to fall 80 percent over the next three years. In January 2000, the average price-to-earnings ratio stood at 44.3.[22] In light of what happened last time around, the market had clearly reached hazardous heights.

The divorce between stock price and underlying value was illustrated by the bizarre destinies of individual companies. Some of the market's favorites actually had no earnings whatsoever. Amazon.com, the on-line book and music store, had yet to turn a profit. Its market value nonetheless rose from roughly $430 million when it went public in May 1997 to more than $35 billion by the end of 1999. Such inflated prices meant exaggerated sensitivity to performance numbers. Weak earnings reports were tantamount to bombshells. Apple Computer announced after the market closed on September 28, 2000, that

Figure 1 Stock Prices and Earnings, 1871–2000

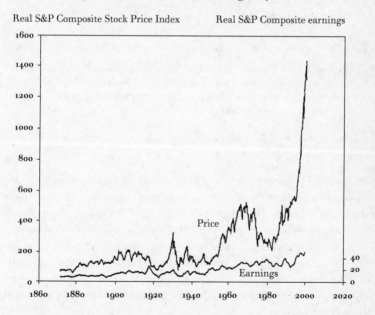

Real (inflation-corrected) S&P Composite Stock Price Index, monthly, January 1871 through January 2000 (upper series), and real S&P Composite earnings (lower series), January 1871 to September 1999.

SOURCE: Robert J. Shiller, *Irrational Exuberance* (Princeton: Princeton University Press, 2000), p. 6.

Figure 2   Price-Earnings Ratio, 1881–2000

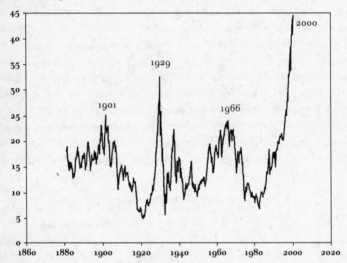

Price-Earnings ratio, monthly, January 1881 to January 2000. Numerator: real (inflation-corrected) S&P Composite Stock Price Index, January. Denominator: moving average over preceding ten years of real S&P Composite earnings. Years of peaks are indicated.

SOURCE: Robert J. Shiller, *Irrational Exuberance* (Princeton: Princeton University Press, 2000), p. 8.

its fourth-quarter earnings would fall short of expectations by about 10 percent. Rather than earning $1.87 per share for the fiscal year, Apple would earn about $1.71 per share. If prices moved in step with price-earnings ratios, Apple stock should have dropped about 10 percent. Instead, it plunged from roughly $53 to $26 a share on September 29, losing 50 percent of its value and closing the day at the general levels at which it traded in the early 1990s. What better evidence that the market was rising and falling on hopes and fears, not on sound economic analysis?

The boom of the 1990s glaringly resembled the bull market of the 1920s in other worrisome respects. As during the twenties, the upward climb of the Dow fueled a sharp rise in margin buying. Tempted by the prospect of returns that were running well above the costs of borrowing, investors during the 1990s relied heavily on loans to purchase equities. Debt owed to New York Stock Exchange member firms rose 62 percent from December 1998 to December 1999, reaching nearly $230 billion. By September 2000, margin debt had climbed an additional 10 percent (a 78 percent increase from the end of 1998). In March 2000, margin loans accounted for 16 percent of total consumer borrowing, compared to 7 percent in 1995. Among online brokerage firms, estimates indicate that margin debt as a percentage of market value rose 459 percent between 1995 and 2000.[23] As New York Senator Charles Schumer told the House Banking and Financial Services Committee on March 21, 2000, "Today margin debt is a greater share of total market capitalization than at any point since the Great Depression."[24]

The market was once again being driven up by borrowed money, risking a collapse should creditors get jittery. The plunge in technology stocks that occurred during the spring of 2000 and again later in the year was caused in part by the selling of stocks by investors who needed to liquidate assets to cover loans. The Nasdaq eventually stabilized as bargain-hunters stepped in, but not before dropping almost 40 percent. Technology companies were particularly hard hit, with Qualcomm falling 55 percent, Cisco plunging 35 percent, and America Online losing 21 percent between early April and the end of May. The slide then returned later in the year, the calling in of loans again contributing to the steep decline. The Nasdaq by April of the following year had fallen almost 70 percent from its highs—from roughly 5,100 to 1,640. Oracle, one stock that had weathered well the spring drop, plunged more than 65 percent between September 2000 and April 2001. Amazon's market value by April was about $5 billion, down roughly $30 billion from the end of 1999.

Again paralleling the 1920s, the demand for capital stimulated by America's booming stock market and its growing economy led to an inflow of foreign investment. The U.S. economy's effect on global finance had effectively become that of a sponge. In the early 1990s, about 20 percent of all capital from countries with a current account surplus (countries that export more goods and services than they import) made its way to U.S. capital markets. By the end of the decade, that figure had risen to almost 70 percent. Between 1995 and 1999, foreign purchases of U.S. corporate bonds increased threefold and of U.S. stocks almost tenfold. Foreigners by the end of the decade had financial claims on the United States amounting to roughly

$6.5 trillion, representing some 35 percent of the Treasury market and 20 percent of the corporate bond market.[25] That foreign investors found the U.S. economy so appealing certainly bolstered the heady times and the boom in the stock market.

The global rush to invest in America, however, did not come without its costs. Although masked by the stellar performance of the U.S. market, growing international imbalances all the while enhanced the global economy's vulnerability to significant shock. Much of the capital flowing into the United States was coming from Europe, contributing to the 25 percent decline in the value of the euro that occurred during 1999–2000. The low euro cheapened European exports, substantially adding to America's trade deficit, which had already ballooned as a result of the financial crisis in East Asia and the devaluation of the region's currencies. America's trade deficit climbed from $167 billion in 1998, to $262 billion in 1999, to $376 billion in 2000.

America's dependence on foreign capital to finance this trade deficit in turn caused the dollar to appreciate, only exacerbating the problem and producing a vicious cycle. The euro declined. Europeans invested in the United States to hedge against the possibility of further devaluation, strengthening the dollar. America's trade deficit rose, stimulating further demand for foreign capital, causing the euro to drop further. This cycle, along with the appeal of the U.S. economy to foreign investors, explains why the United States became so dependent on securing capital from abroad and how foreigners came to have financial claims on the United States of $6.5 trillion—an amount that was more than 60 percent of America's gross domestic product. Carrying such a large amount of foreign debt in the short-term bolstered the American economy and improved the quality of daily life. But the country was living beyond its means and accumulating a level of debt that continues to eat away at future prosperity.

The booming market had one other troubling effect. The annual personal savings rate in the United States shrank to a postwar low. For 2000, it was 1 percent, the lowest level since 1933. Americans were saving less of their wealth in part because the times encouraged them to live large. And the constraining effects of low savings on growth were masked by corporate investment and the influx of capital from abroad. But as the U.S. economy slowed, corporations scaled back on investment, and foreign capital headed elsewhere, America began to feel the effects of a population that loves to consume and hates to save.

The American economy, although touted as a model for the world throughout the 1990s, was, just beneath the surface, in serious jeopardy. The U.S. stock market became dangerously overvalued. Although it came down from its dizzying heights with only isolated pockets of frenzied selling, the record of the past few years makes all too clear the potential for speculative boom and bust. At the same time, foreign debt mounted, both fueled by and fueling a large trade deficit and an overvalued dollar. To make matters worse, these two economic fault lines intersected. The stock market was overvalued in part because foreigners both directly invested in it and provided the liquidity in the credit markets necessary for others to do so. And the dollar was overvalued in part because of the strength of the stock market and the desirability of investing in American equities, treasuries, and bonds. Should the stock market and the dollar have begun falling together, a drop in one would have reinforced a drop in the other, potentially leading to a cascading decline in both.

The Transmission of Bad Times

The stock market and the economy as a whole cooled off with welcome calm in light of the excesses built up over the 1990s. By the spring of 2001, the average price-to-earnings ratio on the S&P Index had settled in less dangerous territory. But as the past makes all too clear, any number of unforeseen developments could have turned a relatively benign environment into an economic maelstrom. And the effects of a U.S. economy in distress would surely be felt throughout the global economy. The same features of globalization that Friedman finds so attractive—its speed, depth, scope, and low cost—make it a safe bet that bad times in America will be transmitted to the rest of the world with impressive efficiency.

This is a central point. Globalization itself is a neutral phenomenon made possible by the expanding infrastructure—the plumbing—of the global economy. In good times, this infrastructure quickly transmits prosperity and stability. But in bad times, it just as quickly transmits impoverishment and volatility. The effects of globalization depend entirely upon what is running through its fast and wide pipes.

The East Asian financial crisis gave us a good taste of just how quickly and ruthlessly trouble can spread through the global economy. The trouble began in Thailand in the middle of 1997, when fear that the Thai economy had become overvalued and overheated led to capital flight. The value of the Thai baht promptly fell about 20 percent.

The Philippine peso was next in line. Within a matter of weeks, the Malaysian ringgit and the Indonesian rupiah were also declining. The rupiah proceeded to lose 30 percent of its value in the space of two months. The crisis expanded to northeast Asia by the fall. Taiwan devalued its currency in October, after which speculation against the Hong Kong dollar immediately followed. Massive currency reserves and good management enabled financial authorities to maintain the value of the currency. But doing so required hiking interbank lending rates to 300 percent, which helped send the Hong Kong stock market into a nosedive, tumbling almost 25 percent over four days. The South Korean won was the next casualty, falling from 850 to the dollar to more than 1,000 to the dollar by mid-November.

Although scholars disagree about the initial causes of the crisis, they are in complete accord that it extended so quickly and widely precisely because it was running through the efficient piping of the global economy. Here is how Stephan Haggard, a professor at the University of California at San Diego and a leading expert on Asian economies, describes the contagion:

> The process of deeper financial integration constituted a necessary condition for the crisis to occur. . . . When such crises start in one country, there are a variety of channels through which they can be propagated to other countries, including fears of competitive devaluation or financial linkages of various sorts. . . . Thailand begat Indonesia and Malaysia; Taiwan's devaluation begat the market meltdown in Hong Kong in late October; and that meltdown begat South Korea, which in turn resonated back through the Southeast Asian markets at the end of 1997.[26]

The trouble soon moved beyond East Asia. By the following May, global investors had begun to pull out of Russia, causing a sharp drop in the country's stock and bond markets. The Central Bank raised interest rates to 150 percent and the International Monetary Fund came forward with emergency loans, propping up the ruble and the markets. But only temporarily. By August, Russia's stock market was again declining, this time taking the ruble with it. On August 17, the Kremlin announced that it was devaluing the ruble and suspending repayment of foreign debt. News of Russia's default sent global stock markets reeling. The impact on the daily life of the average Russian was devastating. The ruble had fallen from roughly 6 to the dollar to

18 to the dollar. The percentage of Russians living below the poverty line almost doubled between 1997 and 1999. Pensioners living on a fixed income were especially hard hit, many of them yearning for a return to the relative prosperity of the communist era.

Russia's default raised fears that emerging markets worldwide might be collapsing, inducing investors to start pulling out of Latin America. Brazil's central bank in September raised interest rates to 50 percent to stem capital flight, but investors continued to withdraw their funds. An international rescue package calmed markets, but again only temporarily. The rout of Brazilian markets continued into December, inducing the government to float the real in January. Over the course of the following month, the currency fell from 1.25 to 2.15 reals against the dollar.

Not even the United States was immune from the crisis. In late October 1997, when it became clear that the troubles in East Asia were not just "glitches in the road" (as President Clinton initially called them), the Dow Jones Average dropped 554 points, setting a new record for the biggest daily point loss. Steep declines occurred the following August in response to Russia's worsening fortunes. Brazil's woes deepened worries on Wall Street, again sending the Dow sharply down. News that Long-Term Capital Management (LTCM), one of America's largest hedge funds, was on the verge of collapse also rattled the market. Calm was restored only after the New York Federal Reserve pushed a consortium of leading U.S. banks and investment firms to provide a $3.5 billion bailout to LTCM. Federal Reserve authorities and private firms agreed that the collapse of LTCM, because of its debts to the world's leading banks, could well have jeopardized the international banking system. U.S. officials now admit that in late September 1998 the global financial system was days, if not hours, from a liquidity crisis and meltdown.

This is a frightening story, exposing the mutual and inescapable vulnerabilities that accompany an integrated world market. A small crisis in Southeast Asia worked its way through the global economy, turning the Asian miracle into the Asian nightmare, ravaging the currencies of Russia and Brazil, and then almost bringing America to its knees. That this crisis occurred during good times makes the story all the more worrisome.

With the international economy this vulnerable to shock even during a period of global growth, imagine what might happen during bad times. Imagine, for example, what might transpire if a crisis were to begin in the United States, the global economy's core, rather than in Thailand, the global economy's periphery. The U.S. dollar and Wall Street, rather than the Thai baht and the Bangkok exchange, would start to slide. The sell-off would quicken as investors seek to contain losses and dump dollar-denominated assets. We already know what the effect would be on foreign equity markets. With the U.S. stock markets making up about 40 percent of global equity markets, foreign exchanges essentially take their cue from Wall Street. When the Dow and Nasdaq plunge, so too do markets in London, Frankfurt, Tokyo, Singapore, and just about everywhere else. And they do so almost instantaneously. By the time New York traders arrive home after a bruising day on Wall Street, the sell-off has already begun in Tokyo. While investors in Tokyo are still assessing the damage done, markets in Europe will already be on their way down.

A financial crisis that begins in the core would also be much harder to control. The global economy enjoyed considerable stability during the 1990s largely because of American stewardship. Washington more or less set the rules, effectively ran the institutions that monitor and enforce these rules, and responded to emergencies when they arose. When the Mexican economy began to stumble in 1994, it was the United States that intervened to stabilize the peso. When the Asian crisis started to expand, it was the U.S. government that took charge, deliberately shooting down a Japanese proposal to manage affairs from Tokyo. And it was the New York Federal Reserve that organized the bailout of LTCM when it, along with global capital markets, was on the verge of collapse. The good judgment of the likes of Robert Rubin and Lawrence Summers at the Treasury Department, coupled with the abundance produced by a booming America, turned back potent threats to the global economy.

But Rubin and Summers are gone, as are the auspicious times. And George W. Bush's first choice for the Treasury, Paul O'Neill, made clear early on that he favored a very different approach to the management of the international economy—a hands-off strategy that involves letting the market take its course. Economic crisis, according to O'Neill, "doesn't have anything to do with the failure of capitalism. It's to do with an absence of capitalism." The prospect of rescue packages and other types of international intervention is part of the problem, not the solution, because it encourages reckless behavior by reducing risk. "Why do we have to intervene? Especially, why do we have to intervene on a crisis basis?" O'Neill asked soon after taking office.[27] He did set aside these reservations and approve IMF assistance for Turkey, Brazil, and Argentina in 2001. But had O'Neill been in command in 1998, the crisis in East Asia might well have been much wider and deeper.

An America in the midst of an economic downturn also dramatically changes the politics, not just the philosophy, of managing the international economy. Even if the Treasury were in activist hands, those hands would be tied by a different politics than existed during the 1990s. Absent a booming stock market and unprecedented budget surpluses, the U.S. government would be much less inclined to lay out resources for bailing out the peso or stabilizing the baht. Indeed, the United States initially refused to contribute to an Asian bailout in 1997 because of domestic political opposition. U.S. policy changed course only after the gravity of the crisis became apparent.

If such parsimony governed policy during an economic boom, consider how Washington might react under leaner conditions. As it has done during previous economic crises, the United States might well turn to protectionist trade policies and go-it-alone monetary policies to cordon itself off from the international economy. America has benefited greatly from globalization and has therefore been its main proponent and manager. But its open embrace of global markets has been a direct function of the benefits it has reaped. When the economy and the employment rolls were both growing steadily, American workers displaced when their factories moved to Mexico had little trouble finding new jobs—often at higher wages. With a sluggish U.S. economy, however, and laid-off workers who cannot find new and better-paying jobs, the country's enthusiasm for globalization is likely to wane. As less fortunate times prevail and globalization is seen as a source of unemployment and cheap imports rather than jobs and economic growth, America may well be one of the first to opt out. A widening economic downturn combined with a spirit of *sauve qui peut* could in short order send the global economy into turmoil. That is exactly what happened during the 1930s.

Optimists think this scenario far-fetched. They contend that we now know enough about the global economy and have erected sufficient safeguards to prevent a repeat of the 1930s—the last time America served as ground zero for a global depression. Financial markets certainly are better regulated than they used to be. The Investment Company Act of 1940 makes today's mutual funds safer than the investment trusts of the 1920s. Circuit-breakers and automatic curbs that kick in on especially volatile days do serve to limit swings in the market. And the Federal Reserve and the Securities and Exchange Commission (SEC) have introduced at least some measures to limit margin buying, however inadequate.[28]

Although such innovations have certainly helped matters, they hardly inoculate the market against either the known excesses or the unknown weak points that could lead to an unwelcome turn of events. During the market's heady days, even Federal Reserve Chairman Greenspan and Treasury Secretary Rubin admitted that they feared stocks had climbed to dangerously high levels. In December 1996, Greenspan cautiously asked, "How do we know when irrational exuberance has unduly escalated values, which then become subject to unexpected and prolonged contractions as they have in Japan over the past decade?"[29] Rubin was more circumspect while in office, but then voiced his concerns soon after leaving the Treasury. "Our stock market may be undervalued, for all I know," Rubin cautiously told Charlie Rose in an interview in June 2000, "but by convention on the traditional standards, it looks like it is certainly high." He went on to say that the strength of the U.S. market could be the product of "a series of excesses supporting each other," and that "real and serious risks . . . are being underrated in most people's thinking about financial decisions."[30] SEC regulations and curbs on day traders may alleviate the worst volatility and the most egregious speculative excess. But they did little to tame a market that lost sight of the importance of keeping share price in sync with underlying value.

The digital revolution and the resulting speed and scope of financial flows also make the management of markets more difficult. The Internet and the "new economy" are certainly contributing to globalization and the interdependence it has engendered. But globalization's novelty and its rapidly changing character make even the best economic models and management techniques obsolete by the time they are implemented. LTCM, after all, was run by two renowned economists (Robert Merton and Myron Scholes are both Nobel laureates) using some of the most sophisticated analytic techniques available. The country's best minds produced models that took their company to the verge of collapse.

Economists and policy-makers are similarly at a loss on basic questions of policy. No consensus exists on the causes of the East Asian financial crisis. Some analysts argue that the core of the problem was economic mismanagement, particularly on exchange rates. Others contend that speculation and contagion initiated the downward spiral. Nor is there agreement on whether the IMF's intervention alleviated the crisis or only made it worse. Some assert that its restrictive monetary and fiscal policies stabilized the situation, others that the IMF's reaction deepened the descent.[31] Confusion also reigns on why Russia's economic reforms went awry and its economy into a tailspin, with some economists suggesting that Russia moved too quickly on privatization and liberalization, and others arguing that Russia did not move quickly enough. Such fundamental differences of opinion are the norm, not the exception.

With so little clarity on the basics, it is hardly surprising that the United States and its main partners have made little progress on reform of the global financial architecture. Public officials, economists, and the investment community all agree that the global economy is rife with vulnerabilities and has the potential to act like a conduit for instability. But no one is sure what to do about it. Greenspan was again blunt in expressing his worries about weaknesses in the existing financial architecture. In July 2000, he lamented that "the accelerating expansion of global finance . . . appears to require ever-newer forms and layers of financial intermediation," thereby raising "questions about the inherent stability of this new system." In encouraging the creation of new financial mechanisms to prevent future instability, Greenspan called for "flexible institutions that can adapt to the unforeseeable needs of the next crisis, not financial Maginot Lines that endeavor to fend off revisiting previous crises that will not be replicated."[32] But he offered no concrete proposals.

Finance ministers and central bankers from around the world gathered in Prague in the fall of 2000 determined to make some headway on crisis management and prevention. But after several long days of debate, they returned home empty-handed. One U.S. official admitted that "probably the best we can say right now is that we've upgraded the plumbing." As for whether the delegates made progress on creating mechanisms for managing future economic crises, Berkeley professor Barry Eichengreen commented, "It's hard to give them even a passing grade."[33] Princeton Professor Robert Gilpin, one of the country's leading analysts of the international economy, agrees that "efforts to create effective regulations governing international capital flows and financial matters have progressed very little, if at all."[34]

It is of course possible that an updated and more responsive global financial architecture will never be needed. But it is unlikely. Although no one knows what to do to prepare for it, few doubt that the next economic shock is far off. America did rise to the occasion and do an admirable job of containing the main financial crises of the 1990s. But if an episode of major instability occurs at a time when the United States is less willing or able to be the guardian of global markets, the outcome may be altogether different. In today's globalized economy, adversity could come with little warning and spread with extraordinary speed.

Should globalization run off its tracks, the geopolitical implications may not look all that different from those of the 1930s. Fragile regimes in Russia and China, under the duress of economic shock, could well give way to militaristic and nationalistic alternatives. Both countries bear some resemblance to the fledgling democracies that fell prey to fascism when hit by the Great Depression. The world's other major nations—the United States, Britain, France, Germany, and Japan—have all enjoyed decades of stable democracy, probably inoculating them against backsliding toward a more nativist and dangerous politics. They are each fully capable, however, of running for cover in the face of trouble, just as did the Atlantic democracies when confronted with Germany and Japan during the 1930s.

The Uncertain Effects of Interdependence and the Information Revolution

Even if a self-regulating global market maintains its stability and the preceding discussion of economic fault lines turns out to be nothing more than needless anxiety, we should still resist the proposition that globalization provides a sure pathway to peace and prosperity. The reason is that Friedman substantially overstates its pacifying potential. The most potent peace-causing effect of globalization, its proponents contend, is the economic interdependence it fosters. The basic logic is straightforward. As trade and investment between two states grow, the greater their mutual interest in preserving peaceful relations. Globalization thus raises both the benefits of peace and the costs of war. States in an interdependent world economy have better things to do than take up arms against each other.

Although the logic seems impeccable on the surface, the argument becomes less compelling as soon as geopolitics enters the picture. Economic interdependence does promote shared interests, but it also creates shared vulnerabilities. Whether mutual dependence induces states to move in lockstep or instead fuels fear and a desire for more autonomy depends on the political context in which such interdependence is situated. When trading with a trusted partner, deeper economic ties are self-reinforcing; the parties enjoy shared gains at minimal risk, encouraging them to come back for more. When trading with a potential adversary, however, more interdependence often translates into less security. In an adversarial context, shared interests provide opportunities for exploitation, not mutual gain.

It was precisely this calculation that propelled Japan's drive toward economic self-sufficiency during the 1930s and its eventual attack against Pearl Harbor. The Japanese saw their dependence on U.S. imports as a vulnerability, not as source of good relations with the United States. Everything else being equal, more interdependence between countries is better than less. But everything else is rarely equal. In the end, geopolitical imperative regularly trumps economic opportunity. If it were otherwise, Paine, Mill, and Angell would have been proved right, and war would have become obsolete long ago.

The historical record also makes clear that even when states are comfortable enough with each other to allow high levels of economic interdependence to emerge, the resulting ties are no guarantor of lasting harmony. International communities knit together by their integrated economies can unravel with surprising speed. Consider Europe during the decade prior to World War I. Trade and investment inside Europe were, in relation to the size of national economies, greater one hundred years ago than they are today. Germany was Britain's second-most-important trading partner (after the United States), and Britain was the top market for German exports. Lloyds of London was a leading insurer of the German ships that the Royal Navy would seek to sink if the two countries were to find themselves at war.[35] Borders in the early 1900s were permeable. Europeans moved freely from country to country, without passports and without having to bother with border controls.

Such intense levels of interdependence, however, did not avert Europe's rapid descent into World War I. Germany's bid for primacy and the geopolitical competition that followed had little trouble overwhelming the mutual interests resulting from economic integration. If economic interdependence could not save Europe from war in 1914, there is no compelling reason to be confident that globalization would do any better at preserving a stable peace today. History suggests that the large volume of goods and capital now flowing across the Atlantic is no guarantee against geopolitical competition between America and a rising Europe.

The recent breakup of multiethnic states provides further evidence of the capacity of political passion to prevail over economic expediency. Throughout the 1990s, economic interdependence meant little in the face of awakened nationalist yearnings. The Slovaks wanted out of Czechoslovakia despite the certainty of facing economic hardship. Slovenia, Croatia, Bosnia, Kosovo, and Macedonia all sought to secede from Yugoslavia despite the economic dislocation that would follow. Since the end of the Bosnian war, the country's Serbs, Croats, and Muslims have shunned rebuilding economic links with each other. They prefer poverty to trading with the enemy. Many of the former Soviet republics have faced severe hardship as they distance themselves from the Russian economy. They have nonetheless proceeded in their search for more autonomy. Whether interdependence breeds trust or instills resentment depends entirely upon the political context in which economic integration takes place.

Overestimation of the political consequences of the information revolution has led to further exaggeration of the peace-causing effects of globalization. Digital technologies have unquestionably made it much more difficult for states to seal off their societies from outside ideas and to resist penetration by the global market. Fax machines, cell phones, the Internet, satellite television and radio, high-resolution reconnaissance—these innovations at once bombard states with information and enable the outside world to examine the internal affairs of those states.

The effects have been profound. The unraveling of the Soviet Union and the end of the Cold War were due in no small part to the Communist Party's loss of control over the flow of information, ultimately exposing the Kremlin's political rot and ideological bankruptcy. Milosevic was similarly brought down by a groundswell of popular opposition made possible by the free flow of information. And there are surely plenty of dogs that did not bark because the free flow of ideas sidelined them before they could do great damage. Dangerous ideologues like Vladimir Zhirinovsky in Russia and Istvan Csurka in Hungary did their best during the past decade to advance their political fortunes by peddling nationalist myths. They were stymied, however, by a marketplace of ideas that neutralized their appeals to darker political instincts.

These auspicious stories aside, it would be a mistake to assume that the information revolution is in the midst of producing a world populated by like-minded liberal democracies. New information technologies may have helped bring down Milosevic, but they also played an important role in fueling the bloodshed that accompanied Yugoslavia's dissolution. Milosevic and Croatian President Franjo Tudjman both made ruthless use of the media to whip up nationalist passions. For most of the 1990s, the media were a tool of ethnic cleansing, not a check against excess.[36]

In China, the Internet and the cell phone have fast been making inroads. But the Communist Party has maintained its grip, blocking access to certain Web sites (such as that of the *New York Times*) and regularly eavesdropping on phone conversations. Nor have new telecommunications technologies brought peace to the Middle East. Cell phone use is common in the oil-rich countries of the Arabian peninsula, but democracy is hardly the beneficiary. Israel long ago became one of the world's high-tech centers, but the Israel-Palestine dispute remains as entrenched as ever. The Palestinian Authority may be using the latest desktop publishing program in preparing its new textbooks. But if those texts present a skewed historical account of the Middle East conflict, they serve only to ensure yet another generation of alienated and resentful Palestinians.

The point here is not that the digital revolution is on balance fostering instability, but that the free flow of information under some circumstances does more harm than good—and certainly is no guarantor of tolerance and democratic governance. New information technologies provide irresponsible leaders with a capacity to propagate virulent ideologies. And it is not only states unfortunate enough to be governed by the likes of Milosevic that could fall prey to excessive bouts of public mobilization. Should the United States and China one day find themselves in an adversarial situation, it is all too easy to imagine the media whipping up public passions. After a midair collision and the emergency landing of a U.S. spy plane in China in April 2001, both the U.S. and Chinese governments played down the incident, fully aware of the potential for the media to help turn an accident into an international crisis. After all, when Harry Truman unfurled the Truman Doctrine in a speech on March 12, 1947—before most Americans had access to television—he had no idea that he was helping to lay the groundwork for McCarthyism and its excessive brand of anticommunism. The international effects of the information revolution, just like those of economic interdependence, depend upon the broader political context in which these technologies are deployed.

The Wrath of Inequality

That only a small percentage of the world's population actually has access to modern communications technology further mutes the beneficial geopolitical consequences of the information revolution. The digital era may well have given birth to a global village. But it is a small village, populated only by those lucky enough to live in a country that is wired into international markets. At present, only about 6 percent of the world's inhabitants have access to the Internet, most of them residing in North America and Western Europe. And the distance between the haves and the have-nots is growing by the day. The income gap between the fifth of the world's population in the richest countries and the fifth in the poorest countries grew from 30 to 1 in 1960 to 74 to 1 in 1997. Four-fifths of the globe's population lives in countries that earn only one-fifth of world income.

The wealthier countries of the world are all too prepared to live comfortably with the gross inequalities that now exist between the North and the South. It will trouble few in the United States, Europe, or Japan that large swaths of the globe have been excluded from the digital revolution. At the same time, this revolution is having important spillover effects that promise to raise the stakes of growing inequality. The gradual diffusion of technology to the developing world gives it new capacities to do damage to the developed world. Control over much of the globe's oil supply has in the past been the South's main source of leverage over the North. But knowledge will ultimately prove to be a more potent weapon than material resources.

The Internet and the expanding availability of information make it easier for those who want it to get the technical specifications for weapons of mass destruction and their delivery systems. The Internet itself could also be turned on the country that invented and constructed it. By penetrating the networks of the Pentagon, tapping into Microsoft's latest software programs, or disseminating e-mail viruses that wreak havoc with the global information infrastructure (all of which have recently happened), a lonely, disaffected computer hacker could do America a great deal of damage. In May 2000, two Filipino programmers disseminated the "Love Bug" virus, which in twenty-four hours infected 10 million computers worldwide and destroyed $10 billion in data. The have-nots will be able to do much more than in the past to express their resentment about being left behind.

At least as worrisome as the inequality between states is the mounting inequality within states. Many countries now contain two segregated economies—a fast, high-flying one for a select few, and a sagging, sluggish one for the rest. Shanghai may be swarming with cell phones and Internet advertisements, but a good portion of China's population lives in the interior of the country, where villagers may not have access even to basic services. Tverskaya Street, one of Moscow's main avenues, is lined with many of the world's high-end shops, but they cater only to foreigners and Moscow's ultrarich. Much of the city's population struggles to make it through the day.

Even Israel, a relatively wealthy country in terms of per capita income, is facing an ever-widening social divide. Herzliya, a northern suburb of Tel Aviv, is becoming a mini–Silicon Valley. One segment of the Israeli population works in this high-tech sector, is fully plugged into the Internet, and is reaping the benefits. But much of the region's population is excluded from this part of Israel's economy. Most ultra-Orthodox Jews shun engagement in globalization and the secularization that often accompanies it. Jewish immigrants from North African countries often lack the educational opportunities needed to enter the high-tech sector. And the Palestinians, who on a good day are allowed to cross into Israel as low-wage laborers, can do little more than look on with a combination of envy and rage.

Such inequalities have the potential to breed a rash of problems. China is already facing a dangerous divide between its coastal cities and the agrarian interior. The road and rail links between the two are poor, and social and cultural differences are widening. If the hinterland remains at the subsistence level while the coast explodes with growth, the country's integrity could be at stake. Concern about keeping China intact already feeds into Beijing's unwillingness to liberalize the political system, in turn risking resentment among the more cosmopolitan urban population.

In Russia, not only has the standard of living declined since the collapse of communism, but the populace has watched a new elite abscond with sizable portions of the country's wealth. Money has not been the only asset leaving Russia. Many of the best and brightest are emigrating to countries where their skills are in greater demand. A globalized labor market is thus making it difficult for Russia to build the middle class it so desperately needs as a foundation for political stability. And in Israel, growing economic inequality often falls along ethnic lines, dividing Ashkenazim (European Jews) from Sephardim (Oriental Jews), the religious from the secular, and Arab from Jew. Israeli society has become especially polarized as a result, adding to the difficulty of moving forward on the peace process.

The disaffected are angry not just at those who are better off, but also at globalization itself. Malaysian Prime Minister Mahathir Mohammed spoke for many when he blamed international financiers for the inequities and the austerities imposed by the global market. Many Russians now equate capitalism with corruption. As they watch the country's new oligarchs speed through Moscow in shiny limousines protected by armed guards, they have good reason to believe that the wealthy as a matter of course make their money at the expense of the poor. Millions of Muscovites are not partaking of globalization or are only glimpsing its benefits as they walk past stores they do not dare enter. The excluded are angry as a result, and because they associate globalization with America, much of that anger gets directed toward the United States.

The terrorist attacks of September 11, 2001, made clear just how vengeful the backlash against globalization can be. Osama bin Laden and his associates were angry about numerous issues—America's military presence in Saudi Arabia, the cultural influence of the West, the Arab-Israeli conflict, the impoverishment of the Islamic people. Inequalities within the countries of the Middle East and between these countries and the West have provided a fertile breeding ground for such disgruntlement. At the opening of the twenty-first century, average income in the world's advanced countries was $27,450, compared to $3,700 within the belt of Islamic countries running from Morocco to Bangladesh.[37] In the aggregate, bin Laden's grievances stemmed from a pervasive sense that Islamic society had been left behind by history, enfeebling its people and its values. The mission was to strike against the purported sources of this disempowerment—America's economic and military might. Hence the symbolic resonance of attacking the World Trade Center and the Pentagon. Hence the extent to which the attacks, although almost universally condemned, did tap into a strong current of anti-American sentiment that runs through much of the developing world.

Osama bin Laden was not just fighting against globalization, he was also exploiting it. A number of the terrorists that carried out the attacks of September 2001 were educated in Europe. Several of those who flew the hijacked planes were well trained in U.S. flight schools. As they planned the attacks, the perpetrators often communicated by sending each other e-mails from computer terminals in public libraries. The terrorists did an admirable job of exploiting America's porous borders, its lax immigration policies, its modern communications infrastructure, and an air transit system that privileged efficiency at the expense of security.

Friedman is hardly oblivious to this darker side of globalization. Indeed, he recognizes the superempowered angry man as both a product of and a principal threat to the era of globalization. But he goes too far when he declares the battle against terrorism "the equivalent of World War III," whose long-term geopolitical consequences will be to produce "new orders and divisions."[38] Terror attacks certainly can do grievous damage. They produce fear, shock, and revulsion. And preventing them requires intense countermeasures. But the appropriate analogy for the battle against terrorism is the war on drugs or the effort to combat organized crime, not the battle against Nazi Germany or the Soviet Union. Terrorism is to geopolitics what a strong wind is to geography—a potent, spectacular, and destructive element, but one that affects surface features, not underlying tectonic forces and the location of fault lines.

That criminal gangs, not organized states, are the perpetrators of terrorism has much to do with its limited geopolitical consequences. If globalization were to spawn superempowered angry states, rather than individuals, however, then it would begin to take on more geopolitical import. This prospect, unfortunately, is not one that can be altogether dismissed.

States and their citizens do not like it when they are whipsawed by the invisible forces of the global marketplace. That, however, is a logical consequence of an international economy in which on an average day some $1.5 trillion changes hands in global currency markets—a sum that is forty-eight times the daily value of world trade, and about equal to the annual economic product of France.[39] States and their citizens do not like it when their welfare becomes beholden to strangers living in countries thousands of miles away. That, however, is a logical consequence of an international economy in which the average American can sit at home and, with the click of a mouse, withdraw funds from a mutual fund invested abroad. It is hard to refute the claim that globalization has antidemocratic effects when Americans have more say in Malaysia's economy than the country's tax-paying, voting citizens.

The danger here is that states and their peoples will only take so much shoving around from the global economy before they eventually start pushing back. Even if a nation's economy is on balance benefiting from being wired into the global marketplace, national authorities may well pull the plug if they feel they are losing control and watching their domestic popularity slip away. Even worse, they may seek to centralize public institutions and rule with a heavy hand, risking the emergence of a new generation of authoritarian states. Karl Polanyi in *The Great Transformation*, his classic account of the rise of fascism during the twentieth century, traced the roots of totalitarian government to the gold standard and the extent to which it exposed states to the full brunt of the unpredictable and unremitting forces of the global economy.[40] The accompanying social dislocation, Polanyi persuasively argued, eventually produced a vengeful political backlash in the form of fascist regimes in Germany, Italy, and Japan.

Today's global economy, via the golden straitjacket imposed on those it embraces, is at least as intrusive as the marketplace of the early twentieth century. It is precisely its penetrating character that gives globalization the potential to induce liberal reform and encourage all countries to adopt lean and nimble laissez-faire economies. But the straitjacket also has the potential to do just the opposite and produce populist and statist regimes running on the fuel of economic nationalism and strategic rivalry. Globalization's success may well sow the seeds of its own demise.

Globalization Without Americanization

Finally, there is the problem of the relationship between globalization and Americanization. Many of globalization's critics maintain that the potential for further backlash against it stems from the misperception that globalization is inseparable from Americanization. When French farmers protested that the global economy was undermining traditional French culture, they did so by throwing bricks at McDonald's. When opponents of globalization flocked to Davos, Switzerland, to harass the economic elite as they gathered for the World Economic Forum, they too went after the Golden Arches. When Mahathir railed against global financiers, he fingered New York–based George Soros, not the many hedge fund managers working out of London. When Osama bin Laden struck, he aimed primarily at U.S. targets. As the global economy chugs ahead, the argument runs, America's economic and cultural reach will continue to rally those interested in stopping globalization in its tracks.

A thorny problem does exist on this front, but it is the opposite of the one identified by conventional wisdom. Americanization is not holding back globalization. On the contrary, the international economy has been expanding with such vigor precisely because it *is* inseparable from Americanization. The strength and stability of the global market have been direct by-products of America's willingness to design and manage it. Many countries of the world have been converging around a common set of business practices and economic ideologies not because of their intrinsic appeal, but because these practices and ideologies have been propagated by the world's only superpower. The United States has been setting the rules and unabashedly using globalization to remake the world in its image. Most countries have been playing along because they have had no choice. Friedman is right that at present states can either don their golden straitjacket (which happens to be tailored in the United States) or become roadkill on the information highway.

From this perspective, the most serious threat over the long term stems not from the link between globalization and Americanization, but from the prospect that the two will soon part ways. The threat of terrorism provides new and urgent reason to be concerned about anti-American sentiment arising from the backlash against globalization. But a much greater menace to international order stems from the likelihood that the American model will start to lose its luster as globalization fuels the rise of Europe and Asia. These two regions, after all, practice different brands of capitalism than does the United States. Finance, industry, and the state are more closely linked in Europe and Asia than in the United States, and Asia's focus on investment and savings contrasts starkly with America's focus on consumption. When Europe and Asia have the ability to do so, they will contest the logic as well as the dominance of the American way. As Martin Wolf astutely commented in the *Financial Times,* "For all its success, it is unlikely that the US offers the only workable way to organize an advanced economy."[41]

When power is more equally distributed around the globe, there will be much more disagreement about the fundamentals of managing the international monetary system, financial transactions, and the flow of goods and services. And even when there might be agreement over substance, there will be much more competition over leadership and status. The interwar period, when there was no dominant nation to hold sway over the international economy, is again instructive. Commenting on the policy differences between the U.S. Federal Reserve and the Bank of England, one historian of the period noted that "at the back of such disagreements on policy matters there were also political rivalries. The special relationship between Great Britain and the United States was not always so very special, for they were rivals as far as the domination of the global financial network was concerned."[42] Kindleberger's worry about "the United States and the E.E.C. vying for leadership of the world economy" may ring all too true.

The global economy, just like the geopolitical landscape, will soon suffer from too little America, not too much. As Europe and Asia rise, their resentment of America may diminish, but so will the stability of the international marketplace. American preeminence brings out the best in the global economy. As unipolarity wanes, so will globalization's more benign effects.

The current economic order thus has only an illusory durability. America's economy has already disproved the invincibility attributed to it during the 1990s. And even if the United States were able to stave off the prolonged cyclical downturns that history suggests are unavoidable, the international economy will transmit wealth and influence to others, at once widening inequalities between and within countries and undermining America's preeminence and its ability to keep globalization on course. Either way, Friedman's map of the world will soon be obsolete.

DEMOCRACY AND NATIONALISM

WITH GLOBALIZATION no guarantor of a benign future, we turn to one final set of arguments about the causes of peace—Fukuyama's claims about the pacifying effects of democracy. In asserting that the arrival of liberal democracy represents a historical end point that will rid the world of interstate war, Fukuyama draws on a distinguished body of scholarship. Immanuel Kant was the first to build a systematic argument as to why the rise of republican government had the

potential to promote "perpetual peace."[43] Many contemporary scholars have picked up on Kant's insights and formed what is now called
the "democratic peace" school.[44] This school has in fact had a substantial impact on U.S. policy, with Bill Clinton repeatedly basing America's interest in exporting democracy on the claim that "the habits of
democracy are the habits of peace."[45]

Proponents of the democratic peace school argue that the historical
record confirms the peace-causing effects of democratic government.
Democracy started to catch on during the eighteenth century. Although there are now more than 120 democracies in the world and
frequent episodes of violent conflict (during the course of the last
decade, an average of twenty-eight major armed conflicts took place
each year), democratic states have yet to go to war with each other.
Scholars back up their historical interpretations with several logical
arguments. The propensity of democratic states to fight wars with
each other should be diminished both by popular opposition to incurring the costs of conflict (unlike in authoritarian states, those who do
the fighting also do the voting) and by the tendency for democratic
debate to produce centrist and moderate policies. In addition, states
that abide by the rule of law at home are likely to abide by established
norms of behavior in the conduct of their foreign policy, enabling
democracies to accord each other respect and to develop a special
sense of affinity.

Critics justifiably question the validity of the historical interpretations offered up by the democratic peace school.[46] Democracy simply
has not been around long enough to draw definitive conclusions.
Until the latter half of the twentieth century, democratic states were
a rarity, making the random chance of war between them close to
zero. The absence thus far of war among democracies therefore proves
little.

Furthermore, there are a few troubling historical cases. Democratic institutions and practices in America and Great Britain were
admittedly in their early stages at the time, but the two countries did
clash in the War of 1812. America's Civil War, although it was a conflict within an existing country, also challenges the proposition that
democratic units will not fight each other. Neither these nor other
questionable cases constitute a clear-cut refutation, but the ambiguity of the historical record does provide reason for withholding
judgment—or at least limiting how much confidence one places in

the claim. With the past providing only inconclusive lessons, the best case for the pacifying effects of democracy rests on logical arguments about the tendency of democracies to pursue centrist policies and to cultivate with each other unusual levels of mutual respect and affinity.

It is precisely on this issue of mutual respect that Fukuyama's work intersects with the democratic peace school. To recall Fukuyama's logic, "Liberal democracy replaces the irrational desire to be recognized as greater than others with a rational desire to be recognized as equal. A world made up of liberal democracies, then, should have much less incentive for war, since all nations would reciprocally recognize one another's legitimacy."[47] As democracy becomes universal, satisfied states should all accord one another recognition and dignity, ultimately eradicating war.

By connecting the mutual respect individuals accord each other in a democracy with the mutual respect democratic states accord each other in the international system, Fukuyama is able to assert that the ability of democracy to pacify politics within the state also applies to politics between states. This is a deft analytic move, allowing him to claim that liberal democracy will lead to the disappearance of traditional geopolitical competition and hence bring history to an end. But herein also lies a principal misconception in Fukuyama's treatise.

The international system, even if it were entirely populated by liberal democracies, is not itself democratic and egalitarian. Strong and wealthy states hold much more sway over international affairs than weak and poor ones. The United States and Norway are both democracies, but their status and weight in the international arena are hardly equal. China is not a democracy, but it has a much greater voice than many of the world's democracies. Unlike inside a state, the international system has no constitution or bill of rights to assure one country one vote, to codify the equal rights of all states, or to lay out the principles of fair and just governance. On the contrary, the international system is unruly and unequal, much like domestic life prior to the taming and leveling effects of democratic rule.

As within the feudal state, order in the international system is based on might, not right. Life is dangerous, competitive, and unequal. Even the United Nations, the institution that comes closest to providing a forum for global governance, is anything but egalitarian. The U.N. Security Council is essentially a great-power club, giving its permanent members much more influence than all other states. The architects of the U.N. recognized from the outset that they had to grant strong nations the prerogatives they expect. To have done otherwise would have relegated the U.N. to irrelevance. And even with its elevated status, the United States rarely does important business at the U.N. because it does not want to be hampered by its procedures and the institutional checks on America's freedom of action.

Liberal democracy may well satisfy man's yearning for recognition and status, but the international system, precisely because it does not play by the rules of liberal democracy, does not satisfy the nation-state's similar yearning for respect and equality. Nations exhibit many of the same drives as the humans that populate and govern them. They want and need more than just material comfort. They also desire and need psychic comfort. That psychic drive manifests itself in the form of nationalism. In the absence of a democratic international system that accords all nations the rights and status they seek, nationalism impels them to continue the struggle for recognition, thus serving as an endemic source of competition.

Fukuyama seems to recognize that the presence of nationalism poses a challenge to his vision. He sidesteps the problem, however, by arguing that nationalism in the contemporary era will lose its bite and its political salience. Fukuyama accepts that "the post-historical world would still be divided into nation-states," but he contends that the world's "separate nationalisms would have made peace with liberalism."[48] Here, Fukuyama relies too heavily on Hegel—to the exclusion of other German philosophers of the time. Had he also consulted Johann Gottfried von Herder, Johann Gottlieb Fichte, and some of the other founding fathers of modern nationalism, he would likely have seen the intimate connection between the advent of liberal democracy and the rise of nationalism.[49] The same political force that Fukuyama argues will bring the end of history—liberal democracy—is also what drives nationalist passions and hence denies liberal democracy its peace-causing effects.

The emergence of the idea of nationhood followed logically from the introduction of consensual politics for a simple reason. If common people were to begin active participation in the political life of the state, they had to have some emotional connection to that state. Identities and allegiances that had been focused on the nuclear family or the feudal lord had to be raised to a much broader level—that of a nation-state embodying the collective will of the people. Nationalism emerged as the medium for doing so by creating an imagined political community based on bonds of ethnicity, culture, language, and history. As the national idea took root, it created a shared identity and shared destiny that were essential to the cohesion of the liberal democratic state. It also instilled a strong sense of belonging and allegiance—important inasmuch as the national state was soon to ask its citizens to die in its defense. Mass conscription was possible only because the masses had begun to identify with the nation. It then helped consolidate the construction of political community at the national level by drawing citizens into a collective mission that evoked passion and self-sacrifice.

Propelled forward by the French Revolution and the establishment of the United States as a federal republic, nationalism, at times in excess, spread in step with democracy; they were the twin sisters of the nineteenth century. Nationalism has been the binding glue of modern democracy ever since, providing the social cohesion and the common purpose without which consensual politics would have foundered. The national ideal also took hold in the developing world, carrying with it the gospel of self-determination, which soon brought to an end the era of colonial empire.

Nationalism, however, also has its adverse side effects. States whose legitimating ideology rests on the nation and its primacy tend to find themselves in competition with other states that have their own legitimating national identity. One's nation, after all, is a meaningful political community only because it is distinct from other nations. Nationalism thus defines not just which community one belongs to, but also which communities one does *not* belong to. As such, it draws lines and as a matter of course sets distinct, self-interested national groupings against each other. Nationalism thus serves as a foundation for the world's primary political units but also as a source of competition among them. Nationalism may help pacify politics inside states, but it does the opposite for politics between them.

Prior to the rise of the nation-state, many of history's great wars were primarily predatory conflicts over wealth and power. Since the birth of nationalism, the world's major wars have also been about ideology and competing national ideals. The Napoleonic Wars, World War I, World War II, the Cold War—these great struggles were born of nationalism and pitted against each other rival concepts of the ordering of both domestic and international society. The violent breakup of Yugoslavia is only the most recent example of the consequences of a world in which the national idea has so infused political life.

Liberal democracy cannot function without nationalism. It is the critical ingredient that brings the faceless state to life by merging it with the mythical nation, the resulting nation-state then able to embrace the citizen through its emotional allure. But nationalism is also a persistent source of rivalry among the very nation-states that it brings to life. Fukuyama would have us believe that these two functions of nationalism can be separated; it can provide social cohesion internally without serving as a source of competition externally. "Separate nationalisms," he tells us reassuringly, "would express themselves increasingly in the sphere of private life alone."[50]

But this cannot be so. Nationalism is by nature a public affair; it is what connects the private to the public realm. If nationalism were to become solely a part of private life, it would deny liberal democracy its ideological foundation and undo the sense of community and belonging that makes consensual politics viable. A collective, public nationalism is at the heart of liberal democracy. Fukuyama's failure to recognize that the two are inseparable is the central flaw in his map of the world. The indelible link between liberal democracy and nationalism is also one of the main reasons that history will not be ending anytime soon.

Democracy may well extend its reach in the years ahead, meaning that the world's great powers could soon find themselves without non-democracies against whom they can focus their national ambitions. But the logic of nationalism suggests that these democracies will then focus their competitive energies on each other, disappointing the many scholars and politicians who have so ardently defended the democratic peace school. The rise of Europe could pose a particular problem from this perspective. Precisely because Europe is in the process of building a new political community that encompasses a region, not just a state, the EU may well find it convenient, if not necessary, to propagate a new and ambitious brand of pan-European nationalism. If so, we cannot take for granted that America and Europe will remain fast friends. The struggle for recognition and status that Fukuyama correctly places at the center of the human experience could well turn the Atlantic link into a new axis of competition.

Democracy does appear to have at least some pacifying effects. The absence of major war among liberal democracies, while not definitive, provides cause for optimism that war may become less common as representative government becomes more pervasive. The notion of a democratic peace also has logical appeal. Democracies should be more centrist, moderate, and levelheaded than states controlled by a single individual or an authoritarian ruling group whose pathologies are likely to go unchecked. And it makes sense that open, transparent polities should be able to build closer ties with each other than closed, opaque ones.

The problem is that the peace-causing effects of democracy may not be able to prevail over trends pushing the international system in the other direction. Nationalism could counter, if not overwhelm, a democratic peace, as could the changing structure of the international system and the tectonic geopolitical forces that these changes generate. The return of multipolarity promises to stir up competitive instincts that may well make short shrift of democracy's benign effects. At a minimum, we cannot afford to be confident that the spread of democratic governance will serve as a sufficient antidote to the geopolitical tensions brought on by the end of America's unipolar moment.

CHAPTER FOUR

The Rise of Europe

T HE CLAIM THAT EUROPE is an emerging pole and that its rise will hasten the end of America's unipolar moment rests on two main propositions, both of which cut against the grain of conventional wisdom. The first concerns the pathways through which shifts in the global distribution of power take place. Most scholars view uneven rates of economic growth as the main engine behind international change. Centers of innovation and productivity move from one locale to another, eventually enabling a nimble newcomer to overtake a tiring hegemon.[1]

This account, however, fails to capture the main source of change in today's setting. Europe will soon catch up with America not because of a superior economy or technological base, but because it is coming together, amassing the impressive resources and intellectual capital already possessed by its constituent states. Europe's political union is in the midst of altering the global landscape.

The second proposition challenging conventional wisdom concerns the implications of Europe's rise for its relations with America. For most policy-makers and scholars alike, amity among the Atlantic democracies is a fact of life, an unalterable product of their common history and values. That the EU and the United States might part ways borders on the unthinkable.[2]

This book takes a different tack. Throughout the Cold War, the United States and Europe effectively constituted a single pole—the West. Shared values no doubt contributed to the strength of this political community. But Europe and America have been fast friends for the past five decades in part because the Europeans have had no choice. They needed America's help to hold off the Soviet Union. And the scope of U.S. predominance ensured they followed Washington's lead. Now that the asymmetry between the United States and Europe is closing, such harmony cannot be taken for granted. A single pole is gradually separating into two. North America and Europe are likely to engage in the competition over status, wealth, and power that has been—and remains—so much a part of the human experience.

Before examining the EU's emergence as a counterweight to America, we again look to history for guidance. To illuminate the profound effect processes of integration and amalgamation can have on the balance of power, we turn to the unification of Germany during the nineteenth century. After Count Otto von Bismarck joined most German-speaking lands in Central Europe into a single country, the new Germany enjoyed several decades of impressive economic growth, soon followed by a steady rise in its military might and ambition. The unification of Germany irretrievably altered Europe's geopolitics, setting the stage for a new round of rivalry that eventually encompassed the world. Europe as a whole is now engaged in a process of integration and amalgamation that may have similarly profound consequences.

To shed light on what may transpire when a single pole separates into competitive halves, we turn to the Roman Empire. During the third century, the Emperor Diocletian decided to divide the empire into western and eastern realms to facilitate the tasks of administration and defense. Rome remained the capital of the western half, while Constantinople (formerly Byzantium) emerged as its counterpart in the east. Although this administrative innovation initially consolidated imperial rule, Rome and Constantinople soon clashed over matters of security, status, and religion. Despite their common culture and heritage, the Western and Eastern Empires became direct competitors. The replacement of one pole with two as a matter of course replaced hierarchy and order with mounting geopolitical rivalry. Rome's fate does not augur well for a unitary West that is in the midst of separating into distinct North American and European power centers.

THE PAST

THE UNIFICATION OF GERMANY in 1871 joined together communities that had for centuries been independent fiefdoms, principalities, and dukedoms. Austria was the only sizable German-speaking polity missing from the new amalgam. And that was no accident. Prussia and Austria had long been rivals. In addition, Otto von Bismarck, the minister president of Prussia, was relying on an anti-Austrian policy to disarm his opponents in parliament. In his typically blunt formulation, "The Viennese policy being what it is, Germany is too small for the two of us." Under Bismarck's guidance, the unification of Germany was coming to mean the exclusion of Austria.[3]

The establishment of a unified Germany, even without Austria as a part, was to alter the geopolitical map of Europe. Prussia under the capable and ambitious leadership of Bismarck had won three wars in its bid to unify Germany—against Denmark in 1864, Austria in 1866, and France in 1870–1871. Victory in the Franco-Prussian War and the population and resources thereafter at the disposal of the new state confirmed that Germany had overshadowed all challengers, including France, as continental Europe's dominant nation. The force that Prussia fielded in 1870 was roughly twice the size of what France was able to muster; French defenses crumbled quickly. At its founding, Germany's population was already larger than that of France and its population growth rate much higher. By 1915, the German population stood at 70 million, the French at 40 million. Add German discipline and the abundant industrial resources of the Ruhr region, and it was clear that a behemoth had arrived.

German unification dealt France the most immediate blow— defeat and humiliation at the hands of Prussia—but the implications for Britain were also ominous. A unified Germany and its consequent ascent spelled the end of Britain's hegemony and would eventually make obsolete its grand strategy of coupling global naval mastery with the avoidance of major military commitments on the European continent. Britain never dominated Europe as did Rome. But not doing so was the genius of its grand strategy. Britain intervened on the Continent only as needed to maintain a stable balance. With potential rivals thus keeping one another in check, Britain was free to focus on developing and safeguarding its overseas empire.

Not so after German unification. A federated German Reich was officially proclaimed on January 18, 1871, by way of a pompous ceremony in the Galerie des Glaces in Versailles presided over by Kaiser Wilhelm I. British leaders immediately recognized the implications. Only three weeks later, Benjamin Disraeli, the Conservative leader who would soon become prime minister, told the House of Commons that the unification of Germany "represents the German Revolution, a greater political event than the French Revolution of the last century. There is not a diplomatic tradition which has not been swept away. We used to have discussions in this House about the balance of power . . . but what has really come to pass in Europe? The balance of power has been entirely destroyed."[4] The uniting of the German people into a single state, Disraeli feared, would irreversibly upset the European equilibrium, eroding for good the foundation of Britain's grand strategy and setting the stage for the demise of its global dominion.

Disraeli was all too accurate in his predictions. During the three decades following unification, the German economy enjoyed steady growth. Technological innovations gave dramatic boosts to heavy industry. Germany rapidly caught up with and then surpassed Britain in key areas of industrial production such as steel and pig iron. A new industrial and financial elite emerged, which, by allying itself with the traditional landed aristocracy, wielded mounting influence. This alliance between "iron and rye" served as Bismarck's main political base and helped him counter the strength of the rising working class.

Due largely to Bismarck's astute diplomacy, Germany's economic accomplishments did not immediately upset Europe's geopolitical equilibrium. Bismarck avoided any rapid or substantial buildup of the navy and army. Although German traders eventually left him little choice but to take on overseas territories, he initially opposed the acquisition of colonies, concerned that it would alienate Britain and France. And he set up an elaborate system of agreements and alliances that made Germany the diplomatic pivot of Europe. Bismarck shrewdly maximized German influence. But he was always ready to pull in the reins just before Germany's newfound ambition would set off strategic rivalry. Bismarck manipulated the European balance, but he stopped short of overturning it.

After 1890, Germany was governed by less able individuals. They also faced greater political challenges at home. The Social Democrats were on the rise at the same time that the alliance between iron and rye was coming apart. German industry was booming and no longer needed protective tariffs. German farmers meanwhile were pressing for protection against imports of Russian and American grain.

The impetuous Kaiser Wilhelm II, backed by his foreign minister Bernhard von Bülow (who was soon to become chancellor) and his naval chief Alfred Tirpitz, turned to nationalism to unite the country. Germany, its leaders proclaimed, deserved a level of international influence commensurate with its economic might. The country would be able to fulfill its new calling only if it had the necessary tools, including a high-seas fleet. Armed with nationalist fervor and the First Naval Law of 1898, Germany embarked upon its new quest. The industrialists welcomed the lucrative orders for their steel mills and shipyards. The landed gentry were rewarded with grain tariffs for supporting the naval buildup. And the rising voice of the Social Democrats was neutralized, at least temporarily, by the unifying cause of national greatness.

The deft use of foreign policy as a tool of domestic politics, however, came at great cost to European peace. With Germany's decision to translate its economic capability into military might, the countdown to World War I began. As Disraeli had predicted, a stable balance quickly gave way to rivalry and rearmament. Carried along by strong currents of nationalism, Germany's military buildup proved unstoppable. Not even a coalition of Russia, France, and Britain was able to deter Berlin from its bid to dominate Europe. Despite intelligence reports suggesting that Germany did not have the wherewithal to prevail against this troika, the kaiser and his confidants headed steadily toward war. In 1913, as all parties proceeded with full-scale rearmament, the chancellor, Theobald von Bethmann-Hollweg, warned a Reichstag charged with war fever, "Woe be to him whose retreat is not well-prepared."[5] When it became clear that Germany was on an irreversible path, Bethmann uttered with resignation that the country was taking "a leap in the dark."[6]

Germany's defeat in World War I restored only temporarily Europe's equilibrium. The Versailles Treaty exacted painful war reparations, demilitarized the Rhineland, and put a cap on the size of Germany's army. But after Adolf Hitler took office in 1933, Germany rode roughshod over its international obligations and began yet another bid for continental hegemony. Fueled by a more twisted and potent brand of nationalism, a unified Germany on this second attempt at dominating Europe came perilously close to overrunning its neighbors to the west and east. Were it not for Hitler's excessive ambition—his decision to open a second front against Russia in 1941 stretched German resources too thin—and America's eventual willingness to help stop the Nazi war machine, Germany may well have gained lasting control of Western and Central Europe.

Scarred by the two world wars, Germany's neighbors were not about to let history repeat itself. At the close of World War II, the spent but victorious Allies occupied Germany and divided the country into administrative units, ensuring its unified strength could not again plunge Europe into war. Once the Cold War set in, Germany was formally separated into two countries, with the western half joining NATO and the eastern half the Warsaw Pact. The Allies soon permitted West Germany to rearm and rebuild its economy to help counter the Soviet threat. But the return of German power was tolerated only within the binding context of NATO and the European Community. Under no circumstances would America and its allies again allow Germany to pursue its own path.

When the fall of the Berlin Wall raised the prospect of the reunification of Germany, most of Europe recoiled at the thought. In recalling her discussions with French President François Mitterrand, British Prime Minister Margaret Thatcher captured the dominant sentiments of the moment: "I produced from my handbag a map showing the various configurations of Germany in the past, which were not altogether reassuring about the future. We talked through what precisely we might do. . . . [Mitterrand] said that at moments of great danger in the past France had always established special relations with Britain and he felt such a time had come again. We must draw together and stay in touch. It seemed to me that although we had not discovered the means, at least we both had the will to check the German juggernaut. That was a start."[7]

Despite the widespread reservations among Germany's neighbors, reunification ultimately proved unavoidable due to the political momentum behind it in Germany. Fortunately for Europe and the rest of the world, this second coming together of a single German nation-state did not expose the frightful geopolitical fault line that it did last time. Instead, Germany's resources and ambition have been merged with the resources and ambition of Europe and the enterprise of European integration.

The integration of Europe's individual nation-states into a collective whole has provided an antidote to the destructive rivalry that for centuries was the inevitable by-product of Europe's multipolarity. France and Germany, rather than vying for supremacy, have formed a close partnership and now serve together as Europe's anchor. Brussels has become the collective capital, in symbolic and practical terms diminishing the authority of the individual national governments. Europe's smaller countries have arrayed themselves around this benign core, with overlapping economic, political, and social networks binding core and periphery together. The Continent's new democracies are waiting impatiently to join the club. Through the European Union, Europe has finally found a way of safely accommodating a unified Germany.

What is good for Europe, however, may not necessarily be good for everyone else. Collective will and centralized authority promote internal stability, but they also encourage external ambition. An integrated and prosperous Europe may have solved the German question, but it could well emerge as a formidable entity on a new geopolitical map of the world.

IN THE NINETEENTH CENTURY, Europe's geopolitics underwent a profound revolution. The agent of change was the integration of individual entities into a unitary state, creating a Germany that overturned the Continent's stable balance. Europe today is unifying, just as Germany did more than a century ago. The EU is not likely to become a single state—at least not anytime soon. But the economic, military, and geopolitical weight of its individual countries has to be assessed in the aggregate, even if then discounted because its integration is still under way. Although a work in progress, Europe's unification has already begun to transform the international system.

To examine how the rise of the EU is likely to affect its relationship with the United States, the past again provides useful clues. During the fourth century, Europe underwent a revolution as significant as that of the nineteenth century. Except the agent of change was the reverse—the division of a unipolar Roman empire into two entities rather than the merging of individual German polities into a unitary whole. The split of a single imperial realm into separate halves had ominous consequences for Roman rule. The peace sustained by unipolarity quickly gave way to the rivalry brought on by competition for primacy among dueling centers of power.

By the first century A.D., the borders of the Roman Empire stretched west to Spain and the British Isles, north to Belgium and the Rhineland, south to North Africa and Egypt, and east to the Arabian peninsula. Rome was to control much of this territory for the next three hundred years. A hub-spoke pattern of rule provided the foundation for an imperial realm of such scope and longevity. Rome extended its reach over the periphery through overlapping sources of control. The Romans made significant improvements in roadway construction, warfare, and shipbuilding, facilitating the flow of political influence and resources between the imperial center and its distant limbs. They introduced an advanced system of governance that fostered the "Romanization" of new subjects. Small groups of Romans were sent to live in imperial territories to help assimilate conquered peoples and encourage them to take on a Roman identity and way of life. The goal was to cultivate allegiance toward, rather than resentment of, Roman rule; assimilation was a much cheaper and more effective way to extend control than was coercion.

Rome was similarly thrifty in its military strategy. The well-trained legions were kept in reserve and deployed only as needed to put down uprisings or repel invaders. This system provided effective deterrence; the mere prospect of facing the legions was enough to dissuade many potential challengers from attacking.[8] Like America today, Rome enjoyed uncontested primacy and the deference that came with it.

By the third century, Rome was beginning to feel the strain of keeping together such a large imperial zone. The empire's frontiers could no longer be guaranteed against contenders growing in both number and strength. Germanic tribes threatened in the west. Persians and nomads from the Black Sea region pressed in the east. Ammianus Marcellinus, a historian of the late Roman period, made clear that the barbarian tribes, despite their primitive weaponry and organization, posed a significant threat:

> Being lightly equipped and very sudden in their movements they can deliberately scatter and gallop about at random, inflicting tremendous slaughter; their extreme nimbleness enables them to force a rampart or pillage an enemy's camp before one catches sight of them.... You cannot make a truce with them, because they are quite unreliable and easily swayed by any breath of rumor which promises advantage; like unreasoning beasts they are entirely at the mercy of the maddest impulses. They are totally ignorant of the distinction between right and wrong, their speech is shifty and obscure, and they are under no restraint from religion or superstition.[9]

The frequency and intensity of barbarian attacks compelled Rome to change its military strategy. With simultaneous threats emerging on the perimeter, the legions had to be dispatched to the frontier.

Their deployment, however, put an extraordinary strain on troop levels and imperial coffers. Even worse, with the legions no longer held in reserve, but instead stretched precariously thin, they could no longer deter adversaries through intimidation. Attacks on one part of the frontier therefore invited secondary attacks elsewhere. The empire also began to face threats from within. Some of the larger provinces had amassed considerable wealth and were seeking to distance themselves from Rome.

Enter Diocletian, who became emperor in 284, and his bold and innovative solution to the problem of imperial overstretch. The task of managing the empire, Diocletian reasoned, had grown too onerous for a single ruler. Better to divide up the realm and devolve responsibility for its several parts to trusted colleagues. He accordingly elevated one of his generals, Maximian, to the rank of coemperor. Diocletian and Maximian each named a junior emperor, known as a Caesar, who would help run the empire and be in line to succeed his Augustus (supreme emperor). The realm was then effectively divided into two halves, and each half again divided between the Augustus and his Caesar. Diocletian ruled the Eastern Empire with the assistance of his junior counterpart, while Maximian and his Caesar ruled the west. Diocletian also divided the larger, wealthier provinces into smaller units, disarming the threat they posed to the authority of the Augusti. These reforms proved effective in shoring up the security of the realm and enabling both the western and eastern portions of the empire to turn back the barbarian threat.

Diocletian and Maximian stepped down in 305, smoothly handing over control to their Caesars—Constantius in the west and Galerius in the east. But once Diocletian and the authority he wielded were gone, fierce jockeying ensued among would-be Augusti and Caesars, with their supporters taking up arms against each other. Constantine, the son of Constantius, was by 313 able to prevail in the west and took the title of Augustus. Licinius, an ally of Galerius, was meanwhile able to triumph in the east.

Constantine was not satisfied with control of only the Western Empire, and soon took it upon himself to restore the unity of the imperial realm. He eventually did so by defeating Licinius at Chrysopolis in 324. Constantine then made two decisions that altered the course of history. First, he established a new capital for the empire as a whole at Byzantium, changing its name to Constantinople. Strategically situated on the Bosphorus, where Europe ends and Asia begins,

Constantinople enabled Constantine to solidify his control over the eastern reaches of the empire and to deal more effectively with invaders on the eastern frontier. Second, Constantine converted to Christianity, setting the stage for its establishment as the official religion of the realm. He also became a strict enforcer of Christian doctrine, even ordering that his son, Crispus, be executed for adultery.

The restoration of imperial unity was short-lived. When Constantine died in 337, the empire was redivided between his sons. Competition between the western and eastern halves again kicked in, especially because Rome[10] and Constantinople emerged as separate capitals, each seeking to extend the influence and enhance the prestige of its court. The replacement of one political center with two had been formalized. The papacy in Rome and the patriarchate in Constantinople soon joined the fray, entering battle over doctrinal questions and differing as to whether religious authorities in Constantinople were of equal status to their counterparts in Rome. Disputes over language and culture followed; the Western "Roman" Empire was based on Latin culture and language, the Eastern "Byzantine" Empire, on Greek. "New Rome" and "Old Rome" also competed over the style and grandeur of their architecture. The Western and Eastern Empires were becoming distinct political and cultural entities.

Although Diocletian's reforms in the short term facilitated the management and defense of the empire, they thus had quite adverse consequences. The split of the imperial realm, rather than promoting unity, almost immediately led to rivalry between the eastern and western halves. Gibbon notes that "this dangerous novelty impaired the strength, and fomented the vices, of a double reign."[11] The division of the empire also quickened rather than slowed the drain on military resources, with each Augustus and Caesar wanting a loyal army. As Lactantius, a religious scholar of the time, put it, Diocletian "appointed three men to share his rule, dividing the empire into four parts and multiplying the armies, since each of the four strove to have a far larger number of troops than previous emperors had had when they were governing the state alone."[12]

The order that unipolarity had provided was gone for good. The Roman Empire was already experiencing a rapid decline before Diocletian's time; the worsening state of affairs had inspired his reforms. But with authority and resources now divided between east and west, the pace of decline quickened. The Western Empire maintained its integrity only until the death of Theodosius the Great in 395. Thereafter, much of its territory was overrun by Germanic tribes and other challengers. Rome itself was sacked by Goths in 410 and then invaded and plundered by Vandals in 455. Twenty years later, the last Roman emperor, Romulus Augustulus, ended his reign and left Italy in the hands of tribal leaders.

During the Western Empire's decline, Constantinople generally sought to exploit its weakness. Eastern emperors were at times tempted to seek the reunification of the realm under their sole control, a task partially accomplished by Justinian and his able general, Belisarius. But the Eastern Empire had neither the resources nor the inclination to devote its soldiers to this end, instead observing Rome's demise with a certain satisfaction. "The Byzantine court," according to Gibbon, "beheld with indifference, perhaps with pleasure, the disgrace of Rome, the misfortunes of Italy, and the loss of the West."[13] Constantinople also looked with disdain at the dilution of Roman culture that had taken place. Its rulers, however, were in the end too weak and besieged with their own internal and external threats to help out. Faced with armies on their eastern and southern flanks, successive eastern emperors could not spare the troops needed to expel the invaders that had carved up the Western Empire. And the west's inhabitants were hardly prepared to direct their allegiance to Constantinople if its troops could not offer them protection.

The church, which was to have helped secure imperial unity, did just the opposite. From the outset, church authorities in Rome and Constantinople were adversaries; the pope in Rome and the patriarch in Constantinople were in a constant struggle for religious and political influence. Tensions grew so acute that in 484 the papacy and the patriarchate excommunicated each other. Serious doctrinal differences helped intensify the rivalry. Did the Holy Ghost proceed from the Father alone or also the Son? Was Christ one being of divine nature or two inseparable beings, one divine and one human? Should busts and religious images play a central part in worship, or, as in Judaism and Islam, did worshiping figures constitute idolatry? When mingled with personal animosities, these doctrinal disputes were to mire both churches in centuries of competition and intrigue—including murders, kidnappings, and lesser forms of abuse. The church nonetheless stayed nominally unified until 1054, when it formally broke into its Roman Catholic and Greek Orthodox variants.

While Rome and Constantinople, along with their respective churches, grew further apart, the Byzantine portion of the empire fared better than the western half. Whereas the Western Empire was already coming apart within decades of the empire's division, the Byzantine realm managed to remain intact until the early seventh century. In 611, Persian armies conquered Syria and Palestine, and then moved on to Egypt in 616. The Byzantines regained much of this territory, but then lost it again to Arab armies soon thereafter. The capture of these areas had a devastating impact on Byzantium; they had been the empire's main source of grain. The setback for Constantinople was so great that Emperor Constans II considered moving the capital back to Rome. At least a part of Italy's population, especially in Rome, Naples, and Sicily, was at the time still loyal to the Byzantine emperor. Constans II did make it to the port of Syracuse in Sicily. But he was promptly murdered, ending the idea of bringing the capital back to Rome.

Following the setbacks of the seventh century, the Byzantine Empire consolidated its position until the twelfth century, after which time it was progressively dismantled by invaders from both east and west. Constantinople itself managed to hang on until 1453, when it finally gave way to an Ottoman siege. But by then the Byzantine Empire had for decades been in receivership. The fall of Constantinople was just official confirmation of the rise of the Islamic world and the decline of Christian Europe.

The Roman imperium would have eventually come undone; all great empires do. Several sources of decline were at work, especially in the Western Empire. Barbarian attacks necessitated a military buildup that weakened the economy by diverting troops and resources from trade, crafts, and agriculture. A bloated bureaucracy and a materialism born of affluence contributed to corruption and an erosion in public spirit, eventually stripping the Roman ideal of its ideological appeal. The spread of Christianity also appears to have contributed to imperial decline by directing the loyalties of citizens toward the church rather than the state.[14]

Although Diocletian's decision to divide the empire initially helped counter some of these sources of decline, his well-intentioned policy ultimately made matters worse by replacing one center of authority with two. Diocletian's experiment had everything going for it—a common religion, history, tradition, and commitment to the well-being of the Roman imperium. But the shift from unipolarity to bipolarity turned commonality into competition. Resources that once flowed to Rome went to Constantinople. Dual emperors worked against, rather than with, each other. Doctrinal disputes transformed a common religion into a divided church. And the cultural gap between Latin and Greek peoples became politicized. In Gibbon's words, "The national schism of the Greeks and Latins was enlarged by the perpetual difference of language and manners, of interest, and even of religion."[15] Centuries of stable order under Rome's leadership gave way to political turmoil and Europe's eclipse by the civilizations rising to its east.

THESE HISTORICAL reflections constitute warnings about the end of America's unipolar moment and its likely consequences. The EU is an emerging pole, dividing the West into American and European halves. America and Europe have certainly been close partners for more than five decades; it would be natural to conclude that they are kith and kin for good. But consider the Roman Empire and its rapid demise after the founding of a second capital in Constantinople. The Western and Eastern Empires were for centuries one polity. They shared a common religion and had deep cultural links. They faced common enemies. And the division of the empire was carefully planned and carried out by Diocletian. Nonetheless, as soon as two poles of power replaced one, geopolitical competition followed.

America and Europe share a common heritage, have strong cultural links, and for decades faced a common enemy. These conditions have helped them form a coherent and cohesive Western world since the onset of the Cold War. But now that the West is in the midst of being divided, it may well go the way of the Roman Empire. What is happening between Washington and Brussels, however, differs in an important respect from what happened between Rome and Constantinople. Today's division is occurring by default, not by design, raising the stakes and the potential for bad blood.

THE INTEGRATION OF EUROPE

ACCORDING TO most observers, American primacy is here to stay. As Dartmouth College political scientist William Wohlforth sums up the prevailing wisdom, "The current unipolarity is not only peaceful but durable.... For many decades, no state is likely to be in a position to take on the United States in any of the underlying elements of power."[16] Wohlforth is technically correct. In terms of its economy, its military, and its intellectual and cultural capital, America is laps ahead of all other countries, and the gap is not closing.

But America's best and brightest are thinking too traditionally; they are being misled by the past to look only at individual countries as likely challengers. As a result, they fail to appreciate that a collective Europe is next in line—even though it is rising before our eyes. Strategists continue to look right past a united Europe because it is a new animal, a political entity that defies standard categories. The European Union falls short of being a centralized federation like the United States. But it is certainly much more than a loose grouping of sovereign nations. America must figure out just what this new entity is—and start taking it seriously—if the country is to get right its new map of the world.

The integration of Europe is one of the most significant geopolitical events of the twentieth century. It represents a turning point every bit as momentous as the founding of the United States as a federal union, perhaps more so. Europe has taken history into its hands and is sculpting its own landscape. After centuries of rivalry and bloodshed among competing poles, the Europeans have had enough. They are in the midst of a revolutionary process of geopolitical engineering aimed at merging these competing polities into a collective whole, eliminating once and for all war among Europe's national states.

The results have thus far been dramatic. From the decline of the Roman Empire until the end of World War II, the peoples of Europe, interrupted only by short breaks, were at war with each other. After just fifty years of European integration, armed conflict among Britain, France, Germany, and their smaller neighbors has become virtually unthinkable. In progressing from the European Coal and Steel Community (ECSC), to the European Economic Community (EEC), to the European Union, Europe has finally escaped its past.

Most Americans dramatically underestimate—or dismiss altogether—the geopolitical significance of the EU.[17] This misreading is understandable. The major initiatives and activities of the EU have been primarily economic in nature. The ECSC, founded in 1951, aimed at bringing under collective control the coal and steel production of France, Germany, Belgium, Italy, Luxembourg, and the Netherlands. The next step forward came with the establishment of the EEC in 1957, a move that eliminated internal tariffs and established a common external tariff. Member states worked to consolidate this common market during the course of the 1960s.

In 1979, the European Monetary System was launched to regulate exchange rates among members. The Single European Act followed in 1987, removing remaining nontariff barriers, such as national regulations and standards. The goal was to create "an area without internal frontiers in which the free movement of goods, persons, services and capital is ensured."[18] Graduation to the EU took place in 1993. The hallmark of this next step was monetary union—the introduction of the euro and the elimination of separate national currencies. Twelve countries have already joined monetary union, with more to come. Euro notes and coins began circulating in January 2002. The French franc and the German mark are gone for good.

Europe's accomplishments in the realm of economic integration have not been matched on matters of defense—adding to the perception that the EU is an economic heavyweight, but a geopolitical lightweight. The Europeans did have a go at it. The Brussels Treaty (1948), the European Defense Community (1952), and the Western European Union (1954) were all attempts to give a collective Europe a defense arm. But they never got off the ground. Instead, the Europeans turned to the United States and NATO. American resources were needed to help rebuild Western Europe's economies and offset the military might of the Soviet Union. And Western Europe's main states were not yet comfortable enough with each other to begin merging their armed forces and defense policies. They were prepared to integrate their economies and pool authority over trade policy, but integrating defense establishments was deemed too much of an encroachment on national sovereignty. From this perspective, a unified Europe has from early on loomed large on an economic map of the world, but remains only a geopolitical blip.

This account of the European project is woefully off target. There is much more to Europe, as becomes clear by putting European integration in its appropriate historical context. Consider the transition of America's thirteen colonies to a federal union of states. Although nominally a confederation after 1781 and a unitary federation from 1789 onward, the early decades of the United States were devoted almost exclusively to matters of economic integration. Bringing down interstate tariffs, regulating commerce, coordinating foreign-trade policies, and issuing a single currency for use in all the states—these issues dominated political debate. Military integration lagged way behind economic integration. The individual states ensured that the Articles of Confederation preserved the right of each state to maintain a militia. Congress was allowed to build and equip a small navy and had the right to draw on the personnel of the individual states to constitute a modest national army. But the states, not the federal government, held the upper hand.

Although the U.S. Constitution strengthened the hand of the federal government, the states continued to retain considerable autonomy. Americans were at least as worried about the threat posed by an overbearing central authority as they were about that posed by outside enemies. The country's foreign ambition and its military accordingly remained limited throughout the Union's early decades. To the observer of the time, America might have been a potential economic giant, but it was not a major strategic presence. As we now know, however, the amalgamation of the United States would alter the geopolitics of North America and, soon, the world.

German unification was no different. It began quietly and slowly after the end of the Napoleonic Wars in 1815. Trade ties were again in the lead, knitting together the economies of the separate German lands. A formal customs union—the Zollverein—was formed in 1834. Political oversight was provided by a confederal structure known as the Bund, which was founded in 1820. The main purpose of the Bund was to resist liberal political change within its member states. Although the individual states sent representatives to a collective parliament, each maintained the right to form alliances and declare war. The Bund thus did not signify the establishment of a centralized and unitary state that was capable of upsetting the European balance. Nonetheless, a historic process of amalgamation was in train. When this process culminated in German unification in 1871, it had become clear—at least to Disraeli—that "the balance of power [in Europe] has been entirely destroyed."

Unlike the amalgamation of the United States and Germany, the process of integration in Europe could well stop short of a unitary state. But even if it does, its geopolitical implications will still be profound. From the outset, European integration has been all about matters of war and peace. Economic activity has been doing most of the work, but in the service of geopolitical intent. Europe's founding fathers knew all too well that a multipolar Europe would continue to be condemned to competition and conflict. Something therefore had to be done to interrupt the cyclical rise and fall of Europe's great powers and the attendant rivalry and bloodshed.

That something was European integration. If separate poles were destined to compete with each other with disastrous consequences for all, then the only way out was to find some means of binding these poles to each other, making them part of a broader whole. By mingling, merging, and ultimately transcending the separate interests and identities of Europe's national states, the process of integration was to produce a new political entity—a collective European polity.

Robert Schuman, France's foreign minister from 1948 to 1952 and one of the founders of European integration, was explicit about the geopolitical objectives of European integration and the linkages between economic activity and its political consequences. The first task was to overcome the intractable fault line between Germany and France. In Schuman's words, "The coming together of the nations of Europe requires the elimination of the age-old opposition of France and Germany. Any action taken must in the first place concern these two countries." The ECSC was to be the vehicle for attaining this task: "The solidarity in production thus established [by the ECSC] will make it plain that any war between France and Germany becomes not merely unthinkable, but materially impossible. The setting up of this powerful productive unit, open to all countries willing to take part and bound ultimately to provide all the member countries with the basic elements of industrial production on the same terms, will lay a true foundation for their economic unification."

Nurturing common economic interests was only the initial objective of economic integration. A deeper merging of interest and identity was to follow. "That fusion of interest which is indispensable to the establishment of a common economic system," Schuman asserted, was to be "the leaven from which may grow a wider and deeper community between countries long opposed to one another by sanguinary divisions."[19] Jean Monnet, the intellectual architect of the ECSC and the first president of its High Authority, was even more explicit: "We can never sufficiently emphasize that the six Community countries are the fore-runners of a broader Europe, whose bounds are set only by those who have not yet joined. Our Community is not a coal and steel producers' association; it is the beginning of Europe."[20] Germany, France, and the states surrounding them were ultimately to form a new political community that would transcend the national state. As the preamble to the ECSC Treaty explicitly stated, the members were preparing "the foundations for institutions which will give direction to a destiny henceforward shared."[21] The intractable instability of multipolarity was to give way to the unity and harmony of a collective Europe anchored by the Franco-German core.

Europe has from its modest beginnings thus had ambitious goals. Fully aware that economic integration alone would not be enough to realize these goals, Europe's architects also turned to more explicit tools of social engineering. They created a European parliament to symbolize that a collective Europe, not just its individual member states, was a legitimate and representative realm of politics. They instituted educational and cultural exchanges to help break down psychological barriers among societies long hostile toward each other. And they created symbols—a common flag, a common passport, and a common currency—needed to make Europe real to the average citizen and create a collective European space worthy of a sense of loyalty and belonging. As Wim Duisenberg, first president of the European Central Bank, remarked, "The Euro is much more than just a currency. It is a symbol of European integration in every sense of the word."[22]

The European project has been an unqualified success. Not only has war among Europe's nations become unimaginable, but the borders among them are undefended and already being crossed without passport or customs control. Driving from France to Germany is becoming like driving from Virginia to Maryland. Opinion surveys reveal a clear preference among European publics for quickening the speed of integration. Almost half of those polled strongly identify as Europeans, not just as citizens of a national state. And more than 70 percent support a common defense and security policy for the EU.[23] Europe's experiment in geopolitical engineering is working.

Europe's economy has followed suit. The intense focus on regional trade has reaped clear benefits. About 75 percent of the EU's total trade is within Europe. Its major economies are becoming more competitive as they deregulate and as their Social Democratic parties move to the center and distance themselves from their traditional labor base. The German government in 2000 passed important tax reforms intended to stimulate growth. The French followed with a similar, but slightly less ambitious, tax reform. General adherence to the criteria imposed by monetary union and the rising political fortunes of center-right parties are also speeding the emergence of a leaner European economy.

Europe's collective gross domestic product (GDP) now stands at close to $8 trillion, compared with about $10 trillion for the United States. Prospective growth rates for the EU are similar to those forecast for the U.S. Following the sharp decline in the U.S. technology sector, the venture capital that fueled the American dot-com revolution began flowing primarily to Europe, opening up the possibility that the EU will enjoy the boost in productivity that America did during the 1990s.[24] With the impending addition of new members (the next wave of enlargement is scheduled for 2004 and will include Poland, Hungary, the Czech Republic, Estonia, Slovenia, Cyprus, Malta, Slovakia, Lithuania, and Latvia), the EU's wealth may before long pull even with America's.

Airbus (a French, German, British, Italian, and Spanish conglomerate) has already passed Boeing as the world's number-one supplier of civilian aircraft. The largest maker of cell phones in the world is Finland's Nokia, well ahead of America's Motorola. After years of U.S. corporations acquiring foreign companies, the tables are turning. In 2000, British and French corporations ranked ahead of their American counterparts in terms of the aggregate value of their international acquisitions.[25] Germany has also been coming on strong. Bertelsmann is the largest book publisher in the world, having bought Random House and other prominent U.S. houses. Daimler-Benz acquired Chrysler in 1998 and Deutsche Telekom purchased VoiceStream in May 2001.

The euro admittedly lost more than 20 percent of its value against the dollar after its debut in January 1999. The flow of European capital to a booming U.S. economy was one of the main causes of its decline. With the slowdown in the United States, the return of capital to EU financial markets, and the prospects for growth within the EU, the euro has been making a comeback. It is likely to emerge as one of the world's major reserve currencies.[26]

The EU's governing bodies—the Commission, the Parliament, and the Council—have matured in step. The Commission, which grew out of the High Authority of the ECSC, is the union's main bureaucracy, staffed by a multinational civil service and by individuals on loan from member states. Although it has only limited power to make decisions, the Commission controls the agenda, formulates specific policy proposals, and is responsible for implementation of decisions. The size and jurisdiction of the Commission have expanded considerably over time as the EU has widened the range of policy issues over which it has authority.

The policy agenda is divided into three so-called pillars—community affairs (matters pertaining primarily to the operation of the single market), foreign and security policy, and justice and home affairs.[27] The Commission's powers are strongest in the first pillar, with authority over economic matters divided between the Commission, which handles trade and competition policy, and the European Central Bank, which sets monetary policy for the union and is run by the presidents of the member states' national banks. The individual member states still control their own macroeconomic and fiscal policies within the constraints of EU-wide guidelines. The European Court of Justice plays an important role in enforcing decisions and resolving disputes between member states and EU institutions. When at odds, EU law trumps national law.

The European Parliament grew out of the ECSC's Common Assembly. All member states send representatives, elected since 1979 by direct suffrage. The Parliament initially had only consultative powers, but its authority has grown steadily since the 1970s. It now has the right to amend proposals drafted by the Commission and to work with the Council to find mutually acceptable policies. The Parliament also approves the composition of the Commission, can demand its resignation, and, together with the Council, has final say over the union's annual budget. The broadening authority of the Parliament has been central to reinforcing the democratic character of a supranational Europe.

The Council, in its first incarnation the Council of Ministers of the ECSC, is the EU's main decision-making body. It consists of the ministers of the member states, who attend when the issue for which they are responsible is under discussion. It also meets periodically at the level of heads of state or government. Most issues taken up by the Council require a qualified majority to win approval.[28] Only matters of foreign and defense policy, justice and home affairs, and some domestic legislation, such as taxation, still require unanimity. The presidency of the Council rotates among member states and changes hands every six months. Summits used to take place in the capital of the country holding the presidency, but all of them will soon be held in Brussels, reinforcing the city's position as the capital of a collective Europe.

Nothing speaks to the success of Europe and its evolving institutions more than the ongoing clamor for entry into the club. Britain, Denmark, and Ireland joined in 1973, followed by Greece in 1981, Spain and Portugal in 1986, and Austria, Finland, and Sweden in

1995. Even after joining, Britain kept its distance from the Continent, trying to serve as a bridge between North America and Europe. But Prime Minister Tony Blair has changed course and is intent on making Britain a leading member of the EU. It is only a matter of time before Londoners will be buying their fish and chips with euros, not pounds. Blair fully recognized that Britain would find itself marginalized—in economic *and* geopolitical terms—if it did not become part of the European mainstream. As he explained in November 2001, "We must be whole-hearted, not half-hearted, partners in Europe. . . . The tragedy for British politics—for Britain—has been that politicians of both parties have failed, not just in the 1950s but on up to the present day, to appreciate the emerging reality of European integration. And in doing so, they have failed Britain's interests." Blair went on to insist that "Britain has no economic future outside Europe."[29]

Europe's new democracies are meanwhile jostling each other to make it to the front of the line. This yearning for entry enables the EU to exercise a quiet discipline across the dozen or so countries consolidating their transitions from communism to capitalist democracy in preparation for EU membership. Prospective members are privatizing and liberalizing their economies, stabilizing their currencies, protecting their minorities, and resolving outstanding border disputes—in short, getting their houses in order so that they can become part of the broader European home. The EU has democratized and pacified Europe's west. It is now poised to do the same for Europe's east.

Europe's accomplishments notwithstanding, an assessment of the EU's future must be tempered by the recent setbacks that integration has suffered and by the enormity of the challenges that lie ahead. Europe over the past decade has certainly had its fair share of disappointments. The EU failed miserably when in the early 1990s it tried to stop the slaughter in Bosnia. Norway in 1994 decided against membership. Denmark, Sweden, and Britain have chosen for now to stay out of the euro-zone. The Nice Summit in December 2000 was to have made substantial progress on institutional reform in order to pave the way for enlargement, but it fell well short of expectations. Despite the limited ambition of the reforms it contained, the Nice Treaty failed to pass a referendum in Ireland in June 2001, revealing the public's lack of enthusiasm for enlargement into Central Europe.

These are serious stumbles. But for a number of reasons, they do not provide cause for doubting the EU's ability to face down the challenges that lie ahead. Even under the best of circumstances, processes of integration and amalgamation are slow and difficult; after all, the states coming together to form a new polity are being asked to give up what they most cherish—their sovereignty and autonomy. America, Germany, and Italy, to name a few, all came together from their constituent units in fits and starts. Europe's ongoing integration has been, and will continue to be, no different. The EU will have good days and bad days. It will at times appear to be losing its momentum and the support of its member states and their citizens. But, as it has done over the past five decades, Europe is then likely to muster the will to take its next step forward.

It is also important to keep in mind that processes of integration tend to accelerate after they pass through a certain inflection point. Political centralization in the United States proceeded slowly until the late 1800s—and then took off. The 1890s saw notable growth in the authority of the executive branch, the size of the U.S. Navy, and the scope of the country's foreign ambition. In similar fashion, German integration proceeded slowly at first, but by the turn of the century moved into a new phase characterized by rapid centralization and expanding naval strength. It is impossible to predict if or when the EU might enter such a phase of accelerated integration, but, as discussed below, the prospect of impending enlargement might well be the precipitating factor.

Optimism about the EU's future also arises from the weakness of the arguments put forward by the euro-skeptics. Many observers, especially in the United States, continue to dismiss the EU's geopolitical significance, claiming that Europe will never coalesce as a serious international actor. They point to four main obstacles. First, Europe's supranational institutions lack democratic legitimacy. As the EU tries to deepen, it will therefore bump up against this "democratic deficit."[30] Second, the EU's population is aging, confronting Germany and other members with the prospect of a dwindling workforce and a bankrupt pension system. Third, the eastward enlargement of the EU, expected to begin by the middle of this decade, will dilute the union and hamper the further evolution of its collective character. Fourth, the EU has been and is likely to remain a military weakling, preventing it from taking on a more weighty geopolitical role.

The EU undeniably has a democratic deficit. Despite the recent adoption of measures to strengthen the role of the Parliament and to encourage the formation of EU-wide political parties, the nation-state retains a strong grip on political life. Linguistic differences and distinct national cultures make the national realm of politics especially durable, raising questions among ordinary citizens about the legitimacy and representative character of EU institutions. As Joschka Fischer, Germany's foreign minister in the center-left government that was elected in 1998, admitted, the EU is often "viewed as a bureaucratic affair run by a faceless, soulless Eurocracy in Brussels at best boring, at worst dangerous."[31] The citizens of EU member states, skeptics contend, are not about to entrust their fate to the EU Commission and its unaccountable staff.

This is a justified and credible critique, but it becomes less potent when put in historical relief. The legitimation of a supranational realm of politics always lags considerably behind the evolution of supranational institutions, which itself is a laborious and incremental process. Their fear of an unaccountable executive led America's founders to set up a system of constitutional checks and balances and to protect the rights of individuals to bear arms. It was not until after the Civil War, decades into America's life as a unitary federation, that the national realm decisively surpassed the individual states as the primary source of political identity and chief target of political loyalty.

Consider the poignant words of Robert E. Lee, an officer in the U.S. Army and an ardent opponent of secession, as he chose sides on the eve of the Civil War: "With all my devotion to the Union, I have not been able to make up my mind to raise my hand against my relatives, my children, my home. . . . If the Union is dissolved, and the Government disrupted, I shall return to my native State and share the miseries of my people."[32] Europe may have a democratic deficit, but it is one through which all integrating polities must necessarily pass as they evolve.

Europe's elites understand that they must make the EU more democratic and are beginning to take steps to address the problem. The adoption of an EU constitution is now under consideration, with many Europeans viewing the process of drafting, debate, and ratification as a means of cultivating deeper public engagement. Roughly two-thirds of the EU's population favors the adoption of a constitution. In March 2002, the EU opened what is effectively a constitutional convention, with former French President Valéry Giscard d'Estaing serving as its chairman. The group's mandate is to prepare proposals for consideration at the major conference on EU reform scheduled for 2004. A constitution would likely provide a clearer demarcation of the respective powers of the member states and EU institutions. It might also expand the authority of both national parliaments and the European Parliament in order to enhance democratic accountability.[33]

Germany's recent willingness to take the lead on institutional change improves the prospects for reform. Bonn for decades deferred to other European capitals as part of its post–World War II effort to reassure and pursue reconciliation with its neighbors. As a sign of its regained comfort with leadership, the seat of government returned to Berlin in 1999, and Germany has been at the forefront of efforts to guide the EU's evolution and redress its democratic deficit. As Fischer explained in a much-acclaimed speech in May 2000, "A tension has emerged between the communitarization of economy and currency on the one hand and the lack of political and democratic structures on the other, a tension which might lead to crises within the EU if we do not take productive steps to make good the shortfall in political integration and democracy, thus completing the process of integration."

Fischer was explicit about just what productive steps are needed. "There is a very simple answer," he said: "the transition from a union of states to full parliamentarization as a European Federation . . . and that means nothing less than a European Parliament and a European government which really do exercise legislative and executive power within the Federation." This federation would "be a Union which the citizens could understand," he continued, "because it would have made good its shortfall on democracy." Fischer reassured that "all this will not mean the abolition of the nation-state. Because even for the finalized Federation the nation-state, with its cultural and democratic traditions, will be irreplaceable in ensuring the legitimation of a union of citizens and states that is wholly accepted by the people. . . . Even when European finality is attained, we will still be British or German, French or Polish."[34]

A few months later, Chancellor Gerhard Schröder proposed the establishment of a two-chamber structure of governance, with an upper house of ministers from each country and a parliament consisting of popularly elected representatives. As in Fischer's scheme, Europe's nation-states would continue to retain important political powers, but institutions of collective governance would be considerably strengthened. Whether or not the precise formulations of Fischer and Schröder come to fruition is much less important than the fact that the EU's most populous and wealthy member has been actively promoting a federal Europe and articulating a pathway for getting there.

Britain too has shown more flexibility on the question of the EU's institutional evolution. Tony Blair has already orchestrated a dramatic about-face in British policy. After decades of skepticism about Europe, London has recently been seeking to establish itself as part of the EU's core. In the prime minister's words, Britain must be a "leading player, a strategic partner" within the union. Blair was behind the new push on the defense front. And he has indicated that he would like to orchestrate Britain's entry into the euro-zone during his second term. William Hague, the Conservative candidate in the 2001 election, made opposition to the euro a centerpiece of his campaign—and his party was badly defeated.

Although Blair has stated his opposition to Europe's evolution into a federal "superstate," he has made clear that he supports "a strong Britain in a strong Europe"—essentially a brand of European supranationalism in which the individual member states coexist comfortably alongside EU institutions.[35] In similar fashion, Blair has been tentative about the notion of an EU constitution, but he has proposed a "Statement of Principles" that would be "a political, not a legal document," and "therefore be much simpler and more accessible to Europe's citizens." Blair has also called for the creation of a second chamber of the European Parliament to enhance democratic oversight.[36] His views have not exactly tracked those of Schröder and Fischer, but they have all recognized the need to generate a debate over the EU's institutional future and to work toward a more democratic and effective form of governance.

France has been more tentative about the EU's evolution, in part because of the *cohabitation* government in office from 1997 until 2002. President Jacques Chirac and Prime Minister Lionel Jospin hailed from different parties and held different views. Chirac was supportive of deeper integration, especially on matters of foreign and security policy. He was also an outspoken proponent of an EU constitution, arguing that "such a text would bring Europeans together, allowing them to identify with a project through a solemn act of endorsement." During the summer of 2001, Chirac said he hoped a constitution would be ready for ratification by 2004.[37]

Jospin was more guarded. In May 2001, he countered Germany's federalist inclinations, announcing in a speech on Europe's future, "I want a Europe, but I remain attached to my nation. Making Europe without unmaking France, or any other European nation—that is my political choice."[38] This position is a paradoxical one for France, given its role in founding European integration and guiding its evolution for decades. Monnet and Schuman, after all, were strong backers of federalism even when they were just beginning to formulate Europe's earliest steps.

But the remnants of Gaullism continue to hold a perverse sway over French politics, producing a brand of nationalism that at once has great ambition for the European enterprise and stands in the way of realizing that ambition. France's position of late has been to call for a Europe that is strong in terms of its role in the world, but weak in its governing institutions—a logical and practical impossibility. Europe cannot be decentralized and fragmented, but at the same time pursue geopolitical ambition. Nonetheless, a uniquely French combination of vulnerability and grandeur has produced this contradictory stance. France is no longer strong enough to project its voice on the global stage, and hence looks to Europe to do so instead. But that same sense of weakness denies the French the confidence to move forward on integration and further sublimate the national state to the European project. France's foot-dragging on institutional reform also stems from a certain discomfort over Germany's new willingness to take a leadership role.

France's ambivalence toward the deepening of EU institutions is unlikely to endure, if only because it is untenable over the long run. An externally strong Europe cannot be weak internally. In addition, Jospin's defeat in the 2002 presidential election should bolster Chirac and his more pro-European stance. France will also face pressure from Germany and other EU members as matters of institutional reform gain urgency in preparation for eastward enlargement. When faced with the prospect of putting the integrity of the union at risk or getting on with the deepening of institutions, the choice will be an easy one even for the étatist French. The European project is too important and the stakes, especially for France, too high.

Finally, even if Europe's democratic deficit does eventually put a cap on further integration, that would not mean that the EU is never to become a serious counterweight to the United States. The EU already presents a challenge to U.S. influence; it need not evolve into a tight federation before it becomes a center of global power. An EU that encompasses Western and Central Europe and whose wealth rivals that of the United States is in and of itself a counterpoise to America. Of course, the more unitary and collective its character, the better able will Europe be to project a single voice and stand its ground. But even the looser Europe that exists today, especially in combination with America's shifting strategic priorities, is an emergent pole in a changing global system.

The EU's demographic problem is no doubt a serious one. Declining birth rates during the post–World War II era mean that Germany, for example, will by 2020 have one worker for every pensioner.[39] The engine of the EU's economy risks being choked by an inadequate workforce and pension obligations that outstrip employee contributions. One study completed in 2000 estimated that the German pension system, if left unchanged, would move into deficit in 2019, with pension debt reaching 50 percent of GDP by 2032. Pension systems in France and Italy are in even worse shape.[40]

Although there will be no easy fix to offset the economic implications of an aging population, EU members are fully aware of the potential crisis that looms ahead and are beginning to take steps to avert it. The German parliament in 2001 passed legislation providing tax breaks and other incentives intended to encourage workers to invest in private pension plans as a way of alleviating the burden on the national system. EU members are also debating how to liberalize rules on the inflow of foreign labor. Germany, for example, has begun relying on guest workers to meet shortfalls in its information technology sector. In August 2000, Berlin enacted a special immigration program to attract 20,000 computer engineers, primarily from India.

The eastward enlargement of the EU has the potential to help matters considerably. Central European countries have a large labor pool that promises to ease shortfalls in some EU countries. Turkey's younger population also makes it a prime candidate for supplying workers. To enhance labor mobility within the EU, which still remains relatively low, the Commission is examining various measures, including improving language education; facilitating the transfer of unemployment, pension, and health benefits across member states; and standardizing academic and professional qualifications.[41]

These developments promise to ameliorate, but by no means solve, the problems arising from the EU's aging population. More ambitious reforms are still needed, including better coordination of fiscal policies among EU members—no easy task with national governments loath to give up control over taxation policy, and trade unions resisting measures that promise to reduce retirement benefits. Improving the social integration of immigrants also deserves urgent attention.

As for enlargement, Europe's critics claim that the prospective inclusion of more than a dozen new members has the potential to dilute the union and paralyze its decision-making structures. The concern is not just that the growing number of member states will complicate governance, but also that the new entrants will have had relatively little experience in democracy and will bring to the EU divergent political cultures and economies at different stages of development. Enlargement also promises to saddle the EU with rising expenses in the form of agricultural subsidies and development assistance.

These concerns are all on point; enlargement does confront the EU with a set of high hurdles. But the challenge may in fact prove to be the EU's saving grace. Enlargement will proceed whether or not the EU has made the necessary preparations; promises have been made to the new democracies of Central Europe and reneging on them is outside the realm of the possible. Deepening the union's institutions may be optional, but widening them is not.

It is precisely because widening without deepening would imperil the ability of the EU to function, however, that enlargement is likely to be the crucial catalyst, the triggering event ultimately forcing the EU to undertake the internal reforms it might otherwise put off indefinitely. Preparation for enlargement creates a sense of urgency and gives EU leaders the domestic leverage they need to get on with the politically difficult task of institutional deepening. Fischer and other politicians have stated as much, acknowledging that enlargement does have the potential to paralyze the EU. "But this danger," he noted, "is no reason not to push on with enlargement as quickly as possible; rather it shows the need for decisive, appropriate institutional reform so that the Union's capacity to act is maintained even after enlargement."[42]

The American experience again provides an important parallel. It was ultimately westward enlargement that obliged the United States to deal with perhaps its weakest link—the cultural and economic divide between the North and the South. During the first half of the 1800s, free states and slave states cut various deals, such as the Missouri Compromise, to prevent their political differences from rising to the surface as enlargement proceeded.[43] In this sense, institutional reform was put off, but at a high cost to the Union's coherence. The continuation of westward expansion, however, eventually brought these underlying political differences to a head, forcing a direct clash between the North and South. The Civil War cost many lives, but it also set the stage for social and political reform and for more effective and centralized governance. Enlargement and the crisis it provoked thus cleared the way for the brand of federalism that remains the ideological and institutional foundation of contemporary America.

Enlargement of the EU fortunately holds little prospect of provoking war, but it does promise to oblige reluctant member states to embrace essential institutional reforms. Strengthening the authority of EU institutions is a must if a union of twenty-five or more countries is to function effectively. That means the extension of qualified majority voting to issues that now require unanimity. It means lodging with the Commission oversight of economic policy and, eventually, of foreign and defense policy. It means expanding the role of the European Parliament. And it may eventually mean establishing a directly elected chief executive of the EU.

Enlargement will also put pressure on the EU to differentiate between an inner core of member states and those whose integration is taking place on a slower, piecemeal basis. More reliance on differentiation—what EU officials euphemistically call "enhanced cooperation"—will enable core members to pursue deeper levels of integration while others opt out or follow long transition periods. The introduction of the euro has essentially followed this model, with a core group of states leading the way and others joining the eurozone when they both muster sufficient political will and meet the specified economic criteria. This multitiered approach will help ensure that the EU is not left always pursuing the lowest common denominator, of paramount importance as the countries of Central Europe begin to enter. In Fischer's words, "Precisely in an enlarged and thus necessarily more heterogeneous Union, further differentiation will be inevitable."[44] This flexibility will not just limit the ability of slow movers to hold back the rest, but it will also free up Europe's core states to press forward with deeper integration, ultimately serving as a political vanguard for the union as a whole.

Finally, enlargement is likely to require long-overdue reform of the EU budget. The Common Agricultural Policy (CAP)—essentially a program of farm subsidies and price guarantees—comprises almost 50 percent of the EU's overall budget. Repeated attempts to reform the CAP have made little progress, largely due to the political clout of French farmers. The size of the agricultural sector in Central Europe, however, makes reform of the CAP a necessity if enlargement is to proceed. The German government has already laid out a number of proposals, including letting each member state deal with farm subsidies on a national basis. Enlargement will also compel reform of the EU's regional assistance program. Development assistance, which comprises almost 35 percent of the EU budget, is another program that has suffered from a combination of inertia and political stalemate. The coming entry of states seeking economic aid will necessitate the program's overhaul. In short, enlargement may be just the shock the EU needs to get it over upcoming institutional hurdles.

Defense is the final issue repeatedly raised by euro-skeptics, and justifiably so. EU members do make important contributions in the security area, but largely through nonmilitary means—giving substantial amounts of economic aid to conflict-prone regions and investing both money and personnel in conflict resolution, democratization, and nation-building. European militaries have been active primarily in peacekeeping missions, with most member states lacking the capability to participate in more demanding operations. The problem is not the lack of soldiers, but the lack of firepower. Although the EU's collective defense budget is well below America's, Europe has many more soldiers under arms than does the United States. Defense budgets go to paying personnel and maintaining large territorial armies, not to buying well-trained and -equipped forces and the transport required to get them where they need to be. Europe has been incapable of undertaking a sizable operation on its own, remaining dependent upon the U.S. military and its impressive logistical infrastructure. The critics are correct that the union is a military weakling.

Times, however, are changing. Europe has arrived at a turning point. For several reasons, its military presence will mount in the years ahead.

For starters, Europe is in the midst of creating more centralized and authoritative structures of collective governance, a necessary precursor to a common defense policy. It is one thing to coordinate trade policy and standardize the size of electrical outlets. It is another to give up your national currency and debate the desirability of an EU constitution—acts that in symbolic and practical terms constitute a true pooling of sovereignty and the lifting up of politics, interest, and identity from the national to the supranational level. And in preparation for the addition of new members, the EU is likely to take steps to further centralize authority. Europe's institutional reforms promise to set the stage for more geopolitical ambition, just as the centralization of America's political institutions did in the late nineteenth century.

Another clear sign of Europe's maturation is its redoubled effort to forge a common security policy and acquire the military capability needed to back it up. In 1999 the EU established the position of high representative for foreign and security policy—in effect, a collective Europe's first foreign policy chief. Javier Solana, the former secretary general of NATO, was selected as its initial occupant. Solana oversaw the development of new political and military councils capable of producing a common defense policy. And the EU committed itself to have ready by 2003 a rapid reaction force of roughly 60,000 capable of being deployed on short notice and sustained in the field for at least one year. The member states thereafter began integrating their defense plans and budgets in order to make good on this pledge.

Euro-skeptics are right to point out that EU defense budgets have been shrinking and that new expenditures will ultimately be needed if Europe is to acquire the level of capability that it has envisaged. But the EU can achieve a great deal by spending more wisely the resources that it already devotes to defense. More coordination among national procurement programs, a sensible division of labor as to which member states fulfill which military tasks, and the switch from poorly trained conscript armies to polished professional units will do much to improve the EU's military capability.

Significant reforms have already been accomplished. France has phased out universal military service. Germany has already conducted a thorough review of its defense establishment and is in the midst of implementing important changes. And new, collective procurement programs have been taking shape. In June 2001, nine European nations (Germany, France, Spain, Britain, Italy, Turkey, Belgium, Portugal, and Luxembourg) committed to buy a total of 212 A400M transport aircraft.[45] The aircraft will be built by Airbus, 80 percent of which is owned by the European Aeronautic Defence & Space Company, a new consortium of European defense contractors. EU members have also agreed to construct their own satellite network, called

Galileo, a move that will reduce European reliance on U.S. assets and technology.

The EU has also begun to flex its diplomatic muscle in unprecedented fashion. In March 2001, the Bush administration indicated it was stepping back from Clinton's forward-leaning stance on pursuing rapprochement between North Korea and South Korea. Concerned about the negative consequences for the region, the EU announced that it would pick up the mediating role from which the United States was walking away. "This means that Europe must step in," said the foreign minister of Sweden, the country at that time holding the rotating presidency of the EU.[46] Later that month, Albanian rebels brought Macedonia to the brink of war, exchanging fire with the Macedonian army in the hills close to the border with Kosovo. The Bush administration kept its distance. Again, the EU stepped in and took the diplomatic lead. Solana and other European officials played a much more important role in resolving the crisis than did their American counterparts. The EU has since taken over command of the peacekeeping mission in Macedonia from NATO. It was the EU that brokered the March 2002 deal in which Yugoslavia's leaders agreed to give their country a new name—Serbia and Montenegro—a move intended to forestall Montenegro's drift toward independence. And during the course of 2002, the EU became deeply involved in negotiations between Israelis and Palestinians—for decades the exclusive preserve of American diplomats—and played a central role in ending the siege of the Church of the Nativity in Bethlehem in May.

"Europe's turn," declared one of Germany's leading newspapers, the *Frankfurter Allgemeine Zeitung,* reflecting on this trend. "A more assertive Europe," commented the *New York Times,* which also noted that the European Union had "gained a new sense of confidence on the world stage, built on Europe's improving economy and its growing political and commercial integration."[47]

Granted, the EU is moving ahead on matters of diplomacy and defense slowly and modestly. But so did the United States, Germany, and every other polity that formed through the stitching together of once-separate entities. States, by their nature, only reluctantly give up their sovereignty and entrust their well-being to a collective union. It is now the turn of Europe's states to make that leap.

That the EU is preparing for a new stage in its evolution is not just a function of time and maturation. Europe is also acquiring greater geopolitical ambition because of the changing ideological role that integration plays in European politics. During the past five decades, elected leaders justified the European project and the sacrifices it entailed on two grounds. First, Europe had to integrate to escape its past. Union was the only way to leave behind rivalry and war. Second, Europe had to band together against the communist threat. NATO was on the front lines, but the EU was all the while building Europe's economic strength and political confidence.

Neither of these justifications for integration now carries much weight. The Soviet Union is gone and Russia too weak to pose a threat to Western Europe even if it wanted to. And now that more than five decades have passed since World War II, escaping the past no longer resonates as a pressing cause for many Europeans. Their historical knowledge aside, younger generations that lived through neither the war nor Europe's reconstruction have no personal past from which they seek to escape. The dominant political discourse that has for decades given the EU its meaning and momentum is rapidly losing its relevance.

In its place is emerging a new discourse, one that emphasizes Europe's future rather than its past. And instead of justifying integration as a way to check the geopolitical ambition of the national state, this new discourse portrays integration as a way to acquire power and project geopolitical ambition for Europe as a whole. French President Jacques Chirac, in a speech delivered in Paris in November 1999, could hardly have been clearer: "The European Union itself [must] become a major pole of international equilibrium, endowing itself with the instruments of a true power."[48] Even the British, who for decades vehemently opposed any EU role in security affairs, have changed their minds. In the words of Prime Minister Tony Blair, "Europe's citizens need Europe to be strong and united. They need it to be a power in the world. Whatever its origin, Europe today is no longer just about peace. It is about projecting collective power."[49]

Integration is thus being relegitimated among European electorates, but paradoxically through a new brand of pan-European nationalism. Europe's individual nations may have rid themselves for good of foreign ambition, but aspirations are returning at the level of a collective Europe. As these new political currents gather momentum, so will Europe's geopolitical ambition.

Strangely enough, America is also providing momentum behind Europe's return to the realm of geopolitics. Europe now finds itself weak and poorly organized on matters of defense because for decades it had the luxury of relying on the United States for its security. The extension of America's strategic umbrella to Europe not only kept the peace during the Cold War, but also enabled the Europeans to expend their main energies on political and economic integration. The United States was buying much-needed time for Europe to get its process of unification up and running. As the years passed, however, strategic necessity turned into an unhealthy dependency. Europe ended up free-riding on America's willingness to be its guardian. Despite all that has changed since 1949, and especially since 1989, Europe has remained dependent on the United States to manage its security.

Europe has thus had a very good deal for a long time. But as most good deals do, this one too is coming to an end. The Cold War bargain struck between a recovering Europe and a hegemonic America is fast wearing thin. And it should. The Cold War is over, Europe's nations are at peace, and the EU is thriving. The U.S. Congress is more than justified in insisting that Europe finally bear a greater defense burden. The battle for Kosovo and the presence of U.S. peacekeepers in the Balkans made clear that the United States is still willing to buy a little more time for Europe to mature. But America could hardly have fought the war over Kosovo with more reluctance. And the Bush administration made plain its ambivalence about keeping U.S. troops in the Balkans indefinitely, a concern only intensified by the added missions stemming from the new focus on homeland defense and fighting terrorism.

There is no better way to get the Europeans to take on more defense responsibilities than to confront them with the prospect of an America that is losing interest in being the guarantor of European security. It is anything but happenstance that Europe redoubled efforts to forge a common defense policy just after the close of NATO's war for Kosovo. The Europeans are scared—and justifiably so—that America will not show up the next time war breaks out somewhere in Europe's periphery. And they are aware that they can either prepare now for that eventuality—or be left in the lurch. They are making the right choice in building up their military capacities. But they are also making a choice that will inevitably give Europe more geopolitical clout—at the expense of American primacy.

This fundamental shift in the strategic relationship between North America and Europe is in its early stages. It will gain momentum in the next few years. And the impetus will come not just from Europe's new ambition, which will gather slowly, but also from America's domestic politics and its schizophrenic reaction to the rise of Europe—a subject taken up in the following chapters.

ROME REDUX

THE PARALLELS between today's world and the world of the late Roman Empire are striking. Washington today, like Rome then, enjoys primacy, but is beginning to tire of the burdens of hegemony as it witnesses the gradual diffusion of power and influence away from the imperial core. And Europe today, like Byzantium then, is emerging as an independent center of power, dividing a unitary realm into two.

It is too soon to tell whether Washington and Brussels will head down the same road as Rome and Constantinople—toward geopolitical rivalry—but the warning signs are certainly present. The United States already feels pressured by the euro and the growing strength of Europe's economy and its top corporations. The EU's geopolitical ambition is still limited, but there are clear signs of wind in the sails. And although America has called for the EU to do more on defense, Washington is none too pleased about having to make room for a more assertive and independent Europe. Perhaps America and Europe are experiencing growing pains. Perhaps the political grandstanding will soon die out. If history is any indication, however, this tentative competition is likely to develop into a more serious rivalry.

Skeptics may object to the analogy drawn between the contemporary Western world and the Roman Empire of the fourth century, arguing that times have changed and politics have moderated; the emerging relationship between North America and Europe will therefore bear no resemblance to the testy confrontation between Rome and Byzantium. It is true that social values have evolved over the centuries and that political and religious violence, especially among liberal democracies, is much less prevalent today than during Roman times. America and Europe have carved out a political community in which war between them borders on the unimaginable. And Europe stood by America after the terror attacks of September 2001, with NATO for the first time in its history invoking the clause in its treaty confirming that an attack on one is an attack on all. It is also the case that even if Europe does move ahead on the defense front, its fighting capability will for the foreseeable future remain modest; the EU is not about to pose a military challenge to the United States.

These considerations admittedly make armed conflict between the United States and Europe an extremely remote prospect. But the likelihood of war breaking out across the Atlantic is too high a standard for gauging whether the rise of Europe and the resulting competition with America will be of geopolitical consequence. Here are just a few of the probable outcomes.

As Europe's wealth, military capacity, and collective character increase, so will its appetite for greater international influence. Just as America's will to extend its primacy stems not just from self-interest, but also from an emotional satisfaction derived from its leadership position—call it nationalism—so will Europe's rise inspire a yearning for greater status. As the United States currently sits atop the international pecking order, the EU's search for greater autonomy and status will, at least initially, take the form of resisting U.S. influence and ending its long decades of deference to Washington.

Some of Europe's leaders have already been vocal in expressing their disgruntlement with America's might and its overbearing ways. French Foreign Minister Hubert Vedrine complained in 1999 that "we cannot accept a politically unipolar or a culturally uniform world, or the unilateralism of the one and only American megapower." President Jacques Chirac was in complete agreement: "We need a means to struggle against American hegemony." Immediately after meeting with Chinese President Jiang Zemin in December 1999, Russian President Boris Yeltsin proclaimed that "we arrived at a conclusion that the unipolar scheme is no good. We need a multi-polar structure."[50]

Such sentiments only intensified after the election of George W. Bush because of the unilateralist substance and tone of his foreign policy. In the wake of Bush's call to widen the war against terrorism to Iraq, Iran, and North Korea, Vedrine called for Europe to speak out against a United States that acted "unilaterally, without consulting others, making decisions based on its own view of the world and its own interests." When asked about how to deal with American preponderance, Gerhard Schröder replied that "the answer or remedy is easy: a more integrated and enlarged Europe" that has "more clout." Valéry Giscard d'Estaing opened the EU's constitutional convention in March 2002 by noting that successful reform of the union's institutions would ensure that "Europe will have changed its role in the world." "It will be respected and listened to," he continued, "not only as the economic power it already is, but as a political power that will speak as an equal with the largest existing and future powers on the planet." Romano Prodi, president of the Commission, agreed that one of the EU's chief goals is to create "a superpower on the European continent that stands equal to the United States."[51]

These statements and others like them have been intended to appeal to domestic electorates as well as to guide European policy. But even as political rhetoric, these exhortations are revealing. That European leaders are calling upon nationalist instincts and urging that Europe act as a counterweight to America underscores the potential for U.S.-European rivalry. Combine the logic of realism with that of a pan-European nationalism and it becomes clear that even in the absence of conflicts of interest between Europe and the United States, there will still be competitive jockeying for position and status across the Atlantic.

There will, however, also be conflicts of interest. Thankfully, the United States and the EU have no outstanding territorial disputes; those were resolved during the nineteenth century through a combination of war and diplomacy. But the two parties are likely to clash over other issues.

The United States and Europe have long gone their separate ways in the Middle East, particularly over Iran and Iraq. Most Europeans opposed America's war to topple Saddam Hussein. Prior to the war, maintaining the sanctions regime against Iraq proved all but impossible. So too have European companies defied Washington's efforts to prevent them from investing and operating in places like Iran and Libya. It is entirely plausible that Congress could at some point insist on sanctions against Europe for its companies' violations of the 1996 Iran-Libya Sanctions Act (ILSA). Congress renewed ILSA for another five years in July 2001. The EU meanwhile adopted a statute making it illegal for European companies to comply with ILSA. The events of September 2001 and the resulting battle against terrorism have further complicated the political environment in the Middle East, making more likely a clash of interests across the Atlantic. The United States and Europe have also taken different approaches to the Arab-Israeli peace process, raising the prospect that the states of the region might play the two sides off each other as Europe becomes more involved as a mediator. European leaders were openly and sharply critical of the Bush administration's support for Israel's crackdown on Yasser Arafat's regime as violence escalated in late 2001 and early 2002.[52]

Consider how the debate over missile defense could play out over the next few years. The Bush administration has made clear that it intends to proceed with development and deployment, and that it may well opt for a broad system that includes interceptors based on land, at sea, in the air, and in space. A system of this scope is unlikely to win support in Europe, opening up the possibility of a significant strategic rift, especially if Russia sides with the EU. Europe simply has a different view of likely threats and how to cope with them. Without the Soviet threat around to keep the alliance intact, a rupture of this sort could well jeopardize America's close strategic partnership with Europe. The relationship may soon resemble that of the interwar period, when America and the European democracies were not adversaries, but they were certainly not trusting allies.

The United States and Europe are also likely to engage in more intense competition over trade and finance. America and Europe today enjoy a remarkably healthy economic relationship, with both parties benefiting from strong flows of trade and investment. A more assertive Europe and a less competitive American economy do, however, make it likely that trade disputes will become more politicized. When the Bush administration announced new tariffs on imported steel in March 2002, the EU vowed to contest the move at the WTO. Pascal Lamy, the EU's top trade official, commented that "the U.S. decision to go down the route of protectionism is a major setback for the world trading system."[53] Europe's restriction on imports of genetically modified foods, a ban that could cost U.S. companies $4 billion per year, has particular potential to produce a major dispute and polarize global trade talks. The emergence of the euro as a reserve currency would also create the potential for diverging views about management of the international financial system. The competitive devaluations and lack of monetary coordination during the interwar period made amply clear that the absence of a dominant economic player can result in considerable financial turmoil and go-it-alone foreign policies—even among like-minded allies.

At issue are competing values, not just competing interests. The two sides of the Atlantic are separated by quite different social models. Despite continuing deregulation across Europe, America's laissez-faire capitalism contrasts sharply with Europe's more state-centered economy. While Americans decry the constraints on growth stemming from the European model, Europeans look askance at America's income inequalities, its consumerism, and its willingness to sacrifice social capital for material gain. The two have also parted company on matters of statecraft. Americans see the EU's firm commitment to multilateral institutions and the rule of international law as naïve, self-righteous, and a product of its military weakness, while Europeans see America's reliance on the use of force as simplistic, self-serving, and a product of its excessive power. Europeans still share a historical affinity for the United States, but they also feel estranged from a society wedded to gun ownership, capital punishment, and gas-guzzling cars. At root, America and Europe adhere to quite different political cultures. And the cultural distance appears to be widening, not closing, putting the two sides of the Atlantic on diverging social paths.

This divergence over values as well as interests is likely to deal a serious blow to the effectiveness of international organizations. Most multilateral institutions currently rely on a combination of U.S. leadership and European backstopping to produce consensus and joint action. The United States and Europe often vote as a bloc, leading to a winning coalition in the U.N., the IMF, the World Bank, and many other bodies. Such coordination quietly and steadily keeps these international institutions on track.

When Europe resists rather than backstops American leadership, multilateral organizations are more likely to be faced with gridlock, if not paralysis. Early signs of such resistance are already visible. In May 2001, EU member states took the lead in voting the United States off the U.N. Commission on Human Rights, the first time Washington had been absent from the body since its formation in 1947. The apparent rationale was to deliver a payback for U.S. unilateralism and to express disapproval of America's death penalty. The same day, in a separate vote of the U.N.'s Economic and Social Council, the United States lost its seat on the International Narcotics Control Board.

The Europeans pressed ahead with the establishment of the International Criminal Court despite U.S. objections. When the ICC came into being on July 1, 2002, the Bush administration made known its displeasure by threatening to withdraw U.S. personnel from the U.N. mission in Bosnia unless American forces were granted protection from prosecution by the court. After Washington defected from the Kyoto Protocol, EU members joined with Japan and 150 other countries to finalize the agreement on global warming in July 2001, their delegates displaying their disapproval when Paula Dobriansky, the Bush administration's emissary, sought to explain America's decision to opt out. In short, a world in which the United States and Europe are no longer closely working together is one in which the day-to-day functioning of international institutions could be put at risk.

None of these scenarios could plausibly lead to armed conflict between the United States and Europe. But any one of them could result in a dramatically different—and much less benign—world than the one we live in today.

The Roman past may shed one final ray of light on the present. Although Byzantium proved to be Rome's chief rival in the near term, it was the rise of non-European powers that ultimately led to the demise of the Roman Empire and its Byzantine successor. The spread of wealth and military might to the Islamic world initially deprived the Byzantine Empire of its main source of grain in the Middle East. Ottoman armies were eventually able to overwhelm Constantinople's walls, formally bringing the Byzantine era to an end. The Ottomans were soon at the gates of Vienna.

In similar fashion, the rise of Asia may in the long term spell more trouble for the West than the return of rivalry between North America and Europe. This book focuses primarily on the rise of Europe, both because the EU's geopolitical significance has been so grossly overlooked and underestimated and because Europe, not Asia, is the near-term challenger to American primacy. It is during this current decade that the geopolitical implications of Europe's ascent will take effect, while the rise of Asia is further off.

But Asia's advance is not that far off. By the third decade of this new century, China will likely arrive on the scene as one of the world's leading nations. If its internal politics have not changed dramatically by that time, the United States will face not just another pole, but potentially a major ideological and geopolitical adversary. In contrast to the European case, the United States could face disputes with China—over Taiwan or the Korean peninsula, for example—that could lead to armed conflict.

Japan too will eventually come out of its economic slump and re-emerge as a global player. Especially because of its estranged relationship with China, Japan is likely to stick by its alliance with the United States and follow Washington's lead on matters of defense. But even within Japan there have been restless stirrings and initial signs that a change of course might be in the offing. Junichiro Koizumi, the prime minister who took office in April 2001, from the outset shrouded himself in both populist and nationalist symbols. He proposed constitutional revisions that would eliminate provisions limiting the role of Japan's military. He selected as his initial foreign minister Makiko Tanaka, a fellow populist who proceeded to skip numerous meetings with visiting dignitaries, including one with Deputy Secretary of State Richard Armitage, the first high-level U.S. official to pay a visit to the new government. In August 2001, he visited the Yasukuni Shrine, a memorial that pays homage to Japanese heroes from World War II. Koizumi also stood by the decision of the Ministry of Education to approve new history textbooks that gloss over the country's wartime atrocities—provoking outrage in China and South Korea.

Japan is not about to make a dramatic change of course and deliberately act as a counterweight to the United States anytime soon. But an ascendant Asia looms on the distant horizon. And coupled with various uncertainties, including the trajectory of North Korea and the fate of Indonesia, the region as a whole will confront both America and Europe with new strategic challenges. By 2025, America and Europe may both be spending much more time worrying about the rise of Asia than about each other.

For now, however, it is Europe that is emerging as America's only major competitor. The implications for the global system and for U.S. grand strategy can be accurately mapped only after examining the other major source of change in the international system—America's changing internationalism.

CHAPTER FIVE

The Limits of American Internationalism—Looking Back

THE RISE OF EUROPE is only one of the two major forces closing in on America's unipolar moment. The other is America's own politics and the country's changing appetite for bearing the burdens that come with global hegemony. That U.S. internationalism will be at once fading and becoming more unilateralist in the years ahead, just like the claim that Europe is America's rising challenger, is a proposition that departs from prevailing wisdom. Most analysts dismiss the possibility of an American retreat from the global stage, arguing that elite and public support for multilateral engagement continues to run strong. Especially in the aftermath of September 11, many foresee the lasting renewal of America's interest in managing world affairs and believe that Washington will readily uphold the mantle of leadership.[1]

In contrast, this book treats the emergence of a more diffident and difficult U.S. internationalism as an inevitable consequence of the absence of a major adversary. Europe will challenge American primacy, but it will not be the type of enemy that evokes America's global engagement. Terrorism will remain a threat to Americans at home and abroad. But even as the United States engages in isolated strikes against terrorists and their sponsors, it will also fortify the homeland and rein in its overseas commitments in an attempt to cordon itself off from such threats. A national economy that has cooled off and demographic change in the United States will also dampen the country's enthusiasm for the expansive, multilateral brand of internationalism that it has practiced for the past five decades. Even if America were to maintain its material preponderance for years to come, a new isolationism and a rising unilateralism would still bring about a major change in the global landscape.

America's past provides compelling support for this assessment. From its founding until its decision to enter World War II in 1941, the United States, with only temporary exceptions, did its best to avoid foreign entanglements outside its hemisphere. The last fifty years of global engagement represent a dramatic departure. And this aberration from the past can be readily explained by the grave threats to American security posed, in the first instance, by Germany and Japan, and later by the Soviet Union. The existence of a clear and present external danger kept at bay many of the political and ideological constraints that had for decades muted America's external ambition and fueled an aversion to participation in international institutions. A sense of common purpose provided a ready foundation not just for an active internationalism, but also for a liberal variant, one wedded to multilateralism and cooperative institutions. With the collapse of the Soviet Union and the unraveling of the domestic consensus forged by the Cold War, it is anything but assured that support for liberal internationalism will continue unabated. Tracking the likely trajectory of America's engagement in the world therefore requires looking to the past and uncovering the domestic forces that are once again coming to have a potent impact on U.S. grand strategy.

Since the Union's founding era, three central debates have shaped the country's internationalism and the grand strategy that has followed from it: whether realism or idealism should guide statecraft; how to reconcile the competing cultures and interests of the country's different regions in formulating grand strategy; and how to manage partisan politics and limit its effect on the conduct of foreign policy. Debate among the founding fathers on these three issues cast an enduring mold—one that continues to this day to shape a uniquely American brand of internationalism.

The struggle between realism and idealism in the formulation of grand strategy reflected the competing ideological impulses enjoined by the nation's founding. Brute strength was central to achieving independence from Britain, ensuring the security of the fledgling Union, and enabling the United States to expand westward. At the same time, many of those who left the Old World to settle in America did so for idealist reasons. Their sense of social and moral purpose carried over into the young nation's foreign policy, with idealists urging that principles temper the exercise of power and that the practice of statecraft be guided by the pursuit of democratic ideals. This tension between realism and idealism remains at the heart of contemporary debate over U.S. grand strategy.

The diverging economic interests and cultures of America's different regions have also had a profound impact on grand strategy since the Union's early days. The northern states, by virtue of the religious communities that settled there, favored a foreign policy governed more by law and reason than by might. The North's idealism gave rise to a liberal strain of isolationism, one that opposed on principled grounds both westward expansion and America's engagement in great-power rivalry. In contrast, the more agrarian and mercantilist South tilted in the direction of realpolitik, and southerners were more comfortable with the use of force as a tool of statecraft, especially to protect the free flow of trade. At the same time, a populist individualism took root in the South, giving rise to a libertarian strain of isolationism based on opposition to an ambitious foreign policy and the strong central government that it would require.

Although not yet relevant because of the republic's self-imposed isolation, in these attitudes also lay the ideological foundation for America's unilateral impulse in the conduct of its foreign policy. If Americans were suspicious of their own domestic institutions, they would be able to muster even less enthusiasm for the international institutions to which their country would later consider submitting its will. Populism would also mix with elements of American idealism, giving rise to the notion of U.S. exceptionalism. The supposition that the United States was a unique nation with a unique calling would further stoke unilateralism and encourage the country to chart its own course when it eventually engaged in efforts to reshape the international system. Hence the complementary, even if paradoxical, nature of America's simultaneous attraction to isolationist and unilateralist extremes.[2]

As westward expansion proceeded, distinctive regional interests and cultures took root in the Midwest, Mountain West, and Far West, adding to the complexity of the country's political geography. The interests and outlooks of America's diverse regions have since changed dramatically. But regional divides continue to play a crucial role in shaping U.S. foreign policy. And liberal and libertarian strains of isolationism, as well as a stubborn unilateralism, remain very much a part of America's broader political culture, even as they wax and wane in America's regions in step with fluid political and economic interests.

Partisan politics has in similar fashion held considerable sway over the formulation of U.S. grand strategy from the nation's outset. The institutional checks and balances insisted upon by the founding fathers produced a workable separation of power among the people, the states, and the federal government. But this decentralization of authority also hampered the steady conduct of foreign policy and exposed it to the vagaries of party politics. Insulating diplomacy from partisan conflict, building internationalist coalitions across party and region, and finding the political middle ground through both creativity and compromise all proved essential to guiding U.S. foreign policy during the early years—and remain so today.

Three historical periods provide a particularly good window on the relationship between America's domestic politics and the evolution of its grand strategy: the founding era and its aftermath, the close of World War I and the country's deliberation in 1919–1920 over its participation in the League of Nations, and World War II and the onset of America's global role during the 1940s. The ideological, regional, and partisan debates that took place during these three periods shed substantial light on where American internationalism has come from and where it is likely to go in the years ahead.

THE FOUNDING YEARS AND THEIR LEGACY

THE MEN WHO guided America to independence and then governed the country during its early years were understandably preoccupied with how to define the new nation's relationship with Europe. Conflicting objectives and impulses complicated the task. Britain was the ostensible enemy, but also the land from which many settlers hailed; strong familial and linguistic ties remained. Trade with Europe was essential to the growth of the American economy. But the United States had to avoid too much interdependence with Europe lest it be lured into the geopolitical rivalries of the Old World. "Any submission to, or dependence on, Great Britain, tends directly to involve this continent in European wars and quarrels," the essayist and champion of independence Thomas Paine proclaimed. In building a new society, Americans would be well served to learn from Europe and draw on its intellectual capital. But the founders were also passionately committed to leaving behind for good Europe's social ills, religious quarrels, and political jealousies.

Early efforts to forge a set of principles to guide U.S. foreign policy failed to produce a meeting of the minds. American leaders divided along idealist and realist lines. In the idealist camp were the likes of Paine and Thomas Jefferson, who felt that the new nation could and should make a sharp break with the past and conduct a foreign policy guided by law and reason, not power politics. America's calling is in commerce rather than war, Paine argued, "and that, well attended to, will secure us the peace and friendship of all Europe."[3] Jefferson firmly believed in the steady progress of mankind and maintained that social and political development was making war obsolete. America had to lead the way toward an "object so valuable to mankind as the total emancipation of commerce and the bringing together all nations for a free intercommunication of happiness." He claimed that war and coercion "were legitimate principles in the dark ages," but that in the new era of democracy and law, relations between nations should be guided by "but one code of morality."[4]

Representing the realist camp, Alexander Hamilton and John Jay took a different approach. In *Federalist 6*, Hamilton acknowledged that "there are still to be found visionary or designing men, who stand ready to advocate the paradox of perpetual peace.... The genius of republics (say they) is pacific; the spirit of commerce has a tendency to soften the manners of men, and to extinguish those inflammable humors which have so often kindled into wars." But he exhibited little patience for the notion of either a democratic or a commercial peace. "Are not popular assemblies frequently subject to the impulses of rage, resentment, jealousy, avarice, and of other irregular and violent propensities?" Hamilton asked. He posed equally sharp questions about the alleged link between trade and peace. "Has commerce hitherto done anything more than change the objects of war? Is not the love of wealth as domineering and enterprising a passion as that of power or glory?" Jay agreed with Hamilton's more pessimistic realism, noting in *Federalist 4* that "it is too true, however disgraceful it may be to human nature, that nations in general will make war whenever they have a prospect of getting anything by it."[5] As far as Hamilton and Jay were concerned, America should be guided by sober self-interest just like any other country.

Despite such profound philosophic differences, the founding fathers did find themselves in agreement on one particularly important issue—that the United States could most effectively safeguard its security by isolating itself from Europe's geopolitical rivalries. Idealists and realists found this common ground for a number of reasons. First and foremost, they maintained that the United States was blessed with a natural security by virtue of its distance from Europe. President George Washington succinctly made the case in his farewell address to the nation in 1796: "Our detached and distant situation invites and enables us to pursue a different course. . . . Why forego the advantages of so peculiar a situation? Why quit our own to stand upon foreign ground? Why, by interweaving our destiny with that of any part of Europe, entangle our peace and prosperity in the toils of European ambition . . . ?"

Washington had originally intended to indicate that America need cordon itself off from Europe only for a number of decades, until it gained in both economic and military strength. But Hamilton convinced the president that avoiding entangling alliances was a dictum based on unchanging geopolitical realities, "a general principle of policy," not a temporary admonition. Hence Washington's eventual decision to refer in his farewell address to a grand strategy of isolation as "The Great rule of conduct for us, in regard to foreign Nations."[6]

The founding fathers were concerned not just about preventing America's entanglement in "all the pernicious labyrinths of European politics and wars," but also about limiting Europe's ability to manipulate and control U.S. policy.[7] John Adams worried that were the United States to form alliances with European nations, they "would find means to corrupt our people, to influence our councils, and, in fine, we should be little better than puppets, danced on the wires of the cabinets of Europe. We should be the sport of European intrigues and politics."[8] The United States should accordingly limit its involvement outside its region and instead seek, in Hamilton's words, "to become the arbiter of Europe in America, and to be able to incline the balance of European competitions in this part of the world as our interest may dictate." Europe would then find itself with decreasing ability to exercise influence on America's side of the Atlantic. "Belligerent nations," President Washington declared, "under the impossibility of making acquisitions upon us, will not lightly hazard the giving us provocation."[9] The United States would consequently be left to rise to a position of primacy in the New World. As Hamilton put it, "Our situation and our interest prompt us to aim at an ascendant in the system of American affairs."[10]

The idealists were as comfortable as the realists with this approach to grand strategy because they believed that the United States could get what it needed—growing commerce—without making enduring political or military commitments to other states. By not choosing sides, the republic would be able to enjoy free trade with all parties. In Jefferson's formulation, "Peace, commerce, and honest friendship with all nations, entangling alliances with none."[11] Paine fully agreed: "As Europe is our market for trade, we ought to form no partial connection with any part of it. It is the true interest of America to steer clear of European contentions."[12] A doctrine that combined the expansion of economic links with the avoidance of strategic ties also appealed to Jefferson's interest in limiting the authority of the federal government and protecting the rights of individual states and their citizens. Inasmuch as a major war would require a large federal army and navy and more centralization, it threatened to do damage not just to America's foreign relations, but also to its domestic institutions and liberties.

The founding fathers brought to the task of launching a new nation a remarkable diversity of ideology, experience, and personality. Their disagreements on fundamental matters of state were numerous and ran deep. But on the question of the new nation's grand strategy, they were of a single mind. As Washington warned in his farewell address, the Union must be guided by the goal of "extending our commercial relations [with other nations] to have with them as little *political* connection as possible."[13]

Fashioning a foreign policy for the new republic entailed reconciling not just the divide between idealists and realists, but also the competing interests of the country's different regions. From their early days, the northern and southern colonies diverged over questions of culture as well as commerce. More religious settlers tended to gravitate to the North. They of course hoped to prosper, but they often put social and communal objectives before economic ones. Through a process of self-selection, the North's culture was thus heavily influenced by Calvinist, Puritan, and Quaker teachings. Ordered freedom, reciprocity, moral rectitude, the progress of mankind—these were the values of northern society. Northerners were also interested in developing a manufacturing economy and therefore sought protective tariffs for their infant enterprises. With these values and interests came a more pacifist approach to foreign policy, one that was generally noninterventionist and predisposed against the use of military force.[14]

The South attracted settlers of a different ilk—those seeking to get away from the constraints of religious authority and moral obligation. Southern plantations were strictly commercial enterprises, not communal projects infused with social purpose. Settlers shunned institutions that might interfere with their daily lives; individual freedoms and liberties took precedence over order and moral progress. Southerners also depended heavily upon the export of cotton and other crops. They therefore tended to oppose the commercial protections sought by some northerners.[15] A distinctly southern culture took shape around libertarian values—a culture that historians have dubbed "Cavalier" in coastal regions and "Scotch-Irish Highland" in the interior.[16] With this culture came a more activist approach to foreign policy. Southerners were generally more interventionist and comfortable with the use of force than their northern compatriots. At the same time, they jealously guarded the rights of states and their citizens, and thus opposed a level of external ambition that would risk centralization and strengthen the hand of the federal government. As America's appetite for international engagement grew over time, this libertarian tradition would also evolve into a potent strain of unilateralism, one insisting that the country fiercely protect its autonomy even as its reach broadened.

During America's early years, the cultural and political differences between North and South had little impact on the issue that stood at the center of debate about grand strategy—the republic's relationship with Europe. There was widespread agreement that the United States should keep its distance from Europe on matters of geopolitics and focus its attention on North America. On questions of policy closer to home, however, significant differences of opinion did emerge. Southerners generally supported the Union's westward expansion, while northerners were ambivalent, if not opposed. And the South, in no small part because of its dependence on seaborne trade, favored a stronger challenge to Britain's military position in Canada and naval strength along the North American coast, a stance that played an important role in the onset of the War of 1812.

Cultural and political differences between North and South, and their impact on foreign policy, were also magnified by the extent to which such differences became intertwined with partisan politics. As Alexander DeConde, a diplomatic historian of early America, has noted, debate over foreign policy "dominated domestic politics and American life as it has at virtually no time since."[17] One of the main reasons that foreign affairs figured so prominently in daily politics is that disputes over policy became personalized and thereby mired in rivalries between leading statesmen and their respective parties.

The confrontation that emerged between Alexander Hamilton and Thomas Jefferson laid bare the complexity and ferocity of such partisan infighting. Hamilton was born in the West Indies to an unmarried couple that had neither the inclination nor the resources to provide for their son. After a teacher and one of his employers stepped forward to help raise and educate the young man, Hamilton left behind his humble roots and joined the northern aristocracy by attending King's College (now Columbia University) and marrying the daughter of Philip Schuyler, a wealthy New York land baron.

Perhaps compensating for his background, Hamilton soon became one of the champions of northern values and interests. He circulated primarily among professionals, bankers, and merchants, favored a strong central government and banking system, and believed that the country should be governed by an educated and privileged elite. Hamilton favored the use of subsidies and tariffs to protect the North's emerging industrial base.[18] And he believed that the United States should look to the English economy as a model as it proceeded with urbanization and sought to build modern industries and social institutions. The party that formed around Hamilton's agenda called itself the Federalists.

Thomas Jefferson, although born into Virginia's landed aristocracy, distrusted the strong federal institutions and elite leadership championed by Hamilton. Fearing the tyranny of centralization, he argued that the federal government should have limited powers and that day-to-day governance should be left to common people, not entrusted to a wealthy and privileged few. Jefferson and his party, the Republicans, came to represent the interests of the small farmer and craftsman as opposed to the banker and industrialist. In his defense of the rights of states and their ordinary citizens and his call for a small and constrained federal government, Jefferson directly challenged Hamilton's views. The two also disagreed on matters of foreign affairs. Jefferson preferred a diplomatic tilt toward France rather than Britain, both because he served in Paris as minister and because he preferred France's agrarian culture to Britain's urbanization and elitism.

The rivalry between Jefferson and Hamilton was stoked in 1789, when President Washington called Jefferson back from Paris and appointed him secretary of state. With Hamilton already serving as secretary of the Treasury, the stage was set for a confrontation of personality and principle. Their dispute also turned into a heated battle between their respective parties, with differences over foreign policy engendering partisan warfare.

Washington had intended to step down after four years. He was, however, so astonished and aggrieved by the "internal dissensions . . . harrowing and tearing our vitals" that he agreed to run for a second term for the sake of the republic's political stability.[19] Washington, who was seen as above partisan politics, easily won the election of 1792. The Federalists and the Republicans ran a fierce contest for the vice presidency, with the Federalist candidate, John Adams, coming out on top, but the Republicans winning a majority in Congress.[20] Jefferson and Hamilton both stayed in the cabinet, their feud continuing.

Foreign policy remained one of the main battlegrounds. At Hamilton's request, John Jay in 1794 concluded a commercial treaty with Britain intended to protect bilateral trade and lock in America's diplomatic tilt toward England. Republicans claimed that America's "funding gentry" would be the only beneficiary of this compact with "the old, corrupt, and almost expiring government of Great Britain."[21] Although Jefferson had by then left the cabinet, he denounced the deal as "nothing more than a treaty of alliance between England and the Anglomen of this country against . . . the people of the United States." Hamilton responded in kind, calling his political opponents "fawning or turbulent demagogues," many of whom were "deeply infected with those horrid principles of Jacobinism."[22] Jefferson was so "electrified with attachment to France," Hamilton charged, that he risked provoking a war between the United States and Britain.[23] For the first time, but hardly for the last, foreign policy had been ensnared in the animosities of partisan politics.

THE DEBATES over foreign policy that emerged during the republic's early years set a steady course for the first century of America's engagement—or, more precisely, its lack thereof—in global affairs. The United States continued to avoid European intrigues for successive decades. Despite help from France during the Revolutionary War, the United States watched from the sidelines when hostilities broke out between Britain and France in 1793. The United States had entered into an alliance with France during the revolutionary period, but many Americans considered it defunct by the 1790s, if not earlier.[24] America's independence and peace with Britain obviated the need for formal military ties with the French. Although fighting continued to plague the Continent until Napoleon was finally defeated in 1815, the United States maintained its distance from Europe's wars.

The U.S. did go to war with Britain in 1812, but only because its leaders and the public thought the British to be unfairly impairing foreign commerce and poaching in America's emerging zone of influence. The Royal Navy was routinely interfering with American shipping as part of its effort to enforce a naval blockade against Napoleon. American resentment was further piqued by Britain's arming of Native American tribes along the Canadian border and the consequent attacks on American settlers.

It is also the case that during the nineteenth century U.S. soldiers sporadically engaged in operations outside the Western Hemisphere. American troops saw action in numerous locations, including Tripoli (1801–1805, 1815), Algiers (1815), Greece (1827), Sumatra (1832, 1838–1839), Liberia (1843), China (1843, 1854, 1856), Angola (1860), Japan (1863–1864, 1868), and Korea (1871). But only small raiding parties were involved, their objectives limited to defending U.S. traders and citizens. Largely to support these operations and to defend its merchant shipping, the United States established cruising stations in the Mediterranean, the Pacific, and the East Indies. But these so-called squadrons consisted of only a handful of ships, often cruising separately. Neither the raiding parties nor the establishment of overseas cruising stations was meant to create a permanent U.S. presence. The United States was interested in protecting commerce, not in shaping the balance of power in distant regions.[25]

In the Western Hemisphere, however, the United States took a more assertive stance, warning European nations to limit their involvement. In his annual address to Congress in 1823, President James Monroe counseled Europeans against interfering with the transition to republican government in South America. Although he acknowledged that the United States would respect existing colonial claims, Monroe asserted that efforts to suppress republicanism would be seen as "the manifestation of an unfriendly disposition towards the United States." The president was also concerned about preventing the spread of balance-of-power dynamics to the Americas, warning European governments that the United States would consider efforts "to extend their political system to any portion of this hemisphere as dangerous to our peace and safety."[26] And he reaffirmed America's hands-off stance toward Europe: "In the wars of the European powers in matters relating to themselves we have never taken any part, nor does it comport with our policy to do so."[27]

President James Polk expanded on these themes roughly two decades later, giving greater form and substance to what became known as the Monroe Doctrine. Polk's main objective was to caution European nations against standing in the way of America's westward expansion. Britain and France had attempted to dissuade Texas from joining the Union, and Polk feared that Spain might try to cede California to Britain so that it would not fall into U.S. hands. "We must ever maintain that people of this continent alone have a right to decide their own destiny," Polk asserted. "Should any portion of them, constituting an independent state, propose to unite themselves with our Confederacy, this will be a question for them and us to determine without any foreign interposition." The president also warned the Europeans to keep their rivalries to themselves, affirming that the balance of power "cannot be permitted to have any application on the North American continent, and especially to the United States."[28] Polk was thus being guided by a blend of idealism and realism. He was standing behind principles of self-determination and at the same time muscling out Europe's major nations, ultimately seeking to bring to an end their strategic presence in North America. So too were unilateralist and isolationist impulses at play. America would manage its neighborhood as it saw fit, while steering clear of European intrigues.

America's westward enlargement raised tensions not only between the United States and Europe, but also between the northern and southern states of the Union. The economic and cultural differences between North and South had only intensified since the founding years. To Jefferson's distrust of a strong central government and his defense of states' rights, President Andrew Jackson (1829–1837) added a proud and prickly populism. The populist politics that took hold in the agrarian South and the expanding West clashed head-on with the elite bent of the North. The South supported the War of 1812, the steady extension of the country's western frontier, and the war with Mexico, which resulted from America's annexation of Texas in 1845 and a subsequent dispute over the new state's southern border. Over the next three years, the United States also acquired all or parts of the territory of present-day New Mexico, Utah, Nevada, Arizona, California, Colorado, and Oregon, expanding the country's size by more than 50 percent.

Commercial incentives helped fuel this expansionist fervor. Planters were searching for new farmlands; Texas, in particular, offered prime acreage for producing cotton. To ensure buyers for their products, farmers and traders alike were interested in gaining control over ports on the West Coast to broaden access to markets in East Asia. Security concerns also figured prominently, with the United States seeking to neutralize threats both from Native Americans and from Europe's colonial powers. Domestic politics added to the momentum behind expansion. Southerners were looking to increase the number of slaveholding states and to protect the country's agrarian traditions against industrialization and urbanization. Enlarging the country's territory would offer its growing population an alternative to urban employment, and new export markets would absorb America's rising agricultural surplus.[29]

As before the 1840s, this expansionary impulse was restricted to North America, with the size of the U.S. Army and Navy remaining quite limited despite the country's growing territory. Until the outbreak of the Civil War, the regular army was serving primarily as a domestic police force focusing on the Indian threat. In 1861, this force consisted of only 16,000 men, most of them serving at posts on the Indian frontier. Despite the existence of a large merchant marine, the United States was without a significant battle fleet. Some 7,600 men served in the navy, about one-tenth the manpower of the British navy.[30]

Despite the relatively low costs of expansion, northerners were generally unenthusiastic about America's westward march, the expansion of slavery, and what they saw as the country's growing militarism. They were more interested in developing their industrial base than in acquiring new farmland through violent means. The Massachusetts hero Henry David Thoreau was arrested in 1846 for refusing to pay federal taxes because they would end up financing U.S. troops fighting against the Mexicans. He subsequently wrote his famous book *Civil Disobedience.*

The divergent priorities of the North and South emerged from the fundamental differences in society, culture, and economy that divided the two regions. Westward enlargement eventually brought these fundamental differences to a head, pitting the North against a Confederacy determined to preserve slavery and its traditional social order. That competing regional interests and cultures ultimately led to civil war and the death of more than 600,000 Union and Confederate soldiers is testimony to their consequence and the degree to which they fueled and were fueled by powerful political passions.

Although a turning point for America's domestic politics, the Civil War did not have a major impact on the country's relations with Europe. Britain and France both tilted toward the Confederacy, their textile industries heavily dependent upon the South's cotton and thus suffering from the North's naval blockade of southern ports. Some in Britain favored the independence of the South, arguing that a divided America and an independent, antiprotectionist Confederacy would further British interests. In the end, neither Britain nor France chanced direct involvement in the war, dissuaded by the Union's repeated warnings and the prospect of conflict with its forces. The behavior of Britain and France thus did little more than strengthen the conviction among statesmen in the victorious Union that the United States had to resist Europe's strategic presence in North America.[31]

THE 1890s proved to be a much more important turning point in the evolution of American foreign policy than the 1860s. After more than a century of keeping America's strategic sights focused almost exclusively on its own hemisphere, the United States emerged during this decade as a nation with global ambition, its reach stretching well beyond its immediate neighborhood. The U.S. markedly expanded the size of its navy. When President Benjamin Harrison took office in 1889, the U.S. Navy ranked seventeenth in the world. When he left office in 1893, it ranked seventh. The navy also adopted a more ambitious strategy, building large battleships capable of engaging the world's major fleets rather than smaller cruisers intended to protect commerce and coastlines. America simultaneously redoubled efforts to push Britain and Spain from its sphere of influence, the former through tough-minded diplomacy, the latter by besting the Spanish fleet in a conflict over Cuba, which was deliberately provoked by the United States. Victory in the Spanish-American War whetted the country's appetite for expansion; the United States proceeded during the course of 1898 to establish colonial rule in Puerto Rico, Hawaii, Guam, and the Philippines.

President Theodore Roosevelt, who took office in 1901, continued this expansionary fervor by substantially extending the scope of the Monroe Doctrine, articulating and putting into practice what came to be called the "Roosevelt Corollary." Roosevelt essentially reserved to the United States the right to intervene in other countries of the Western Hemisphere as needed to forestall outside interference. The precipitating event was a financial crisis in the Dominican Republic in 1904 that induced Europeans to threaten intervention to recover their debts (they had forcibly claimed assets in Venezuela in 1902–1903). Roosevelt dispatched American agents to take over the country's customs service and ensure repayment of existing obligations. "In the Western Hemisphere," Roosevelt asserted, "the adherence of the United States to the Monroe Doctrine may force the United States, however reluctantly, in flagrant cases of wrong-doing or impotence, to the exercise of an international police power." The president added in his annual address to Congress in 1905 that the expanded version of the Monroe Doctrine "offers the only possible way of insuring us against a clash with some foreign power. The position is, therefore, in the interest of peace as well as in the interest of justice."[32]

Perhaps the most telling sign of America's new calling was Roosevelt's decision in 1907 to send the Great White Fleet on a world tour. The voyage lasted more than a year. The fleet visited ports in numerous countries, including Brazil, Chile, Peru, Mexico, New Zealand, Australia, China, Japan, Ceylon, Egypt, Algeria, Turkey, Greece, Italy, and France. Roosevelt was making clear to the rest of the world that America had arrived on the world scene. He also took on the task of constructing the Panama Canal, eventually encouraging a Panamanian uprising after the Colombian government rejected an offer for the land. Roosevelt then used U.S. warships to warn off those angry about the revolt and America's unilateral interference.

The new and more adventurous brand of internationalism behind this activism had complex roots. The U.S. economy grew rapidly during the second half of the nineteenth century. Between 1860 and 1900 America's population more than doubled. Its railway network increased from 31,000 to more than 250,000 miles, while wheat production tripled, coal output increased eightfold, and oil production rose by more than 2,000 percent. The growing output of iron and steel established America as one of the world's major industrial economies.[33] Compelled by the search for new markets and enabled by its impressive resource base, the United States by the end of the 1890s had both the need and the means to take on a more expansive role in global politics.

Some historians argue that it was economic misfortune as much as newfound wealth that gave rise to America's imperial impulse. The United States suffered a sharp economic downturn between 1893 and 1895. This trough coincided with the popularization of Frederick Jackson Turner's claim that the closing of the western frontier was sapping America's dynamism.[34] With the completion of the country's continental expansion, Turner's analysis suggested, the United States would have to look overseas to restore its economic vitality. As Walter LaFeber writes, "The American commercial community believed that an expanding overseas commerce would revive the American economy." The colonization of Hawaii and the Philippines may have strengthened America's strategic position in the Pacific, but commercial motivations were paramount. In LaFeber's words, "The United States obtained these areas not to fulfill a colonial policy, but to use these holdings as a means to acquire markets for the glut of goods pouring out of highly mechanized factories and farms."[35]

The search for new markets no doubt contributed to the more ambitious foreign policy that emerged during the 1890s. But commercial incentives offer an incomplete explanation of the switch in strategy. The United States had from the outset pursued foreign markets with vigor, backing up its economic interests with naval power. But now the country was building battleships, not lightly armed cruisers for protecting its merchant marine. It was establishing overseas colonies, not just defending the rights of its traders. As John Bassett Moore, who was assistant secretary of state during the late 1890s, put it, the United States had moved "from a position of comparative freedom from entanglements into the position of what is commonly called a world power. . . . Where formerly we had only commercial interests, we now have territorial and political interests as well."[36] As Moore astutely recognized, America was flirting with a new grand strategy—one in which it would seek not only to defend its global commercial interests, but also to have a hand in shaping the balance of power well beyond its neighborhood.

Two additional factors are needed to explain this change of course: shifting regional alignments and the effect of partisan politics on America's governing institutions. The diverging economic interests of the country's different regions again came to the fore during the 1890s.[37] At this point in time, however, the South and the North paradoxically switched roles. The South, from the outset a strong supporter of interventionism and expansionism, opposed America's discovery of a global calling. The North, long the voice of restraint and nonintervention, became the leading proponent of the country's new international ambition.

The North's continuing industrialization was behind its shifting stance on matters of grand strategy. Economic interests proved more persuasive than regional ideology as political power shifted away from America's planters toward its industrialists and financiers. Northern manufacturers and bankers welcomed the new orders that came with the decision to build a major battle fleet, as well as the new markets that accompanied America's expansion into the Pacific and the opening of a cross-isthmus canal in Panama. Furthermore, the North's dominant party, the Republicans, used foreign policy to build a political alliance with the West. (During the course of the 1800s, the northern Federalist Party had come to be called first the Whig Party and then the Republican Party, and the southern Republican Party came to be called the Democratic Party.)[38] Although the West was largely agrarian, it welcomed an expansionist foreign policy that would open new markets in Latin America and the Pacific. Western farmers also supported the North's call for protective tariffs, seeing them as a tool for forcing open foreign markets.

Southern Democrats, meanwhile, feared that the combination of imperial expansion and tariffs would result in retaliation from Europe, the main export market for southern cotton and other products. A populist fear that excessive militarism would strengthen the center at the expense of state and citizen rights also fed into the South's opposition to the country's growing ambition. The coalition between northern and western Republicans, however, bested the isolated southern Democrats, providing the winning coalition needed to bring to life a more ambitious brand of U.S. internationalism.

Partisan maneuvering reinforced this new domestic alignment and its impact on foreign policy. The popularity of the Democrats had declined sharply as a result of the economic downturn of the early 1890s. After the Republicans took control of both the legislative and executive branches in the 1896 election, President William McKinley exploited the weakness of his opposition to strengthen his hold over foreign policy and enhance the influence of the executive branch in its ongoing game of check and balance with Congress. This move also enhanced Washington's position at the expense of the individual states, a trend that had been deepening since the Civil War. Both developments made it easier for the country's leaders to implement and oversee a more demanding foreign policy—one that required greater centralization and resources. It was thus no accident that the emergence of America's imperial impulse coincided with the emergence of the imperial presidency.

McKinley's decision to go to war against Spain was also affected by party politics, with the president seeking to counter charges from Democrats that he lacked the mettle to guide the country into battle. Mounting war fever in Congress and a jingoistic press added to the domestic pressure, eventually convincing him not only to drive the Spanish from Cuba, but also to acquire a major strategic foothold in the Pacific.[39]

Rhetoric and action combined to instill in many Americans a new form of nationalism predicated upon the notion that it was time for their country to enter the top ranks. The United States had built a first-rate economy; it should therefore have an international voice to match. The prominent Massachusetts senator Henry Cabot Lodge proclaimed that Americans should awaken to their place "as one of the great nations of the world."[40] According to George Kennan, the U.S. diplomat turned historian, many influential Americans of the time liked "the smell of empire and felt an urge to range themselves among the colonial powers of the time, to see our flag flying on distant tropical isles, to feel the thrill of foreign adventure and authority, to bask in the sunshine of recognition as one of the great imperial powers of the world."[41]

The United States thus entered the twentieth century armed with a new internationalism and a new grand strategy to match. It would not be long, however, before the onset of World War I tested this ambition, revealing the limits of America's fondness for the responsibilities that came with its broader reach.

WORLD WAR I AND THE DEFEAT OF THE LEAGUE OF NATIONS

THE INITIAL RESPONSE to the outbreak of war in Europe in 1914 was to return to the dictums of the republic's early years; the United States declared strict neutrality and its intention to continue trading with all belligerents. The public strongly opposed entry into the war. President Woodrow Wilson and his advisers were equally determined to avoid direct involvement. Attitudes changed quickly in early 1917, however, when German submarines began attacking U.S. merchant ships crossing the Atlantic. At Wilson's behest, Congress declared war on April 6, and the United States was thereafter engaged in just the type of conflict against which the founding fathers had so passionately and unanimously warned.

It is hardly surprising that the United States overcame its deep reluctance to involvement in Old World affairs. Wilson had little choice but to abandon neutrality and enter World War I after the German navy started sinking American ships. The political outcry effectively closed off any other course of action. Furthermore, the war threatened to do serious harm to the U.S. economy by shutting down transatlantic trade.

The most interesting and revealing aspect of America's engagement in World War I is thus not how that engagement began, but how it ended. Once an Allied victory appeared in hand, Wilson devoted his presidency to negotiating the Versailles Treaty and designing a postwar order that would provide a foundation for a lasting peace. As preparations for a settlement began, Wilson in 1918 offered his famous "Fourteen Points" as a stark alternative to the past. Open negotiations should replace the secret diplomacy of the past. Trade barriers should be abolished and all trade routes open to every country. The major nations should disarm to the lowest levels consistent with territorial defense and should be guided by the notion of collective security and their willingness to stand together against aggression. Wilson also urged that the principle of self-determination take the place of colonialism and the subjugation of the weak by the strong. To put these ideas into practice, Wilson proposed the establishment of the League of Nations, a global assembly that would at once coordinate collective action against aggression wherever it might occur and serve as a forum for the nations of the world to engage in diplomacy and deliberation.

Wilson's approach to preserving peace can be traced back to his childhood. The son of a Presbyterian minister, Wilson had a strong moral compass. He was four years old when the Civil War broke out; the destruction and suffering he witnessed fueled the intensity of his later determination to help rid the world of armed conflict. He believed that making World War I the "war to end all wars" required nothing less than recasting the foundation of an international system that was irretrievably flawed. And inasmuch as Wilson argued in favor of America's permanent involvement in managing global affairs, his ideas represented a radical departure for the United States.

The debate over whether the Senate would approve U.S. participation in the League of Nations was a defining event for America. The Senate's deliberation mesmerized the country for months and, because it coincided with the presidential election of 1920, broadened into a national referendum on the scope and character of America's engagement in the world. The debate harkened back to precisely those themes pored over by the founding fathers—realism versus idealism, the competing interests and cultures of the country's different regions, and the distorting effects of partisan politics on foreign policy. As such, it tested the more ambitious internationalism that had emerged during the 1890s. So too did it test the country's tolerance for a particularly liberal brand of internationalism, for Wilson was asking Americans to commit to a codified and institutionalized form of multilateral engagement. That the Senate ultimately rejected U.S. participation in the League not only dealt a mortal blow to Wilson's brainchild, but also revealed the fragility of America's new ambition and made clear the country's profound ambivalence about submitting its will to the constraints of a binding multilateralism.

The political battle lines were drawn well before Wilson formally presented the treaty to the Senate in July 1919. In his campaign for reelection in 1916, the president ran on a platform calling for American participation in postwar efforts to preserve a lasting peace. Addressing an October rally in Indianapolis, Wilson stated that "when the great present war is over, it will be the duty of America to join with the other nations in some kind of league for the maintenance of peace."[42] The Republican candidate, Charles Evan Hughes, kept his distance from proposals for U.S. participation in a new international institution; his party was divided on the issue, and he was seeking to distinguish himself from the president. Wilson's margin of victory was small, but many in his camp interpreted the outcome as indicative of growing public support for the country's deeper engagement in world affairs. As one of Wilson's supporters commented, "The President we re-elected has raised a new flag, or, at all events, a flag that no other president has thought or perhaps dared to raise. It is the flag of internationalism."[43]

Armed with an electoral mandate, Wilson decided to lay out his ideas in greater detail. On January 22, 1917, he delivered a formal address to the Senate, noting that "in every discussion of the peace that must end this war it is taken for granted that peace must be followed by some definite concert of power which will make it virtually impossible that any such catastrophe should ever overwhelm us again." Wilson then ventured that it would be "inconceivable that the people of the United States should play no part in that great enterprise."[44] When finished laying out his vision, the president was greeted by rousing applause from Democrats and Republicans alike.

In the days that followed, however, the Republicans began mounting their counterattack. Senator William Borah of Idaho warned that the country should remain true to the isolationist tenets of Washington's Farewell Address. Senator Lodge argued in favor of a more unilateral brand of internationalism, urging that America protect its own security interests before worrying about the collective welfare of the international community.[45] Borah and Lodge were to become two of Wilson's most intractable opponents.

German attacks on U.S. shipping began in early February, cutting off debate about the postwar order and focusing the attention of the president and Congress on preparations for war. After America joined the conflict, Wilson was curiously silent about his plans for the League of Nations, not making a single public speech focused on the issue throughout the remainder of 1917 and most of 1918. Furthermore, Wilson restricted planning for the League to an exclusive inner circle and did not reach out to the League to Enforce Peace or other domestic organizations that had formed to help shape and build support for a new postwar institution.

Public and congressional debate picked up again early in 1919, after Wilson's trip to Europe to help shape the League Covenant. Although the document was still in draft form and not yet ready for the Senate's consideration, Lodge took the lead in gathering thirty-seven signatures in support of a resolution indicating that the treaty provisions as they stood at that time were unacceptable. This move sent a clear message to the president that he would not be able to garner the two-thirds majority needed for ratification. Wilson then headed back to Europe to continue the negotiations, winning from his European colleagues their acquiescence on new provisions exempting domestic matters from the purview of the League and acknowledging that the United States, as articulated in the Monroe Doctrine, held unchallenged sway in its neighborhood. Both changes specifically addressed concerns raised by the Senate resolution.

Wilson then returned to the United States with great fanfare. The presidential liner *George Washington* pulled into New York harbor on the morning of July 8. Wilson was greeted by an armada of naval vessels carrying, among many others, members of the cabinet and Congress. Immediately after disembarking, Wilson was driven to Carnegie Hall, his motorcade passing through city streets crowded with cheering supporters. He there delivered a speech about his efforts in Europe "to save the world from unnecessary bloodshed." The weary president that same evening boarded a train for Washington, arriving at Union Station to find, despite the late hour, another boisterous gathering of some 10,000 well-wishers.[46]

Two days later Wilson made his way from the White House to Capitol Hill, where he officially submitted to the Senate the treaty containing the Covenant of the League of Nations. As soon as the president finished making his case, it became clear that a bruising battle lay ahead. The Democrats responded with a rousing ovation, but the Republican majority could barely muster a mild applause. From the outset, the two-thirds majority needed for ratification looked anything but assured.

The problem for Wilson was not the so-called irreconcilables—the hard-core isolationists who wanted nothing to do with the League and would vote against it in any form. Such individuals did exist—Senator William Borah of Idaho was their outspoken leader—but not in sufficient numbers to sink the treaty. The real obstacle was the Republican mainstream and its insistence on changing the treaty through a series of "reservations." Senator Henry Cabot Lodge, the leader of Republican efforts to modify the Covenant, proposed fourteen reservations in all. The crux of the debate focused on Article X, the provision obligating signatories of the Covenant "to respect and preserve as against external aggression the territorial integrity and existing political independence of all Members of the League."

For Wilson, Article X was the heart of the treaty, in principle and practice the foundation of a workable system of collective security that would preserve peace by obligating members to take joint action against aggressors. To water down this provision in order to get it past the Senate, Wilson contended, would "not provide for ratification but, rather, for the *nullification* of the treaty."[47] The Republicans begged to differ. An ironclad commitment to defend all states against aggression would only drag the United States into unwanted and unwise wars. Furthermore, only Congress, not some supranational body, could choose when and where to send the U.S. military into battle. America should not compromise its autonomy by empowering an international institution to make decisions on its behalf. Hence Lodge's careful stipulation in his second reservation that the United States "assumes no obligation" to come to the defense of other countries unless Congress specifically decides to do so.

Wilson refused to budge, asserting that it was "better a thousand times to go down fighting than to dip your colors to dishonorable compromise."[48] Instead, the president decided to take his case to the American people, embarking by train for a tour of the heartland and Far West—precisely where opposition to the League was running strongest. Wilson's whistle-stop appeal to America was unprecedented. The president gave speeches by day and often slept on the moving train at night. The trip lasted almost the entire month of September and included major speeches in the following cities: Columbus, Indianapolis, St. Louis, Kansas City, Des Moines, Omaha, Sioux Falls, St. Paul and Minneapolis, Bismarck, Billings, Spokane, Seattle, Portland, San Francisco, Los Angeles, San Diego, Reno, Salt Lake City, and Denver.

Wilson intended to continue on to Wichita, Oklahoma City, Little Rock, Memphis, and Louisville, but he collapsed in exhaustion after his speech in Pueblo, Colorado. His doctors insisted upon canceling the remaining stops. The president's train then set off on the two-day ride back to Washington. Four days after returning to the White House, Wilson suffered a stroke. He was to spend the next several months in bed, rarely able to muster the strength to continue his fight for the League or to deal with any other pressing matters.

Wilson's personal sacrifice for the sake of the League of Nations proved to be in vain. Despite his trip and months of rancorous debate that engulfed much of the nation, the two-thirds majority needed for ratification remained beyond reach. The Republicans refused to support the treaty *without* Lodge's reservations. The Democrats, on orders from Wilson, refused to support the treaty *with* Lodge's reservations. The Senate finally moved to a vote on November 19. Neither the original treaty nor the treaty with Lodge's revisions won even a simple majority. The following March, the Senate voted again on Lodge's modified treaty. Forty-nine senators voted for and thirty-five against, a simple majority but well short of the votes needed for ratification.

Wilson's last recourse was to appeal to the public one more time. At his insistence, the 1920 election was portrayed as a "solemn referendum" on American internationalism, with the fate of the League one of the main issues dividing the two parties. The man selected by the

Democrats to carry the Wilsonian banner, Ohio Governor James Cox, was easily defeated by the Republican challenger, Warren Harding, extinguishing any hope for American participation in the League. In his inaugural address, Harding cleared up any ambiguity about his approach to American internationalism: "The recorded progress of our Republic, materially and spiritually, in itself proves the wisdom of our inherited policy of non-involvement in Old World affairs." "This is not aloofness," Harding concluded, "it is security."[49]

AMERICA'S collective deliberation about its role in the postwar world bore striking resemblance to the debates that ensued at the country's founding. The themes that guided the formulation of grand strategy during America's early days showed remarkable resilience, despite the country's transition from weak newcomer to major power.

The debate over the League resurrected the traditional divide between idealists and realists. In the Jeffersonian tradition, Wilson believed in the capacity of reason, law, and social progress to lead to a just and peaceful world. This belief was the foundation for Wilson's confidence in the League and in the capacity of a global system of collective security to avert war. Article X was for Wilson the backbone of the League Covenant, not because of its legal implications, but because it entailed a moral obligation. The president accepted a permissive interpretation of Article X on legal grounds; the U.S. government, not the League of Nations, would be the ultimate arbiter of when and where American forces would go into combat. But as a signatory of the League Covenant, the United States would have a moral obligation to act against aggression, an obligation that in the end was more important than any legal technicality. When Warren Harding in the midst of the Senate debate over ratification asked Wilson why the United States should honor a moral obligation, Wilson shot back, "Why, Senator, it is surprising that that question should be asked."[50]

Wilson's idealism ran head-on into the legacy of Hamiltonian realism. It was one thing for the United States to get involved in a European war when its ships were being attacked by German submarines. It was a different matter, however, to make an enduring commitment to engage in conflicts whenever and wherever they might occur. Senator Philander Knox of Pennsylvania worried that the League would drag the United States into unwanted conflicts and lead only to "centuries of blood-letting." Irreconcilables and more moderate Republicans alike frequently invoked the founding fathers in building their case against Wilson's vision. Lodge charged that America was being asked "to move away from George Washington to . . . the sinister figure of Trotsky the champion of internationalism."[51] Opponents of the League were in agreement, according to one historian of the period, that "Washington would stir uneasily in his tomb at Mount Vernon if he should learn that we were going to underwrite a League of Nations and keep an army of American boys ready to fight strange peoples in strange lands—all at the behest of some superbody."[52]

As the preceding quote makes clear, Republicans also deployed populist and unilateralist themes in their assault on the League. It was bad enough that an overweening federal government was encroaching upon the liberties of the individual states and their citizens. Wilson was now going a step further, compromising the very sovereignty of the United States by subjugating it to a supranational institution. As Harding put it soon after taking office, "In the existing League of Nations, world-governing with its superpowers, this Republic will have no part."[53]

The Republicans sought to portray the League as a threat not just to the country's sovereignty, but also to the spirit of American nationalism. As Senator Lodge told his colleagues, "We are asked . . . to substitute internationalism for nationalism and an international state for pure Americanism."[54] At times, this line of attack even took on racial and religious overtones. Senator James Reed of Missouri complained that whites would be outnumbered by blacks in the League, while Senator Lawrence Sherman of Illinois worried about the predominance of Catholics and the pope's consequent influence over international affairs. Wilson tried to counter such charges by claiming that the League Covenant was a "thoroughly American document" and a "people's treaty." But he was little match for orators such as Borah, who called the defeat of the treaty in the Senate "the second winning of the independence of America" and the "greatest victory since Appomattox."[55]

Although the positions staked out by the protagonists in the League debate tracked closely the themes dwelled on by the founding fathers, the lineup of regional cultures no longer followed the pattern of the republic's early years. The South had been the breeding ground for populism and its libertarian tradition, while northerners were believers in moral and social progress and the importance of elite governance. By 1920, the ideological alignment was just the opposite. The

South was firmly behind Wilson, with every senator from below the Mason-Dixon line voting for ratification. Meanwhile, the North and West were the strongholds of opposition, the northerners straying far from their previous commitment to bettering both domestic and international order through law and reason.

This novel alignment of ideology and region was partly a function of partisan politics. The South was solidly Democratic and thus backed Wilson out of party loyalty. The Republican alliance between North and West that emerged during the 1890s meanwhile held together, with the party staking its fortunes on defeating Wilson and his liberal brand of internationalism. But economic interests also contributed to this new regional alignment. The South remained in favor of free trade and against expenditure on the military—goals that would be furthered by U.S. participation in the League. An industrializing North and a West in search of new markets, in contrast, backed higher military spending, protective tariffs, and overseas colonies—goals that ran counter to the intent of the League. Furthermore, the heartland and the West had become the new home of the frontier spirit and the inheritor of the populist aversion to government interference. It was no accident that many of the irreconcilables hailed from these areas.

The alignment between ideology and region was thus anything but static. Rather, liberal internationalism as well as potent strains of isolationism and unilateralism had all become fundamental elements of a fluid political discourse. Which outlook took root in which region at any given point in time was a function of a complex mix of economic interest, party affiliation, and culture.

The partisan tone of America's deliberation over participation in the League stemmed as much from personal rivalries as from regional alignments. Of most importance was the intense dislike that developed between Wilson and Lodge. The animosity between them predated the debate over the League. In February 1915, after differing with the president on how America should handle the war in Europe, Lodge confided to Theodore Roosevelt that "I never expected to hate anyone in politics with the hatred I feel towards Wilson."[56]

Matters only worsened once the League debate was under way. Wilson made the mistake of appointing not a single senator and only one minor Republican to the peace commission he brought with him to Europe for consultations during the treaty negotiations. William Howard Taft, the incumbent Republican whom Wilson defeated in the 1912 election, was the head of the League to Enforce Peace and thus an obvious candidate to join the delegation. But Wilson passed him over. An angry Lodge retaliated by stacking the Foreign Relations Committee with Republicans, including several irreconcilables. The partisan rancor grew by the day, with the *Piedmont*, a daily newspaper in Greenville, South Carolina, concluding that "the Senate's chief objection to the League idea is that Wilson is a Democrat."[57]

Wilson's stubborn self-reliance exacerbated his rift with the Republicans. His failure to reach out to Taft and other potential allies stemmed at least in part from concern about retaining control over both the design of the League and the effort to bring it into being. In so doing, he squandered the opportunity to tap into an important source of political support. The paucity of public diplomacy similarly emerged from Wilson's distrust of his opponents and his desire to restrict debate over the League to his confidants. As *The New Republic* commented, the president "preferred the lone hand to the effort of building up an informed and energetic public opinion in America to back him up." Although this strategy ensured that Wilson was in charge, it also denied him the popular support that he eventually needed to salvage the League. By the time he started his appeal to the public late in 1918, it was too late. As Thomas Knock comments, "No preparatory groundwork had been systematically laid—for he had not permitted any."[58]

In the lead-up to America's deliberation about its participation in the League, Wilson managed to alienate not just internationalist Republicans, but also a substantial number of his supporters on the left. Although liberals and socialists helped the president win reelection in 1916, voters on the left defected from the Wilsonian camp during the war. Some were die-hard pacifists and opposed America's direct involvement. Many others lost faith in Wilson because of the wartime constraints he imposed on civil liberties—including the arrest of leftist activists and censorship of the press. Still others walked away from the progressive coalition because they found the League and the peace treaty at odds with the idealist agenda—the former because it was too conservative and the latter because it was too punitive.

The unraveling of Wilson's leftist coalition cost him few votes in the Senate; most Democrats remained loyal to the president. But it did take a toll on the broader public debate. Influential publications, such as *The New Republic* and *The Nation*, both of which had initially backed the League, withdrew their support just at the time that Wilson was seeking to garner popular momentum. In March 1919, *The New Republic* came out against Article X, claiming that its pledge to preserve existing territorial boundaries was unjust and reactionary. The following month J. A. Hobson published an article in *The Nation* calling the League "A New Holy Alliance" of the five great powers, while another of the magazine's authors characterized the arrangements decided at Versailles as a peace of "intrigue, selfish aggression, and naked imperialism."[59]

It is of course impossible to determine whether the League might have met a different fate had the Senate debate not become so deeply infused with partisan politics and had Wilson done a better job of reaching out to potential allies on the left and right. The poisonous political atmosphere clearly contributed to the uncompromising stance of Democrats and Republicans alike. Lodge wanted nothing more than to humiliate Wilson and oblige him to acquiesce to his reservations. Wilson preferred seeing the League Covenant go up in flames to giving in to Lodge. Even when Wilson's closest confidants pressed him to compromise, the president stood his ground.

In an attempt to save the League from defeat, a few Democrats eventually defied Wilson's stubbornness and backed Lodge's modifications. But the defectors were too few in number. Partisan politics combined with America's limited appetite for internationalism to deny the League the participation of one of the world's strongest countries. The League never recovered from the setback.

Americans rejected the liberal brand of internationalism that Wilson had offered them at the close of World War I, but they did not immediately retreat from the global stage. Washington played a leading role in negotiating disarmament agreements and helped design and manage a new international monetary system. The United States did, however, steer clear of alliances and commitments to collective security, mustering enthusiasm for only anodyne agreements, such as the Kellogg-Briand Pact of 1928, which condemned war and committed signatories to the peaceful resolution of disputes.

After the onset of the global depression and the rise of militarism in Germany and Japan, isolationist forces gained in strength. In 1935, President Franklin Roosevelt decided in favor of U.S. participation in the World Court, but isolationist and unilateralist instincts prevailed when the agreement was sent to the Senate for ratification. A congressional commission examining World War I concluded that America's involvement was unwarranted and blamed the arms industry and bankers for forcing the country into the conflict. Congress proceeded to pass a succession of neutrality acts prohibiting trade with belligerent nations, seeking to ensure that the United States would not again be drawn into great-power rivalries. By the second half of the 1930s, America had found the comfortable perch from which it watched in illusory quietude as the world again began a slow but steady descent toward war.[60]

WORLD WAR II AND THE ONSET OF AMERICA'S GLOBAL CALLING

AT FOUR-THIRTY in the afternoon of June 26, 1945, President Harry Truman delivered the closing address to the weary delegates who had just finalized the United Nations Charter. "By this Charter," Truman told the crowd gathered in San Francisco's War Memorial Opera House, "you have given reality to the ideal of that great statesman of a generation ago—Woodrow Wilson. If we had had this Charter a few years ago—and above all, the will to use it—millions now dead would be alive." At ten in the morning on July 28, the U.S. Senate convened to deliberate over the document that had emerged from the San Francisco conference. By a vote of 89 to 2, the Senate assented to America's entry into the United Nations.

In 1920, the Senate rejected the principle of collective security and America's participation in a global institution designed to manage international order. In 1945, the Senate did just the opposite, ratifying almost without objection a treaty committing the United States to the notion of collective security and multilateral involvement in managing global affairs. This striking turnabout in U.S. policy was anything but accidental.

America's new course was the product of years of careful planning and shrewd political maneuvering by President Franklin Roosevelt. Wilson's debacle with the League of Nations provided Roosevelt and his advisers important lessons about the stubborn constraints on American internationalism. As a result, even as World War II was raging, the administration set as a top priority the task of building domestic support for America's participation in a postwar security system. Furthermore, Roosevelt realized that realism and idealism had to be kept in careful balance if he was to craft a sustainable internationalism and ensure that the United States did not again opt out of global engagement. In 1941, Roosevelt wrote that "it is not advisable at this time to reconstitute a League of Nations which, because of its size, makes for disagreement and inaction."[61] Roosevelt thus lowered his sights and aimed at a workable, even if less ambitious, system for preserving peace, rather than aiming high and ending up, like Wilson, empty-handed.

Although the United States did not formally enter the war until attacked at Pearl Harbor, Roosevelt took steps to help the Allied cause well before the end of 1941. In November 1939, he dropped the arms embargo against belligerents, enabling Britain and France to purchase weapons in the United States as long as they transported them across the Atlantic on their own vessels. The following August, Roosevelt issued an executive order making it possible for Britain to purchase old U.S. destroyers. In return, the United States was granted access to bases on British possessions in the western Atlantic. Lend-Lease followed early in 1941, a program that provided naval vessels and other war-making capability to cash-strapped Allies. At roughly the same time, American and British officials began discussing joint war plans, and FDR ordered the U.S. Navy to help protect convoys in the Atlantic by tracking German vessels and reporting their positions to the British.[62]

The United States also started planning for a new postwar order in advance of its entry into World War II. Whether or not Americans would ultimately join the fight, many in Washington concurred that the Atlantic democracies had made costly mistakes during the 1930s. As Truman made clear in his closing address in San Francisco, U.S. statesmen firmly believed that the war might well have been avoided had the world's democracies banded together from the outset and taken resolute steps to block German and Japanese aggression. Rather than follow in Wilson's footsteps and risk a repeat of the 1930s, this time the United States would get an early start on postwar planning and the establishment of a viable mechanism for collective action.

In August 1941, Roosevelt traveled to Newfoundland to meet Britain's prime minister, Winston Churchill. High on the agenda was not just the conduct of the war in Europe, but also the shape of a desirable postwar order. As they worked over the text of the Atlantic Charter that emerged from their meeting, Churchill passed to Roosevelt a draft committing their two countries to "seek a peace which . . . by effective international organizations will afford to all States and peoples the means of dwelling in security." Roosevelt immediately deleted the reference to "effective international organizations," preferring instead to call for the disarmament of aggressors and to make only a vague reference to "a wider and permanent system of general security."[63] Mindful of the minefield of American politics, Roosevelt wanted to avoid language that would only invoke domestic "suspicions."[64]

The discussions widened to other parties during the following months, leading in January 1942 to the signing of the Declaration of the United Nations by the United States, Britain, the Soviet Union, China, and twenty-two other nations that had joined the war against the Axis powers. The Declaration committed the signatories to stand together until the defeat of their adversaries was ensured, and stated their common commitment to "life, liberty, and independence." Roosevelt and Churchill explicitly chose to refer to the pact as the Declaration of the United Nations rather than as an alliance in order to head off opposition from isolationists in Congress.[65]

Their tact, however, backfired. The liberal *New Republic*—whose editors had opposed the League of Nations because it did not go far enough in building a postwar order based on idealist principles—welcomed this move toward "a dynamic international union for the benefit of all." Roosevelt then had to rectify such misconceptions, insisting that the purpose of the Declaration was restricted to consolidating the coalition against Germany and Japan. He explicitly shunned any discussion of postwar international organizations.[66]

Responding to Roosevelt's carefully chosen rhetoric, most Americans assumed the U.S. government was preoccupied with the prosecution of the war. This perception induced anxious internationalists to pressure FDR to start building public support for America's involvement in managing the postwar order. But the president was deliberately holding off on public diplomacy, keeping quiet that U.S. officials were in fact working quite hard on postwar planning.

At the end of December 1941, Roosevelt had approved the formation of the Advisory Committee on Postwar Foreign Policy, a group that was to consist of both government officials and outside experts, enabling it to tap into the work being done at the Council on Foreign Relations, the Carnegie Endowment for International Peace, and other organizations interested in contributing to the formulation of foreign policy. The Advisory Committee began its work in February 1942. The secretary of state, Cordell Hull, explicitly charged the group with combating the "sinister influences" of isolationism and making "better preparations for world peace than was [sic] made at the close of the First World War."[67] The existence of the group and its work were kept out of the public eye. Better to formulate and carefully implement a strategy for building domestic support than to rush to the public with the administration's planning and risk stirring up the political battles that ultimately sank the League.

Within Roosevelt's inner circle, there was a firm consensus that the preservation of peace in the postwar world would require the establishment of a new international organization and America's participation as one of its leading members. Beyond that, however, opinions diverged widely. The principal disagreements concerned the nature of the obligations that member states would make to collective action, how decisions to combat aggression would be taken, and whose armies would do the fighting. At one end of the spectrum were the die-hard Wilsonians, who envisaged binding commitments to collective security and multinational forces that would stand at the ready. Vice President Henry Wallace was an outspoken proponent of this version of the United Nations, calling it a "second opportunity to make the world safe for democracy."[68] If economic sanctions failed to stop an aggressor state, Wallace argued, a multinational squadron of aircraft under the control of the United Nations "must at once bomb the aggressor nation mercilessly."[69]

On the other side were those, including Roosevelt himself, who were skeptical that the scheme envisaged by Wallace was either workable or politically feasible. Although he campaigned vigorously for American entry into the League of Nations, Roosevelt found Lodge's reservations sensible and admitted in 1919 that "I have read the draft of the League three times and always find something to object to in it."[70] Roosevelt thus gravitated toward a much more diluted notion of collective security, one that depended principally on cooperation among leading states—and would therefore fit more easily within the dictates of power politics and America's potent domestic constraints. Idealism and multilateralism had a place in U.S. foreign policy, but they had to be tempered by a strong dose of realism and respect for national autonomy.

Roosevelt's search for a compromise between an ideal form of collective security and the unadorned practice of realpolitik led him to the notion of the Four Policemen. Regardless of the nature of the institutions eventually built to preserve peace, Roosevelt reasoned, the strongest nations would still hold sway and exercise more influence than the rest. Rather than resist this unalterable reality, the cooperative management of the international system by the world's major states—the United States, Great Britain, the Soviet Union, and China—should be the guiding principle for designing the postwar order. Roosevelt's realist leanings led him to conclude that the great powers not only had to be in charge, but also that their different interests would put limits on the scope of cooperation, particularly in the military realm. Each nation was likely to care much more about its own sphere of influence than about developments far afield; a grave threat to one state might seem only a peripheral distraction to another.

Roosevelt accordingly had little interest in the likes of Wallace's scheme for a joint U.N. force. He was straightforward on this issue in his discussions with foreign leaders about the nature of a new postwar institution. In November 1943, Roosevelt told Joseph Stalin that Russia and Britain would have to provide the ground troops for peace operations outside the Western Hemisphere, with U.S. participation likely limited to air and naval support. Again, Roosevelt was searching for a middle ground—a security system ambitious enough to preserve peace, but not so demanding that it violated the bounds of America's national interests or its restricted appetite for liberal internationalism. "He is after workable minimums, not impossible maximums," a journalist for the *Saturday Evening Post* wrote of Roosevelt's plans for the postwar order after interviewing the president in March 1944.[71]

Roosevelt's vision evoked numerous objections. Sumner Welles, undersecretary of state and confidant of the president, feared the Four Policemen concept would alienate and arouse opposition from the world's smaller nations. Cordell Hull worried that each of the four powers would end up holding sway over its sphere of influence rather than collectively managing the whole. Britain's foreign minister, Anthony Eden, shared this concern, asserting that he "did not much like the idea of the Chinese running up and down the Pacific."[72]

Welles drafted a compromise memorandum in March 1943, sketching out an organization that tried to do justice to Roosevelt's ideas without violating the spirit of collective security. His outline called for an executive body restricted to the four great powers, an eleven-member council consisting of these four plus seven other countries selected to represent different regions, and a general assembly open to all nations. The United Nations that eventually came into being in 1945 bore close resemblance to Welles's early draft.[73] Roosevelt had found his middle ground.

.   .   .

ROOSEVELT exercised caution and pragmatism not only in designing a new postwar order but also in managing the domestic politics of securing U.S. participation. Whereas Wilson retained tight control over the League debate and failed to reach out to the supporters he would need to ensure ratification, FDR took a different course—he early on crafted a political strategy for building a bipartisan consensus behind the U.N. Like Wilson, Roosevelt was reluctant to engage in public debate as his ideas were taking shape. But while Wilson was acting out of stubbornness and concern about authorship, FDR was implementing his strategy, addressing the design and function of the U.N. only in vague and generic terms, and explicitly avoiding contentious topics, such as whether the United States would undertake binding commitments to joint military action.

The administration was particularly careful in its dealings with Congress. Roosevelt kept the issue of postwar planning off the congressional agenda until 1943. The House and Senate then debated resolutions that had been meticulously vetted and cleansed of language that could incite partisan combat. The House version, which passed in September by a vote of 360 to 29, called for "the creation of appropriate international machinery, with power adequate to establish and maintain a joint and lasting peace, among nations of the world, and as favoring participation by the United States therein through its constitutional processes." In stipulating the importance of America's "constitutional processes," the sponsors of the resolution were deliberately preempting objections from unilateralists and others concerned about U.S. sovereignty and autonomy.

The Senate then took up the issue, the *New York Times* noting that it was "the most important Senate debate on international affairs since the rejection of the Versailles Treaty and League of Nations Covenant nearly twenty-four years ago." The resolution was devoid of any mention of an international military force and of any more general American commitment to joint military action. It passed by a vote of 85 to 5. Senator Arthur Vandenberg, a potential skeptic who ended up playing a leading role in securing Republican support for the United Nations, made a statement that could have been Roosevelt's: "I am hunting for the middle ground between those extremists at one end of the line who would cheerfully give America away and those extremists at the other end of the line who would attempt a total isolation which has come to be an impossibility."[74]

From late 1943 until the end of the war, the administration pursued a dual track, mapping out detailed plans for the U.N. while working to strengthen the bipartisan consensus supporting U.S. participation. Roosevelt continued to tread a fine line between realist and idealist impulses and to prepare the political groundwork for the U.N., thus seeking to evade Wilson's ideological and tactical errors. Rather than design the ideal institution and set out to sell it to the American people, Roosevelt appreciated the inherent limits on America's appetite for engagement abroad and crafted his goals and his political strategy accordingly. Rather than pick fights with potential skeptics, he studiously avoided raising issues that he knew would engender opposition. Rather than insist that America make binding commitments to collective security, he preferred ambiguous and contingent commitments—precisely because he understood they would resonate with America's unilateralist impulse and its ambiguous and contingent brand of internationalism. As the president reassured potential skeptics during a news conference in 1944, the U.N. would create the mechanism for "talking things over with other Nations, without taking away the independence of the United States in any shape, manner, or form."[75]

Roosevelt's success in coaxing America out of its isolationist posture was a product not just of his legendary political skill. Ongoing industrialization helped his cause by leading to a realignment of regional interests that proved favorable to a more ambitious internationalism. In 1920, the North and West allied against the South to defeat the League. In 1945, the North and South allied against the West to ensure just the opposite—ratification of America's participation in the U.N.

This important realignment came about in the following manner. The South backed Roosevelt because it was still the stronghold of the Democratic Party and continued to be an ardent supporter of an open international economy. During the 1920s, the South had exported more than 60 percent of its annual cotton output. By the early 1940s, that figure had dropped to less than 20 percent because of the global protectionism of the 1930s and the disruption caused by the war itself.[76] Restoring the economic vitality of the region thus depended not only on winning the war, but also on rebuilding an open and stable international order of the type promised by the U.N.

The South had also warmed up to the idea of a military buildup and the stronger federalism that accompanied it. New bases and defense industries had opened in the southern states, bringing them a greater share of defense spending. And whereas the militarism of the late 1890s and early 1900s had been an outgrowth of imperial aspirations, which the South opposed, the militarism and enlarged government of the 1940s were needed for a more legitimate end—to defeat Germany and Japan. Although not ready to embrace an open-ended internationalism, the South was certainly prepared to combat the fascist regimes threatening world peace and the global economy. Furthermore, Roosevelt self-consciously kept civil rights off the national agenda to ensure the continued political support of southerners.

The most significant change in regional alignment took place in the Northeast, which had emerged as one of the world's leading centers of trade and finance. With its businesses now globally competitive, the Northeast was no longer protectionist and instead wanted full access to global markets and the international stability conducive to the free flow of capital. Ongoing urbanization also changed the political complexion of the North's electorate, with the inflow of immigrants and southern laborers giving the Democratic Party a much stronger foothold than before. Converging economic interests combined with the gaining strength of the Democrats to give Roosevelt an unprecedented opportunity to build a coalition between North and South. Despite a political and cultural rivalry that dated back to colonial times, and despite the strong strains of isolationism that had existed in both regions, the North and South finally came together to support a new brand of American internationalism.

The West and parts of the heartland were the primary holdouts. Farmers in the West continued to focus primarily on the domestic market and were less dependent than their southern counterparts on exports. Limited urbanization also meant the preservation of more traditional agrarian values, including libertarian strains of isolationism and unilateralism. Senator Gerald Nye of North Dakota harkened back to Jefferson's and Jackson's concerns about the tyranny of the center. The real danger to America, Nye insisted, did not come from Germany or Japan, but from "the encroachments upon our constitutional status, and the impairment of the regular process of our government by the forces within the Government itself."[77] Representative Stephen Day of Illinois was more concerned about potential encroachments on American sovereignty, accusing those favoring U.S. participation in the U.N. of seeking "to consummate the surrender of our American independence and the return of the United States into the British empire."[78] Such strident appeals, however, found fewer adherents than they had during the debate over the League of Nations. And without the North as a political ally, the West had insufficient population and political clout to turn back the rising tide of liberal internationalism.

The final ingredient in Roosevelt's plan for ensuring America's full engagement in shaping and running the postwar order was his astute management of partisan politics. Whereas Wilson snubbed the Republicans and the Senate from the outset, Roosevelt did just the opposite. He co-opted them through engagement. In 1940, FDR appointed two internationalist Republicans to his cabinet—Henry Stimson as secretary of war and Frank Knox as secretary of the navy. In 1942, the administration invited two senators to join its secret advisory group on postwar planning. One, Warren Austin of Vermont, was a Republican.

Roosevelt also enlisted Wendell Willkie, the Republican candidate whom he had defeated in the 1940 election, to help build an internationalist center within the Republican Party. Especially after Pearl Harbor, Willkie devoted his public life to the internationalist cause, convincing the Republican National Committee to adopt a resolution in 1942 acknowledging that after the war "the responsibility of the nation will not be circumscribed within the territorial limits of the United States." The *New York Times* consequently credited him with "removing the brand of isolationism from the Republican party."[79] When the Republicans, including some prominent isolationists, did well in the 1942 elections, Roosevelt again turned to Willkie, asking him to undertake a world tour to attract public attention to foreign affairs. Upon his return, Willkie published *One World*, part travel chronicle and part advocacy for U.S. internationalism, which quickly became an influential best-seller.

Roosevelt resorted to similar tactics to ensure that partisan politics did not interfere with ratification. At the request of Hull, the Senate in April 1944 formed the Committee of Eight to consult with the administration as plans for the U.N. began to take final form. The committee consisted of four Democrats, three Republicans, and one Progressive. When American, British, Russian, and Chinese diplomats gathered in August at Dumbarton Oaks, an elegant Georgetown estate, to work out the details, Hull consulted regularly with the Committee of Eight. And when it came time to select a delegation to send to San Francisco the following year, Roosevelt insisted that it include equal numbers of congressional Republicans and Democrats. In a cable to London from his post at the British embassy in Washington, Isaiah Berlin noted that the U.S. delegation "in fact looks almost as carefully balanced though possibly not so well together as a rowing eight."[80]

Such careful attention to building bipartisan support could not disarm the die-hard isolationists and unilateralists, who still feared that the United States was submitting its will to a "godless, soulless, international Frankenstein."[81] But it did succeed in insulating debate about America's role in the world from the worst of party politics. John Foster Dulles, an internationalist Republican who would soon become President Eisenhower's secretary of state, lamented the loss of his party's candidate to Roosevelt in 1944. But he was pleased, he told his brother Allen, that "we succeeded in keeping the world organization out of politics. I think that was, at least, one important precedent established."[82]

Roosevelt's task was made infinitely easier by the many private organizations that had emerged to support liberal internationalism among the American public. In contrast to Wilson, who had shunned the League to Enforce Peace, Roosevelt made good use of these available sources of political support. Already active during the 1920s and 1930s, these associations increased in number and in the scope of their programs in response to the war and the second chance it offered to guide the United States into some type of collective security system. The Council on Foreign Relations, the Foreign Policy Association, the Committee to Defend America, and the United Nations Association, to name a few, worked closely with the administration to alter public attitudes. "Public opinion must be mobilized now," one of the leaders of the internationalist movement said in March 1941, "so that America will play an effective part in the organization of a lasting peace and will this time see the job through."[83]

The work of these groups complemented official efforts. During the six months following the Dumbarton Oaks conference, State Department officials made some three hundred speeches across the country. The department also tapped Alfred Hitchcock to direct a movie on postwar foreign policy and the role of the United Nations. The movie, entitled *Watchtower over Tomorrow,* was written by Hitchcock and the playwright Ben Hecht, and narrated by Edward Stettinius, who succeeded Hull as secretary of state in December 1944. In the words of Stettinius, the film "dealt with the proposed international organization in dramatic form by projecting into the future and telling the story of its operation in stopping an unnamed potential aggressor about the year 1960."[84]

This partnership between private groups and public officials had a telling impact on American opinion. In May 1941, only 37 percent of the public favored joining an international institution to preserve peace at the war's end. That figure climbed steadily over the next four years, reaching 55 percent in 1942, 72 percent in 1944, and 81 percent in March 1945.[85]

By the time the Senate voted on the U.N. treaty in July 1945, Roosevelt, despite his untimely death in April, had succeeded in laying the groundwork for ratification. He had constructed a U.N. that contained equal parts realism and idealism, appealing to the middle-of-the-road internationalism he thought sustainable. He stitched together a political coalition of North and South, marginalizing the isolationist and unilateralist instincts that still held sway in the West. He worked tirelessly to build bipartisan support for the U.N., sidestepping the political rancor that had plagued U.S. foreign policy from its early days. And he helped orchestrate a campaign of public education to convince the American people that the time had come for them to accept the responsibilities of international leadership. More than 150 years into the life of the United States, more than 50 years after the country's arrival as a great power, Roosevelt had built a brand of internationalism sturdy enough to maintain America's steady, multilateral engagement in shaping and managing global affairs.

FDR CRAFTED a bipartisan consensus that was to serve the country well for the next half century. The internationalism he forged provided a political foundation not just for America's struggle against fascism and its entry into the U.N., but also for the long and trying years of the Cold War. Furthermore, Roosevelt succeeded in convincing Americans of the merits of not only global engagement, but of a liberal, multilateral brand. After enthusiastically joining the U.N., the United States proceeded to fashion a broad network of political and economic institutions to help manage the international system. America had overcome its isolationist roots as well as its aversion to institutional entanglements. It would be premature, however, to conclude that Roosevelt in fact brought about a permanent change of course, enabling America to leave behind isolationism and unilateralism for good. For it is important to keep in mind the role that a major external threat has played in underwriting the liberal internationalism of the last six decades.

The United States was a strategic spectator during the 1930s, watching idly as militaristic regimes in Germany and Japan rearmed and engaged in repeated acts of aggression. Not even the outbreak of the war in Europe was enough to secure America's direct involvement, which came only after Japan's surprise attack on Pearl Harbor. The war then served as an ideal backdrop for Roosevelt's efforts to build a new internationalism, arming him with a compelling case that the United States had to take urgent steps both to defeat the Axis nations and to put in place a postwar mechanism for preserving peace. Had it not been for the threat posed to America's welfare by the prospect of German and Japanese control of much of the industrialized world, the United States may well have remained in its comfortable shell.

Despite America's contribution to the war effort and its enthusiastic entry into the U.N., it is by no means clear that the internationalist fervor that mounted during the course of the war would have been sustained had it not been for the speedy emergence of a new threat from the Soviet Union. Unmistakable signs of the beginning of a retreat arose soon after the war ended. During the two years following the end of hostilities, defense spending fell from $81 to $13 billion, and troop levels from 12.1 to 1.6 million. President Truman ran up against congressional opposition when trying to win approval for foreign assistance to Allies struggling to rebuild their economies. And when it became clear that the Soviet Union was emerging as America's new adversary, the administration had to resort to scare tactics to mobilize public support for the task of containing communism.

In laying out the Truman Doctrine in March 1947, the president deliberately overstated the threat posed by the Soviet Union in order to rouse the public. Truman told his advisers that winning support for the more ambitious foreign policy needed to stand up to the Soviets would require the "greatest selling job ever facing a President." Cold War historian John Gaddis called the Truman Doctrine "a form of shock therapy: it was a last-ditch effort by the Administration to prod Congress and the American people into accepting the responsibilities of . . . world leadership."[86]

Truman's efforts worked well to galvanize the support of the public behind economic aid, rearmament, and the formation of the alliance network needed to contain communism. Indeed, his salesmanship worked too well, stoking a fervent anticommunism and helping provide a platform for Senator Joseph McCarthy's efforts to purge the country of those engaging in "un-American" activities. But amid the excesses, the Truman administration's public outreach—coupled with growing Soviet intransigence, the communist victory in China in 1949, and Moscow's test of an atomic weapon that same year—helped to create a solid and durable domestic consensus behind America's global engagement.

The Vietnam War did crack that consensus, encouraging the American public to question the merits of global engagement and weakening the internationalism that had firmed up with the onset of the Cold War. In 1964, only 18 percent of the public agreed with the statement that "the United States should mind its own business internationally and let other countries get along as best as they can on their own." By 1974, 41 percent of respondents agreed with this statement.[87] It was in this more fluid political environment that President Richard Nixon decided to pursue détente with the Soviet Union and establish ties with China. Nixon also offered up his own doctrine, one intended to reduce the burdens stemming from America's overseas commitments by expecting regional allies to rely more heavily on their own manpower should local conflicts break out.[88] Even as the domestic backlash against the Vietnam War made room for this more flexible diplomacy, however, it did not erode America's internationalist foundations. The ongoing East-West divide, the Soviet invasion of Afghanistan in 1979, and the continuing need to contain the spread of communism kept Americans vigilant and engaged.

Now that the Cold War is over, the Soviet Union gone, and communism struggling to survive in only a handful of countries, America must craft a new internationalism that befits a new world. In the wake of the events of September 11, 2001, many observers were quick to pronounce that the attacks against New York and Washington would serve as the Pearl Harbor of the twenty-first century, with the battle against terrorism providing a new foundation for American internationalism. But logic suggests otherwise.

The struggle against terrorism will be long and difficult, with many of the countermeasures taking place beyond public view. Although the military component of the battle—its most visible element—went well when fighting the Taliban and Al-Qaeda in Afghanistan, the direct application of superior force will not always be possible. Success will therefore be hard to measure, risking that patriotism will gradually turn back into indifference. Furthermore, when America does act, it may well feel compelled to do so alone, forsaking the international institutions that it worked so hard to put in place after World War II. At home, America now patrols its borders, shores, and public spaces with far more vigilance, raising its guard against outside threats. And should attacks on American targets continue abroad and in the U.S., the voices in favor of retrenchment may well grow stronger. As the founding fathers vigorously and repeatedly asked, why should America involve itself in distant lands and their troubles if doing so ultimately brings harm to America's shores?

America's current predicament thus provides much cause for concern. As a rule, the United States has kept to itself. Only when confronted with a grave threat to its security has it contravened the admonitions of the founders and become directly involved in shaping the balance of power outside its immediate neighborhood. There are two exceptions: the late 1890s, when the United States flirted, quite temporarily, with formal imperialism; and the 1990s, when the internationalist momentum left behind by the Cold War and America's predominance kept the United States globally engaged virtually by default. As the nation enters this new century, it faces a serious threat from international terrorism. But this threat is both elusive and sporadic, meaning it may over the long term do more to erode liberal internationalism than to rebuild it. It is in this context that America's past provides a sobering backdrop to its future.

CHAPTER SIX

The Limits of American Internationalism—Looking Ahead

ABOUT 5 PERCENT of America's present population is old enough to have been an adult during the early 1940s and to have witnessed firsthand the quiet revolution in U.S. internationalism that took place over the course of World War II. It is hardly surprising that most of the country, after four decades of the Cold War, one more coasting along in unchallenged supremacy, and then the shock of a terrorist attack on the homeland, voices support for continued international engagement and remains none too worried about the prospect of a world absent its global guardian.

But amid this complacency, there are quiet signs that America's past is catching up with its present. It was not without reason, after all, that Alexander Hamilton counseled President Washington that America's predisposition against involvement in Old World affairs was a "general principle of policy" based on geopolitical realities, not a function of temporary conditions. Hamilton was of course right; the risk of terrorist attacks notwithstanding, the United States still has benign neighbors to its north and south and protective oceans to its east and west. Hamilton also counseled that America should aim at becoming "an ascendant" primarily in its own hemisphere. That George W. Bush from his early days as a candidate made clear his intention to focus U.S. foreign policy on the Americas certainly has historical resonance. President Bush's first two meetings with foreign leaders were with Canadian Prime Minster Jean Chrétien and Mexican President Vicente Fox. His first major international meeting was a Summit of the Americas in Quebec.

Furthermore, populist themes have been making a comeback, at least in certain areas of the country.[1] They have less traction in coastal cities, where most policy-makers and foreign affairs analysts spend much of their time. But they have strong appeal in the agrarian South and Mountain West, where those same elites rarely venture. Bush's ability to tap into these political currents clearly played an important role in his victory in the 2000 election. His personal style and his policy positions harkened back to central elements of the populist tradition: defending states' rights, limiting the authority of the federal government, reducing taxes, distrusting Washington's entrenched elites, reining in America's foreign commitments, and backing away from liberal internationalism and multilateral institutions. One need only glance at the electoral map to detect the strong correlation between traditional regional divides and the appeal of Bush's message. Al Gore carried the more urbanized states on the coasts and much of the Midwest, while Bush won the rest.

The emergence of a more reluctant and unilateralist brand of internationalism is not, however, a temporary phenomenon born of the momentary predilections of a president who happens to hail from Texas. Rather, American internationalism and the grand strategy that emerges from it have been in the process of adapting to fundamental geopolitical change. The end of the Cold War and the absence of a major adversary have been gradually cycling through domestic politics, slowly but surely eroding support for the global activism of the recent past. Americans have justifiably been starting to ask whether it is fair that they should continue to shoulder an inordinate share of the burden of managing international order. Without the disciplining effects of the communist threat, America's traditional aversion to entangling institutions is returning as well, pushing aside the enthusiasm for multilateralism that emerged amid World War II.

America's political landscape is also changing in ways that will affect the country's engagement abroad. Younger Americans who did not live through the defining events of World War II or the Cold War are now rising to positions of prominence. Economic interdependence, the information revolution, and international terrorism will likely inoculate them against isolationism, but they will not be automatic internationalists like many of their elders. The population and political influence of the South and Mountain West are growing, strengthening the constituency in favor of a more unilateralist foreign policy and potentially leading to a widening cultural and political gap with the coasts. Building internationalist coalitions across region and party may well grow more difficult. The country's Hispanic population is also expanding dramatically. Especially because Americans of Hispanic descent tend to concentrate in important electoral states like Texas, Florida, and California, Central and South America are likely to figure much more prominently in the formulation of U.S. foreign policy. Taken together, international and domestic changes are bringing back the more contingent and contentious brand of internationalism that guided America for much of its past.

A RELUCTANT AMERICA

AMERICA'S growing ambivalence about the scope of its global role does have its upside. The current absence of great-power competition stems not just from America's might, but also from its political character. The United States has had sufficient strength to coerce and exploit at will, but instead has coupled its extraordinary capability with relatively benign intent. That is why other countries have not been rushing to join arms to counter a predominant America. And this restrained behavior explains why even Mexico, a nation long suspicious of the bully to its north and well versed in anti-American politics, has altered course and is studiously trying to link its economy and its identity to the United States. As President Fox made clear, he wants his country and the United States to "become real friends, real partners, and real neighbors."[2]

It is to the benefit of all that the only superpower around has been by historical standards a restrained one, but there is a worrisome downside. Cultural and political limits on the country's appetite for internationalism help produce a centrist and moderate policy abroad. If America's appetite were to diminish too far, however, then a policy of moderation could become one of neglect. Today, America is more a reluctant sheriff than a hungry hegemon.[3] If the United States loses interest in being the sheriff, there would be no one to form the posse.

Consider the record of the last decade. Saddam Hussein's army invaded Kuwait in the summer of 1990. In response, Washington amassed some 700,000 troops, including 540,000 Americans, proceeded to expel Iraqi forces from Kuwait, and spent the rest of the decade boxing in the Iraqi regime. The same went for the Balkans. Slobodan Milosevic, Europe's most recent ethnic cleanser, turned his twisted ambition to Bosnia and Kosovo. An American-led coalition eventually stepped in, stopping the bloodshed in Bosnia and then driving Serb troops from Kosovo. Washington proceeded to support Serbia's democratic opposition, which eventually overthrew Milosevic, arrested him, and sent him to the war crimes tribunal in The Hague. American forces remain in the region to monitor the uneasy peace. So too did Washington respond with speed and vigor to the terrorist attacks of September 2001. Within days of the calamity, thousands of U.S. troops, hundreds of aircraft, and dozens of warships were on their way to the Middle East.

But there were also clear limits to U.S. action. Saddam Hussein and his repressive regime survived military defeat because the elder George Bush was not willing to run the risks of invading and occupying Baghdad. Although oil supplies were at stake, the Senate resolution authorizing the war against Iraq passed by only a few votes (52 to 47). Colin Powell, then chairman of the Joint Chiefs, opposed going to war against Iraq.[4] Bill Clinton's unwillingness to send ground troops to Yugoslavia to protect Kosovo and topple Milosevic stemmed from similar concerns about whether the interests at stake warranted the risk of high U.S. casualties. Even with Clinton's pledge to avoid the introduction of forces on the ground, the U.S. House of Representatives made clear its lack of enthusiasm for the war.

America's response to terror attacks against the homeland admittedly met with none of this reluctance. Congress and the American people firmly backed military retaliation. These circumstances were, however, unique. It was the United States itself that had been attacked and wounded, not an oil-producing ally in the Persian Gulf or a struggling minority group in the Balkans. Furthermore, the new demands of the war against terrorism are likely to cut into America's willingness to take on more traditional missions.

If America's politics soon come to rein in its foreign policy, the United States might well bow out before others are prepared to fill the void. With no one around to mind the store, incremental threats of the sort that recently emerged in the Middle East and the Balkans would go unchecked. No other country has the combination of military capability and political clout needed to put together a campaign of the size that drove Iraqi troops from Kuwait, forced the Yugoslav army from Kosovo, or brought down Saddam Hussein's regime. Had the United States not reined in Hussein, he might still be in power today, perhaps with control over much of the region's oil. And had the United States not intervened in the Balkans, the peninsula could well have descended into turmoil, destabilizing southeastern Europe and irreversibly damaging the credibility of the European Union.

THIS DESCRIPTION of the future is no fantasy. It is the world toward which we are likely headed. Fittingly enough, even the end of America's unipolar moment may be made in America. Along with the history of the nation's reluctant engagement in world affairs, basic suppositions about the determinants of grand strategy reinforce the claim that U.S. willingness to shoulder the burdens of global engagement will be diminishing in the years ahead.

Figuring out how America's domestic politics will affect its behavior abroad necessitates clarifying what motivates external ambition to begin with. And here it is important to distinguish between satisfied and rising powers. Satisfied powers are those that have reached the top of the pecking order, are happy with their lot, and are primarily interested in preserving the status quo. In contrast, rising powers are states on the move. They are not satisfied with their lot, are usually struggling for recognition and influence, and are therefore looking for ways to overturn the status quo. In general terms, satisfied states extend commitments abroad when they must, not when they can. They are motivated by necessity rather than opportunity. Rising states extend commitments abroad when they can, not when they must. They are motivated by opportunity rather than necessity.

The United States is a satisfied power. It worked hard to construct the current international system, and it is one that for the most part safeguards and extends American interests and values. America should therefore be prepared to invest in preserving the status quo and in combating threats to its homeland. But it should not be looking to take on a new array of commitments. On the contrary, it should be looking to shed some of the heavier responsibilities that it accumulated during the demanding years of the Cold War.

From this perspective, there is something wrong about the story of the 1990s. The Cold War ended when Russia let go of its satellites in Eastern Europe. The Soviet Union then broke up and Russia itself lapsed into disrepair. The central rationale for America's extensive network of overseas commitments was gone. Nonetheless, the United States not only maintained its numerous and wide-ranging Cold War commitments, but actually enlarged them.

NATO, which by treaty obligates all members to defend each other, recently took in three new countries and is already preparing for the next wave of entrants. In the aftermath of the war for Kosovo, much of the former Yugoslavia has essentially become a ward of NATO. America's strategic commitments in Europe have thus increased markedly since 1990—and are still growing. In East Asia, the United States has expanded the scope of its defense alliance with Japan, and the U.S. Navy has been augmenting its access to bases in Southeast Asia. In Latin America, the United States has been drawn into the conflict between Colombia's government and its drug-running rebels. And all this occurred before the events of September 2001 refocused the country's attention on matters of foreign affairs. Strange behavior for a satisfied power that, according to geopolitical logic, ought to be reining in its commitments, not multiplying them.

The best explanation for this odd behavior is that the past decade has been an anomaly rather than a good indicator of the future direction of U.S. policy. The Cold War is over, but American officials and elected representatives have still been operating according to the old assumptions. After all, most of the individuals running foreign policy since 1990 cut their teeth during the long years of the Cold War: On Capitol Hill, Lee Hamilton, Joseph Biden, and Jesse Helms. In the first Bush administration, James Baker, Brent Scowcroft, and Richard Cheney. Under Clinton, Warren Christopher, Les Aspin, and Anthony Lake. And under George W. Bush, Cheney, Donald Rumsfeld, and Paul Wolfowitz. After spending most of their careers fighting the Soviet Union, these individuals have brought to the table preconceptions of an expansive American role in the world.

The past decade was in another important respect an aberration rather than a good predictor of the future. America during the 1990s enjoyed an unprecedented economic boom. Awash in budget surpluses, neither Democrats nor Republicans were pushing hard to trim the defense budget. In an era of plenty, husbanding resources was not a priority. The country was flush with cash and feeling good about it—a state of being conducive to an activist, expansive, and expensive foreign policy.

The 1990s were remarkable in one final respect. American forces were regularly deployed in combat, but they suffered few casualties. Half a million Americans were involved in the Gulf War. Thankfully, only 147 were killed in action. During the Clinton years, U.S. personnel saw combat in the Middle East, Africa, the Balkans, and Haiti. In Somalia, 18 servicemen were killed in a firefight, and Clinton promptly withdrew U.S. troops. Everywhere else, the U.S. fought without losing a single soldier in combat. Quite a testimony to the quality and superiority of America's military, but also an illusory test of America's mettle.

The three conditions that helped make America so magnanimous and expansive during the 1990s are anything but durable. Turnover is changing the complexion of Capitol Hill. More than 50 percent of current senators and more than 60 percent of current representatives first took office after 1992. Americans who entered college after the fall of the Berlin Wall are already occupying positions of influence. They will not bring to the table the potent historical memories— Munich, Pearl Harbor, the rebuilding of Europe, the Iron Curtain— that have served as the intellectual and political foundation of U.S. internationalism over the past five decades. And as Karl Mannheim noted in his classic essay on the political effects of generational change, "Early impressions tend to coalesce into a *natural view* of the world," one that colors attitudes and shapes how individuals interpret incoming information throughout their lives.[5]

Public opinion surveys reveal that age cohort has a significant impact on attitudes toward social and cultural issues, but less impact on attitudes toward foreign policy.[6] Most of the data used in these polls was collected during the Cold War, however, when one would expect the East-West conflict to reproduce similar positions across different generations. The end of the Cold War should mean, after a decent time lag, changing perspectives among younger Americans. Opinion polls have already begun to indicate that Americans between eighteen and twenty-nine years of age are less concerned about international affairs than their elders.[7]

The cause of this diminishing enthusiasm for internationalism goes beyond the absence of a major external challenger. Younger Americans are also devoting less time to the study of history than did older generations. A 1999 survey of America's top fifty-five universities and colleges revealed that none of them required students to take a course in U.S. history, and that 78 percent of them did not require any history courses at all. Of seniors at these institutions participating in the poll, only 35 percent could name the U.S. president in office when the Korean War broke out, and only 40 percent knew that the Battle of the Bulge occurred during World War II. National exams have also revealed a very poor command of history among high school seniors.[8]

Younger Americans are unlikely to be isolationist; they have more opportunities for travel than their elders and many of them are partaking of the globalized economy with gusto. But being cosmopolitan and worldly is not the same thing as being internationalist. It took war against Germany and Japan and the struggle against Soviet communism, after all, to instill America's midcentury elite with internationalist fervor. Furthermore, that generation's professional class regularly served in the armed forces. Not so among today's rising economic and political elites. Nor will the searing images of hijacked planes flying into the World Trade Center offer a steady backdrop for rebuilding internationalism similar to that provided by World War II or the Cold War. For better or for worse, Americans coming of age after 1990 will have tasted the fear of terrorism, but they will not have known geopolitical urgency firsthand. And many of them will not even know it through the study of history. As these individuals become the principal shapers of opinion and policy, the reflexive internationalism of the 1990s is likely to dissipate.

The boom of the 1990s also came to an end. Support for free trade, difficult to come by during the 1990s, is therefore likely to be in short supply. George W. Bush did win the House's approval of fast-track negotiating authority in July 2002, but only by a few votes and only after acquiescing to new protection for the textile industry. Parsimony will gradually spread into the security realm, intensifying the domestic debate over burden-sharing and calls within Congress for America's regional partners to shoulder more defense responsibilities. After the terrorist attacks of September 2001, it took Congress only a few days to approve—by unanimous votes in both chambers—$40 billion in emergency funding, much of which went to the military. But these were extraordinary times. As budget deficits replace surpluses, largess is likely to give way to relative austerity, and activism to a more moderate and diffident engagement. It is worth noting that before the events of September 2001, Secretary of Defense Rumsfeld, despite the conservative and promilitary orientation of the Bush administration, was engaged in a battle with the White House and Congress to secure financial support for his program of defense reform.

Finally, the human toll that comes with the role of global guardian will eventually mount. It may be a suicide bomber targeting an American barracks, as in Lebanon in 1983. It may be that America finds itself in battle against an adversary more worthy than Iraq, Yugoslavia, or the Taliban. Whatever the scenario, whoever is in office, the political backlash could be severe. In laying the groundwork for the military component of the struggle against terrorism, President Bush went out of his way to warn Americans that U.S. casualties were likely. Nonetheless, the initial attack against Afghanistan was conducted largely from the air, with the United States limiting its combat presence in the country to special units, instead relying heavily on local opponents of the Taliban to carry out ground operations. U.S. soldiers entered Afghanistan in significant numbers only after the Taliban was already near collapse. And even after the enemy's main forces had been defeated, the Pentagon restricted the mission of U.S. troops and did not task them with searching caves and other hideouts in the Tora Bora region, perhaps contributing to the ability of the Al-Qaeda leadership to slip away. Similar restrictions were not in place during the 2003 campaign against Iraq, with U.S. ground troops entering the country in large numbers. American casualties were fortunately low. But should they mount in a future conflict, the toll on America's appetite for intervention could be considerable.

These trend lines are more than hypothetical. Numerous warning signs suggest that U.S. internationalism is already in retreat. The terror attacks on New York and Washington did evoke national unity and an outpouring of enthusiasm for military action. But this was only a temporary spike in bipartisan support for internationalism and should not be allowed to mask the broader trends. Here is the picture that was emerging prior to the events of September 2001—and the picture that will likely reemerge as those events slowly recede into the past.

America's diplomatic corps, once a magnet for the country's best graduates, had lost much of its professional allure. Many of the more talented Foreign Service officers that the State Department did attract during the 1990s left in frustration after only a few years. According to the *New York Times*, "The State Department, the institution responsible for American diplomacy around the world, is finding it hard to adjust to an era in which financial markets pack more punch than a Washington-Moscow summit meeting. It is losing recruits to investment banks, dot-com companies and the Treasury and Commerce Departments, which have magnified their foreign policy roles."[9]

Public opinion surveys paint a similar picture. Regular surveys by the Chicago Council on Foreign Relations and other bodies indicate that Americans remained generally internationalist throughout the

1990s.[10] However, the public's interest in foreign affairs did decline sharply. During the Cold War, a pressing geopolitical issue of the day usually ranked near the top of the public's concerns. By the end of the 1990s, only 2 to 3 percent of Americans viewed foreign policy as a primary concern. When Americans were asked to name the "two or three biggest foreign-policy problems facing the United States today," the most popular response was "don't know." A solid majority indicated that events in other parts of the world have "very little" impact on the United States. As James Lindsay of the Brookings Institution summed up the situation in *Foreign Affairs,* "Americans endorse internationalism in theory but seldom do anything about it in practice."[11] At the opening of the twenty-first century, Americans thus did not oppose their country's engagement in the world. They had just become profoundly apathetic about it.

It is precisely because of this attention deficit that newspapers, magazines, and the broadcast networks dramatically cut back foreign coverage. In a competitive industry driven by market share and advertisement fees per second, the media gave America what it wanted. The spillover into the political arena was all too apparent. With foreign policy getting so little traction among the public, it had all but fallen off the political radar screen. Virtually every foreign matter that came before Congress, including questions of war and peace, turned into a partisan sparring match. Peter Trubowitz, a political scientist at the University of Texas, has documented that partisan conflict over foreign policy rose dramatically in the recent past.[12] Clinton's scandals and his repeated standoffs with an alienated Republican leadership no doubt played a role in pushing relations between the two parties to the boiling point. That even foreign policy was held hostage, however, made clear that America's politics and priorities had entered a new era.

Partisan politics trumped the demands of international leadership with worrisome regularity. Important ambassadorial posts remained empty throughout the Clinton years because Republicans on the Senate Foreign Relations Committee refused to confirm the president's nominees. In August 2000, Peter Burleigh resigned from the State Department after waiting nine months for the Senate to confirm his appointment as ambassador to the Philippines.[13] Burleigh was widely recognized as one of America's most accomplished diplomats. America's dues to the United Nations went unpaid for most of the decade to keep happy the antiabortion wing of the Republican Party, which thought the U.N.'s approach to family planning too aggressive. The

Senate in 1999 rejected the treaty banning the testing of nuclear weapons despite the administration's willingness to shelve it. Better to embarrass Clinton than to behave responsibly on matters of war and peace.

In the wake of these episodes, Senator Chuck Hagel, a Republican from Nebraska, tried to offer a reassuring explanation of his party's behavior. Reflecting on the apparent assault on internationalism, Hagel commented that "what this is about on the Republican side is a deep dislike and distrust for President Clinton."[14] But these are hardly comforting words. A considered and sincere isolationism is preferable to the cynical disregard of matters of global importance due to partisanship.

The battle for Kosovo, largely because it entailed sending U.S. personnel into combat, provided an excellent vantage point from which to view this new and more ambivalent brand of American internationalism. Posturing and positioning were all too easy when debating NATO expansion, treaty commitments in East Asia, or defense spending—issues that in the near term require primarily paper commitments, pledges of good faith, and budget authorization. Putting lives on the line was a better litmus test of internationalism's limits.

On the surface, NATO's battle for Kosovo appeared to confirm the durability of American internationalism. The United States led NATO into battle, Washington effectively ran the air campaign, and Clinton held course until Milosevic caved in and withdrew from Kosovo. Upon a closer reading, however, a different picture comes into focus.

The United States spent the first half of the decade trying to avoid entanglement in the bloodshed spawned by the breakup of Yugoslavia. The ineffectiveness of intervention by the U.N. and the EU and the American public's mounting unease about the ongoing slaughter—the massacre at Srebrenica in July 1995 and the shelling of Sarajevo's outdoor market the following month were turning points—eventually induced Clinton to approve the use of force. A few days of U.S. air strikes against Bosnian Serb positions, coupled with a ground offensive by Croat and Muslim armies, finally brought the parties to the negotiating table in 1995. The Clinton administration then fashioned the Dayton Accords, which halted the violence, but only by confirming the position of Slobodan Milosevic, the mastermind behind the breakup of Bosnia, as the region's power-broker.

When Milosevic next turned his sights on Kosovo in 1998, the United States again sought to avoid military involvement. But the deepening crisis encouraged Clinton to resort to coercive air strikes for a second time, the air campaign beginning on March 24, 1999. Washington expected Milosevic to capitulate within a matter of days, similarly to Serb forces in Bosnia. When he did not, the Clinton team was in a state of virtual paralysis.[15] Despite weeks of an air campaign that only expedited the humanitarian crisis in Kosovo, Clinton kept U.S. aircraft at 15,000 feet—where they were relatively immune from ground fire, but also much less effective against intended targets. He also kept the introduction of NATO ground troops off the table, even though doing so weakened NATO's coercive leverage and encouraged Milosevic to ride out the air campaign.

Nor was Congress any help. A month into the war, the House voted overwhelmingly to refuse funding for sending U.S. soldiers to Yugoslavia without congressional approval. The House could not even muster the courage to pass a resolution endorsing the bombing campaign (the vote was 213 to 213). Despite the eventual success of the air operation and the absence of a single NATO combat casualty, the Senate's main reaction to the war was to pass a resolution berating Europe for its military weakness.

Since the end of the Kosovo conflict, the United States has tried to limit the extent of its involvement in monitoring the uneasy peace. The EU has had no choice but to contribute most of the troops to the peacekeeping mission (KFOR) in Kosovo and to take the lead on economic reconstruction. Even before the end of the fighting, Clinton promised Americans in his 1999 Memorial Day address that "when the peacekeeping force goes in there [Kosovo], the overwhelming majority of people will be European; and that when the reconstruction begins, the overwhelming amount of investment will be European."[16] When KFOR was deployed shortly thereafter, American troops (which represented less than 15 percent of the total) were sent to the east of Kosovo, where the likelihood of violence was presumed to be lower. In February 2000, a small contingent of U.S. soldiers was dispatched to the northern city of Mitrovica to help quell ethnic violence. When they were stoned by angry Serbs, the Pentagon responded by ordering them back to their sector, making clear that Washington was prepared to undercut the KFOR commander on the ground and put U.S. forces under special restrictions.[17]

Despite the unusual protections afforded U.S. troops, American lawmakers continued to complain about the need for Europe to do more. Republican Senator John Warner, chairman of the Armed Services Committee, in March 2000 pledged to withhold half of the $2 billion appropriation for American troops in Kosovo unless European nations augmented their financial contributions to the U.N. efforts there.[18] Democratic Senator Robert Byrd proposed that the United States should turn over to the EU the peacekeeping and reconstruction effort in Kosovo and withdraw U.S. troops from the region in a timely fashion.[19] Congress certainly appeared to have lost interest in underwriting European security.

The election of George W. Bush only strengthened these basic sentiments. Vice President Cheney made clear during the campaign that "troops on the ground, in Europe, in the Balkans in particular . . . strikes me [as] an appropriate role for our European friends and allies."[20] After months of equivocation on the topic—and protests from America's European allies—President Bush finally announced that U.S. troops would remain in the Balkans after all. But when fighting broke out in Macedonia in March 2001, despite the potential for a bloodbath between Macedonian Slavs and the country's sizable ethnic Albanian minority, the Bush administration essentially vetoed direct American involvement. NATO's secretary general, Lord Robertson, asked member states to enlarge their military presence in Kosovo to help prevent the flow of arms and personnel to Macedonia. The United States passed on that too. And when NATO sent troops into Macedonia in August to disarm the Albanian rebels in the wake of a peace accord, the United States took on a minimal role. Only U.S. troops already stationed in the country to support peacekeeping operations in Kosovo joined in, and their mission was restricted to providing European troops logistical support and intelligence. Soon thereafter, Secretary of Defense Rumsfeld suggested that NATO start making preparations for reducing its presence in Bosnia by one-third.

The battle for Kosovo and its aftermath made clear that the domestic consensus behind America's dominant strategic role in Europe had cracked. Democrats and Republicans alike came to the realization that Europe's strategic dependence on the United States was neither fair nor politically sustainable. Europe would be unwise to interpret the warnings continuing to come from Washington as idle threats emerging from yet another passing preoccupation with burden-sharing. The Soviet Union has collapsed, the EU is thriving, and Europe had better realize that it may well be on its own. The Bush administration's initial efforts to scale back America's role on the Korean peninsula, in the Middle East, and in other hot spots suggest that Europe may not be the only region to feel the effects of America's dimming interest in retaining the role of global guardian.

A UNILATERAL AMERICA

THE WANING OF U.S. internationalism will have major consequences for a world that has grown accustomed to American primacy. Its impact will be magnified, however, by the fact that a diminishing appetite for international engagement is being accompanied by a second potent trend—increasing unilateralism. At the same time that the United States has been tiring of its global role, it has also been gravitating toward a go-it-alone attitude.

A stingy internationalism combined with a prickly unilateralism is a lethal mix, the worst of both worlds. The United States has been retreating from the stage and distancing itself from troubles abroad, but then refusing to work with others to fill the gap, fearful that deferring to other states means diminished influence. But Washington cannot have it both ways. It must either range widely and run the show, having good reason for telling others to join in or get out of the way. Or it must step back and shed some of its international burdens, but then work with others to pick up the slack—and accept the resulting loss of influence. Furthermore, other nations have not hesitated to express their discontent with U.S. unilateralism, making clear that it will hasten the return of a more divided and difficult international environment. If confronted with a unilateral America, an ascendant Europe and a rising Asia are sure to set their gaining strength against the United States.

America's unilateral impulse has deep roots, going back to the founding fathers and their fears of the young republic's entanglement in the dangers of great-power rivalry. After World War II, Americans of necessity shed some of their aversion to multilateral engagement; building a cohesive community of liberal democracies and managing the Western world required an elaborate network of institutions. But even during the Cold War, unilateral urges often prevailed. On issues ranging from the tenor of diplomacy with the Soviet Union, to the

Arab-Israeli conflict, to arms control, to international trade, the Western allies frequently complained of a wayward America all too often acting alone.

Absent the constraints of the Cold War, this unilateral impulse has been growing stronger. Despite awareness of a profound global interdependence, politicians from the left and right have been encouraging the United States to forsake its role as a builder of consensus and coalition. Even the Clinton administration, although in principle committed to a multilateral brand of international governance, frequently felt compelled to stand alone.

Clinton in 1997 refused to sign an international treaty banning landmines that had won the support of 123 nations. Among the other holdouts were exemplary countries like Afghanistan, Iraq, Libya, China, Russia, and North Korea. The Clinton administration in 1998 signed the Kyoto Protocol but then demurred on implementation. In November 2000, 175 countries gathered in The Hague for a follow-up meeting to finalize agreement on measures to curb global warming. The United States found little common ground with its interlocutors; the meeting ended in a stalemate. Clinton also withheld America's support for the International Criminal Court until the waning days of his presidency. Three weeks before leaving office, he reversed course and signed the ICC Treaty, but also counseled Bush not to send it to the Senate until certain modifications would improve the prospects for ratification.

The election of George W. Bush toughened this unilateral inclination. Many of his top foreign policy advisers—Richard Cheney, Donald Rumsfeld, Paul Wolfowitz, Richard Armitage, and John Bolton (an undersecretary of state)—have been well known for their hawkish, unilateral bent. Rumsfeld has been a leading supporter of a national missile defense (NMD) system, unabashed about his willingness to defy international treaties and the objections of allies to build such a system. In his confirmation hearing, Rumsfeld declared the ABM Treaty to be "ancient history."[21] Bush himself, in his keynote speech at the Republican convention, asserted that "now is the time, not to defend outdated treaties, but to defend the American people."[22] At Bolton's confirmation hearing, Republican Senator Jesse Helms remarked, "John, I want you to take that ABM Treaty and dump it in the same place we dumped our ABM co-signer, the Soviet Union—on the ash heap of history."[23]

The Bush team also made clear from early on that it opposed the

International Criminal Court. Rumsfeld signed a joint letter in December 2000 warning that "American leadership in the world could be the first casualty" of the ICC.[24] Bolton has long been one of the court's most ardent opponents. He played a leading role in convincing the administration to announce in May 2002 that Clinton's signature on the treaty was no longer binding and that the court should expect no cooperation from the United States. Neither the Comprehensive Test Ban Treaty nor an emerging body to verify the Biological Weapons Convention passed muster. Similar attitudes have prevailed on environmental issues, with the Bush administration withdrawing from the Kyoto Protocol and announcing plans to drill new oil wells in the Alaskan wilderness. And in early 2003, the United States attacked Iraq—despite its inability to win the backing of the UN Security Council.

These moves astonished America's allies. Bush's action on the Kyoto Protocol evoked sharp criticism. "If one wants to be a world leader," commented Romano Prodi, president of the European Commission, "one must know how to look after the entire earth and not only American industry." *Le Monde*, France's influential daily, called the move "a brutal form of unilateralism."[25] As the Bush administration started its third month in office, here is how one of England's leading journalists summed up the view from London: "From here, the main voices in Washington seem to be working their way toward a host of fresh assessments: abrasive toward old enemies, mistrustful of internationalist compromise, America First when it comes to global threats, admonitory toward allies, disdainful rather than constructive in face of the messy complexities that have replaced the neat old bipolar world on which most of them cut their teeth."[26]

This schizophrenic combination of diminishing enthusiasm for international engagement and growing unilateralism presents the world with confusing signals. One moment, the United States is complaining about excessive burdens, asking its partners to shoulder their fair share, and stepping back from its expansive global role. The next, it is disregarding its partners, going off on its own, and reacting with affront when others seek to fill the vacuum left by a weary hegemon.

These contradictions lie at the heart of the impasse on European defense that soured Atlantic relations following the Kosovo war. In the wake of that conflict, the United States and the EU agreed that it was time for Europe to improve its military capabilities. The war revealed to Europeans their serious military shortcomings and their level of strategic dependence on the United States. And Washington expressed disgruntlement with the EU's inability to carry a greater share of the burden. The Europeans responded by embarking on efforts to build a rapid reaction force capable of operating independently of the United States.

The Clinton administration's reaction was revealing. The Europeans had complied with America's request, and the United States on the surface welcomed the effort. Deputy Secretary of State Strobe Talbott insisted that "there should be no confusion about America's position on the need for a stronger Europe. We are not against; we are not ambivalent; we are not anxious; we are for it."[27] Behind the scenes, however, Washington was sending a different signal. Secretary of State Madeleine Albright warned the EU not to duplicate existing NATO assets, something the Europeans had to do if they were to develop a meaningful level of autonomy. Assistant Secretary of Defense Franklin Kramer asserted that "there can be no question of an 'EU Caucus' inside NATO," a must for the Europeans if they were to develop a coherent policy.[28] Secretary of Defense William Cohen added that Europe risked turning NATO into "a relic of history."[29]

In effect, the United States was telling Europe to acquire more defense capability, but not to expect more voice or autonomy. America wanted Europe to do a better job of sharing the burden, but had no interest in reciprocating by sharing more influence with the Europeans. The EU's defense efforts, however, were all about acquiring just that—more influence and autonomy. This misfit explains why, in the words of the *Guardian*, "to put it mildly, this scheme [for European defense] is driving the Americans nuts."[30] When push came to shove, the Clinton team simply was not prepared to step aside and make room for a more assertive Europe.

America's schizophrenia continued under the Bush administration. Rumsfeld was initially dismissive of Europe's efforts, not even making mention of the EU during his first official visit to Europe to attend a security conference in Munich in February 2001. As for the new defense force, the test of its merits was whether it strengthens NATO, not Europe. And on this question, Rumsfeld pronounced, "I do not quite see how it strengthens [NATO]."[31] Bolton told the House International Relations Committee in testimony in 1999, "We should openly acknowledge that the aim to align the foreign and defense policies of the EU's members into one shared and uniform policy is at times motivated either by a desire to distance themselves from U.S.

influence, or in some cases by openly anti-American intentions."[32] Secretary of State Powell was more receptive to the EU defense force and President Bush himself voiced some sympathy for the idea, stating after a meeting with Tony Blair that the British prime minister had "assured me that the European defense would [in] no way undermine NATO," and "so I support what the Prime Minister has laid out."[33] Bush's positive statement notwithstanding, his administration, like the one before it, has been avowedly uncomfortable with the notion of a stronger and more independent Europe.

There is no better way for the United States to poison its relations with a rising Europe than to ask the Europeans to become more self-reliant, only then to take umbrage when they comply. Washington is right to give notice that a more discriminating internationalism is in the offing. But to combine this message with a bristly unilateralism is to risk alienating friends and foes alike. If the world that comes after America's unipolar moment depends on partnership and equitable sharing of risks and responsibilities, then an America that prefers acting alone spells trouble for the future. The United States may have the luxury of being headstrong while it still enjoys primacy; smaller states have little choice but to play along. But when America's dominance is less pronounced and other centers of power have the wherewithal to stand their ground, its unilateral impulse will serve only to guarantee the return of global geopolitical rivalry.

TERRORISM AND AMERICAN INTERNATIONALISM

AT LEAST IN THE short term, the terror attacks of September 2001 reversed these worrisome trends. The drift toward a new brand of isolationism gave way to vigilant engagement. America set about tracking down terrorists on a global basis, deploying the military, diplomatic, legal, and economic instruments at its disposal. Foreign policy became the nation's top priority. A nation galvanized by its sudden vulnerability replaced public apathy. Partisan wrangling disappeared overnight, with Democrats and Republicans setting aside their differences in the name of national unity.

America's growing unilateralism was also tamed by terror. Washington sought to patch together as broad a coalition as possible to fight back. President Bush and Colin Powell worked the phones while Donald Rumsfeld went to the Middle East to enlist support. The United

States even reached out to Russia, China, and Iran, states that the Bush administration had previously held at arm's length. Most nations responded favorably and were ready to join the fight, at least in principle. Both NATO and the Organization of American States invoked the collective defense provisions in their charters. One foreign leader after another came to Washington to show support and offer a helping hand. The Bush administration seemed to have rediscovered the merits of multilateralism.

In the long run, however, terrorism is likely to have a quite different impact on American internationalism, one that promises to reinforce the unilateralist and isolationist trends that were already picking up steam before September 2001. Rather than serving as a collective threat that brings America back to the center line, terrorism will probably play like a wild card, at times provoking America to lash out, at other times inducing it to retreat behind protective barriers. Instead of encouraging America to be a more steady partner, the threat of terror may well make the country a more difficult, unpredictable, and stubborn actor.

Despite its inclusive rhetoric, the United States was not as avowedly multilateralist as it appeared on the surface. The U.S. certainly wanted as wide a coalition as possible, affording American forces access to bases in the Middle East and providing international legitimacy to the retaliatory attack on Afghanistan. But Washington did not welcome the constraints on its room for maneuver that would have accompanied coalition warfare. The Bush administration preferred "à la carte multilateralism," a phrase earlier coined by Richard Haass, director of the State Department's Policy Planning Staff. It asked different countries for specific forms of assistance but did not engage in the broader consultation that is the true test of multilateralism. Here is how one American journalist summarized the view from Europe as America was building the coalition:

> The United States has put together an extremely broad, loosely defined coalition to fight terrorism, and backed it up with very specific support from the United Nations Security Council, the European Union and NATO. . . . But if this is the United States' moment of multilateralism, or its humbled new geopolitics, it is managed the American way, and in a manner so carefully controlled that it appears to be causing real European distress. It has become obvious that while President George W. Bush has won extensive support for

his with-us-or-against-us approach to terrorism he is quietly enforcing the subtext that there is only one captain and one playbook for the team he has formed. The new American multilateralism—with U.S. soldiers and diplomats handing out specific tasks like securing overflight rights or furnishing logistical support to coalition associates—has nothing of a discussion forum of equal voices. Rather, it is more a gathering hall where the United States gives precise assignments, careful not to ask too much of most allies, and even wounding some by asking for nothing.[34]

On October 7, 2001, the day the military campaign against Afghanistan commenced, Washington did not bother to inform Belgian Prime Minister Guy Verhofstadt, whose country then held the EU presidency, that the bombing was about to begin. The Bush administration enlisted Tony Blair's help in sustaining the coalition as the fighting proceded, but it kept tight hold over the prosecution of the war and the accompanying diplomacy. An international poll conducted about a month into the war revealed that two-thirds of opinion leaders outside the United States felt that America was acting without taking the interests of allies into consideration.[35]

In similar fashion, the international solidarity that emerged immediately after the attacks on New York and Washington was comforting and helpful, but it did not run deep. America's partners were willing to share intelligence and cooperate on law enforcement. But when it came to the question of military retaliation, the coalition was wavering virtually from the start. Within a few days of September 11, America's European allies were already skittish and cautioning restraint, playing down talk of war. Saudi Arabia, Washington's closest ally in the Persian Gulf, announced that U.S. planes were welcome to use its airspace, but that they would not be permitted to carry out offensive strikes from Saudi bases. The Saudis initially refused even to freeze the bank accounts of suspected terrorist groups.

When the air campaign actually began, the United States was accompanied only by the British. And Britain's participation in the air war was limited; its main contribution was the launching of a few cruise missiles on the first evening of the campaign and the deployment in Afghanistan of a handful of special units. Other European countries voiced support for the operation, but their troops were not at risk. Most Arab nations distanced themselves from the campaign, offering either no reaction or a veiled rebuke. Russia did step forward as never before, strongly backing the U.S.-led operation and providing intelligence and military support. But Russia had a clear incentive for doing so—it saw Islamic radicalism as a threat to its security. Russia has been bogged down by a bloody struggle to pacify separatist Muslims in Chechnya, and it shares a border with several predominantly Muslim countries. Moscow was motivated by self-interest, not by a newly discovered altruism.

A similar picture emerged during the second phase of the campaign. After the collapse of the Taliban in the north of Afghanistan, the United States deployed some 2,000 ground troops and established a major operating base in the south to help defeat remaining Taliban strongholds and to coordinate the hunt for Osama bin Laden. A limited number of special forces from other countries participated, but the ground campaign, like the air war, was almost exclusively an American operation. Several European countries offered to deploy regular troops in the north to help maintain order and assist with the delivery of humanitarian aid, but Washington declined, fearing that their presence would complicate operations. Only after the main battles were over did forces from Europe, Turkey, Canada, Australia, and New Zealand arrive in significant number to serve as peacekeepers and help eliminate remaining pockets of resistance in the mountains.

It should not be surprising that America was largely acting alone in the war against the Taliban and Al-Qaeda. Although terrorists pose a collective threat, they single out specific countries when they strike. Understandably, the attacked country has a much stronger motivation to hit back than others. The relative absence of foreign attacks against the U.S. homeland explains why Washington was not more engaged in the battle against terrorism prior to September 2001. Israel has faced terror strikes on its territory for decades, but it has been alone when it responds. The same goes for Britain and its struggle against the Irish Republican Army, and for France and its fight against terrorists from North Africa and the Middle East. For better or for worse, the type of threat posed by terrorism is more likely to stoke unilateral action than to tame it.

The incentives toward unilateralist behavior also stem from the political context in the Middle East. To fight terrorism in the region is to stray into a labyrinth of political, ethnic, religious, and national divides, each of which has the potential to ensnare outside actors. It is true that all Arab nations save Iraq initially condemned the attacks of

September 11. But it is also the case that Palestinians paraded in the streets in celebration, and that in the ensuing days anti-American protests broke out in Afghanistan, Pakistan, Somalia, Oman, Nigeria, and Indonesia.

Amid this volatile environment, and in light of the economic interests at stake in the Middle East, individual states have strong reasons to tread lightly. Fear of inviting terrorist retaliation, provoking a backlash against the West, and destabilizing moderate regimes within the Arab world works against the durability of a broad antiterror coalition. The same self-interest that motivated Russia's cooperation early on persuaded many other countries to keep their distance from America's military action even as they voiced support for retaliation.

The distance between the United States and its putative partners only increased after Bush described Iraq, Iran, and North Korea as an "axis of evil" and suggested that they would be the next targets in America's war against terrorism. This pronouncement elicited widespread opposition abroad. Even Britain and Germany, two of America's steadiest allies, voiced their discontent. Tony Blair cautioned Washington against attacking Iraq. The German foreign minister warned Washington that "Alliance partners are not satellites." The daily *Süddeutsche Zeitung* lamented that "Poor Gerhard Schröder," who was about to embark on a visit to the United States, would have "to appear at the throne of the freshly anointed American Caesar." On the evening of Bush's May 2002 trip to Europe, the *Berliner Zeitung* lamented that in the aftermath of September 11, the United States, far from renouncing unilateralism, had "used the opportunity to strengthen its selfish superpower position." "Never has a president of the United States been so foreign to us," the newspaper opined, "and never have German citizens been so skeptical about the policies of their most powerful of allies."[36] Despite Britain's eventual decision to join the war against Iraq, the conflict strained Atlantic relations to the breaking point.

As for the claim that terrorism will serve as a welcome antidote to America's isolationist instincts, the opposite may prove to be the more likely outcome. The central question is how America will deal with its new sense of vulnerability and the realization that its dominating role in the world puts the security of the homeland at risk. Here, Americans are admittedly entering uncharted waters. Pearl Harbor, after all, was an attack on a naval base located thousands of miles from the

U.S. mainland. In contrast, the strikes of September 11 and the bioterrorism that followed hit the commercial and political heart of the American nation.

"Isolationism is dead," proclaimed Andrew Sullivan five days after the attacks, insisting that its vulnerability will rid America of any illusions about geographical immunity. "We are all Israelis now," declared another commentator, referring to Israel's resolute battle against terrorism.[37] Far from retreating in the face of terror, Israel has stood firm, responding to repeated attacks by retaliating against both the perpetrators and the sponsors of terrorism.

Israel's experience with terrorism is not, however, a particularly good indicator of how America will respond over the long run to its newfound vulnerability. Israel's terror comes from within, the purveyors of violence living together with Israeli Jews and residing in territory effectively controlled by Israel. The country consequently has no choice but to stand firm and face down terror; its very existence is at stake.

A better historical analogy for the predicament facing America is the experience of other global powers that have suffered terrorist attack as a result of their preeminence and their strategic presence in distant lands. This historical record paints a more ambiguous picture, suggesting that asymmetric threats have at times effectively negated the overwhelming military superiority of leading nations. Such threats have also proved difficult to counter and suppress, producing frustration and exacting high political costs. Although it is difficult to trace the complex motivations that figure into decisions to extend and retract strategic commitments, the evidence does indicate that terror attacks have succeeded in wearing down resolve and inducing states to scale back the scope of their international ambition.

Consider Britain's experience in Palestine. The League of Nations made Palestine a British mandate after World War I. During the early mandate period, the British maintained a significant military presence in Palestine to forestall violence between Jews and Arabs. As the likelihood of war in Europe mounted during the second half of the 1930s, the British attempted to reduce the empire's drain on resources and therefore tried to placate Palestine's Arabs through concessions that ultimately jeopardized the Jewish population's quest for a homeland. Although many Jewish leaders continued to work closely with the British, some extremists responded by organizing terrorist attacks against British targets, culminating in the bombing on July 22, 1946, of Jerusalem's King David Hotel, which housed high-ranking British officials. More than 90 people were killed.

These attacks hastened Britain's retreat from the region. In 1947, with a year left on its 1923 mandate, the British turned over the Palestine problem to the U.N. When the U.N. asked the British to extend its mandate past the 1948 expiration date, London refused, indicating that it planned to withdraw from Palestine altogether. The costs were too high, and the prospects for a peaceful settlement too remote. As Chancellor of the Exchequer Hugh Dalton wrote to Prime Minister Clement Atlee even before the strike against the King David Hotel, "The present state of affairs is not only costly to us in manpower and money, but is, as you and I agree, of no real value from the strategic point of view—you cannot in any case have a secure base on top of a wasps' nest—and it is exposing our young men, for no good purpose, to abominable experiences." Britain's colonial secretary similarly referred to Palestine as "a mill-stone around our necks."[38]

Britain's experience in Aden followed a similar course. The British established a naval base there during the middle of the nineteenth century. An oil refinery and airfield were eventually added. The port of Aden became a formal colony and the surrounding area was established as a protectorate in cooperation with local sheiks. Opposition to Britain's presence in the Arabian peninsula grew during the 1950s, with terrorist attacks against civilian and military targets beginning in the early 1960s. In 1964, the British announced their support for the establishment by 1968 of an independent South Arabian Federation, although they also indicated that they would retain control over the port at Aden and would leave troops in the region to help defend the new state. Terrorist raids only intensified—including a grenade attack on a children's party taking place on a British air base. In 1966, London announced that it would quit the region altogether. The last British forces withdrew in 1967.

Terrorism did not always have the effect of wearing down British resolve. In Malaya, for example, Britain held its ground and stamped out terror attacks, withdrawing according to its own timetable and giving control to parties of its choosing. Terror attacks against homeland targets by the Irish Republican Army also proved ineffective in inducing a British retreat. Despite years of sporadic bombings in London, Britain has kept a strong military presence in Northern Ireland and worked toward a negotiated settlement. This case is closer to the Israeli one, however, inasmuch as Northern Ireland is a part of the

United Kingdom, not a distant appendage of the empire. Further-more, the majority of its population is Protestant and prefers that Northern Ireland remain in the U.K. London sees itself as standing by the country's territorial integrity and its democratic traditions, not defending a remote colony, and has thus been prepared to bear the costs of terror attacks against the homeland.

Algerian attacks against targets in mainland France provide a bet-ter test case of how great powers react to terrorism against the home-land stemming from their overseas commitments. Amid Algeria's struggle for independence from France during the 1950s and early 1960s, terrorism took place in both Algeria and metropolitan France. Although a good portion of the violence occurred among competing Algerian factions, Algerian rebel groups carried out strikes against French targets in Algeria and in France proper. On November 1, 1954, the Front de Libération Nationale (FLN) struck at French military installations and garrisons throughout Algeria, marking the begin-ning of a sustained campaign of terror. Perhaps the most dramatic attack in metropolitan France took place on August 24, 1958, when Algerian rebels, in a coordinated operation, blew up oil depots near Marseille that were being used to supply the French army in Algeria, derailed a train, and hit police stations in Paris and Lyon.

It is difficult to trace the precise effects of these events on French policy. The French community in Algeria was emboldened, itself resorting to terrorism against Algerians and pressing Paris to use all the means at its disposal to suppress the rebellion. But the conse-quences in metropolitan France itself were more complicated. As the bloodshed mounted in Algeria and spread to the mainland, anti-war sentiment grew. Recognition that Frenchmen were themselves using terror tactics against suspected rebels strengthened opposition to the war.

Although the French army had by 1960 all but won the war against the rebels, continuing outbreaks of violence and sporadic ter-rorism wore down French resolve. As Martha Crenshaw, a professor at Wesleyan University, concludes, "Terrorism succeeded for the FLN initially as a way of putting the nationalist struggle on the national and international agendas, as a symbol of the intensity of resistance, and then as a tactic in a war of attrition, part of a protracted insur-gency. Throughout the conflict it served as a constant reminder to the French government and the French public that security in Algeria was tenuous and that the two communities could never be united, even if a military victory was within French grasp."[39] That the French populace was deeply divided about how best to resolve the Algerian question added to the political costs.

After his return to the presidency in June 1958, Charles de Gaulle became convinced that France's withdrawal and independence for Algeria offered the only way forward. "Decolonisation is our interest, and, therefore, our policy," de Gaulle explained. "Why should we remain caught up in colonisations that are costly, bloody and without end?"[40] Four years later, France concluded negotiations that led to the withdrawal of its forces and Algerian independence. "FLN obstinacy and its capacity to continue a low-level war of attrition paid off," writes Crenshaw. "The French accepted not only full independence and recognition of the FLN but also conceded the two FLN demands that had prolonged both the negotiations and the terrorism that accompanied them—the rights of the future European minority in Algeria and the control of oil in the Sahara."[41]

America's reaction to terrorism against U.S. targets abroad lends further support to the proposition that such attacks have the potential to lead to retrenchment rather than renewed engagement and internationalist fervor. In October 1983, terrorists bombed the barracks of U.S. Marines serving as peacekeepers in Beirut, killing 241 servicemen. The United States promptly withdrew its troops from Lebanon. Secretary of Defense Caspar Weinberger soon announced that the country would thereafter engage in military intervention only when its "vital interests" were at stake and "with the clear intention of winning." The promulgation of this doctrine effectively served to rein in America's overseas commitments by limiting engagement in peacekeeping missions and in conflicts in peripheral areas.

In 1993, U.S. forces suffered fatalities in Somalia. The soldiers fell in combat, not in a terrorist attack, but the opposing fighters had ties to Osama bin Laden's network. Furthermore, the bodies of several servicemen were dragged through the streets of Mogadishu in front of television cameras, intensifying the political impact in the United States. Again, Washington withdrew its troops from the country, and the Clinton administration's initial enthusiasm for peacekeeping quickly dwindled.

America pursued a similar course of action in response to the October 2000 bomb attack on the USS *Cole* while it was anchored in the port of Aden, Yemen. The U.S. Navy put an effective stop to the use of the port. A team of FBI investigators was dispatched to Yemen to investigate the incident. Before it was able to complete its work, however, Washington withdrew the agents from the country because intelligence reports warned of the potential for terrorist attack. U.S. Marines concurrently engaging in joint exercises with the Jordanian army abruptly ended their maneuvers and left the country. And U.S. ships anchored at Bahrain, the headquarters of the Fifth Fleet, evacuated the harbor and put to sea. As Thomas Friedman remarked in the *New York Times*, "There is a military term for all this; it's called a 'retreat.'"[42]

These actions were generally consistent with standard operating procedures. When the security situation in foreign countries deteriorates, the United States usually encourages its citizens to leave, withdraws all nonessential diplomatic personnel, and erects barricades around its embassy. When the bombing campaign against Afghanistan began, the United States closed its embassy in Saudi Arabia and reduced its diplomatic staff in other Muslim countries. These measures are understandable and justifiable. America should not run undue risks and should seek to protect its own from danger.

But it is precisely this logic that suggests that terrorism in the long run has the potential to erode, rather than bolster, American internationalism. The price a population is willing to pay for the autonomy of its homeland is usually higher than the price an outsider is willing to pay to maintain its presence on that land. That is one of the main reasons that colonial empires eventually crumbled. It is why the United States has departed from military outposts where it was not wanted—such as in the Philippines. And this logic explains why America is likely to decide that the costs of at least some of its overseas commitments exceed the benefits.

The United States is certainly wanted more than it is resented in most regions of the world, including the Middle East. A large part of the reason is that the United States is not an imperial state with predatory intent; it is more concerned with enhancing regional stability and security and protecting international trade than enlarging its power at the expense of others. And America certainly has strong reasons for staying fully engaged in the Middle East, preserving access to the region's oil and ensuring the security of Israel among them. Terrorist attacks and other manifestations of anti-American sentiment are unlikely to convince Washington to question its commitment to these priorities anytime soon. The history of the twentieth century makes clear that America is a tenacious enemy when provoked.

But U.S. history also makes clear the political and emotional appeal of an inner voice urging America to stay out of the affairs of other countries so that they stay out of America's affairs. Should the costs of global engagement rise and continue to result in attacks against the homeland, calls for the country to distance itself from the troubles of the Middle East may intensify. Even if on some level defeatist, there is logical appeal to the notion that the best way to avoid terrorism is to avoid the behavior that might invite it to begin with.

Amid the patriotic fervor that followed the terror attacks on New York and Washington, there was little discussion of how America might alter—or limit—its engagement in the Middle East to dampen anti-American sentiment in the region. The national mood initially made editors of U.S. newspapers reluctant to publish articles on the subject.[43] But an extensive dialogue on this issue and an effort to reduce America's exposure in the Middle East are natural and inevitable consequences of the events of September 11 and their aftermath. That is one of the main reasons that Israeli Prime Minister Ariel Sharon warned the United States not "to appease the Arabs at our expense," adding, in a reference to Western Europe's appeasement of Hitler during the 1930s, that "Israel will not be Czechoslovakia."[44] That is also why, especially after the military campaigns in Afghanistan and Iraq had removed the Taliban and Saddam Hussein from power, Americans began to debate whether to reduce the U.S. military presence in Saudi Arabia.[45]

The new focus on homeland defense, albeit unwittingly, is likely to contribute to the emergence of a more inward-looking America. Measures to improve the security of the homeland are certainly necessary. But in two important respects they effectively distance the United States from the rest of the world. First, America has surrounded itself with higher barriers and tighter borders. Aircraft and warships patrol the coasts. More restrictive immigration policies and more surveillance have meant less porous borders. In their intention and their result, these steps wall off the United States and provide it a protective buffer against foreign threats. Second, the new resources committed to defending the homeland will at least to some extent come at the expense of the resources committed to overseas missions. The more time American soldiers and aircraft spend in or near the United States, the less time they will devote to keeping the peace farther afield.

A final question concerns how terror attacks against the homeland are likely to affect America's broader public mind and the appetite of the electorate for internationalism. The short-term effects were clear. The U.S. public fully backed military retaliation. The nation came together and demonstrated both resolve and unity. Opinion surveys revealed renewed trust in government.[46] The surge in volunteer activities and charitable giving marked a dramatic rise in civic spirit.

The prospects over the longer run, however, point in the opposite direction. Most of the activities involved in the long battle against terrorism do not lend themselves to galvanizing the nation. The most effective countermeasures involve law enforcement, intelligence, and covert operations; there was and there will be no D-Day. America's military might will on occasion be brought to bear—as in Afghanistan and Iraq. But its superior strength will at times be offset by a shadowy enemy, making victory hard to gauge and creating the prospect of a long and frustrating struggle. By any measure, the United States handily won the war against the Taliban and Al-Qaeda, but many in their ranks slipped away and are still at large. Furthermore, the greatest successes will be nonevents—terrorist attacks that are averted or never even planned—and thus they will go unreported.

Nor will the nation collectively be involved in the struggle. In the months following the attacks, there were flags in the windows, but no lines at the recruiting stations. Airlines sent hundreds of aircraft to storage facilities because there were no passengers to fill them; people preferred to stay at home. And rather than being asked to head to the factories to contribute to the war effort, many Americans were laid off as a result of the economic slowdown exacerbated by the terrorist strikes. For better or worse, the struggle against terror may well intensify, rather than ameliorate, unilateralist and isolationist instincts.

CRAFTING A NEW AMERICAN INTERNATIONALISM

WHILE THE PAST and the emerging present suggest that isolationism and unilateralism will be on the rise in the years ahead, they also reveal that a rejection of liberal internationalism is by no means foreordained. The challenge is to find a new equilibrium, a level of U.S. engagement abroad that is in keeping with a new politics at home. Doing so will require finding the right mix of realism and idealism, balancing competing regional interests and cultures, and insulating foreign policy from the partisan wrangling that has distorted it since America's earliest days.

Today's leaders must therefore follow Franklin Roosevelt's example, finding the middle road between doing too much and doing too little. To err on the side of either extreme is equally dangerous. On the one hand, an unchecked unilateralism would turn allies into opponents. It would also be to overextend by pursuing a level of foreign engagement for which there is insufficient political support, risking a backlash and a precipitous return to isolationism—exactly what happened to Woodrow Wilson. On the other hand, to retreat from the outset and dramatically reduce America's global role would only fuel complacency and a gradual drift toward the illusory seclusion that the American nation has found all too appealing throughout much of its history. In between is the middle ground, a new and more discriminating brand of liberal internationalism upon which a new and more selective grand strategy can be built and sustained over the long term. Workable minimums, as Roosevelt would have it, not impossible maximums.

The first order of business in accomplishing this goal is to realize the magnitude and the importance of the task at hand. It will be impossible to find a new equilibrium in the absence of a deliberate effort to do so. A new internationalism and a grand strategy to match will not emerge of their own accord. Nonetheless, the Clinton administration seemed oblivious, misled by the strength of the American economy and the sense that the unipolar moment was here to stay. The Bush team is likely to focus on combating terrorism—a worthy cause, but also one that will continue to distract attention from other equally important issues. And even as Bush does return to a broader agenda, he is likely, as at the outset of his administration, to oscillate between doing too much and doing too little. Bush's advisers and the Republican Party more generally have been divided between opposing camps that represent these two extremes.

On one side have been the neoconservatives like Wolfowitz and outside analysts William Kristol, Robert Kagan, and Richard Perle. Hawkish conservatives like Cheney and Rumsfeld have tended to line up with the neoconservatives. They have backed a foreign policy that favors the unilateral use of U.S. force and that aims at preserving American hegemony as long as possible through actively resisting the rise of alternative centers of power. On the other side are more centrist heartland conservatives like Condoleezza Rice and Colin Powell. They have been more circumspect about the projection of U.S. power, believing that America should recognize its own limits, husband its resources, focus on homeland defense, and devote attention to the major players—the EU, Russia, and China.

President Bush himself initially leaned toward the heartland conservative, do-less camp. He has throughout his career demonstrated little interest in foreign affairs. And as a candidate, Bush's main message was that he would be more selective than his predecessor in taking on foreign commitments. "I would be guarded in my approach," Bush said during the presidential debate in Boston. "I don't think we can be all things to all people in the world. I think we've got to be very careful when we commit our troops."[47] Since September 11, Bush appears to have embraced the more hawkish stance of the neoconservatives. But precisely because Bush is relatively inexperienced in foreign affairs and does not bring to the table strong inclinations, he is likely to be pulled back and forth between the unilateralism of the neoconservatives and the inward-looking instincts of the heartland conservatives.

Bush will be confounded not just by the need to arbitrate between opposing wings of the Republican Party. He will, as all presidents before him, also need to mediate the conflict between realist and idealist impulses. Clinton actually did an admirable job of blending the two. After a rough start, he handily managed the traditional security agenda, repeatedly sending U.S. soldiers into combat in the Balkans and the Persian Gulf. Clinton brought back into the U.S. arsenal the option of limited war, gradually becoming comfortable with the use of limited force in a manner proportional to the limited interests at stake. In so doing, he effectively overturned the Pentagon's previous all-or-nothing approach left behind by Colin Powell's tenure as chairman of the Joint Chiefs.

At the same time, Clinton developed a new agenda that had clear idealist overtones—managing globalization, protecting the environment, addressing health crises in the developing world, and enlarging the role of international institutions. He also understood that the rise of other centers of power could ultimately redound to America's benefit—even if he had trouble acting on that understanding with regard to Europe's defense force. As Samuel Berger described Clinton's views, "He understood that the old paradigm of win-lose that had dominated the Cold War was no longer sufficient. If Europe got stronger that was good for us, not bad. If Latin America integrated, that was good for us, not bad."[48] One commentator identified Berger himself as the source of this balance between realism and idealism: "He had declined to be a Wilsonian idealist or a Henry Kissinger realist. He has refused to choose between go-it-alone conservatism and liberal internationalism."[49]

Although members of the Clinton team effectively blended realism and idealism in practice, they never did so self-consciously—that is, they never articulated a set of guiding principles that could serve as the conceptual foundation for their actions. Without such conceptual coherence, the whole of Clinton's foreign policy ended up being much less than the sum of the parts. The administration may have gotten right many specific policies, but those policies did not add up to a coherent grand strategy. Furthermore, precisely because Clinton failed to arm himself with a clear set of guiding strategic principles that he could impart to the electorate, he was not able even to begin the task of laying the foundation for a new American internationalism.

Bush's problem has been different. He has been adhering to a realist agenda unleavened by idealist aspirations, and is therefore poised to pursue a monolithic foreign policy ill suited to the present. His team was initially focused almost exclusively on a traditional balance-of-power agenda: rebuilding America's military strength, deploying missile defenses, reinforcing long-standing alliances with Europe, Japan, and Taiwan, and preparing for competition with China. It was then compelled by events to reorient its agenda, the war against terrorism becoming the top priority. The realist bent continued. Wolfo-witz promised to "end" states that supported terrorism. The Bush team warned countries around the world that they had to make a stark choice—whether they were with America or against it. Amid the search for states against which America could retaliate, *The Onion*, a satirical newspaper, quipped, "President Bush made a direct plea to Osama bin Laden to form a nation the U.S. can attack."[50]

Bush did back away from the bellicose instincts of his team, exercising patience and opting for a measured military response. But his stark brand of realism remains anachronistic. Although it may prove well suited to the few parts of the world in which the traditional security agenda still dominates, such as northeast Asia, it has much less to offer the rest of the world. Europe's geopolitical fault lines are gone for good. Latin America and Southeast Asia are focusing on regional integration, not the balance of power. Multilateralism prevails in all three regions, explaining why America's unilateralist proclivities are unwelcome.

Bush's brand of realism is also inappropriate for dealing with the Middle East, the region that has proved to pose the most imminent threats to U.S. security. Terrorism has its roots in social and religious cleavages, not geopolitical ones. And although most people in the Middle East do not support terrorism, anti-American sentiment does run strong and many regimes face domestic threats from their own Islamic radicals. Political life in the Middle East is not black and white; states have no choice but to pursue a balancing act, at times siding with America, but at other times keeping their distance. So too might America on occasion find it expedient to cooperate with regimes linked to terrorist activities—such as the Palestinian Authority or Iran. In similar fashion, Africa faces tough times ahead, but its problems stem from religious and ethnic strife, poverty, and disease, not traditional geopolitical rivalry. Wars are certain to break out in the world's developing regions, but they are likely to be precisely the smaller ethnic and civil conflicts in which the Bush team has said it does not want to engage. Try as it might to make the world conform to a starkly realist template, the Bush team will find that its approach to global affairs has become obsolete.

The realist bent of the Bush administration also stands in the way of its ability to craft a new U.S. internationalism. Realism offers an attractive formula for educating the public. It is easy to grasp because it portrays the world in clear friend-or-foe terms. And it mobilizes political support effectively because of its black-and-white approach to global problems. Peripheral threats and the new security agenda— the environment, peacekeeping, health, and economic development—are not America's business, so the public can happily tune out. Major threats to its well-being are the nation's calling, and when they emerge, they readily engender full public attention and sacrifice.

But again, the world will not lend itself to such simplicity. An either/or approach to U.S. engagement is fanciful in a world characterized by great complexity. Realism may provide a ready foundation for a new American internationalism, but it will be a brand poorly suited to the challenges facing the country. The central issues will turn not on whether to engage, but on how and to what degree. In this sense, America's leaders have no choice but to share with the electorate the careful assessments and judgments required to guide foreign policy. The United States lives in a world in which fault lines are for now blurred, the identity of allies and enemies uncertain, and the main perpetrators of violence against America able to slip into mountain hideouts even before they have done their damage. This world is a difficult one for politicians in search of a tag line. The only responsible alternative is confronting political ambiguity with conceptual clarity.

Rethinking the nature of the country's foreign commitments has an important role to play in this regard. Here, history again provides a useful lesson. Wilson failed to secure U.S. participation in the League of Nations not because he wanted America to extend commitments to other states, but because of the type of commitments he wanted to extend: binding and automatic ones. The Senate ultimately proved unwilling to countenance such constraints. In contrast, FDR succeeded in winning support for the U.N. precisely because he appreciated that America's commitments under the Charter had to be left loose and open to interpretation if the body was to win public approval. In the absence of a major adversary, Americans do not like to be pinned down.

Bush and Clinton before him have failed to assimilate this important lesson. They continue to rely on alliances containing binding and automatic defense commitments as principal instruments of policy. Such alliances are credible in northeast Asia, where geopolitical fault lines continue to threaten long-standing partners such as South Korea and Japan. But the ongoing expansion of NATO in Europe, where no such fault lines exist, risks running aground on precisely the same domestic political shoals that sank the League of Nations. If Bush is skeptical about keeping American troops in the Balkans, then he is surely going to have a hard time explaining why he wants to grant codified defense guarantees to the ten or more countries now aspiring to NATO membership. The United States is more likely to stay engaged in Europe if it can pick and choose its fights than if Americans soon find themselves extending ironclad commitments to countries they cannot find on a map. As Bush tests the limits of a new internationalism, he would be wise to heed Roosevelt's dictum that less is more. It is better to secure workable minimums than to overreach and end up empty-handed.

American hubris will further complicate the task of finding a new and more discriminating internationalism. The United States is faced with a challenge that few great nations have managed to pull off—

accepting the rise of alternative power centers and willingly ceding influence to them. One of the main obstacles to this devolution of influence is domestic politics. Politicians fear they will pay a price if they appear weak or too accommodating, especially when opponents are at the ready to charge them with national humiliation. The American polity, precisely because of its long-standing ambivalence about international responsibilities, might be able to adjust to a less exalted position more easily than others. But American elites and the public alike have grown accustomed to calling the shots, making it likely that the United States will continue to bristle as others challenge its preeminence. Bush and his successors thus face the unenviable task of crafting a more discriminating internationalism without at the same time stoking a stubborn unilateralism. Packaging American strategy as a willful lightening of the load, not a retreat under pressure from others, will help with this aspect of public diplomacy.

CRAFTING A NEW brand of liberal internationalism involves not just getting right its ideological content, but also balancing the competing cultures and interests of America's different regions. The country's past makes clear that isolationist and unilateralist currents have at times run strong in all parts of the United States. Certain regions are neither irretrievably isolationist nor doggedly unilateralist. Rather, isolationism, in both its liberal and libertarian variants, and unilateralism have deep roots in America's creed. Their salience in a given region varies with shifting political and economic forces. Isolationist and unilateralist voices will therefore remain present in political discourse. Politicians and groups of various stripes will gravitate to them for both ideological and instrumental reasons. The challenge will be to neutralize these pockets of extremism through careful management of regional coalitions and by forging a moderate internationalism that disarms the isolationists and unilateralists of their political appeal.

The regional alignments around which internationalist coalitions have taken shape continue to remain fluid. The internationalist alliance of North and South orchestrated by Roosevelt unraveled during the 1970s. The falling out was over the Vietnam War and civil rights. The South was staunchly anticommunist (and thus prowar) and socially conservative. The North tended toward an antiwar and socially progressive stance. The period of détente that followed the end of the Vietnam War temporarily suppressed the political consequences of this unraveling of the North-South coalition. But when détente gave way to renewed Cold War rivalry at the outset of the 1980s, regional alignments again became decisive.

President Ronald Reagan fashioned a new coalition of the South and the West to serve as the political foundation for his military buildup and hawkish policies. This new regional alliance was based on a shared anticommunism, the benefits that military spending brought to both regions, and support for free trade. The more liberal North was meanwhile less convinced of the need for Reagan's hard-line policies, benefited less from military expenditure than the South and West, and had experienced a period of industrial decline that sapped support for free trade. As economic vitality and population moved from the rust belt to the sun belt, so did support for economic openness.[51]

The end of the Cold War and the economic upturn that accompanied it produced a decade in which regional interests generally ran along more harmonious lines. Protectionist pressures were eased by an economy that was booming throughout the country. With the defense sector still reeling from the cutbacks that followed the demise of the Soviet Union and the U.S. government flush with budget surpluses, additional military spending met little opposition. Although the wars to drive Iraq from Kuwait and to bring peace to the Balkans provoked bitter debates in Congress, victory with few casualties limited their immediate impact on support for internationalism. And the country was of a single mind in supporting military retaliation after the terrorist attacks on New York and Washington.

Under these conditions, the alliance between South and West orchestrated by Reagan withstood the disappearance of the "evil empire" against which it took shape. It ably served the Republican Party by securing George W. Bush's victory in November 2000. Harking back to the republic's early days, the South and the interior West were more conservative, more realist, and attracted to Bush's populism, while the North, along with the coastal West, was more liberal, more idealist, and attracted to Al Gore's policy expertise.

The clashes between regional cultures and interests promise to intensify in the years ahead, in part because America's regions are growing apart in political terms. New England used to have a healthy mix of Republicans and Democrats. In 1985, for example, the states of the region (Maine, Vermont, New Hampshire, Massachusetts, Rhode Island, and Connecticut) sent to the House fourteen Democrats and ten Republicans. In 2001, those same states were represented by seventeen Democrats, five Republicans, and one independent. It is increasingly hard to find Republican voters in New England. The opposite is true in the Mountain West. Montana, Nevada, Idaho, Utah, Wyoming, Colorado, Arizona, and New Mexico in 2001 sent seven Democrats and seventeen Republicans to the House—exactly the same mix as in 1985. Despite the region's growing population, it remains hard to find Democratic voters in the interior West. These trends promise to hamper efforts to build coalitions across region and party. Not good news for American engagement, inasmuch as Roosevelt made clear how important such coalitions are to building and sustaining liberal internationalism. Rather than relying on a centrist consensus to steer a steady course, the country's leaders may find themselves stymied by regional divides and buffeted by domestic pressure toward both unilateralist and isolationist extremes.

In similar fashion, America's regions will continue to have diverging economic interests. While the Northeast's main trading partner is Europe, the Midwest's is Canada, the West's is Asia, and the South's trade is almost evenly divided among Europe, Asia, Mexico, and Canada. Regional differences over America's trade agenda result. The composition of a region's economic base and the relative political weight of the industrial, agricultural, and service sectors reinforce regional divisions. As they have since the Union's founding, diverging economic interests produce clashes not just over trade policy, but also over the nature and scope of America's strategic commitments abroad.

A slower economy and higher unemployment promise to exacerbate these regional divides. Growing and lagging regions are likely to differ over free trade. The financial community and the Internet sector in the Northeast and on the West Coast will be pushing hard for liberalization. Meanwhile, textiles and apparel and industrial sectors like automobiles, aircraft, and steel will want protection. American auto manufacturers have been losing market share to imports, and jobs in the sector have been trending downward. Boeing was hard hit by the lowering of demand for commercial aircraft that followed the terror attacks. It was no accident that President Bush, having won West Virginia in the 2000 election and having almost carried Pennsylvania, opted in March 2002 to impose steep tariffs on imported steel in order to protect U.S. manufacturers. The agrarian sector itself will be divided, with grain-producing states in the Midwest generally supportive of free trade, and citrus and sugar producers in Florida against it. Complicated and fragile regional alignments are likely to result.

Regional differences on issues related to the use of force are also likely to widen, both for cultural and economic reasons. The South is overrepresented in the military in several respects. It sends a disproportionate percentage of its population into the armed services. In 1998, for example, the southern states accounted for 35 percent of the U.S. population, but provided 43 percent of the country's new recruits.[52] It is overweighted in terms of military bases. The southern states make up roughly 25 percent of the land area of the United States, but are home to 36 percent of domestic military installations.[53] The South also benefits more than other regions from military spending; in fiscal year 2000, 45 percent of all military contracts went to the region.[54]

Important political implications follow. The military was alienated from the Democratic Party during the Clinton years. Clinton's avoidance of the Vietnam draft made for an unfortunate start. Relations with the services were then further strained by his position on gays in the military and the drain on resources and morale resulting from lengthy deployments abroad. Surveys also revealed an across-the-board gap between the conservative values that predominate in the services and the more liberal positions of the Democratic Party.[55]

The Republicans are likely to continue taking advantage of the estrangement between the Democrats and the services. One of President Bush's first moves in office was to promise a pay hike for military personnel. After initially alienating the services by seeking to push through a series of reforms, Secretary of Defense Rumsfeld backed off and gave them more leeway. The Republicans have also sought to be responsive to the Pentagon's predisposition against involvement in peacekeeping and humanitarian missions. Throughout the Clinton years, the military complained that these tasks distracted the services and their scarce resources from core missions. The new focus on homeland defense and combating terrorism promises to secure the military both higher levels of funding (Bush announced in early 2002 a $48 billion increase in defense spending) and a new rationale for resisting involvement in "nonessential" missions such as peacekeeping.

Bush's efforts to respond to the needs of the military will dovetail nicely with the populist traditions running strong in the agrarian South and interior West. Residents of these regions support high levels of defense spending and are strong internationalists when it comes to fighting major enemies—Nazi Germany, Imperial Japan, the Soviet Union—that threaten America's security.[56] And like most Americans, they enthusiastically supported retaliation against the perpetrators of terrorist attacks against the U.S. homeland.

But this sector of the electorate is much less enthusiastic when it comes to fighting limited wars in areas in which the United States has only limited interests. Part of the reason may be that their sons and daughters would do much of the fighting; lower-income families from the South send many more of their children into the armed forces than do wealthier families from the Northeast.[57] Although initially resolute about fighting terrorism with military might, these voters may well tire of efforts to track down extremists in the mountains and back alleys of the Middle East. And many in the South and the Mountain West were none too happy about the potential effects of terrorism on their domestic liberties. As one resident of Colorado exclaimed, "Here it comes—our government trying to take away freedoms again in the name of a national emergency. They can put a little more surveillance in airports, but beyond that—no."[58] In light of the nature of the threat posed by terrorism and its impact on domestic freedoms, Americans carrying forward the Jeffersonian and Jacksonian traditions may over the long run argue that the best way to deal with terrorism is to raise protective barriers and reduce the scope of America's overseas commitments.

The South and the Mountain West represent President Bush's main constituency; populist proclivities thus promise to induce more restrained Republican attitudes toward the use of force in peripheral areas. Residents of these regions also tend to be suspicious of international institutions, preferring unilateral initiative. The North is meanwhile likely to adhere to its more idealist roots, to favor multilateralism, and to continue its support for humanitarian missions—even as it questions the need for high levels of defense spending. These regional differences came out clearly when Congress voted on the war over Kosovo; the South and Mountain West generally voted against the air campaign, while the Northeast supported it.[59]

That the population of the South and West is growing much faster than that of the North will also give these regions and their populist leanings greater influence over foreign policy. During the 1990s, the population of the northern region grew by 7 percent, while the South rose by 17 percent and the West by 20 percent. In 2000, the North accounted for 42 percent of the U.S. population, while the South and

West accounted for 36 and 22 percent respectively. Estimates suggest that by 2025 the North will account for only 38 percent of the population, with the South and West accounting for 37 and 25 percent.[60]

Changes in the ethnic composition of American society also have the potential to strengthen regional divides. The United States has from the outset been an immigrant country, demonstrating remarkable potential to integrate successive waves of newcomers into mainstream America. Even as immigrants retained strong personal and cultural ties to their motherlands, their political allegiance became distinctly American. Almost every ethnic group admittedly has established a lobbying arm (if not several) in Washington. But Americans of all backgrounds, especially when they have entered the world of foreign policy, for the most part have worked to secure a common notion of national interest, not one that is attuned exclusively to their particular ethnic origins.

The melting pot theory of national interest may, however, be reaching the end of its days. Minority groups will no longer be integrating as fully into a multiethnic mainstream when they become sizable enough to be the mainstream. Non-Hispanic whites constitute an ever-shrinking proportion of the U.S. population. They are expected to fall below 50 percent by 2060 and represent only 40 percent of the population by the end of the century. On the rising side of the ledger are Hispanic Americans, who will represent one-fourth of the population by 2060, and one-third by the end of the century. The rate of growth for non-Hispanic blacks and Asians will be considerably slower. Asians, who now represent 4 percent of the population, will rise to 7 percent by 2025, and 10 percent by 2060. And non-Hispanic blacks are expected to hold steady at roughly 13 percent of the population.[61]

Hispanic and Asian Americans tend to concentrate in specific regions of the country—Hispanics in the Southwest and Asians on the West Coast—making it more likely that among rising generations ethnic identity and interests may weigh more heavily than for previous generations. By 2025, whites will constitute only 33 percent of California's population, with Hispanics representing 42 percent, Asians 18 percent, and blacks 7 percent. Similar changes are occurring in other states. By 2025, Texas will be 46 percent white and 38 percent Hispanic, while New Mexico will be 40 percent white and 48 percent Hispanic.[62]

The concentration of Hispanics and Asians in select states magnifies the political influence of these groups, especially because states such as California and Texas are extremely important in electoral terms. California and Texas together have 86 votes in the electoral college, almost one-third of the 270 needed for a candidate to win the presidency. As the debate over NATO expansion made clear, ethnic concentration in states with a large number of electoral college votes gives ethnic interests considerable sway. If Americans of Polish, Czech, and Hungarian descent had been evenly scattered across many states, they would have had little say when during the second half of the 1990s the U.S. government was considering whether their motherlands should be invited to join NATO. But because they were concentrated in populous swing states in the Midwest and organized effective lobbies, they had considerable impact on the issue.[63] It follows that America's growing Hispanic population should have a major impact on U.S. foreign policy. If candidates for the presidency are to win California and Texas—key electoral prizes—they will need to carry the Hispanic vote.

That different ethnic groups will seek to influence U.S. foreign policy in ways that enhance their special interests is nothing new. They always have and always will. Such is the nature of pluralist democracy in a multiethnic society. But America's changing demographics could give new meaning to ethnic politics and have important consequences for American internationalism.

The size of the Latino population may well have a direct impact on the tenor of U.S. internationalism and the goals of U.S. foreign policy. Opinion polls within the Hispanic community are by no means conclusive. But they do indicate preferences that diverge widely from those of American leaders as a whole. Hispanic leaders, for example, "voice much weaker commitment to traditional defense policy and military alliances." Only 8 percent of Latino leaders, compared with 60 percent of U.S. elites overall, view the defense of allies as a "very important" goal. Eighty-five percent of Hispanic elites believe the United States should pay more attention to its relations with Latin America. America's foreign relations are not zero-sum. But limited resources do mean that greater focus on Latin America is likely to come at the expense of the attention devoted to other areas.[64]

The potential balkanization of America could also complicate the task of crafting a sustainable, common internationalism for the country as a whole. If the Southwest is preoccupied with Latin America, the West Coast with the Pacific, and the East Coast with Europe, it will be difficult to reach a consensus about what constitutes America's national interests. If ethnic and even linguistic dividing lines are added to the cultural and economic dividing lines that have always separated America's regions, regional differences may erode the social fabric and unifying identity essential to forging a sense of national purpose. The likely results are political stalemate, internationalist coalitions that become ever more difficult to build and maintain, and a drift toward isolationist and unilateralist policies.

Labor mobility does have the potential to counteract this strengthening of ethnoregional divides. Shifts in the regional demand for labor have played a major role in making America's melting pot work, sending immigrants and settlers west during the 1800s, bringing laborers from south to north amid industrialization and urbanization during the first half of the 1900s, and sending them back south and west to the sun belt in the later part of the century. The intermixing that resulted played a central role in making the United States a strong and unified polity with a common identity and ethic, and not just a loose federation of states, each with its unique identity and outlook.

The problem is that the digital age does not engender the same labor mobility as the industrial age. The information revolution will not perform the same mixing function as industrialization precisely because it enables people and firms significant flexibility in deciding where to locate. During the industrial era, firms located near the raw materials or transportation links that were vital to their business. The labor pool moved accordingly, essentially forcing people to leave behind their preferred living location in search of work. As Ernest Gellner details in *Nations and Nationalism*, industrialization and the mobility and homogeneity it engendered gave birth to the modern nation-state. Industrialization was the fuel that fired the melting pot.[65]

During the digital era, firms and workers will more frequently settle where they want to, not where they must. In choosing where to live, Americans will rely more heavily than in the past on factors such as lifestyle, proximity to family, cultural milieu, or climate. These considerations mattered even before the widespread use of digital technology. During the 1970s and 1980s, northerners who migrated to the South were more conservative in their political views than the North's population as a whole.[66] The digital economy promises to reinforce such trends, potentially strengthening cultural or ethnic dividing lines among regions. As Michael Lind of the New America

Foundation explains, "The geographic mobility of Americans may actually reinforce regional subcultures by encouraging a voluntary partition, with liberal southerners moving to the North and conservative northerners fleeing Boston or New York for the more congenial environments of Atlanta or Dallas."[67] Regional cultures and interests thus promise to diverge as the digital age proceeds. At a minimum, this picture complicates the task of forging a common American internationalism and resisting isolationist as well as unilateralist extremes. It also underscores the need for a carefully constructed political strategy for doing so.

PREVENTING GROWING regional divides from standing in the way of a new and steady internationalism will require a conscious effort to insulate foreign policy and its domestic roots from partisan politics. As the electoral map of the 2000 presidential election revealed, this will not be easy; there is a strong link between party affiliation and region. That partisan wrangling over foreign policy was on the rise during the past decade is also an ominous sign, as is the short duration of the bipartisan spirit that emerged after September 11. If regional differences over foreign policy do intensify over time, candidates for office will face only added incentives to highlight these differences in fashioning their electoral platforms.

Escaping the distorting effects of partisanship on American internationalism will require nothing less than a self-conscious political cease-fire. The Roosevelt era does provide hope that Republicans and Democrats alike can exercise self-restraint and put nation before party. But Roosevelt did have the war behind him and therefore the help of strategic imperative in eliciting political discipline. Leaders today cannot afford to await the emergence of a new rival to help them along. America would then have missed its current opportunity to avert that threat by fashioning a new grand strategy and a new internationalism to underwrite it. The incentive will have to come from foresight and awareness of the vital issues at stake.

America's leaders must focus on two chief objectives in addition to bipartisan cooperation. One is public education, particularly directed at younger generations. Polling data are not yet picking up striking differences across age groups on questions related to America's role in the world. But initial survey data and common sense suggest that

Americans raised after the end of the Cold War will pay less attention to geopolitics than their elders and be less attuned to the importance of multilateral engagement in global affairs. Most Americans are poorly informed about current events, not to mention the historical episodes that put in relief the high stakes riding on the trajectory of U.S. internationalism. The decline of history requirements in the country's colleges has only made matters worse. An ambitious education campaign is therefore a necessity, requiring everything from prime-time presidential speeches, to targeted programs in high schools and universities, to redoubled efforts by organizations like the Foreign Policy Association and the Council on Foreign Relations.

The second task is to rebuild intellectual capital on matters of grand strategy. The United States has in the past had the foresight to invest wisely in education, particularly in the hard sciences. America's labs, industries, technology firms, and military are second to none as a result. The United States now needs to make a similar investment in training diplomats and strategists, seeking at once to stanch the brain drain to other callings and to nurture a new generation of citizens schooled in matters of grand strategy. Such training should of course encompass exposure to a wide range of new issues—globalization, the Internet, international finance, homeland defense and combating terrorism—which are now central elements of a changing strategic environment. Furthermore, it is essential to ensure that African Americans, Hispanic Americans, Asian Americans, Arab Americans, and other minority groups are strongly represented in such programs. These communities must be fully engaged if an inclusive and representative brand of American internationalism is to emerge.

Yale University has taken an important step in the right direction by launching in 2000 a new program on grand strategy. Both undergraduates and graduates participate. They are exposed to the wide array of analytic tools needed to think about grand strategy as well as to the history of great powers and their successes and failures in managing order. The program's directors are still feeling their way forward, trying to figure out how best to close the divide between the past and the future, between the economist and the military strategist, between thinking and doing. But Yale has embarked on an endeavor that will begin to help fill a critical void.

Assuming that America's leaders rise to the occasion and set out to craft and sustain a new internationalism, what vision should they articulate as they do so? What policies should they pursue to prepare for the transition from a unipolar to a multipolar world? How can the United States lay the groundwork for stability and peace even as power and influence become more equally distributed among North America, Europe, and East Asia? What should be America's new grand strategy for the twenty-first century?

CHAPTER SEVEN

After Pax Americana

THE UNITED STATES cannot and should not resist the end of the American era. To do so would only risk alienating and provoking conflict with a rising Europe and an ascendant Asia. Asking that the United States prepare for and manage its exit from global primacy, however, is a tall order. Great powers have considerable difficulty accepting their mortality; few in history have willfully made room for rising challengers and adjusted their grand strategies accordingly.

If armed with the right politics and the right policies, the United States may well be able to manage peacefully the transition from unipolarity to multipolarity, thereby ensuring that the stability and prosperity attained under its watch will extend well beyond its primacy. At first glance, the past provides only sober warnings, not useful lessons. Multipolar systems have for the most part been breeding grounds for rivalry and war, not good news for America's leaders and their foreign counterparts who will soon have to confront the geopolitical fault lines long held in abeyance by U.S. predominance. But amid the long centuries of bloodshed are a few historical episodes that provide cause for optimism and reason to look again to the past for guidance on how to prepare for the future.

The relevant periods all involve processes of integration in which separate states self-consciously bound themselves to one another to avoid the destructive competition that would otherwise ensue. These historical episodes fall along a continuum that runs from a tight coupling at one end to a loose grouping at the other. At the tight end of the spectrum is America's experience with federation. The thirteen American colonies joined together to attain independence from Britain and then formed a polity that not only prevented rivalry among the separate states, but eventually merged them into a unitary nation. At the other end of the spectrum is the Concert of Europe, which effectively preserved peace in a multipolar system from 1815 until the middle of the nineteenth century. The five nations that participated in the Concert jealously guarded their sovereignty and created only an informal club; they never even considered engaging in the more demanding processes of integration that had occurred in North America. But they did succeed in overcoming the geopolitical rivalry that is usually endemic to multipolarity. In between the experiences of the United States and the Concert of Europe is that of the European Union. The EU is much less than a unitary nation but much more than a loose grouping of sovereign states. Although neither fish nor fowl, the EU represents a historic experiment in geopolitical engineering that has proved remarkably effective in erasing the strategic relevance of Europe's national borders.

A closer look at these historical episodes reveals that the peaceful management of relations among proximate centers of power requires three essential ingredients: the exercise of strategic restraint, the establishment of binding and bounding institutions, and the pursuit of the social integration needed to promote familiarity, trust, and a common identity and purpose.[1] Strategic restraint involves the withholding of power, thereby making room for newcomers and indicating benign intent. Institutions do for international politics what constitutions do for domestic politics—they tame the system and mute competition by binding actors to each other and bounding their behavior through adherence to a common set of rules and norms. Political and economic integration serves as the social glue, channeling competitive urges in a cooperative direction and laying the foundation for a realm of politics that encompasses previously separate states.

THE PAST

A TRAVELER CAN today cross the border from Virginia to Maryland without a passport or identity paper of any kind. Many Americans commute across that border daily without even being conscious that they are traversing a political boundary. In similar fashion, war between Virginia and Maryland is today unthinkable. The University of Virginia Cavaliers and the University of Maryland Terrapins may be archrivals on the basketball court, but there is no strategic competition between the two states. On the contrary, they, along with the other forty-eight states of the Union, are bound to defend each other's security. If Maryland were attacked by a foreign nation, Virginians and Americans from the rest of the country would not have to think twice before taking up arms. Support for military retaliation against Osama bin Laden's network was as strong on the West Coast as on the East, even though Californians were thousands of miles away from the destruction.

Americans take for granted that the states of the Union are at peace and would not hesitate to rush to each other's defense. But such harmony and collective spirit have not always been the case. Rather, they are the product of many decades of political and economic integration. During the colonial period, according to Felix Gilbert, a prominent historian of early America, "each colony felt itself to be autonomous and independent, a world of its own." The colonies also had different political systems. Some had governors appointed in London, some were private land charters, and others were governed primarily by religious authorities. There were at the outset few causes for direct conflict; the colonies were sparsely populated, had plenty of available land, and therefore rarely ran up against each other. But as the population increased, so did disputes over borders and territorial claims. Settlers not infrequently resorted to the use of force to resolve such disputes, and many feared direct warfare between the separate colonial (and later, state) militias. As Gilbert comments, "Their policy would have to be coordinated if they were not to fight each other."[2] At this stage in America's evolution, the colonies were competitors more than they were partners.

The separate colonies also had to address the question of whether they would band together when faced with external threats. They initially resisted collective efforts, preferring to remain independent political units. In 1754, the Albany Plan offered a unified policy and supervisory council for dealing with the threat from Native Americans. The colonies rejected it on the grounds that the plans infringed upon their individual autonomy. Even the prospect of a French invasion proved insufficient to elicit a collective response. When considering whether Maryland should prepare to come to the assistance of Virginia, the Maryland Assembly concluded "that the Situation . . . of our Neighbors of Virginia, with regard to violence or Outrage, threatened or perpetrated against them, by the French, does not require our immediate aid or Assistance, by the raising of an armed Force here."[3]

Replacing the individualism and competitive instincts of the colonies with a collective spirit was no easy task. The key political and conceptual innovation was the exercise of strategic restraint—the notion that checking the strength and autonomy of the individual colonies would ultimately leave them all better off. The practice of strategic restraint was to accomplish three distinct objectives: to tame the ambitions of the colonies toward each other, to constrain foreign countries in their dealings with the emerging American union, and to create a self-checking balance of power among the people, the states, and the federal government, the three political units that made up the Union. Mutual constraint, checks and balances, the moderation of power—these were the core ideas that made possible the transformation of America's politics, turning competition among separate colonies into cooperation among integrating states.[4]

The founders could hardly have been more adamant about the need for the separate states to set aside their jealousies and check their individual ambitions. The *Federalist Papers* delivered countless warnings that the states had to leave their quarrels behind or risk perpetual competition and conflict. John Jay used the experience of Great Britain to make the point. "It seems obvious to common sense that the people of such an island should be but one nation," Jay remarked. But England, Scotland, and Wales remained divided, and therefore "almost constantly embroiled in quarrels and wars with one another." Unless the people of America avoided the same mistake, Jay warned, "they would always be either involved in disputes and war, or live in the constant apprehension of them." The states would end up "formidable only to each other." "When a people or family so divide," Jay added, "it never fails to be against themselves."[5]

Alexander Hamilton was particularly worried about territorial disputes that would arise in the context of westward expansion. "To reason from the past to the future," he wrote, "we shall have good ground to apprehend, that the sword would sometimes be appealed to as the arbiter." The disputes between Connecticut and Pennsylvania over the Wyoming Valley (which is located in present-day northeastern Pennsylvania), Hamilton continued, "admonish us not to be sanguine in expecting an easy accommodation of such differences." Hamilton noted that it was particularly important for large states like New York and Pennsylvania to practice self-restraint in order to ensure that their small neighbors did not see "with an unfriendly eye the perspective of our growing greatness." Only if the strength of large states could be permanently checked would small states comfortably enter the Union. Hamilton argued that the separate states also had to compromise their economic autonomy and abolish interstate tariffs. Otherwise, duties would disrupt the flow of trade and foster commercial rivalries. Resentment would build quickly, Hamilton warned, as a result of "the opportunities which some States would have of rendering others tributary to them by commercial regulations."[6]

Federation would act as a check not only on the individual states of the Union but also on the ambition of foreign countries toward America. Jay stated the case succinctly in *Federalist 5*, arguing "that weakness and divisions at home would invite dangers from abroad; and that nothing would tend more to secure us from them than union, strength, and good government within ourselves." If others "see that our national government is efficient and well administered, our trade prudently regulated, our militia properly organized and disciplined . . . they will be much more disposed to cultivate our friendship than provoke our resentment," Jay explained. The alternative, according to Hamilton, would be for the separate states to "become a prey to the artifices and machinations" of foreign countries all operating on the motto of "divide and impera." The same logic applied in the realm of commerce. If America remained divided, foreign nations would play the separate states off each other and exploit them. Federation, on the other hand, "would enable us to negotiate, with the fairest prospect of success, for commercial privileges of the most valuable and extensive kind."[7]

Strategic restraint was also needed to protect America from itself, to ensure that the creation of a federation would not come to imperil the freedom and liberty of the people and their individual states. Accordingly, the federal government had to be simultaneously empowered and constrained. As James Madison put it in *Federalist 51*, "You must first enable the government to control the governed; and next place oblige it to control itself."[8] The federal government was charged with overseeing the collective welfare of the union of states and ensuring its security. But to protect against the tyranny of the center, state militias, not a large federal army, were to provide the men. Strategic restraint would both enable the Union to come into being and prevent it from becoming a dangerous Goliath.

If strategic restraint was the main idea making possible the American Union, institutions were the main mechanisms bringing that idea to life. Institutions set out the rules of the game and the means of enforcing those rules, replacing rivalry and suspicion with order and reciprocal self-restraint. The principal institution behind the domestication of America's politics was the U.S. Constitution. Spelling out and codifying the rights and obligations of the different spheres of authority were crucial to creating a structure that was centralized and coherent enough to provide effective governance, but decentralized and constrained enough to pass muster with those wary of central authority. The Articles of Confederation adopted by the states in 1781 simply proved too weak. That government consisted only of a legislative body to which each state legislature sent representatives. There was no judiciary, no executive, and a congress that did not have the right to tax, to enforce the few decisions it took, or even to regulate interstate commerce.

The Constitution that entered into force in 1789 rectified these weaknesses by performing the two essential functions of binding and bounding. By binding to each other and making mutually dependent the people, the states, and the federal government, the Constitution mandated the processes of integration and centralization that would make the Union cohere as a single entity. As made clear in its first sentence, the purpose of the Constitution was "to form a more perfect union." It was to this end that it granted to the federal government the authority needed to bind the states to each other and create a whole from the sum of the parts. These core functions included "to regulate commerce with foreign nations, and among the several states," "to coin money, regulate the value thereof, and of foreign coin, and fix the standard of weights and measures," "to establish post offices and post roads," and "to provide for the common defense." All rather mundane tasks, but all central to forming a unitary nation from the several states.

The Constitution amassed collective will through its binding function, but it also countered that will by bounding the powers of each sphere of authority and making them mutually constraining. In so doing, it locked in the checking mechanisms that protected Americans from the very act of federation in which they were engaging. The Constitution vested sovereignty in the people by establishing elections, making elected officials accountable to the public, and specifying the inalienable rights of the individual to, for example, free speech, association, and religion. But it then bounded the power of the citizen by giving the state the authority to raise a militia and put down popular rebellion.

The Constitution empowered the states by giving each of them two senators (originally selected by state legislatures, not popular vote) regardless of population and vesting state authorities with numerous responsibilities, including law enforcement and the maintenance of order. But it then limited the autonomy of the separate states by creating a federal government that stood above them, had the authority to tax, and could regulate interstate commerce.

The Constitution empowered the federal government by making the president the commander in chief and establishing judicial and executive institutions that gave America a unitary character. But it then restricted the authority of these institutions by giving Congress the right to declare war, ratify treaties, and control the budget. By binding together the people, the states, and the federal government while simultaneously bounding the power of each, the Constitution provided an institutional framework that tamed the separate ambition of the states as well as the ambition of the federal government, paving the way for union.

That joining the United States had considerable appeal across North America was a testament to the Union's power-checking devices and the comfort they engendered in the territories considering statehood. America was anything but restrained in dealing with Native Americans, Mexicans, and others who stood in the way of westward expansion. But once settlers were in control of the land, the self-restrained nature of the U.S. government made it much easier for them to opt for statehood. Although declaring neutrality or allying with Britain held initial appeal for some territories, the realization that they would retain important aspects of autonomy helped tip the balance toward joining the Union. As Senator Robert Walker of Mississippi remarked in making the case for the accession of Texas to the Union, "Each state, within its own limits, controls all its local concerns," with the federal government confining itself "to commerce and . . . foreign relations."[9] America was not in the business of annexing new states and absorbing them into a preexisting country. Rather, new states were becoming part of an ongoing experiment in nation-building even as they preserved a significant degree of self-government.[10]

The third ingredient that made possible the taming of America's political system was social integration and the framing of a common national identity. America from the start had a distinct advantage in overcoming competition among its individual states—they were not divided by ethnic or linguistic boundaries. And precisely because many settlers had immigrated to America in search of religious and political freedom, the states shared a common commitment to developing a republican civic identity. The essence of American identity was not ethnicity or religion, but commitment to the national project and its core values of liberty and democracy. As President Andrew Jackson told Americans in his farewell address, "Providence . . . has chosen you as the guardians of freedom, to preserve it for the benefit of the human race."[11] Norms of self-restraint, fairness, and moderation were also part of the civic identity that was propagated through political activities, the mass education system, public ceremonies, and literature to help develop a national identity that would subsume, or at least stand alongside, separate state identities and loyalties.[12]

The spread of this national identity went only so far. It was held back by the weakness of the center, the limited mobility of many Americans, and the consequent persistence of local and state loyalties. And although growing trade did mean more contact across state boundaries, greater economic integration was not sufficient to reverse the gradual separation between the North and the South that resulted from their incompatible social orders. Slavery had become an institution in the South, one that was a part of the region's culture, not just its economy. In the lead-up to the Civil War, southern leaders began to develop and disseminate a distinctive southern identity, with a separate flag, folklore, and cultural heritage. When the continuing admission of new states into the Union shifted the political balance against slave states, it was therefore the South's way of life and core values that came under threat. The sense of commonality stemming from a shared commitment to a republican civic identity was no match for the passions invoked by the estrangement between North and South.

In the aftermath of the war that resulted from these passions, social integration proceeded in unprecedented fashion. The Civil War and its outcome strengthened the federal government, the executive branch in particular. Industrialization and the expansion of a transportation network also led to greater mobility and economic integration, furthering the process of building a centralized national government supported by a strong national identity. Prior to the Civil War, Americans almost always followed the name of their country with a plural verb ("the United States are . . ."). During the years following the war, they began to use a singular verb ("the United States is . . ."), connoting that an important shift in social identity had taken place.

The exertions and national mobilization demanded by World War I and World War II completed the building of the modern American nation-state, creating an extensive public sector, a substantial national security apparatus, and political support for the country's active engagement in world affairs. By the second half of the twentieth century, America had not just turned its multipolar landscape of separate states into a cohesive union, but had also created an amalgamated and centralized polity of unsurpassed economic and military strength.

BRITAIN'S Lord Castlereagh and Austria's Clemens von Metternich, the principal architects of the Concert of Europe, took a different approach to taming multipolarity than did America's founding fathers. Formed at the Congress of Vienna in 1815 and developed further at Aix-la-Chapelle in 1818, the Concert took shape at a time when Europe was populated by sovereign nations separated from one another by distinct political, linguistic, and cultural boundaries. Europe was also ideologically divided, with Britain and France pursuing liberal reforms while Russia, Austria, and Prussia were steadfastly defending conservative monarchy. The conditions were hardly ripe for a stable peace.

The Concert nonetheless overcame the competition that normally accompanies multipolarity, replacing it with community and cooperation among Europe's major states. Despite stark differences with the American experience, the three main ingredients of this novel European peace were the same as in the U.S. case: strategic restraint, binding and bounding institutions, and social integration.

The Concert introduced strategic restraint at three complementary levels. First, the four original members—Britain, Russia, Prussia, and Austria—integrated France into the Concert in 1818, only three years after their adversary's defeat. Despite the temptation to impose on France a punitive and exclusionary settlement, the Concert's leaders held back, realizing that the preservation of peace in Europe could not be attained without French participation.

Second, the two strongest countries, Britain and Russia, deliberately elevated the status of Prussia, Austria, and France in order to put all of Europe's major states on a level playing field. They went so far as to enlarge the boundaries of Prussia to augment its military strength and political clout. By withholding their power and decentralizing influence, Britain and Russia were forming a forum of equals, one that would satisfy the aspirations of second-tier countries instead of provoking their ambition. Castlereagh made explicit this particular brand of self-restraint: "Rather than put herself at the head of any combinations of Courts to keep others in check," he wrote, "it is the province of Great Britain to turn the confidence she has inspired to the account of peace, by exercising a conciliatory influence between the Powers."[13] Stepping back and making room for rising states to punch above their weight was an innovative strategic maneuver that made clear the benign intentions of Britain and Russia and facilitated the formation of an exclusive and cohesive club of Europe's five major nations.

Third, the Concert developed the practice of reciprocal self-restraint; one country would pass on opportunities for individual gain in return for like behavior from the others. If the French refrained from taking unilateral action to enhance their interests in Egypt, for example, the Austrians would do the same in Italy. The purpose, according to one of the British diplomats who helped negotiate the terms of the Concert, was to avoid "any projects of aggrandisement and ambition similar to those which have produced all the calamities inflicted on Europe since the disastrous era of the French Revolution."[14] By agreeing to put harmony and consensus above all else, Concert members were making a tacit compact to let collective welfare prevail over self-interest. In a note to his counterparts explaining why France in 1841 was backing off from policies in Egypt that were alienating the other Concert members, King Louis Philippe wrote, "France wishes to maintain the European equilibrium, the care of which is the responsibility of all the Great Powers. Its preservation must be their glory and their main ambition."[15]

Institutions served as the vehicle for the exercise of strategic restraint, making explicit the rules and norms that would guide the behavior of the members. These institutions took shape through a series of meetings, the most important of which were the gatherings in Vienna and Aix-la-Chapelle. Some of the rules governing the Concert were contained in official documents. Others emerged as shared understandings among the participants.

Like the U.S. Constitution, the institutions of the Concert performed the function of at once binding the members to each other and bounding their individual ambition and influence. The Prussian foreign minister, Friedrich Ancillon, described these dual functions as follows:

> The five great powers, closely united among themselves and with the others, form a system of solidarity by which one stands for all and all for one; in which power appears only as protection for everybody's possessions and rights; in which the maintenance of the whole and the parts within legal bounds, for the sake of peace of the world, has become the only aim of political activity.[16]

A joint protocol signed in 1818 reaffirmed that "the five powers . . . are firmly resolved never to depart, neither in their mutual Relations, nor in those which bind them to other states, from principles of intimate union."[17]

Regular face-to-face meetings of European leaders were perhaps the most important institution of the Concert. High-level emissaries gathered whenever crises or disputes emerged. Decisions were taken only by consensus. The members signed off on the territorial status quo; borders could be changed only through negotiation and the agreement of all five. Mechanisms for orchestrating restraint and inaction were as important as those providing for collective undertakings. Concert members established spheres of influence, buffer zones, neutral zones, and demilitarized zones to preempt competition in volatile areas. It was preferable for all five countries to refrain from intervention rather than to risk strategic rivalry. The Concert also provided for opt-outs as a means of avoiding conflicts of interest. The British opposed joint Austrian, Russian, and Prussian intervention to suppress a liberal uprising in Italy in 1820–1821. But instead of blocking the operation, London kept its distance. Castlereagh agreed to watch from the sidelines rather than stand in the way of his colleagues "provided only that they were ready to give every reasonable assurance that their views were not directed to purposes of aggrandisement subversive of the Territorial System of Europe."[18]

Institutional flexibility was also central to the Concert's effectiveness. The leaders who designed and managed it recognized that too much formality, codification, and institutionalization would do more harm than good. The Concert would have been brittle and short-lived if it had relied on rigid procedures and expected members to take on ironclad commitments to joint military action whenever and wherever a crisis would emerge. Instead, it functioned through informal negotiation, consensus-building, and an occasional bout of diplomatic coercion. Like Franklin Roosevelt, the designers of the Concert were searching for workable minimums, not impossible maximums. A British memorandum from 1818 captured this spirit:

> There is no doubt that a breach of the covenant [of the territorial system of Europe] by any one State is an injury which all the other States may, if they shall think fit, either separately or collectively resent, but the treaties do not impose, by express stipulation, the doing so as matter of positive obligation. . . . The execution of this duty seems to have been deliberately left to arise out of the circumstances of the time and of the case, and the offending State to be brought to reason by such of the injured States as might at the moment think fit to charge themselves with the task of defending their own rights thus invaded.[19]

The final ingredient of the Concert's success was the process of socialization that took place through repeated contact among its members. The leaders of Britain, Russia, Austria, and Prussia, by virtue of the alliance they forged to defeat France, had developed close personal ties even before the founding of the Concert. As Metternich remarked, "The Emperors of Austria and Russia, the King of Prussia, and their three cabinets, were really never separated. The leader of the English cabinets had also generally been with his colleagues of Austria, Russia and Prussia."[20] These personal relationships deepened further through the numerous meetings held to negotiate the peace settlement, map out how the Concert would function, and manage crises as they emerged. A strong sense of camaraderie and common purpose gradually took shape.

The Concert nurtured not just personal ties but also a communal identity. National allegiances were giving way to a growing sense of pan-European community. Members referred to the Concert not only as a compact or alliance, but also as "an intimate union." Europe, according to Castlereagh, had developed a "unity and persistence of purpose such as it had never before possessed." A chief aim of the Concert was to deepen this unity of purpose and sense of solidarity, "to keep down the petty contentions of ordinary times, and to stand together in support of the established principles of social order." Metternich agreed that Europe "has acquired for me the quality of one's own country."[21] The permeability of borders and the flow of people and goods across national boundaries contributed to the intensification of this pan-European identity. Social integration and communal spirit in turn facilitated cooperation and trust among Concert members.

Social integration furthered the cause of peace in nineteenth-century Europe, but its shortcomings also contributed to the ultimate collapse of the Concert and the return of national rivalries. Just as America's experiment with union was stymied by incompatible social orders in the North and the South, the Concert was plagued by the divide between more liberal rule in Britain and France and autocratic monarchy in Russia, Prussia, and Austria. Diverging conceptions of domestic order did not prevent the Concert from forming and functioning effectively for decades; the members took a hands-off approach to each other's internal affairs. But the divide did mean that the liberal revolutions and conservative crackdowns that swept Europe in 1848 dealt the Concert a blow from which it could not recover.

The revolutionary contagion and political unrest of 1848 led to a preoccupation with domestic affairs. France and Russia, in particular, turned to nationalism to promote political unity and legitimacy, contributing to the reemergence of strategic competition. Furthermore, many of the Concert's initial leaders were no longer in office, depriving Europe of the close personal ties, trust, and sense of common purpose they had forged. Because the Concert operated primarily at the level of high politics, social integration did not penetrate deeply. A new crop of leaders therefore meant the effective end of the Concert. By 1854, Europe's great powers again found themselves at war, this time in the Crimea.

THE EUROPEAN Union represents a third approach to taming multi-polarity. The Napoleonic Wars, the Crimean War, the wars of German unification, World War I, World War II—these struggles had made amply clear the destructive potential of rivalry among proximate poles of power. In the face of this long record of bloodshed, Europe's leaders embarked after World War II on efforts to alter permanently the Continent's strategic geography. The scheme they devised for doing so was considerably less ambitious than America's experiment with formal federation, but considerably more demanding than the

Concert and its reliance on ad hoc forms of cooperation. This middle road consisted of an evolutionary process of economic and political integration that would over time knit together Europe's national states and replace strategic rivalry with lasting cooperation. The essential ingredients were again the same—strategic restraint, institutional binding and bounding, and social integration.

Three overlapping tiers of strategic restraint have been at the heart of European integration since the outset. First, Germany, the instigator of World War I and World War II, had to be pacified. Germany's victorious adversaries provided the initial restraints. The Allies occupied the country and, after the onset of the Cold War, divided it into two. In East Germany, Soviet occupation was to continue for decades. In West Germany, the German people took it upon themselves to engage in many different forms of self-restraint, including abolishing the General Staff to check militarism, moving the capital from the grandeur of Berlin to the unassuming quiet of Bonn to signify a change of course, and incorporating in their new constitution provisions making illegal the use of military force for any purpose other than territorial defense. West Germans also dealt openly with their past, accepted responsibility for the atrocities their countrymen committed, and pursued reconciliation with their neighbors, steps important to ridding German society of aggressive nationalism.

Second, France and West Germany entered into a deepening process of economic and political integration, ensuring that the border between them would not again emerge as a geopolitical fault line. The formation of the Franco-German coalition was to induce the two nations to move in lockstep; decisions about common interests were to emerge only through consensus and compromise. The Franco-German coupling, inasmuch as it aggregated the strength and influence of Europe's two largest countries, was an instrument of empowerment. But the pulling and hauling of coalition management also acted as a check on the ambition of both states, exposing them to the restraint of each other's embrace.

Third, the European Union has itself acted as a power-constraint device based on a bargain struck between the Franco-German coalition and its smaller neighbors. The basic deal was that France and Germany agreed to bound their overwhelming might, forgo some of the advantages associated with their size and strength, and expose their behavior to the constraints of a collective Europe. In return, the smaller states agreed to play along, entering a European construction designed primarily by France and Germany. Through this essential bargain, the smaller states received what they wanted—a check against unfettered French and German power. And France and Germany attained what they wanted—a Europe crafted in their image.[22]

Europe took an incremental approach to designing the institutions needed to pull off this bargain. Its bloody past and array of cultural and political dividing lines denied it the opportunity to replicate the American experience and legislate the terms of union from the outset. Instead, Europe has had to take a long and steady series of discrete steps, gradually binding and bounding its way to unity. To drive this process along, the EU's founders turned to economic integration. If Europe were ever to cohere as a collective political entity, it would have to begin life as a collective economic entity. With little else to work with in the desolate and bitter years after World War II, Europe's leaders enlisted economic integration in the service of geopolitical transformation.

Robert Schuman could not have been clearer on this point when Europe was taking its first step, the founding of the ECSC: "Because Europe was not united, we have had war. . . . This proposal [for a coal and steel community] will create the first concrete foundation for a European federation which is so indispensable for the preservation of peace."[23] Despite the decades of incremental evolution to the EEC and then the EU, both the process and the ultimate objective identified by Schuman have remained essentially the same. As German Chancellor Helmut Kohl put it in 1996 when discussing the prospect of monetary union, "In reality, the policy of European integration comes down to the question of whether we have war or peace in the twenty-first century."[24]

Political integration has from the outset lagged behind economic integration. The sectors of society benefiting from economic union have served as the engine behind the European project, dragging along national states more reluctant to give up the prerogatives and trappings of sovereignty. The incremental steps have, however, added up, gradually enhancing the authority of EU institutions at the expense of national governments. The EU is now in the midst of sorting through numerous proposals for the further centralization of political power, including altering voting rules in the Council, streamlining decision-making, and strengthening the role of the European Parliament. Historic in its symbolic and practical implications, the drafting and ratification of a European constitution are under consideration.

Social integration and the salience of a collective European identity and loyalty have contributed to the increasing ability of EU institutions to bind and bound the separate national states. Europeans still feel much stronger attachment to their individual states than do Americans. But the EU's efforts to nurture a collective identity have had a telling impact, with many Europeans now strongly identifying themselves as citizens of Europe, not just of their nation-state. This shift in attitudes and allegiances was partly the natural product of economic integration and open borders. But explicit efforts at social engineering also played an important role. A European flag, a European parliament, a European passport, a single currency, cultural and educational exchanges, the establishment of several European universities—these initiatives have all contributed to the creation of a legitimate realm of politics at the level of a collective Europe.

The EU's magnetic attraction among Europe's emerging democracies is a testament to the appeal of its construction. As in the American case, an expanding union is not causing the countries in its path to run for cover or seek to form an opposing coalition. On the contrary, states not yet part of the union are impatiently awaiting membership. Far from seeing Europe as a predatory institution that will threaten their sovereignty and well-being, the new democracies justifiably see entry into the EU as their ticket to prosperity and security. The EU promises to do for Central Europe what it has already done for Western Europe—replacing a war-prone multipolar landscape with the binding and bounding effects of peaceful union.

THE FUTURE

NOTHING COULD be more perilous than entering the emerging period of geopolitical transition under the illusion of geopolitical stasis. Nonetheless, that is precisely what the United States is poised to do. America is likely to be preoccupied with the battle against terrorism, a focus that will come at the expense of the attention paid to the challenges posed by the return of a multipolar world. America's unipolar moment is also coming undone in a deceptively quiet fashion, with most observers and policy-makers failing to appreciate the geopolitical significance of Europe's rise. That the shifting character of American internationalism will contribute to the pace of global change further masks the unraveling of unipolarity. Diminishing political will is much harder to detect and measure than diminishing military might. So too is it hard to measure the quiet alienation engendered by America's unilateralism.

Accustomed to hegemony and overlooking the subtle but potent forces altering global politics, most American strategists remain confident that unipolarity is durable. The size of the U.S. economy and its dominating defense establishment help sustain this illusion. Indeed, confidence in the longevity of American primacy contributed to the dangerous mix of unilateralism and isolationism that shaped the initial outlines of the foreign policy of President George W. Bush.

Managing the return to multipolarity will be difficult and fraught with dangers under the best of circumstances. To overlook the global diffusion of power, focus on homeland defense and combating terrorism, and otherwise continue with business as usual would ensure the worst outcome. The United States would antagonize Europe and other aspirants, ensuring that the return of a world of multiple poles leads to estrangement and rivalry. Were America to seek to extend unipolarity beyond its time, it would also overreach, setting the stage for popular discontent and the country's ultimate retreat. A fragmenting international system coupled with a sudden bout of American isolationism would likely result—exactly the conditions that during the 1930s cleared the way for war.

Instead, the United States should get ahead of the curve and seek to shape the global transition that is now under way and picking up speed. The central question is not how much longer the unipolar moment will last, but whether the multipolar world that lies ahead emerges by default or by design. If by default, multipolarity will likely bring with it renewed instability and conflict. If by design, America has at least a reasonable chance of getting it right.

The return of a world of multiple power centers necessarily means the return of geopolitical fault lines. The chief challenge for the United States is therefore to find ways to minimize the strategic consequences of these fault lines, to build bridges across them, to check ambition in order to mute the competitive instincts they engender. As America's own history reveals, strategic restraint, institutions, and social integration have been the crucial ingredients of successful efforts to tame multipolarity in the past. These three ideas should serve as the foundation of a new liberal internationalism and form the conceptual core of a new American grand strategy.

Strategic Restraint

To exercise strategic restraint is to withhold power, to give ground, to make room for others. It is a strategy that is by no means universally applicable. To demonstrate restraint when dealing with an implacable enemy would be an act of folly and an invitation to exploitation. Britain, for example, had no business appeasing Nazi Germany during the 1930s—and suffered for doing so. The United States today confronts a serious threat from terrorism—and should show no restraint in meeting that threat. But America does not currently face a major adversary. Instead, it confronts an array of potential challengers whose intentions are still in their formative stages. The United States therefore has a rare opportunity to help shape those intentions, push them in a benign direction, and channel rising strength so as to dampen the competitive effects of new fault lines. In this context, to exercise strategic restraint is to give ground in order to gain ground, to expend less power, but paradoxically to realize more influence in doing so.

The practice of strategic restraint would further these goals through several pathways. The United States would make clear its benign intentions, sending a signal to others that it is more interested in preserving peace than in preserving domination. Potential partners would then be able to respond in kind, setting in motion the reciprocal acts of self-restraint that are the foundation of trust. By making room for other centers of power, the United States would also be able to shape when and how they assume more international responsibility. America would engage potential challengers rather than bump up against them as they eventually tire of answering to Washington and seek to shirk off its influence. Just as Britain and Russia during the Concert of Europe made satisfied nations of Austria, Prussia, and France, so can America elevate the status of today's rising aspirants and grant them the voice that preempts resentment. The child who rebels against overbearing parents is usually much more trouble than the one who is weaned of dependence and develops a mature responsibility and self-reliance.

EUROPE

What does a grand strategy predicated upon strategic restraint mean in practice? In the first instance, it means accepting Europe's yearning for greater voice and autonomy. History is coming full circle here. During America's early days, its citizens bristled at European superiority and the arrogance that accompanied it. As Hamilton wrote in *Federalist II*, "The superiority she [Europe] has long maintained has tempted her to plume herself as the Mistress of the World, and to consider the rest of mankind as created for her benefit. Men admired as profound philosophers have, in direct terms attributed to her inhabitants a physical superiority, and have gravely asserted that all animals, and with them the human species, degenerate in America— that even dogs cease to bark after having breathed awhile in our atmosphere."[25]

But then the tables turned. Europe's arrogance waned as it was eclipsed by a rising America. Europe wisely stepped aside, but over time came to resent American dominance and the conceit that has come with it. According to the German weekly *Der Spiegel*, "The Americans are acting, in the absence of limits put to them by anybody or anything, as if they own a blank check in their 'McWorld.' Strengthened by the end of Communism and an economic boom, Washington seems to have abandoned its self-doubts from the Vietnam trauma. America is now the Schwarzenegger of international politics: showing off muscles, obtrusive, intimidating."[26]

Now the tables are turning yet again. Europe is integrating and rapidly catching up with America. It behooves America to step aside. The United States has much to learn from the previous transfer of power and influence from one side of the Atlantic to the other. That transfer occurred peacefully largely because Britain exercised strategic restraint and made room for America. Americans did fight against the British in the War of Independence, and again in the War of 1812. But America's displacement of Britain as the hegemon of the Western Hemisphere—the real passing of the baton—occurred without the firing of a single shot.

During the closing decades of the nineteenth century, London accommodated U.S. demands on a series of divisive issues. Britain dramatically reduced its military strength in Canada, backed down on a dispute concerning the borders of Venezuela, supported the United States during the Spanish-American War and U.S. expansion into the Pacific, and reduced its naval presence throughout the western Atlantic. The United States reciprocated by effectively demilitarizing its side of the Canadian border, agreeing to settle all disputes with London through neutral arbitration, and changing the tenor of its diplomacy toward Britain from hostility and suspicion to friendship and trust. By the early 1900s, policy-makers and observers on both sides of the Atlantic agreed that affinity between the two countries had grown so strong that conflict between them would have "the unnatural horror of a civil war."[27]

It is a historical anomaly that Pax Britannica gave way to Pax Americana without direct conflict between Britain and the United States. Most great powers step aside only after brutal defeat by the rising challenger. Britain and America had a common heritage and democratic culture going for them. And the rise of Germany and the threat it posed to European stability gave London a strong incentive to seek rapprochement with the United States, enabling Britain to recall its Atlantic fleet to deal with challenges closer to home. Commonality and strategic incentive, however, are hardly sufficient to ensure a peaceful handoff. Rome and Constantinople shared a common heritage, religion, and system of governance. They each faced pressing external threats. And the third-century division of the Roman Empire into western and eastern halves occurred by design, not by default. Nonetheless, theirs was a history of bloodshed and struggle for primacy, not accommodation and peace.

The actions of the United States will be the primary determinant of whether the end of Pax Americana resembles the peaceful handoff from Britain to the United States or parallels the bloody experience of the Romans and Byzantines. As was Britain during the 1800s, America is the reigning hegemon and therefore holds the cards. It must tender the first offer of accommodation and make room for the newcomer if the United States and Europe are to follow a path of reciprocal restraint rather than confrontation. America is fortunate to have in Europe a willing partner. The two have a long history together and share some common values. And Europe is anything but an aggressive predator that needs to be rigorously contained; the EU is bent on finding a stronger geopolitical voice, not on conquest and domination. Should America prove able to tame its unilateral impulse, Europe's limited ambition provides cause for cautious optimism about the prospects for reciprocity and accommodation.

The Clinton administration took an important step in the right direction by being more supportive of European integration than its predecessors. During the Cold War, Democrats and Republicans alike expressed public support for integration, but an undercurrent of suspicion that European strength would come at the expense of American influence always limited Washington's enthusiasm. The Clinton team fought against this tradition, mustering strong and sincere support for Europe's single currency and for an EU that would enjoy greater unity and a larger membership. Clinton understood that a stronger and more self-confident Europe could in the end work to America's advantage.

There were, however, limits to the Clinton team's ability to tolerate a stronger Europe. When the EU in 2000 embarked on efforts to build an independent defense capability, the administration proved unable to let go of old habits. Bush's advisers have been equally tentative about Europe's defense aspirations—even as they have made known their intention to downsize America's strategic commitment to Europe. Control over security matters is, after all, the decisive factor in setting the pecking order and determining who is in command.

Washington's generally skeptical reaction to Europe's geopolitical ambition makes clear just how difficult it will be for America to cope with its unraveling primacy. To resist the maturation of the EU is, however, to make less likely a smooth and peaceful transition to a multipolar world; the United States is missing an opportunity to channel growing European strength so that it emerges as a complement rather than a challenge to the United States. Instead, America should welcome European integration in all its facets, including defense, using strategic restraint as an instrument for engaging Europe and shaping the trajectory of its geopolitical aspirations.

To move past the current impasse and the ill will it is generating, Europe should get on with the task of building a military force able to operate autonomously. The EU must oversee the further coordination and integration of national defense policies, seeking to map out on a collective basis the procurement programs and reforms required to give Europe more capability. European governments also need to begin laying the necessary political foundation for these new defense programs. Moving from conscript to professional armies, upgrading equipment and training, merging the planning and procurement processes of individual states, raising defense expenditure—these are tasks that will require public understanding and a new level of collective will.

The United States should reciprocate by ceasing its carping about Europe's moves and offering a new bargain: capabilities for influence. America agrees to accord Europe greater voice in step with its greater capability. The United States should make clear that it is prepared to uphold its end of the bargain by actively seeking ways to devolve more responsibility to the EU. Giving Europeans more influence in the

NATO command structure would be a step in the right direction. NATO's decision in January 2000 to grant European forces operational command of the mission in Kosovo was a positive gesture.

As Europe's defense capacities and its collective will evolve, the United States should look for ways to forge a more mature strategic partnership with the EU. This means more diplomatic contact with Europe as a single entity rather than working primarily through national capitals. It means consulting fully with the EU before pursuing important policy initiatives rather than acting unilaterally and briefing Europe after the fact. And it means a public education campaign to ensure that Congress and the American people come to see Europe as an emerging equal, not as a strategic burden or a strategic adversary.

As THEY SEEK to forge a new and more balanced Atlantic link, America and the EU should work together to complete two remaining tasks: the consolidation of peace in southeastern Europe and the integration of Russia into the European project. Europe's southeastern flank remains its most troubled zone. The historical developments that helped democratize and pacify northern Europe—industrialization, the formation of classes that cut across ethnic boundaries, the separation of church from state—have made less headway in the southeast. Ethnicity, religion, and competing historical claims are therefore still entangled in politics.

Despite the largely peaceful revolution that swept Yugoslav President Slobodan Milosevic from office in 2000, the union of Serbia and Montenegro is still fragile and could fragment yet again. The Dayton Accords have kept the peace in Bosnia for six years, but only because NATO troops stand at the ready. Were the international community to depart, fighting would likely return to Bosnia. Albania is a state only in name; the central government does not have effective control of large portions of the country and corruption runs rampant. Greece and Turkey are still uncomfortable neighbors, their politicians regularly exchanging barbs and their aircraft regularly engaging in mock, but still hostile and dangerous, dogfights over the Aegean. Unless these festering disputes are resolved, they will continue to bog down the EU and drain its diplomatic and military resources. If this decade is to serve as a transition period for America to devolve to Europe primary responsibility for managing its own security, the United States and the EU must first work together to ensure that these historical divides are permanently on the mend.

Peace in the Balkans is now being held together by a combination of coercion (provided by NATO peacekeepers), political trusteeship (provided by the U.N. and the international community's Office of the High Representative), and economic assistance (provided primarily by the EU). The hope is that the gradual integration of the region into the EU will work its wonders, ultimately rendering insignificant the ethnic and political borders that at least for now still invoke passion and conflict. Although sensible in principle, this strategy has a major timing problem. It will take a generation, if not two, for the broken states of the Balkans to be ready for entry into the EU. In the mean-time, ethnic hatreds will continue to fester; children who watched their parents slaughtered by their neighbors do not easily forgive and forget. In this sense, America and the EU are stuck in a holding pat-tern in the Balkans that does not offer the prospect of a stable end point in a reasonable time frame. The United States and the EU may well run out of patience and resources before processes of integration into Europe have made a lasting difference.

Even as integration of the Balkans into the EU remains the ulti-mate goal, measures will therefore be required in the nearer term to bring the region to a stable, albeit interim, plateau. This interim objec-tive should be a regional order that is self-sustaining, or least much less dependent upon legions of outside troops, administrators, and aid workers. Attaining this goal means acknowledging that the preserva-tion of multiethnic societies throughout the Balkans, however laud-able in principle, is not working in practice. States that enjoy the most ethnic homogeneity—Slovenia and Croatia—are the farthest ahead on political and economic reform. States with large ethnic minorities have already come undone violently and are hanging together by the loosest of threads. Kosovo is now independent from Serbia in all but name. Bosnia has been divided into Serb, Croat, and Muslim sec-tors; they barely tolerate each other and pretend to be part of a unitary state only under the duress of the international community. Macedo-nia, which throughout the 1990s was able to avoid the bloodshed, in 2001 fell prey to violence between its Slav majority and Albanian minority.

A day of reckoning therefore awaits, one that will likely involve the redrawing of borders and a new territorial settlement that offers hope of bringing a lasting stability. Kosovo will ultimately have to be cleft from Serbia and recognized as either an independent state or an autonomous region. Macedonia has a chance of remaining a multi-ethnic state, but its integrity will require careful monitoring by the international community as well as earnest efforts by the government to improve the rights and social status of the Albanian minority.

Bosnia presents a much greater challenge. It is stuck in a political no-man's-land. The international community has essentially attached itself to Bosnia like a barnacle, sitting atop the state, attempting to govern through the same political parties and patronage systems that oversaw the bloodletting. The Dayton Accords were supposed to provide a framework for repairing ethnic divides and encouraging Serbs, Croats, and Muslims to live again in each other's midst. But few refugees have returned to villages in which they would be in the minority. And the three polarized communities would rather receive economic aid from the EU than rebuild economic ties that cut across ethnic boundaries. The sad truth is that Bosnia has already been ethnically partitioned and that reconciliation is nowhere in sight.

If Bosnia is to become other than a ward of the international community, America and the EU must either take two steps forward or two steps back. Stepping forward requires giving the Office of the High Representative the authority to govern with a heavy hand and to break the logjam that continues to confound Bosnia's government. It means changing the country's electoral system to deny nationalist parties their stranglehold over politics, making room for candidates willing to reach out across ethnic lines. It would mean instructing NATO troops to arrest all indicted war criminals rather than look the other way as some remain free. And moving forward would necessitate more serious efforts to return refugees to their original homes, restoring at least some multiethnic character to towns and villages that were ethnically cleansed during the war.

If the international community is not prepared to run the risks associated with these actions, it must take two steps back and cut its losses. This approach would necessitate giving up on maintaining the integrity of a multiethnic Bosnia, scrapping the Dayton Accords, and letting the Croats affiliate with Croatia and the Serbs with Serbia. Better to face reality and let pragmatism trump principle than to expend scarce resources and political capital under the pretense that they are paying off.

Consolidating rapprochement between Greece and Turkey is the final piece of unfinished business in southeastern Europe. The two parties made significant progress during 1999 after they helped each other recover from earthquakes that hit the region. Turkish Foreign Minister Ismail Cem and Greek Foreign Minister George Papandreou exchanged visits and built a sincere personal rapport. Greece at the end of the year took an important step forward by supporting Turkey's bid to start negotiating with the EU over ultimate accession. The Turks, however, failed to reciprocate with a gesture of similar import. The budding rapprochement then stalled, and Greece's optimism turned into resentment.

America and the EU should use whatever leverage they can to encourage both parties to pursue reconciliation and trade concessions rather than barbs. Drawing Turkey more fully into Europe's markets and institutions—and making such integration contingent upon a more forthcoming stance on relations with Greece—offers the best hope. Nothing would do more than rapprochement to set the stage for the end of southeastern Europe's long era of cleavage and confrontation. Reconciliation between Ankara and Athens would also help bring a stable peace to Cyprus, an island for decades plagued by hostility between its Greek and Turkish communities.

The attachment of Russia to a broader Europe is the other crucial step needed to complete the European project and prepare the EU for more self-reliance. Since the rise of the modern state system in the seventeenth century, Russia has been an integral part of Europe's geopolitics. It helped defeat Napoleonic France and then was a leading member of the Concert of Europe. Russia also played a central role in the defeat of Germany in World War II.

The past illuminates not only Russia's prominent role in shaping the Continent's geopolitics, but also the importance of attaching Russia to contemporary Europe. As the experience of the Concert made clear, victors must reach out to a defeated adversary when fashioning a new order. The Concert was able to preserve peace for decades in no small part because it had the foresight to include a defeated France in its ranks. France therefore reemerged as a cooperative power, not a humiliated and resentful one. In similar fashion, the genius of the post–World War II settlement lay in incorporating a defeated Germany into NATO and the European project, paving the way for a democratic, prosperous, and reunified Germany to emerge as one of the anchors of the EU. In stark contrast, the Versailles Treaty imposed a punitive peace on Germany after its defeat in World War I, leading to impoverishment and alienation and setting the stage for the sequence of events that put Hitler and the Nazis in control of much of Europe.

We seem to have forgotten these important lessons and have been in the midst of proceeding with the construction of a Europe that risks excluding Russia. Rather than doing our utmost to draw Russia into the territorial settlement that followed the end of the Cold War and the collapse of the Soviet Union, the United States and its allies have been doing just the opposite—expanding NATO despite the vociferous objections of Moscow and building a wider Atlantic security order that still treats Russia like an outsider.

Sparing Europe the emergence of a new dividing line requires a definitive change of course. The enlargement of NATO, rather than amassing American and European might against Russia, should serve as an instrument for binding and bounding Russian strength and channeling it toward Europe. Just as the United States must exercise restraint and make room for Europe if competition across the Atlantic is to be muted, NATO must make room for Russia in its ranks if a new division of Europe is to be avoided. This approach would also make it much easier to integrate the Baltic and other Central European states as enlargement proceeds; they will be joining with rather than against a Russia that has come to see NATO not as a threat, but as integral to its security.

NATO is the appropriate tool for the job both because American power and leverage are needed to draw Russia westward and because the alliance serves as the leading edge of the historical processes of democratization and pacification that have gradually extended eastward across Europe. NATO prevents war and sets in motion reconciliation and integration; the EU then picks up where NATO leaves off, making integration irreversible and locking in peace among its members. Russia is still decades away from having an economy and polity ready for formal membership in the EU. But it may well be only years away from meeting the standards that would make it eligible for entry into NATO, an important first step in finding Russia a place in a new European order. And as its cooperation in the battle against terrorism made amply clear, Russia has a great deal to contribute to the collective security of the NATO countries.

As NATO members prepare for the further enlargement of the alliance, they must therefore alter their sights, transforming enlargement from a strategy aimed at stabilizing Central Europe to one that makes Russia's integration into Europe its top priority and ultimate objective. Expanding Russia's role in NATO deliberations, a step taken in the wake of Moscow's help in combating terrorism, was a move in the right direction. But measures short of full membership will ultimately prove insufficient; Russians justifiably balk at being treated as second-class citizens. The next round of enlargement should proceed as planned. But concurrently, NATO should begin a serious dialogue with Russia about its eventual membership. A time-table should be drafted; perhaps 2010 would serve as an initial target date for Russia's accession.

It is entirely plausible that Russian reform will fail, foreclosing the option of joining NATO and entering Europe. But at least the West will have made a sincere effort to bring Russia in and expose it to the pacifying effects of military and political integration. The risks are low; Russia will have a full say in NATO only as its reforms advance. But the payoffs of success would be substantial—Russia's democratization, pacification, and integration into Europe.

A NATO that includes Russia would admittedly bear little resemblance to the alliance that existed during the Cold War. Rather than being focused on the territorial defense of members, it would serve as a vehicle for coordinating peacekeeping, countering terrorism, and carrying out other military activities across Europe. It would be looser and more flexible, abandoning defense guarantees in favor of the informal habits of cooperation and consensus that were the lifeblood of the Concert of Europe. This is the only kind of NATO that can fulfill the task of attaching Russia to Europe, a primary goal for the United States as it seeks both to reduce its strategic commitments on the Continent and to construct a new relationship with a Europe at peace. And, as Americans realize that they are no longer interested in extending automatic guarantees to countries in all quarters of the globe, it is also the only kind of NATO that has a chance of sustaining the support of the U.S. Congress and the electorate.

Getting right this devolution of responsibility from America to Europe should be a central objective of U.S. grand strategy. The risk of overlooking it is high, precisely because it is a more subtle challenge than, say, bringing down the Taliban or managing relations with China. But the stakes are considerable. The Atlantic link has been the mainstay of Pax Americana; Europe has been the principal partner of the United States on virtually every front. Neither side can afford to take for granted that this relationship will outlast a more equal distribution of power across the Atlantic. On the contrary, more competition is inevitable. But foresight and willingness to accept a new and more balanced relationship can help ensure that even as Europe and America become competitors, they do not become adversaries.

EAST ASIA

In East Asia, America faces a different strategic challenge, even if a more familiar one. Unlike in Europe, countries in East Asia have not taken advantage of America's protective umbrella to pursue regional integration and repair geopolitical divides. As a result, American forces and diplomacy still play an important role in preserving a stable balance. Europe is now ready to run on its own steam in part because of Germany's willingness to deal openly with its past; denazification went hand-in-hand with regional reconciliation. Meanwhile, Asian countries harbor age-old antagonisms, with China and Korea justifiably unsatisfied with Japan's halting and reluctant approach to addressing the darker moments in its history. The Germans in 2001 opened a Jewish museum in Berlin, one whose searing design memorializes the Holocaust and the fate of German Jews. In contrast, the War Memorial Museum on the grounds of the Yasukuni Shrine in downtown Tokyo glorifies World War II; the main exhibit hall shows off Japan's infamous suicide torpedoes and aircraft. East Asia has not yet owned up to its past.

Uncertainty about China's long-term intentions adds a further complication. America can afford to, and indeed must, make room for Europe precisely because of confidence that the EU will not evolve into a predator. It is likely to flex its muscles and stand its ground with greater regularity, but unlikely to develop imperial aspirations. It is in this sense that Britain's accommodation of a rising America is the appropriate historical analogy. Britain presumed that the United States would not do it harm, and therefore had the confidence to engage in the acts of strategic restraint that, in combination with American reciprocity, ultimately led to a lasting partnership.

Britain's standoff with Wilhelmine Germany, not its rapprochement with the United States, may well be a much more appropriate historical analogy for America's contemporary engagement with China. During the decade prior to the outbreak of World War I, Britain faced in Germany not just a rising power, but also one bent on dominating Europe. The kaiser's resort to nationalism as a means of forestalling democratization and co-opting the working class produced a dangerous mix of military strength and geopolitical ambition. For Britain to have made room for Germany would have been to invite aggression—exactly the result of London's policy of appeasement in the 1930s.

At this point in China's development, it is impossible to predict how its intentions will evolve and whether its relationship with the United States will track the benign course of Anglo-American rapprochement or the malign trajectory of Anglo-German rivalry and war. Accordingly, the United States does not yet have enough information to decide whether it should make room for China's ambition or resolutely seek to block its path. For Washington to accommodate China in the same fashion that it should give way to the EU would be naïve; Beijing's intentions may well necessitate constraint. But to assume that China is already an adversary requiring rigid containment would be equally unfounded—and likely would become a self-fulfilling prophecy. In the great debate over China's future that is now taking place, both the optimists and the pessimists are off the mark.[28] It is simply too early to pronounce China either a strategic partner or an implacable adversary.

Furthermore, America can afford to adopt a wait-and-see attitude toward China. The alarmist claims of the pessimists notwithstanding, China does not have the economic and military might to be America's main competitor. China's GDP in 2001 was $1.3 trillion, while America's was $10.2 trillion—almost eight times larger. The economy of California alone is bigger than that of China.[29] At the end of the 1990s, China's defense budget was roughly 5 percent of that of the United States, and it has not kept pace with America's rising expenditures. The $48 billion increase proposed by President Bush in 2002 was itself more than twice the size of China's entire military budget.[30] America has twelve aircraft carriers in its fleet and is adding a thirteenth. The Chinese navy does not have a single carrier. If all goes well, China will be a respectable middle power within a decade, but it will not be America's principal challenger anytime soon.

Rather than rush to premature judgment, America should at this stage focus its efforts on shaping the character of China's growing ambition and channeling its increasing strength in benign directions. Washington should send a signal to Beijing that by moderating the scope of its ambition it will in fact expand its leverage and room to maneuver. This task means engaging rather than isolating China, and elevating Beijing's status and voice to satisfy its yearning to move up the international hierarchy. The goal should be to find ways of accommodating China's gradual emergence as a major power, while at the same time hedging against the possibility of an aggressive turn in Chinese intentions. America must seek to bind and bound China, but remain guarded about the possibility that China might refuse to play along.

Putting this strategy into practice means dividing U.S. policy into three categories. First, the United States should identify issues of special sensitivity to China on which it would seek to tread especially lightly. Washington should redress the widespread impression among Chinese that America looks down upon them and holds their country in low regard. "We do not expect equality," a senior diplomat explained during a recent conversation on the campus of Beijing University, "but we do expect respect. We could accept an America that treats China like a rich man treats a poor man. But we cannot accept an America that treats China like a rider treats a horse."

Rectifying this impression requires not only a change in the general tenor of U.S. diplomacy, but also the exercise of strategic restraint on specific issues. The United States can stand by Taiwan without arming the island with the latest generation of weapons and without taunting statements from Congress and the White House. Washington must also handle the issue of missile defenses with great care, consulting with China as development and deployment proceed. If China believes that its primitive nuclear arsenal will be neutralized by a defensive system, it will substantially augment its nuclear capability. To overlook Chinese concerns could not just poison Sino-American relations, but also lead to a new buildup of nuclear arms.

Second, the United States should identify the core issues on which it is prepared to stand firm. The aim is to set an outer boundary within which China needs to contain its behavior and to set standards by which to judge Chinese intentions. For Beijing to cross these boundaries would serve as an indication of aggressive intent and warrant a switch in U.S. policy from engagement to containment. China's use of force outside its borders, including against Taiwan, would clearly constitute a breach of this outer boundary. So would the transfer of weapons of mass destruction to rogue regimes or terrorist groups.

Third, the United States should seek to broaden and deepen areas in which it already shares common ground with China. Both parties have a strong interest in ending the division of the Korean peninsula. Washington and Beijing should cooperate more closely on the issue, with the United States working through Seoul, and China capitalizing on its special influence in Pyongyang. Trade is another obvious area of common interest. American corporations are keen to gain greater access to China's market. Chinese companies are already benefiting from more than $100 billion in annual sales to the United States.[31]

Europe has a potentially important role to play on the economic front. Whereas the EU's military reach is likely to be limited to its own region for the foreseeable future, its economic engagement is global in scale. In 1996, the EU and ten Asian countries established the Asia-Europe Meeting (ASEM) to pursue cooperation on economic, political, and cultural issues. Especially because the EU does not bring with it the political liabilities associated with America and its hegemonic posture, it may be able to play an important role in drawing China into global markets.

The potential payoffs extend well beyond the shared benefits of expanded trade. The economic liberalization that accompanies China's integration into global markets has the potential to produce political liberalization as well. Facilitating this process is the large and growing number of Chinese students studying in the United States, some of whom return to work in China's main urban centers. It is no accident that booming cities like Shanghai also have the most liberal politics. Competing in international markets and attracting foreign capital necessitate not just transparent accounting procedures, but also a congenial political atmosphere. China's Communist Party is not yet prepared to loosen its grip, and economic liberalization is no guarantor of political change. But the steady, continuing integration of China into the global economy holds out much promise of inducing reform and an incremental transition to democracy.

Regional integration offers another potential area for greater Sino-American cooperation. Successive U.S. administrations have generally stood in the way of the formation of regional forums in East Asia that do not include the United States. Washington opposed the creation of an Asia-only trade pact in the early 1990s, blocked Japan's attempt to set up an Asian fund to manage the region's financial crisis in 1997–1998, and has consistently resisted efforts to create an Asia-only security forum. Instead, the United States has erected a hub-spoke diplomatic structure, effectively establishing itself as East Asia's core and the main conduit for relations between the region's major states. This strategy maximizes U.S. influence and facilitates America's ability to preserve a stable balance in the region. But it also impedes regional integration and hinders the processes of reconciliation and rapprochement that must move forward if East Asia is to erect an order that is less reliant on the United States.

Rather than blocking Asia-only regional integration, Washington should welcome it, even if it comes at the expense of U.S. influence. America cannot permanently assume responsibility for keeping the peace. The region will ultimately need a self-sustaining order, and repairing political and ideological cleavages is a task only regional states themselves can perform. In addition to welcoming and facilitating more direct contact among all East Asian countries, the United States should press Japan and China in particular to set aside the grievances still lingering from World War II and proceed with rapprochement. Just as the Franco-German coupling has been the key to locking in peace in Europe, so too do East Asia's two main nations need to close ranks if the region is to enjoy a lasting stability.

It is admittedly premature, if not fanciful, to make mention of a Sino-Japanese coalition. The two countries are anything but partners; they are locked in adversarial dialogue and posturing, with America's military presence keeping the parties at bay. But reconciliation between France and Germany was equally implausible in 1945. The Franco-German coalition exists today only because of leaders who had the courage to imagine it, to practice strategic restraint, and to set in motion the processes of integration that brought it to life.

Jump-starting reconciliation and integration in East Asia would require not just bold leadership, but also Japanese willingness to deal more openly with its behavior during World War II. The Japanese have in recent years become somewhat more forthcoming in acknowledging and expressing remorse for their country's aggression against its neighbors. But guarded apologies and halfhearted acknowledgments have also been accompanied by actions that serve only to reopen old wounds.

Early in 2001, Japanese officials released a new junior high school textbook that justified Japan's conquests in East Asia and omitted mention of its wartime excesses, including the system of sexual slavery the military set up in Korea. In response, the Chinese government canceled a high-level visit to Japan, claiming the text "denies Japan's history of aggression." South Korea temporarily recalled its ambassador from Tokyo. And South Korea's foreign minister, Han Seung Soo, noting that "we've been on the receiving end of history's misfortune from Japan," lamented that "this textbook case threw cold water" on the emerging rapprochement between the two countries.[32] Prime Minister Koizumi's August 2001 visit to the Yasukuni Shrine, which honors Japanese militarism during World War II, aroused a similarly harsh response. South Korea announced that its president, Kim Dae Jung, would call off a meeting with Koizumi unless he formally apologized for Japan's wartime atrocities and acknowledged the inappropriate content of the new textbooks. China's President Jiang Zemin also balked at meeting with Koizumi.[33]

A true opening between Japan and China first requires a true opening and accounting of Japan's past—one that involves the rewriting of history textbooks, an extensive public dialogue, and reconsideration of whether certain museums and shrines appropriately memorialize the country's wartime behavior. As the recent history of Germany makes clear, internal reflection is a necessary precursor to external reconciliation. In addition, Japan should seek to enlarge its investment in and trade with China, enabling economic incentives and more contact to draw the two countries closer together. Investment in energy and transportation infrastructure would be particularly welcomed by the Chinese.

China also has work to do if its relationship with Japan is to move beyond cold peace. Beijing should respond with enthusiasm if Japan were to address its past more openly. It would be particularly important for Beijing to take advantage of a resolute accounting and apology to shape public opinion and moderate the resentment toward Japan that still runs deep in Chinese society. According to a public opinion survey in 1997, more than 40 percent of Chinese have a "bad" impression of Japan, while 44 percent have an "average" impression, and only 14 percent have a good impression. More than 80 percent of respondents indicated that Japan's invasion of China and its behavior during World War II remain their main association with Japan.[34] Loosening the domestic constraints stemming from these public attitudes is necessary to clear the way for rapprochement.

Negative attitudes toward China among the Japanese public, although more muted than anti-Japanese sentiment in China, place similar constraints on Tokyo's room for maneuver. Since the Tiananmen incident in 1989, when more than 150 students were killed during the government's suppression of popular protests, Japanese public opinion has been especially sensitive to China's domestic politics. In this respect, Beijing's willingness to liberalize further the country's political system and improve its record on human rights would help

Tokyo sustain an opening to China. At a minimum, a positive gesture from Beijing would build support for rapprochement among Japanese liberals, for whom China's stained human rights record is one of the main obstacles to closer relations.

China could also be more receptive to regular, high-level contact with Japan's politicians and its defense establishment. The two countries established diplomatic relations in 1972, but it was not until 1998 that a Chinese head of state traveled to Japan. And President Jiang Zemin's visit ended up doing more harm than good because the Japanese government refused to make mention of an apology for the past in a joint communiqué. Jiang then turned the issue into the centerpiece of his trip. High-level meetings have nonetheless continued, but they have done little to build momentum behind a real political opening.

Contact between the Japanese and Chinese militaries, although picking up in frequency, has been sparse, contributing to estrangement between Beijing and Tokyo. After years of isolation, China's People's Liberation Army has only recently agreed to engage in regular exchanges of information and personnel. If decades of mutual suspicion are to be overcome, China will need to demonstrate its readiness to participate in broader and more frequent bilateral activities, including joint military exercises. The two countries should also take advantage of the regular regional forums hosted by the Association of Southeast Asian Nations (ASEAN) to advance their bilateral agenda.

Numerous obstacles stand in the way of rapprochement. Sino-Japanese estrangement is as much a part of life in China and Japan as was East-West rivalry a part of life in America and Russia during the Cold War. Furthermore, the Japanese and Chinese political systems are anything but adaptive. An entrenched patronage system in Japan blocks much-needed domestic reform. That is one of the main reasons Japan's economy has been in the doldrums for more than a decade. The Chinese government is equally averse to change. It is threatened by the demise of communist regimes in most other parts of the world and by the liberalizing demands of globalization. It lacks the confidence to take the risk of reaching out to Japan. And authorities in Beijing may well face incentives to resort to nationalist appeals to bolster their waning legitimacy. These obstacles are not insurmountable, but they do make clear how important U.S. encouragement and pressure are likely to be in getting Japan and China to begin repairing East Asia's principal divide.

Sino-Japanese rapprochement, regional integration, and the ultimate taming of East Asia's multipolar landscape are distant prospects. Nonetheless, they offer the only alternative to a regional order that remains heavily dependent upon American guardianship. America is unlikely to withdraw anytime soon; the interests at stake and the threats to those interests remain high. America's changing internationalism will therefore have fewer immediate consequences for Asia than for Europe.

It would be a dangerous illusion, however, to assume that the status quo in East Asia is sustainable indefinitely. Should reconciliation between North Korea and South Korea move forward, it would likely have considerable impact on the scope and tenor of American strategy in the region. Although the North Koreans have suggested that they might welcome the presence of U.S. troops even after unification, the absence of a geopolitical divide on the Korean peninsula could undercut the principal mission justifying America's forward posture in East Asia. If that mission disappears, it may be hard to make the case—in the United States as well as among America's regional allies such as Japan—that this forward strategy should continue in its current form. Prudence warrants the beginning of a serious dialogue between the United States and East Asia's major countries on how to move toward a more self-sustaining and stable regional order.

SHOULD EAST ASIA eventually embark on reconciliation and integration, the resulting global system would consist of three main blocs— one in North America, one in Europe, and one in East Asia. On the surface, this vision has the potential to be a recipe for clashes between three regional behemoths, not a pathway to global stability. But in reality, integration on a regional basis offers the best hope for the peaceful return of a multipolar world. War and peace begin locally, not globally. Only if neighbors enjoy peace with each other will they be able to build stable and cordial relations with countries farther afield. It was only after Germany and Japan conquered their neighbors during the 1930s, after all, that they amassed sufficient strength and ambition to pose a wider threat. A realistic plan for building peace on a global scale must begin, to use the terminology of Harvard professor Joseph Nye, by constructing "peace in parts."[35]

Processes of regional reconciliation and integration, precisely because they are made possible by the exercise of strategic restraint and the use of power-checking devices, will produce regional blocs with only limited geopolitical ambition. America's ambivalence toward global leadership has its roots in the political culture and constitutional constraints left behind by the decades of compromise and debate that accompanied the forging of a federation. The EU's geopolitical ambition will continue to be constrained by the pulling and hauling that goes on between its supranational institutions and its member states. The external ambition of a regional bloc within East Asia would be similarly limited by the self-checking nature of coalition between China and Japan and the binding and bounding bargains that would be necessary to facilitate integration among the region's individual countries. In Asia, as in Europe, linguistic and cultural dividing lines would slow centralization and ensure that a regional bloc not turn into a unitary state with predatory ambition. If processes of regional integration are handled correctly, the prospect is thus not one of clashing behemoths, but of regional organizations more focused on managing their internal relations than on projecting their influence on the global stage.

THE DEVELOPING WORLD

Building peace in parts makes sense for one final reason. Regional zones of stability offer the best hope not only for furthering harmony among the more advanced nations, but also for promoting political modernization and economic growth in the developing world. The challenge ahead is how to convince the North to engage the South rather than to turn its back and cordon itself off from poverty and disease. The answer lies in two realities—that interests are more persuasive than altruism in engendering action, and that interests, even in the digital age, still intensify with proximity.

The United States is more interested in bringing peace and prosperity to Latin America than is either Europe or Asia. When poverty and instability send drugs and refugees northward, the U.S. pays a heavy price. In contrast, when Latin America's emerging markets thrive, the United States benefits from the expansion in trade and the declining flow of northbound migrants. Interests also explain why the countries of Central and South America are actively seeking to enlarge the free trade zone that has emerged in North America. They understand that there is no better route to prosperity than attaching themselves to a project of regional integration. An expanding zone of peace and free trade in the Americas thus represents the best hope of gradually closing the gap between the haves and the have-nots.

The same logic applies in Europe and Asia. Europeans are much more interested in the affairs of North Africa than are Americans or Asians. If violence or political collapse were to engulf the region, it is to Europe that the waves of refugees would head. The EU accordingly has a direct and pressing interest in fostering development on its southern periphery. So too is Europe's periphery intent on attaching itself to the EU, whether through membership or more informal political and economic ties. A potent centripetal force thus extends outward from the EU's core, reaching well beyond its formal borders into Eastern Europe, the Middle East, and Africa.

Regionalism in Asia lags behind that of Europe and North America. But if deeper regional integration does get off the ground, it would have a similar effect on the surrounding periphery. Attaching India to an expanding zone of prosperity in Asia promises to help integrate the world's second-most-populous state into the global economy, perhaps bringing Pakistan along with it. Their troubled relationship would benefit, just as did that of Spain and Portugal when they joined the process of European integration. China's border with India gives it a direct interest in the country's welfare and the stability of South Asia as a whole. In similar fashion, it is no accident that throughout the 1990s Japan consistently spent at least 60 percent of its foreign assistance budget in Asia or that most of the peacekeepers deployed in East Timor in 1999 came from Australia, New Zealand, Thailand, Malaysia, and other nearby countries.[36] Proximity matters. The formation of wealthy zones of regional peace in North America, Europe, and Asia is not a panacea for the developing world. But attaching poorer nations to proximate zones of prosperity offers them a much brighter future than the alternative—being left behind.

Even as regional zones of peace and prosperity extend their reach toward their neighboring peripheries, the United States has a special role to play in the Middle East. Ensuring access to the region's oil, protecting the security of Israel, and combating terrorism and its sources give the U.S. a direct interest in remaining fully engaged. At the same time, thinking through how Washington can modify its policy toward the Middle East is not to bow to terrorism or legitimate its perverse objectives, but only to recognize the complicated political terrain of the region and improve America's ability to navigate through it.

The main sources of anti-American sentiment in the Middle East stem not from the behavior of the United States, but from the region's own failures—poverty, income inequality, political repression, state-controlled media, ethnic and religious rivalries, and poor education systems. The regimes confronted with these conditions have primarily themselves to blame. But politicians, clerics, and extremist groups manipulate and exploit the alienation. They divert responsibility to Israel, the United States, and the West, and then seek to capitalize upon the resulting mobilization to further their ends. This anger toward the West frequently gets intermixed with religious fundamentalism, creating an explosive mix. The region's troubles are thus indigenous and have deep historical and political roots. Regardless of the behavior of Washington and the status of the Arab-Israeli conflict, Islamic countries will continue to vent at least some of their wrath toward America and the West. For these reasons alone, the United States would be wise to decrease its dependence on the region's oil by curbing consumption and developing alternative energy sources.

Nonetheless, America can and should take steps to deflect this anger, direct it toward the local parties mainly responsible for the poverty and inequality, and work to limit the social discontent upon which extremist groups prey. Especially if Washington finds itself using coercive means to eliminate terrorist cells based in the Middle East—which it must—it should be sure to take simultaneous steps to avoid a backlash and deepening resentment.

Helping to secure a peaceful resolution of the conflict between Israel and the Palestinians is a crucial first step. The United States cannot afford to distance itself from the dispute, as the Bush administration initially attempted to do. Whether justified or not, America is widely seen throughout the Islamic world as a staunch supporter of Israel, which in turn is perceived as an alien outpost of the West in Islamic lands. That perception will not change as a result of incremental shifts in U.S. policy. Instead, a peace settlement and the ultimate establishment of a Palestinian state offer the only solution.

Anti-American sentiment and terrorism are by no means a direct by-product of the Arab-Israeli dispute; Americans therefore should not labor under the illusion that these ills would disappear in the wake of a peace deal. On the contrary, extremist groups have regularly opposed a negotiated settlement and have explicitly sought to scuttle efforts to achieve one by carrying out terrorist attacks against Israel, thereby hardening Israeli attitudes, strengthening its right wing, and hampering compromise. The motivation behind this strategy is nothing other than self-interest. Extremist groups expand their ranks and derive their political momentum from disaffection. The more bitter and intractable the Arab-Israeli dispute, the better these factions fare.

But it is precisely because terrorist bands feed on discontent that a peaceful solution to the dispute between Israel and the Palestinians is so crucial. A peace settlement would eliminate at least one source of the anger that much of the Arab world feels toward the United States and the West more generally. It would mean that Arab leaders would have to begin answering for their failures, no longer able to blame outside forces. And it would make it easier for the United States to pursue other objectives in the region; America's presence would no longer be equated with the suffering of the Palestinians.

The United States should also seek to diminish anti-American sentiment in the Islamic world by demonstrating greater sensitivity to the suffering of peoples in the region. Dropping humanitarian assistance to the Afghani people amid the bombing campaign against the Taliban and Al-Qaeda was a useful move. The United States could reduce the visibility of its military presence in the Arabian peninsula without eroding the capabilities it needs to protect the flow of oil and prosecute the war against terrorism. And America should take steps on the public relations front, making its own case to peoples in the region through cultural and educational exchanges and broadcasting in local languages.

In short, the United States should be more aware that, even when it pursues well-intentioned policies, it is often perceived in the Middle East as a domineering, imperial power. That perception is to some extent inevitable; it comes with the terrain and America's position of global primacy. But Washington can certainly do much more to ameliorate the intensity of the resentment. Strength and vigilance in the struggle against extremist groups thus need to be carefully balanced with the practice of strategic restraint.

A final initiative involves formulating a long-term plan for gradually eliminating the underlying sources of disaffection throughout the developing world. This plan should aim at political liberalization, the growth of a middle class, the improvement of educational opportunities, and the modernization of social institutions. A long-term solution to the tension between the haves and the have-nots ultimately requires closing the gap between those at the front of history and those lagging much further behind. The extension of regional zones of prosperity to their poorer peripheries is a must in this respect, but so is reform of the North's broader approach to development assistance.

Reform means recognizing that regions vary widely as to the sources of poverty and lagging development. Most countries in Latin America and the Caribbean have the resources and infrastructure needed to attain higher levels of prosperity. They have been held back, however, by poor economic management, corrupt judicial systems, and wide social inequalities. Despite per capita incomes well above those in other developing areas, one-third of the region's population lives in poverty.[37] Although additional aid is needed to upgrade health care and education and to deliver basic needs to the poor, improving governing institutions and the judicial system is a priority. The region's gradual incorporation into a free trade area of the Americas can help reduce poverty and encourage reform, just as entry into NAFTA has done for Mexico.

Promoting development among the impoverished nations of Africa and South Asia is a more difficult challenge. Many of these countries have only a rudimentary economic and political infrastructure. Oppressive poverty is widespread, with education and health care systems primitive or, in some areas, nonexistent. In sub-Saharan Africa, less than a quarter of girls living in poor rural areas attend primary school. Africa is home to 90 percent of some 500 million clinical cases of malaria worldwide, a disease that results in an annual average of 1 million deaths. A child born in Zambia or Zimbabwe is more likely than not to die of AIDS.[38]

Africa's plight does not mean that the billions of dollars of aid that have flowed to the continent have been altogether ineffective. On the contrary, there are cases—Ghana and Mozambique are examples—in which outside assistance has clearly helped alleviate poverty and promote growth. Furthermore, social services in Africa have expanded markedly since the 1960s. Enrollment at primary school jumped from 40 to 70 percent of eligible children between 1965 and 1990, with literacy rates rising from roughly 15 to 50 percent. Between 1960 and 1990, the ratio of nurses to total population doubled. Life expectancy at birth has increased from thirty-nine to fifty-two years.[39]

These isolated successes aside, development efforts in Africa have generally fallen well short of expectations. Here is how Carol Lancaster, formerly a senior official in the United States Agency for International Development, summarized her conclusions in a book about the effectiveness of aid to Africa:

The amounts of foreign aid to most countries of sub-Saharan Africa have been among the largest in the world relative to the size of their economies.... For most African countries, the relatively high levels of aid had extended over several decades. Nevertheless, economic development has been disappointing in most of Africa. Average per capita income in the region is nearly the same in the 1990s as it was in the 1960s. Nearly half of Africa's 570 million people live on only one dollar per day. This percentage has not changed over the past decade or so. As a consequence, population growth has added 30 million people per year to the ranks of the impoverished. Moreover, the degree of impoverishment is greater in Africa than in any other part of the world.[40]

Such disappointing results have several causes. One is the inability of the recipient country to take advantage of available assistance due to the weakness of public institutions, corruption, and mismanagement. If the national government is pursuing flawed fiscal and monetary policies to begin with, then inflows of aid are unlikely to help the economy. They may even make matters worse by offsetting the ill effects of misguided policies, thereby reducing the pressure on leaders to change course. The donor community has also been at fault. Aid is frequently administered by bureaucracies in Washington, New York, or Geneva that have little knowledge of conditions in recipient countries. There is insufficient coordination among individual donor nations, bodies such as the World Bank and the United Nations, and the many nongovernmental organizations involved in providing development assistance. Political, strategic, and commercial motivations often crowd out humanitarian ones, meaning that even when assistance does stimulate economic growth, the benefits may not reach those most in need—the poor.

These shortcomings in performance and process underscore the need for substantial reform. Despite the importance of tailoring development programs to the specific problems of each locale, the world's wealthier nations must come together on the broad outlines of a new approach if they are to help redress the underlying sources of underdevelopment. Furthermore, the events of September 2001 and their aftermath provide new reason for seeking to relieve poverty and the disaffection it breeds. Although policies crafted to meet humanitarian needs will have better results than those aimed at countering strategic threats, programs that achieve their development goals will have the added benefit of helping to moderate the South's hostility toward the North.

A more effective program of assistance means devoting equal attention to the three building blocks of development—human capital, economic infrastructure, and political capacity. Human capital is the foundation; a literate and healthy population is vital to social and economic progress. Without it, a polity does not have the capacity to absorb outside assistance, with aid dissipating through society much like water runs through a sieve. Education and health also reinforce each other. Educated women have smaller, healthier families than do those without schooling. Education also appears to decrease child mortality and HIV infection rates.[41] China is today enjoying much higher economic growth than India at least in part because the Chinese government, even before it began to encourage the emergence of a market economy after 1979, invested in the country's schools and its health care system.[42]

The international community should devote much more attention and money to improving primary education throughout the developing world. Oxfam estimates that it would cost roughly $8 billion—less than 3 percent of America's annual defense budget—to provide universal education by 2015. Donors should offer national and local governments matching funds to encourage them to raise spending on primary schools and to magnify the effects of such spending. Steps should also be taken to improve universities, including partnerships and faculty exchanges with developed nations. And the United States and other countries with strong university systems should do more to encourage foreign students to return to their homelands for at least part of their careers, perhaps by making student visas or scholarships contingent upon a commitment to do so.

Improving access to education will have positive effects on health, both because more knowledge correlates with more prevention and care and because schools provide a centralized location for administering vaccines and distributing medicines. But direct intervention is also urgently needed. Whereas the construction of a modern health care system will take generations, the international community can take immediate steps to address the most acute diseases—and at moderate costs. The absence of a vaccine or cure, the high rate of infection, and its devastating effects on young adults make combating HIV a top priority and a unique challenge. Initial steps include providing better information about prevention, especially among social groups most vulnerable to the disease, and convincing pharmaceutical companies to provide medicines at much-reduced cost. Decreasing the incidence of tuberculosis, diarrhea, and malaria is easily within reach as long as more resources are made available for the purchase and distribution of medication.

The international community's main contribution to economic infrastructure comes in the form of aid and trade. Enhancing the effectiveness of aid in alleviating poverty and promoting growth requires revamping the relationship between donor and recipient. Rather than implementing programs designed and administered by the donor community, officials and private citizens in the recipient country should generate their own proposals, which would then be vetted by the assistance community on a competitive basis.

Relying more heavily on this "demand-driven" approach would have several advantages. It would vest initiative, responsibility, and accountability with local citizens rather than with bureaucrats thousands of miles away. Programs would be better suited to existing conditions and reforms more likely to last; innovative ideas and policies that come from within will be embraced more readily than those imposed from outside. Direct funding of specific projects would reduce the need for large and expensive staffs in both donor and recipient countries.[43] Cutting out intermediaries and targeting grassroots projects would also make it more likely that aid reaches communities in the most need. And competitive funding works against corruption and mismanagement; agencies or groups that have misused assistance would no longer receive it.[44]

More efficient use of aid would give donor countries a new incentive to increase their development budgets. U.S. spending on international assistance has been in relative terms very low, hovering at only 0.1 percent of GDP. The average African nation has been receiving from the United States about $20 million per year (a single jet fighter costs the U.S. about $30 million). On a per capita basis, each American has contributed about $29 per year to development and humanitarian aid, while citizens in other industrialized countries spend about $70 per year. In March 2002, the Bush administration announced that it planned to gradually augment annual spending on foreign assistance, raising the budget from roughly $10 billion to $15 billion by 2006—a significant increase, but one that will still put America well below the norm.[45]

Greater flows of trade must follow aid to ensure a stable foundation for continuing development. The United States and other wealthy countries should eliminate remaining commercial barriers with developing nations. Doing so would have a minor impact on an advanced economy, but could significantly stimulate export-led growth in smaller, developing economies. Opening the North's markets would, in aggregate terms, substantially outstrip the value of benefits provided through assistance programs. As one economist noted, "Developed countries have their highest trade barriers in precisely those industries, such as agriculture and apparel, where poor countries would have the best chance to work their way out of poverty."[46]

The United States should also increase the use of enterprise funds—publicly supported investment funds supervised by private boards of directors accountable to Congress. These instruments proved effective in supporting the growth of small business in Central Europe. Partnerships between donor organizations and private companies should also be used more regularly to expand the private sector in developing economies. Doing so is essential to teaching modern management skills and creating a middle class with a vested interest in economic stability and good governance. An influential domestic constituency, not just pressure from the international community, is ultimately required if economic and political reform is to gain momentum.

Political capacity is the final ingredient needed to help the South escape pervasive poverty. Economists have found a strong link between good governance and the ability of economic aid to stimulate growth.[47] In contrast, poor governance and counterproductive policies have stood in the way of development even in countries endowed with an educated public and abundant natural resources, such as Brazil, Argentina, and Russia. In Africa and South Asia, the costs of mismanagement are even higher, with the decisions taken by officials affecting not just the standard of living, but the viability of the state and the ability of its citizens to secure their most basic needs. As Lancaster notes, "It is difficult for foreign aid to bring about beneficial and sustainable changes where economic growth itself is stymied by government policies that discourage investment, by ineffective or corrupt public institutions, or by political repression and instability."[48] Many African governments, for example, continue to rely on high trade taxes for a sizable portion of fiscal revenue even though doing so significantly impairs commerce and dampens growth.

Political reform can to some degree come from the top down,

through a combination of local leadership, pressure from the international community, and the creation of a cadre of well-trained technocrats. But especially because officials are often reluctant to deviate from established practice and risk the perquisites of office, reform must also come from the bottom up. Some of the most striking episodes of political and economic reform in recent years have started at the grassroots level. In Russia, regional officials and local entrepreneurs have taken the lead in pursuing democratic and market reforms—despite resistance from the Kremlin.[49] The rapid growth of independent associations committed to civil society played an important role in supporting the transition to democracy in Central Europe. At the same time that it encourages institutional reform in national capitals, the international community should therefore target aid at local organizations, supporting projects that encourage public participation, provide social services, and nurture civic engagement.

Although important in their own right, such efforts would have the added benefit of countering Islamic extremism. The funding of local primary schools is a case in point. Greater access to schools promises not only to encourage economic progress and social mobility, but also to moderate religious extremism. Many Pakistani children have been attending *madrasas*—schools run by fundamentalist clerics—because they have no other option. To invest in primary education is therefore to invest in pluralism and religious tolerance.

The connection between education and pluralism leads to a broader point about Islam and political modernization. In the aftermath of the attacks of September 2001, many commentators suggested that Islam itself has given rise to extremism and has been responsible for blocking political and economic development throughout the Middle East.[50] The causal arrow, however, points in the opposite direction. It is weak political and economic institutions that have given rise to Islamic fundamentalism. Religious absolutism and the violence that often accompanies it are less prevalent in Christian and Jewish societies precisely because those societies have been exposed to the liberalizing effects of the Reformation, the Enlightenment, the scientific and industrial revolutions, the rise of democracy—in short, the historical advances that separated church from state and pacified religion's effects on political life. Economic and political development in South Asia, the Middle East, and Africa can expose Islam to these same liberalizing, restraining, and pacifying forces.

Helping the developing world build human capital, economic infrastructure, and political capacity will take considerable time and money. Even with substantial reform, many assistance programs will continue to fall short of expectations. But keeping at the task offers the best—perhaps the only—means of closing the cultural, as well as the socioeconomic, gap between North and South.

International Institutions

If strategic restraint—selectively and prudently applied—is the core logic that should inform an American grand strategy for managing the transition to a multipolar world, institutions are the core instruments for putting that logic to work. Just as constitutions counter disorder at the domestic level, institutions are an antidote to geopolitical competition at the international level. They tame the system by binding and bounding powerful actors, by replacing anarchy with rule-based order, and by promoting governance based on right rather than might. Institutions are constitutions in only nascent form; sovereign states would have it no other way. Nonetheless, they are the building blocks of international community and the indispensable instruments that make possible the transformation of realms of conflict into zones of peace.

Institutions also promise to fulfill another important function—that of guiding America down a multilateral path that offers a critical middle ground between unilateralism and isolationism. The divide in the Republican Party between neoconservatives and traditional conservatives, coupled with a national politics polarized along both party and regional lines, risks producing an America that oscillates between a unilateral and an isolationist impulse. The multilateralism inherent in international institutions promises to counter both of these extremes. Multilateral engagement neutralizes unilateralism by binding America to other nations and providing joint solutions to common challenges. It also counters isolationism by sharing the burden of global management with like-minded partners, undercutting those who argue that America's engagement in the world is too costly. Investing in institutions thus offers a means of simultaneously taming the international system and finding a political middle ground on which to build a new brand of liberal internationalism that is at once discriminating and durable.

Americans have from early on had a strong aversion to institutions, whether domestic or international in character. The colonies initially settled for a loose confederation because they were unwilling to tolerate the strictures of a more ambitious institutional structure. Americans acquiesced and accepted a constitutional federation only under duress, when it became clear that the institutions agreed upon in 1781 were too weak to sustain the Union. Since then, and especially in the aftermath of the Civil War, America has developed into one of the most institutionalized and legalized countries on earth. The populist aversion to strong federalism aside, most Americans have come to accept a nation replete with multiple layers of local, state, and federal government, countless nongovernmental organizations, and a ubiquitous legal system. America now has roughly one attorney for every six hundred people because navigating the nation's maze of rules and institutions requires their expertise.

Early America was even more suspicious of international institutions than it was of domestic ones. The founding fathers' dictum against entangling alliances was, after all, a more general admonition against America's involvement in institutions that might ensnare the country in the perils of great-power politics. As it focused on its internal construction, westward expansion, and economic and military ascent, America wanted nothing to do with either the binding or the bounding role of international organizations. The Senate's rejection of U.S. participation in the League of Nations was only the most glaring example of the depths of this impulse.

The lessons of the 1930s, the shock of World War II, and Roosevelt's skills in public diplomacy wore down America's opposition to engagement in international institutions. During the first postwar decade, the United States actively set out to fashion a new international order and turned primarily to institutions to complete the task. At Dumbarton Oaks and then at San Francisco, the United States took the lead in founding the U.N. as a global collective security organization. A conference at Bretton Woods, New Hampshire, led to new institutions for managing the international economy. With the onset of the Cold War, the United States formed alliances around the periphery of the Soviet Union, setting up security pacts in Western Europe, the Middle East, Southeast Asia, and northeast Asia. The hard work of the United States during the 1940s and 1950s put in place an institutional infrastructure that still serves as the foundation for multilateral cooperation in many parts of the world.

Despite America's heavy reliance on institutions to shape and manage international order, Americans have never embraced them with the enthusiasm that they have mustered for their domestic institutions. The same concerns that left the founders wary of entangling alliances and that sank the League of Nations continue to have considerable traction. Contemporary critics of international institutions regularly return to themes that resonate strongly with the past—institutions compromise American sovereignty and autonomy, diminish the country's room for maneuver, and often conflict with constitutional principles by encroaching on the authority of Congress.

Senator Jesse Helms decided in 2001 that five terms in the Senate were enough. Nonetheless, his many conservative allies will continue his war against the U.N. As Helms wrote in *Foreign Affairs,* "With the steady growth in the size and scope of its activities, the United Nations is being transformed from an institution of sovereign nations into a quasi-sovereign entity in itself. That transformation represents an obvious threat to U.S. national interests."[51] Republican Senator Rod Grams of Minnesota in 1998 voiced similar hostility toward the International Criminal Court: "I hope that now the administration will actively oppose this court to make sure that it shares the same fate as the League of Nations and collapses without U.S. support[,] for this court truly I believe is the monster and it is the monster that we need to slay."[52]

Not all international institutions meet with such disapprobation. Alliances such as NATO enjoy strong support across the political spectrum, largely because America controls them by virtue of its military might. Washington has few problems with the G-8, another body in which the United States is in a commanding position, or with the IMF, where the United States has a larger say than any other country and can usually get its way.

As for institutions in which the United States has to answer to others, however, even liberal politicians are generally wary. Few Democrats would support putting U.S. troops under U.N. command. The International Criminal Court has only a limited number of strong backers in Congress. The Bush administration rejected outright the Kyoto environmental accords, but even the Clinton administration was reluctant about implementation. The Bush administration showed little remorse—in fact, it portrayed the decision as a test of its mettle—in proclaiming its intention to do away with the ABM Treaty through unilateral withdrawal.

Getting the United States to accept arbitration and stand by decisions that run counter to its interests is usually an uphill battle. Washington generally has an easier time complying with trade rulings than with those that involve matters of security. In 1984–1985, for example, the United States refused to abide by the findings of the International Court of Justice that America was violating international law by mining Nicaragua's harbors. The U.S. contested the Court's jurisdiction when Nicaragua first brought the case. When the Court ruled against the contest, the United States gave notice that it was terminating its 1946 declaration accepting the Court's general jurisdiction.

America's Janus-faced approach to international institutions could not be more shortsighted. At present, the United States may be able to afford to turn its back on institutions within which it cannot have its way; it is strong enough to act unilaterally when it so chooses. The problem is that America will not always have the luxury of going off on its own whenever it sees fit. As its unipolar moment passes, the United States will more frequently find itself turning to precisely those institutions that its unilateralist behavior is now undermining.

When management of the international system depends on consensus and compromise rather than on American leadership, the United States will lament that it taught by example norms of self-interest rather than norms of reciprocity. When the dollar is no longer the dominant reserve currency, Washington will wish that it could turn to an international institution to help stabilize the international financial system. When America's military is busy meeting challenges in the Middle East or Asia, and ethnic conflict again breaks out in Europe, the United States will want an EU force capable of operating independently of NATO. When the coal-and-oil-burning industries of emerging economies are operating at full capacity a decade or two from now, Americans may well regret that their government, when it had the leverage to do so, failed to take decisive steps to shape an effective global environmental regime to contain pollution.

Instead of relying on its primacy to stand aloof, the United States should do just the opposite—use its influence to fashion the institutions upon which it will soon have no choice but to rely. The United States should give up some of the prerogatives of its dominance in return for locking in institutions that will work to its advantage when it no longer has the capability to act unilaterally. This approach necessitates sacrificing short-term gains for long-term benefits. It means exercising strategic restraint to embrace institutions in which the United States will have to share rights and responsibilities with partners. It means using these institutions to bound American strength while at once binding America to other centers of power.

This is precisely the bargain that large colonies like Virginia and New York agreed to in order to pave the way for a federal union. It is the same deal that Germany and France struck as the opening gambit in building the European Union. And it is the same logic that Georgetown University's John Ikenberry has identified as being central to stable postwar settlements:

> If the leading state calculates that its heightened postwar power advantages are only momentary, an institutionalized order might lock in favorable arrangements that continue beyond the zenith of its power. In effect, the creation of basic ordering institutions is a form of hegemonic investment in the future. If the right type of rules and institutions become entrenched, they can continue to work in favor of the leading state even as its relative material capabilities decline—gains that the leading state would not realize in a noninstitutionalized order.[53]

The United States must give up its autonomy ahead of schedule if the institutions needed to tame multipolarity are to be ready in time, holding out hope that the best of Pax Americana long outlasts the unipolar moment. As it heads in this direction, Americans should invest in institutions that fulfill three broad functions.

To begin, the United States should seek to establish a directorate of major states focused on managing relations among the world's main centers of power. The U.N. Security Council ostensibly provides such a forum. But the Security Council, because of the formality of the U.N. and the veto wielded by its five permanent members, is more a forum for decorous—and sometimes indecorous—speechmaking than for hardheaded diplomacy.

A global directorate should function along the lines of the Concert of Europe, not the U.N. or the League of Nations. Its founding members should be the United States, the European Union, Russia, China, and Japan. Major states from other regions—Indonesia, India, Egypt, Brazil, and Nigeria would be top candidates—should also have a seat at the table. Like the Concert, this directorate would serve as an informal forum for discussion and coordination. Decisions would be reached through consensus; no party would have a veto. Coordinating inaction and strategic restraint would be as important a function as coordinating joint action. The directorate would meet on a regular basis and as needed to deal with emergencies. Like the Concert, it would be guided by the goals of promoting cooperation among the world's main power centers and managing regional crises.

The United States should also seek to cultivate a second tier of institutions whose function would be to embed in the international system an established set of rules and norms. Daily life inside most countries is peaceful and predictable because of the rules and norms that have become second nature and guide individual behavior. Daily life between countries is much less tame, in large part because those rules and norms are considerably more primitive and rudimentary. This need not, however, always be the case. Institutions give the international system a social character. They lay down the markers and set the rules that guide state behavior. To the extent that sovereign nations are willing to invest in institutional infrastructure, they can make international life more peaceful and predictable.

Some of this institutional infrastructure already exists; it has been put in place by the United States during the past five decades. But the many institutions still dependent upon U.S. leadership should be adapted so that they continue to function effectively even after they are no longer controlled by Washington. America also needs to support many other institutions that it now sidesteps and views as too constraining. Mustering more enthusiasm for the U.N. would be an important symbolic step. The goal would be not just to enhance the U.N.'s ability to deliver humanitarian aid and carry out peacekeeping missions. An indication of U.S. support for the global forum would itself send an important message about America's willingness to invest in institutions and to play by the same rules as other countries.

Strong institutions are also needed to manage specific components of international life. For starters, globalization makes it essential to improve mechanisms for managing trade, financial, and monetary relations. The World Trade Organization and its dispute-settlement system represent a good start, but monetary and financial matters have yet to be addressed. Especially as the euro begins to compete with the dollar as a reserve currency, monetary policy cannot be left to the system of ad hoc coordination that exists today. And additional financial mechanisms are needed to prevent the spread of sectoral and regional shocks. Whether such mechanisms take the form of emergency funds to stabilize economies in free fall, circuit-breakers to contain panic and contagion, or international restrictions on margin debt or capital flows, the United States and its partners should construct a new financial architecture and not wait until the next crisis sweeps through the global economy.

Building the international system's legal infrastructure is another step needed to enhance global stability and predictability. Recourse to law enforcement plays a major role in the pacification of domestic life; it can do the same in the international arena. The International Court of Justice, the Permanent Court of Arbitration, the International Criminal Court, and the war crimes tribunals established under the auspices of the U.N. have each helped extend the rule of law into the realm of international politics. Next steps include expanding the authority of the dispute-settlement panels set up under the auspices of the WTO and other organizations. The United States must resist the temptation to distance itself from these institutions or opt out of them altogether, putting itself above the law now because it can afford to do so. If those institutions are not at the ready when a less predominant America needs to rely on them, Americans will have no one but themselves to blame.

A third tier of institutions should be focused less on day-to-day management and more on countering long-term threats. Most current threats to the United States are collective in nature—that is, they are the same threats faced by many other nations and they can be effectively countered only through joint efforts. This is true even in the traditional realm of security, where location used to matter more. There are still dangerous neighborhoods in the world, South Asia and the Middle East among them. But full-scale war, even in these regions, is still less likely than acts of terrorism, the isolated detonation of a chemical or biological device, and cyber warfare, threats that know no geographic boundaries.

The most effective way to deal with these threats is through international coordination. Institutions are needed to interdict the proliferation of nuclear materials and missile technology, especially from the former Soviet Union. In light of the ease with which chemical and biological weapons can be acquired and delivered, international sharing of intelligence and joint surveillance and penetration of terrorist groups are the best antidotes. The retaliatory strikes against Afghanistan were an important component of the effort to eliminate Al-Qaeda and other terrorist networks. But Al-Qaeda reportedly had cells operating in more than fifty countries. The long-term struggle against terrorism will require institutionalized collaboration among the intelligence, police, and immigration agencies of many countries.

If the Bush administration proceeds with the deployment of a missile defense system, it should pursue a multilateral program that provides wide-ranging protection. Developing boost-phase technology and focusing on joint deployments would be appropriate steps. A boost-phase system, by intercepting missiles soon after launch rather than as they approach a target, protects all potential target states, not just the one setting up the system. In this sense, its benefits are broadly shared and its development therefore more likely to diminish rather than raise the chances of a new arms race. Boost-phase intercept is also more difficult to circumvent than intercept later in flight. Deployment of joint, multilateral systems will further ease fears that the United States is seeking to protect only itself or gain unilateral strategic advantage. The United States should accordingly explore with the EU, Russia, and perhaps China proposals for the sharing of early warning systems and intercept technology.

Conventional security threats also more regularly lend themselves to collective responses. War among the world's major nations is a remote prospect, at least for the foreseeable future. Most violent conflict is therefore likely to resemble the ethnic and civil wars of the sort that have recently afflicted Bosnia, Serbia, Azerbaijan, Rwanda, and East Timor. With the United States having already made clear that it will decline direct involvement in many of these wars, Washington should actively develop alternative sources of prevention and intervention.

The most promise lies with forces from the region, whose countries will have the greatest interest in preventing and stopping conflict. Readying local organizations in Africa, Southeast Asia, and other regions for these tasks will require a substantial investment in building institutional infrastructure and training personnel. Even the peacekeeping mission in Kosovo, which had the firm backing and involvement of NATO and the U.N., had great difficulty finding personnel adequately trained to carry out policing and local administration. The U.N. has to both expand its stable of individuals available for deployment on short notice and improve its linkages with regional organizations.

More effective assistance programs in the developing world are also an important investment in conflict prevention. The prospect of chaos and war in many parts of Africa is a direct outgrowth of the region's dire economic conditions, the scarcity of resources, and the spread of AIDS and other diseases. More generous and better-administered foreign assistance can make a quantum difference. To wait until social crises develop into security crises is a recipe for paralysis; it is when deprivation leads to violence that the North is most likely to cordon itself off from the South's plight.

Finally, collective efforts are urgently needed to protect the global environment. Global warming, the depletion of the ozone layer, water scarcity, deforestation—although scientists differ as to the precise timing and severity of the impact of these different forms of environmental degradation, they agree that current efforts to combat them are inadequate and that the trend lines suggest worsening, not improving, conditions.

Here is just one plausible scenario of what is in store. Carbon emissions from already industrialized countries, coupled with the continuing industrialization of populous developing countries like China and India, promise to hasten global warming. An increase of one meter in ocean levels, which could happen by 2100, would displace tens of millions of people in Bangladesh. It would also substantially decrease world food production. A rise of only fifty centimeters in ocean levels would flood 50 percent of North American coastal wetlands. Higher temperatures would also increase by one-third (from 45 percent to 60 percent) the proportion of the world's population vulnerable to tropical diseases such as malaria. In areas where malaria is already common, annual infection rates would rise by between 50 and 80 million people.[54]

A global agreement is needed, one that ensures institutionalized enforcement of across-the-board reductions in pollutants. The main obstruction is the temptation to pass the buck; with future generations bearing the brunt of the adverse consequences, politicians all too easily put off making the economic sacrifices that accompany efforts to curb pollution. Only seven weeks into his presidency, George W. Bush abandoned his campaign pledge to put new caps on emissions of carbon dioxide, citing the excessive strains such regulations would place on the energy industry. That different countries are at different levels of economic development and contribute to environmental degradation in different ways is another obstacle, making it more difficult to reach a consensus on what constitutes a fair agreement. But the longer the wait, the more the damage done. The United States should lead efforts to find common ground on how best to protect the environment now, while it still wields the leverage that comes with primacy. Reaching such an agreement will only grow more difficult over time as a more equal playing field produces a more divided and contentious international system.

America need not and should not sign up to every international institution that exists or may soon be created.[55] Many organizations have their flaws. Even strong backers of the Kyoto Protocol admitted that the agreement was hardly perfect. But when Washington feels compelled to withhold its participation, it should not just pursue its own course, declaring America's narrow self-interest as its guiding light. Instead, the United States should propose alternatives and compromise with others to fashion a mutually acceptable agreement. The spirit of multilateralism is at least as important as the fact. Only if America backs international institutions and the solidarity they signify will those institutions have a chance of offsetting the competitive instincts of a multipolar world.

Social Integration

Social integration is the most elusive component of a grand strategy aimed at taming a world of multiple power centers. The United States almost came apart in the 1860s precisely because northerners and southerners had created incompatible social orders with their own identities and cultural attributes. The Concert of Europe similarly unraveled because the revolutions of 1848 brought to the surface the political divide between liberalizing regimes and conservative monarchies, exposing the risks of a shallow social integration that never reached beyond the diplomats. In contrast, the vitality of the American Union during the twentieth century was due in no small part to the inclusive civic identity that forged a cohesive nation of disparate regions. The success of Europe's ongoing experiment with integration is also directly related to the EU's ability to construct political identities and allegiances that subsume the national state in a broader European polity. Social integration and the common identity that follows from it close the deal; they make the building of community and the elimination of strategic rivalry irreversible.

Constructing social fabric among neighboring countries is easier than among those separated by long distances. A shared identity requires extensive social contact, something facilitated by proximity.

And neighbors often enjoy common linguistic and cultural attributes, providing a foundation for a strong sense of affinity. Samuel Huntington is wrong to argue that different civilizations are destined to clash with each other, but he is right that culture matters. Everything else being equal, it is easier to nurture a sense of community among states that share a common culture than among states that do not. It is no accident that the areas in which social integration has gone the farthest—North America, the Nordic area, Western Europe—are those that enjoy a significant level of cultural commonality. From this perspective, social integration is likely to proceed much further within regions than among them. This is another reason for building peace in parts and establishing regional zones of stability as stepping-stones on the path to a broader peace.

It is nonetheless worthwhile for the United States to seek to extend a social character, even if a thin one, well beyond its immediate region. America and Europe have carved out a nascent Atlantic polity over the past five decades, one in which cooperation has become a habit of the mind. This accord will be much harder to sustain when Europe is more assertive, the United States has turned inward, and more competition results. But the maintenance of a shared identity can serve both parties well, muting the confrontations that will inevitably emerge. Cultural and educational exchanges, regular visits of congressmen and parliamentarians, common memorials and holidays, and high levels of transatlantic commerce are all wise investments.

The United States also has more instruments at its disposal for encouraging international socialization than during previous periods. The spread of democracy may not guarantee peace, but it does provide a set of shared norms and values upon which a sense of community can be based. More agreement on matters of human rights, legal procedures and standards, and dispute arbitration could advance this sense of commonality. Gatherings of the world democracies, like the one held in Warsaw in 2000, have both symbolic and practical potential; they reinforce communal identity and provide a forum for furthering social and political convergence. The United States should do more to enhance contact with nondemocracies as well. Even if greater interaction with the Muslim world does not lead to social convergence, it could certainly encourage mutual understanding.

The digital era opens up new opportunities for both public and private contributions to social integration. Advances in transportation and communications technology are making social interaction less dependent upon geographic proximity. Air travel facilitates direct contact among distant peoples; between June 1999 and June 2000, U.S. and foreign air carriers transported 137 million passengers between the United States and other countries.[56] And creative use of the Internet, such as organizing international referenda or multinational town meetings, could offer novel ways to deepen public engagement across national boundaries.

International institutions provide another venue for furthering social integration. Participation in forums like NATO and NAFTA enhance a sense of shared identity among elites and publics alike. China's entry into the WTO has the potential not just to promote trade, but also to further the perception both within China and elsewhere that the country is joining a community of nations, all of which should play by similar rules. Strengthening the democratic accountability of international institutions and increasing their transparency would help deepen their socializing role. Expanding the authority of parliamentary oversight groups would give greater legitimacy to the work of bureaucrats and negotiators.[57]

Just as the members of the Concert of Europe did during the nineteenth century, today's major states should seek to cultivate a sense of common purpose and shared destiny that cuts across political and cultural dividing lines. By believing in the Concert as "an intimate Union," its leaders cultivated the notion that they, in Castlereagh's words, "have not only a common interest, but a common duty to attend to."[58] The United States needs to begin cultivating among emerging centers of power that sense of intimate union, common interest, and common duty.

CHAPTER EIGHT

The Rebirth of History

THE VANTAGE POINT of modern society affords a view of history that is distinctly progressive and evolutionary. Advances in knowledge and technology have made possible steady improvement in the quality of life, replete with comforts and opportunities not even dreamed of only a century ago. A progressive notion of history is also embedded in our intellectual and cultural institutions. Charles Darwin's account of human evolution informs disciplines ranging from medicine to geology to economics. Judeo-Christian culture, despite its ancient roots, offers a similarly progressive perspective on the human predicament, with the Bible offering an account of creation that is both sequential and cumulative.

This evolutionary conception of history is the foundation for many of the more optimistic assessments of the state of world affairs. It is elemental to Francis Fukuyama's assertion that history is coming to a happy end as well as other claims about the ability of democracy and globalization to usher in a lasting era of peace. After centuries of struggle and incremental advance, man has finally reached his ultimate destination. Markets will satisfy his material needs, and democracy, his psychic needs. History has run its course.

This book rests on a very different foundation, one that views history as having a cyclical as well as an evolutionary character. As innovation and discovery propel mankind forward, such progress privileges certain types of political and social formations, only then to render them obsolete as changes in the mode of production and communication continue their onward march. The result is the cyclical rise and fall of particular historical eras even as history as a whole maintains its forward motion.

Nomadic society gave way to the agricultural era as the plow and irrigation ditch proved more effective than the spear in providing nourishment. Roving bands were replaced by settled villages and eventually by agrarian empires, and animism was replaced by organized religion. Agricultural society then gave way to the industrial era as factories proved more effective than farms in producing wealth. Villages were overshadowed by urban centers, the empire gave way to the democratic republic, and organized religion, although it remained a significant part of private life, lost to nationalism its role as the dominant source of communal identity. Changes in the underlying mode of production have had profound political and social consequences, producing the cyclical transitions from the nomadic to the agricultural to the industrial eras.

A new era is now opening—the digital era. The technologies driving this historic transition are microchips capable of processing and storing vast amounts of information and an infrastructure of cables, transmission towers, and satellites that provide inexpensive and virtually instantaneous communication on a global scale. The introduction of digital technology marks a fundamental change in the means of communication, not the means of production. But the shifts in the means of communication and information-processing brought on by the digital era represent a transformation sufficient in both quantitative and qualitative terms to alter the underlying mode of production.

Industrial society is therefore beginning to founder as digital technology and information-based enterprise replace the factory production line. The opening of the digital era and the decline of industrial society will have a major impact on the main political and social formations produced by industrialization—republican democracy and nationalism. Indeed, the passing of the industrial era and the ongoing shift to a digital economy promise to shake the foundations of the democratic nation-state. One cycle of history is closing, but another is just beginning.

From this perspective, the end of the American era is not just about the end of American primacy and the return of a world of multiple centers of power. It is also about the end of the era that America has played such a large role in shaping—the era of industrial capitalism, republican democracy, and the nation-state. Fukuyama mistakes the end of history itself for what is only the end of a particular cycle of history. He therefore sees the onset of liberal democracy as marking a stable and peaceful end point rather than a historical phase that, like those before it, will soon give way to further advances in the mode of production. Epochal turning points usually bring with them turbulent times, suggesting that the end of this current cycle of history, rather than producing a democratic peace and global quiescence, will result in profound changes in political and geopolitical life.

Before laying out this argument in more detail and examining the potential consequences of the shift from the industrial to the digital era, we turn briefly to history to illuminate the extent to which means of production are intimately linked to political and social institutions. The setting is early America, and the relevant debate is that which took place among its leaders about what type of domestic economy would best serve the interests of republican ideals.

THE PAST

THE BITTER RIVALRY between Thomas Jefferson and Alexander Hamilton, although it extended into the realm of foreign policy, had its roots in their differing perspectives on how America's economy would affect its political institutions. Controversy over the impact of economic life on American democracy produced some of the young republic's most impassioned and divisive debates. As Michael Sandel chronicles in his book *Democracy's Discontent*, dispute about "the political economy of citizenship" remained at the heart of American politics well into the twentieth century.

Jefferson and James Madison were the leading proponents of building a primarily agrarian economic base. Both believed that working the soil would instill among Americans the qualities of character—personal responsibility, integrity, civic virtue—needed to make republican government function efficiently. Jefferson wrote that "those who labour in the earth are the chosen people of God, if ever he had a chosen people, whose breasts he has made his peculiar deposit for substantial and genuine virtue."[1] Madison similarly insisted that "the class of citizens who provide at once their own food and their own raiment, may be viewed as the most truly independent and happy. They are more; they are the best basis of public liberty and the strongest bulwark of public safety. It follows, that the greater the proportion of this class to the whole society, the more free, the more independent, and the more happy must be the society itself."[2]

Jefferson, Madison, and a Republican Party that embraced their views were not opposed to all manufacturing. Rather, they believed that Americans should focus on small-scale production of household commodities and crafts. The lifestyle of artisans and craftsmen, like that of farmers, would promote values of self-reliance and dignity essential to republican notions of citizenship. In contrast, factories, the production line, and urbanization would erode civic virtue, deny workers their self-respect, and lead to corruption and immorality. As George Mason pointedly asked, "If virtue is the vital principle of a republic, and it cannot long exist, without frugality, probity and strictness of morals, will the manners of populous cities be favorable to the principles of our free government? Or will not the vice, the depravity of morals, the luxury, venality, and corruption, which inevitably prevail in great commercial cities, be utterly subversive of them?"[3] Fearful of the political and social implications of city life and convinced of the connection between agrarian society and civic virtue, the Republicans called for an economic policy focused on both the republic's westward expansion to incorporate more farmland and the further opening of international markets to U.S. agricultural goods.

Although Hamilton agreed with Jefferson that the character of the American economy would affect its political and social institutions, he had a different view of the type of economic base that would best serve the country's interests. Hamilton conceded that agrarian life provided a "state most favourable to the freedom and independence of the human mind."[4] But he believed that the functioning of democracy required an educated and professional elite, not just farmers and artisans, however virtuous they may be. Hamilton also envisaged an America that would emerge as a great power. He therefore favored industrialization, urbanization, and the gradual reduction of the domestic market's dependence on foreign imports. Although George Washington was concerned about "the luxury, effeminacy, and corruptions" that accompany commercial life, he agreed with Hamilton that "the spirit for Trade which pervades these States is not to be restrained."[5]

Under Hamilton's guidance, the Federalists called for the tariffs and public subsidies that they thought necessary to speed industrialization. Hamilton sought to establish a federal banking system, hoping to create a class of wealthy investors with a direct stake in public finance and to amass the funds needed for capital investment. While the Republicans complained that a federal bank would only breed corruption and strengthen the hands of elites, Hamilton argued that it would help generate national unity by checking the self-interested behavior of the separate states and private creditors. The Federalists also opposed rapid westward expansion, fearing that it would come at the expense of industrialization and dilute the strong federal institutions and sense of unity that Hamilton was seeking to encourage.

The debate between Hamilton and Jefferson was settled more by the passage of time than by deliberation and decision. Ongoing commercialization and industrialization soon made anachronistic Jefferson's conception of an agrarian America. The maturation of the U.S. economy did not, however, close off debate about how the country's economic base would affect its political life.

Picking up on Jeffersonian themes, Jacksonian Democrats during the 1830s and 1840s worried about the growing concentration of wealth and influence in the hands of merchants, industrialists, and bankers. By diminishing the political power of laborers, craftsmen, and farmers, the rise of an industrial and financial elite posed a risk to the vitality of American democracy. The Federalists, who by then called themselves Whigs, countered that large-scale investment in roads, railways, and the public school system would both contribute to economic development for the country as a whole and foster greater national unity. As one newspaper put it, "Truly are rail roads bonds of union, of social, of national union."[6]

By the middle of the 1800s, the issue of slavery came to dominate discussion of the country's political economy. The debate went to the heart of competing notions of the link between economic production and republican government. Southerners defended slavery to preserve their wealth and agrarian lifestyle, but they also claimed that it was a lesser evil than the system of wage labor that was emerging in the North. Senator James Henry Hammond of South Carolina argued that northern workers had become the slaves of industrial capital: "The difference between us is, that our slaves are hired for life and well compensated; there is no starvation, no begging.... Yours are hired by the day, not cared for, and scantily compensated."[7]

Northern abolitionists responded that slavery was immoral and inconsistent with America's founding principles. Many other northerners, however, opposed slavery on more pragmatic grounds, fearing that its spread would deny wage laborers the opportunity to move west and ultimately become self-reliant. Although many northerners accepted the onset of wage labor, they viewed it as a way station on the road to eventual self-employment and economic independence. As a spokesman for the Republican Party explained, "A young man goes out to service—to labor, if you please to call it so—for compensation until he acquires money enough to buy a farm...and soon he becomes the employer of labor."[8] Access to new farmlands would both offer laborers the option of an agrarian lifestyle and improve wages and working conditions for those who decided to remain in the industrializing East.[9] Stopping the expansion of slavery was thus central to preserving an economic base conducive to independent labor, civic virtue, and republican ideals.

In the wake of the rapid industrialization that took place in the decades following the Civil War, deliberation about how to protect the independent laborer and his civic character was replaced by debate over how to protect the factory worker and counter the ill effects of industrialization on republican government. Labor leaders proposed legislation limiting the workday to eight hours. A primary rationale was to preserve the dignity and moral character of laborers and to ensure they had time to devote to civic duties. Congress and the courts began to debate the merits of antitrust legislation, hoping to check the large corporate monopolies that threatened to wield their influence at the expense of working America.

How to mediate between the political and social effects of industrialization and the requirements of republican government figured prominently in the election of 1912. The dominant themes of the campaign echoed those articulated by Jefferson and Hamilton. Woodrow Wilson, the Democratic candidate, argued in favor of economic decentralization, the protection of small enterprise and the independent worker, and the preservation of local community life. If future generations "open their eyes in a country where they must be employees or nothing," Wilson insisted, "then they will see an America such as the founders of this Republic would have wept to think of."[10] Theodore Roosevelt, the Progressive candidate, countered that corporate influence had become a fact of life; the only way to contain it was through big government and federal regulation. Rather than resist the centralizing effects of industrialization, the government should harness it in the service of creating greater national unity and social cohesion. In Roosevelt's mind, it was "a spirit of broad and far-reaching nationalism," no longer the civic virtue of the self-employed worker, that would serve as the foundation for republican government.[11]

Although Wilson won the election—defeating both Roosevelt and William Howard Taft, the incumbent president and Republican candidate—Roosevelt's conception of America's political economy proved a more accurate vision of the country's future. The two world wars sped along not only industrialization, but also the propagation of a brand of American nationalism that instilled public sacrifice, fostered civic engagement, and furthered social cohesion. The era of industrial capitalism, republican democracy, and nationalism—the American era—was coming into full bloom.

A THEORY OF HISTORICAL CHANGE

IT IS NOT only in the United States that the nature of economic activity has had a profound impact on political life. The engine behind historical progress is advance in the dominant mode of production and its effect on institutions of governance and communal identity. Even though economic transformation generally occurs in a progressive fashion, historical change overall has both an evolutionary and cyclical character. A particular mode of production gives rise to a particular institution of governance and a particular form of communal identity—the three main dimensions that define an era. But progress in the underlying mode of production then undercuts and delegitimates those same political and social institutions, bringing that era to an end and opening the next. As Stephen Jay Gould puts it in his book on the evolution of the field of geology, "History moves inexorably forward as it cycles."[12]

Figure 3 lays out history's principal eras and identifies the economic, political, and social characteristics that distinguish them. The logic behind this account of history's evolution is straightforward.[13] The mode of production drives history because it constitutes the fundamental activity through which humans meet their basic physical needs and desires. The way in which humans provide for their needs then gives rise to institutions of governance and communal identity that are suited to daily life. During the nomadic era, hunters formed small bands and governed themselves through informal consensus. Communal identity was provided by kinship and a primitive animism. During the agricultural era, settled populations of growing size required the emergence of a ruling class to provide governance and a codified religion to promote a common identity and social cohesion. During the industrial era, the economic and political empowerment of the masses led to republican democracy. Nationalism was the logical corollary, providing the common identity and social glue needed to legitimate the democratic state.

Figure 3 Historical Eras

ERA	NOMADIC Before 8000 B.C.	EARLY AGRICULTURAL 8000–3000 B.C.	AGRICULTURAL 3000 B.C.–1700 A.D.	INDUSTRIAL 1700–2000	DIGITAL 2000–?
Mode of Production	Hunting, Gathering	Hunting, Horticulture	Cultivation	Industrial Capitalism	Digital Capitalism
Dominant Institution of Governance	Band	Tribe, Chiefdom	Kingdom, Coercive State	Democratic Republic	?
Dominant Institution of Communal Identity	Animism	Nature Worship	Organized Religion	Nationalism	?

It is feedback between the mode of production and the political and social institutions that follow from it that gives history a cyclical as well as evolutionary character. Advances in cultivation and irrigation, for example, furthered the onset of settled communal life and the social differentiation that came with it. The emergence of a clerisy, a state bureaucracy, and a merchant class in turn fostered the expansion of literacy and the beginnings of an intellectual and commercial elite. The scientific and technological advances produced by this intellectual elite and the political empowerment of a merchant class, however, eventually undermined agricultural society and set the stage for the industrial era. These cycles lead to cumulative historical progress through a process of natural selection. As modes of production advance, and political and social institutions evolve in step, societies are better able to provide sustenance and defense, enabling them to prevail over and eventually replace the polities that came before.

Figure 4 represents an account of historical evolution driven by change in the mode of production and the consequent rise and decline of dominant political and social institutions. Simplified for the purposes of clarity and brevity, the following narrative elaborates upon this theory of historical change.[14]

During the nomadic era, humans lived in roving bands of roughly twenty-five members.[15] Males hunted for wild animals, while females gathered edible foodstuffs. The groups were fairly egalitarian and had no formal political institutions, although the most able hunters often

Figure 4 The Cyclical Evolution of History

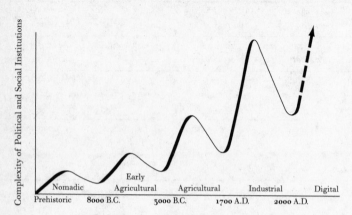

emerged as de facto leaders. Communal identity emerged from the close-knit quality of group life and from primitive rites based on animal and vegetable spirits.

The transition to early agricultural society was driven by both the demand for more stable food supplies and the development of horticulture and animal husbandry. Archaeologists have found agricultural settlements in southwest Asia and the Middle East dating to roughly 8000 B.C. Although most of the food supply still came from wild animals and plants, these early communities cultivated wheat and barley, and the main domesticated animals were sheep and goats. Early settlements in China, along with millet and rice cultivation and the domestication of dogs and pigs, date to roughly 6000 B.C.

The shift from hunting and gathering to horticulture produced important changes in political and social life. Settled societies required more governance than had nomadic ones; decisions had to be made about where to locate, what crops to plant and when to do so, and who would hunt and who would farm. A primitive political hierarchy consequently evolved, usually involving the designation of a tribal leader or chief. Chiefdoms were somewhat more complex than tribal societies, often exhibiting greater social stratification and hereditary succession. Communities were still relatively small in size, enabling direct contact to serve as the main source of social cohesion. Spiritual practices, however, came to include more rites involving the sun, the moon, the weather, and the earth—reflecting the greater role of agriculture in daily life.

The onset of the agricultural era was again the product of a mixture of demand and supply. Growing population and the dwindling number of wild animals raised demand for cultivated foodstuffs. And innovations such as the ox-drawn plow, irrigation, and crop rotation made possible the transition to societies that survived almost exclusively on farming. After 3000 B.C., agricultural society took root contemporaneously in Asia, Europe, the Americas, and Africa.

The emergence of agriculture as the main mode of production transformed prevailing institutions of governance and communal identity. The multiple tasks of irrigation, planting, food storage, and communal administration led to social differentiation. Society also became stratified between those who owned the land and those who worked it. The demand for more extensive governance and the stratification that came with agricultural society led to nascent state structures—a ruling class and an administrative bureaucracy. Especially when agricultural communities began to compete with each other for land and labor, the burden of war-making necessitated stronger state institutions. Kings and royal courts, which emerged primarily to prosecute war, eventually took on the task of peacetime governance as well. Most agrarian polities crystallized as imperial kingdoms, feudal states, or some combination of the two.

The onset of an agrarian mode of production set the stage for the emergence of organized religion as the primary institution of communal identity. Cultivation increased the number of people that could live off a given area of arable land, clearing the way for large towns and early cities. Farmers grew more than they could consume, leading to collective storage facilities, market towns, and the expansion of trade routes. Political units expanded in size, encompassing communities that would have little or no contact with each other. These changes made political life more impersonal and meant that social cohesion could no longer rely on ties of kinship and local culture. Agricultural society thus created a demand for institutionalized religion and the sense of common identity that came with it.

The food surpluses produced by cultivation also contributed to the rise of modern religion by making possible the development of a priestly class that could be relieved from working the land. Tithes and other forms of communal support enabled the clerisy to focus on intellectual pursuits and to advance the theological and ritualistic foundations of organized religion. The priestly class also had a vested interest in enhancing its influence through the embrace of belief and ritual, and therefore worked hard to counter earlier folk practices. In addition, priests often became involved in state administration by virtue of their skills and education. The Kohanim and Levites of early Israel, the clergy of the medieval Catholic Church, the ulama of Islam, Hinduism's Brahmins, and China's Confucian scribes—all these religious authorities took on important political and administrative functions.

The political elite had their own reasons for supporting the spread of organized religion. Rulers regularly turned to religion to legitimate their authority and wealth, with kings and emperors often claiming divine lineage and inspiration. Secular leaders also turned to faith to instill loyalty and promote imperial unity. During the fourth century, for example, one of the reasons the leaders of the Roman Empire established Christianity as the official religion of the imperial realm was to promote political cohesion.[16]

Agrarian society elevated the importance of marking time and seasonal change, a development that also contributed to the formation of organized religion. Decisions about when to plant, irrigate, and harvest were vital to communal welfare, heightening society's consciousness of past and future and its awareness of time and the means used to measure it. The advent of "empty, homogenous time" in turn created a psychic need for links to ancestors and a conception of the afterlife— a need fulfilled by organized religion.[17] That religious authorities were usually the ones charged with marking seasons, announcing the sighting of the new moon, and fulfilling other time-related tasks reinforced the connection between faith and agrarian society.

The Hebrew Bible is in many respects a chronicle of the historic transition from nomadic to agricultural society. The Jews began as desert wanderers, torn between the animism of the Golden Calf and the monotheistic teachings of Moses. With settled life in the land of Israel came a priesthood supported by obligatory communal contributions, the institution of the king-warrior, and the development of religious learning and practice. Secular and religious authorities together staffed the institutions of the state. Judaism provided a compelling social bond, especially important after foreign conquerors dispersed the Jewish population. Judaism's holidays, most of which were related to the agricultural cycle, and its practice, much of which connected daily life to the past and future, were well suited to the social and psychic needs of agrarian society.

Like nomadic society before it, agrarian society fostered changes in the mode of production that would eventually bring on its demise. Two developments led to underlying economic change and the consequent deterioration of the dominant political and social institutions of the agricultural era. One was the formation of a merchant class whose interest in free trade and the accumulation of capital set it against the absolutist and centralized state. Relying on its wealth and growing autonomy, this commercial class gradually undermined the ability of dynastic rulers and landed nobility to monopolize political power. Merchants also invested in research and technology, expanded trade routes, and helped develop early financial instruments. The commercial class thus prepared the way for both political and economic liberalization.

The second development contributing to the demise of agrarian society was the diffusion of learning. Especially after the printing press came into use during the 1500s, literacy and scholarship were no longer the preserve of the clergy. Science and the rationalism that accompanied it challenged the dominating social role of organized religion and set in motion a gradual process of separation between church and state. Entrepreneurs and craftsmen, helped along by the technological progress that dramatically picked up speed during the course of the 1800s, produced the spinning wheel, the steam engine, the railroad, and other innovations central to the growth of modern industry. Scientific advance ensured that industrial capitalism, not just commercial capitalism, followed the agrarian era.

Commercial capitalism evolved during the course of the sixteenth and seventeenth centuries, primarily in Europe and Japan, where decentralized feudal states were particularly conducive to the rise of a relatively autonomous merchant class.[18] Industrialization then took off in Britain during the second half of the eighteenth century, and extended to continental Europe, North America, and Japan during the nineteenth century. In 1789, farming accounted for 40 percent of Britain's national product and industry for 21 percent. By 1900, agriculture generated only 7 percent of Britain's output, compared with 43 percent for industry. By the middle of the 1800s, three-quarters of

Britain's adult male workforce was already employed outside the agricultural sector.[19] Industrial manufacturing rapidly replaced agriculture as the leading mode of production.

The industrial era brought with it a new form of governance—republican democracy.[20] Industrialization led to the rise of consensual politics for three main reasons. First, it created an influential constituency of industrialists, financiers, merchants, and shopkeepers interested in gaining more control over economic and political life. The economic empowerment of a middle class both heightened its demand for political empowerment and enhanced its ability to marshal the resources and leverage necessary to back up those demands. It was this growing middle class that served as the vanguard of the French Revolution and that ultimately led the fight for republican democracy across much of Western Europe.

Second, an industrial economy required a literate and mobile workforce, which in turn necessitated a system of mass education. For the state to educate the masses, however, was also to bring them into the political arena and threaten rule by the industrial and landed elite. In addition, to uproot workers from agrarian settings and bring them to cities was to foster class-based alliances that cut across diverse cultures, languages, ethnicities, and religions. The rise of an educated, organized working class thus hastened the transition to republican government and universal suffrage.

Third, capitalism and the industrial mode of production were predicated upon a set of ideas whose logical corollary was democratic government. The primacy of the individual, economic competition and perpetual growth, the operation of the free market, the liberalization of trade—these concepts went hand in hand with the notion of political liberty. That the state would serve the interests of its citizens and maximize their welfare was also consistent with the emphasis on rationalism and efficiency emerging from the scientific revolution.

The industrial era brought about a similarly profound change in the dominant institution of communal identity—the rise of modern nationalism. Nationalism was a logical consequence of the onset of industrial society and consensual politics. Religion's dominating social role had been delegitimated by scientific inquiry and the separation of church and state. A new social glue was required to attach the citizen to the secular state, a task fulfilled by nationalism and the sense of common identity and purpose it engendered. Through the national idea, the faceless, administrative state was turned into the emotive and inclusive nation, a political community worthy of loy-alty, belonging, and sacrifice. The intermixing produced by industri-alization and a system of mass education furthered this binding together of state and nation by creating what Ernest Gellner calls the "homogeneous breathing tank."[21] The high school, the newspaper, the production line, the railway, the conscript army—these were the homogenizing institutions of industrial society that at once necessi-tated nationalism as a new form of communal identity and made pos-sible its rapid spread.

The industrial era is now poised to give way to the digital era. As a result of technological progress, industrial manufacturing has lost its place as the dominant mode of production. In 1950, the manufactur-ing sector employed 34 percent of America's nonfarm workforce and produced 29 percent of the country's economic product. By the end of the 1990s, the manufacturing sector employed only 15 percent of non-farm workers and produced only 16 percent of the country's economic output.[22] On the rise have been the information, financial, and service sectors. And the agricultural and manufacturing sectors are them-selves being transformed with the emergence of bioengineered seeds, automated development and production, and other innovations made possible by digital technology.

This shift to a digital mode of production is still in a nascent phase. But as the digital era unfolds, it promises to cause fundamental change in prevailing political and social institutions, just as did previ-ous epochal transitions. America is the primary founder of this new era and has fast been incorporating digital technology into its society, economy, and military. Moreover, it has embraced a set of next-generation principles revolving around finance capitalism, informa-tion technology, and globalization for keeping itself at the forefront of this new era. Paradoxically, however, the digital age may well com-promise the core political and social institutions that have served America so well during its rise to global dominance.

AMERICA IN THE DIGITAL ERA

ONLY WITH the advantage of hindsight is it possible to confirm the closing of one era and the opening of another. Technological progress occurs almost daily, but most innovations have a quantitative rather than qualitative impact on the mode of production. The introduction of the telephone, for example, constituted a major advance in communications technology. It certainly enhanced the efficiency of industry by facilitating management and putting producers in instantaneous touch with suppliers and consumers. But the telephone did not alter the fundamentals of industrial production and thus did not engender significant change in political and social institutions.

It is too soon to be able to claim with certitude that the diffusion of digital technology represents a qualitative shift in the mode of production and consequently marks the opening of a new era. But the financial and service sectors already represent between 40 and 70 percent of U.S. economic output, depending upon how broadly these sectors are defined.[23] And there are several characteristics of digital technology that may well give it a transformative capacity sufficient to constitute a historical breakpoint:

- Unlike the spinning wheel or the telephone, which were discrete innovations, digital technology represents an operating system that affects virtually all types of economic activity. It is simultaneously automating the production line, making possible the genetic engineering of crops and animals, and altering financial instruments and flows. In this respect, it is a generic innovation, similar to the creation of the engine and its ability to convert heat into energy, a discovery that at once transformed agriculture, manufacturing, and transportation.

- Digital technology may make possible increases in productivity and decreases in cost on a scale comparable to those associated with the introduction of the steam engine and electricity. Between 1990 and 1997, goods producers intensively employing information technology enjoyed advances in productivity nearly twice those of firms relying on more traditional technology. In the 1980s, it took U.S. automobile companies four to six years to develop and manufacture a new car model. Digital technology has reduced the cycle time to just over two years. Booking an airline ticket through a travel agent costs the airline $8, while doing so over the Internet costs $1. Within the high-tech sector itself, productivity growth per worker was as much as twenty times greater than in other sectors of the economy.[24] Furthermore, digital technology is penetrating leading economies much more quickly than did earlier innovations. From initial public availability until penetration of 30 percent of U.S. households took forty-six years for electricity, thirty-eight years for the telephone, and seventeen years for the television. The Internet reached 30 percent of U.S. households in seven years.[25]

• Digital technology is at once increasing and decreasing economies of scale. The speed, scope, and integrated nature of the global economy are encouraging larger enterprises whose production sites, workforce, and investments span national boundaries. At the same time, small biotech firms and Internet start-ups may well be the key nodes of innovation in an economy in which knowledge is the primary ingredient of growth. The centralized state of the industrial era may be undermined from above and below.

• Digital technology is weakening the link between geographic location and production site that was a hallmark of the industrial era. Access to raw materials and transportation networks is of diminishing importance to information-based enterprises. Growing numbers of workers are relocating out of choice rather than necessity. The result is the decline of industrial cities, less intermixing of populations than during the industrial era, and a more atomized and individualized mode of production.

It is too early to draw a definitive causal link between the digital age and the signs of stress now showing in American democracy. Nonetheless, that this shift in the underlying mode of production is beginning to take a toll on America's political and social institutions strengthens the case that the country is nearing a historical switching point. Other forces are probably at play—the decline of the traditional family, economic inequality and insecurity, the additional hours Americans spend at work—all combining to give the country's political system its sluggish feel. But the falling off of civic engagement and the weakening of the nation-state—trends detailed below—are consistent with the notion that America's institutions are growing brittle and unresponsive in the face of the political and social changes accompanying the transition from an industrial to a digital economy. As during previous historical cycles, it appears that a change in the mode of production is causing the delegitimation and deterioration of society's dominant institutions.

America's founding fathers argued passionately about how the nature of daily life would affect the functioning of the country's political institutions. Even though Jefferson and Hamilton differed as to whether an agrarian or an industrial economy would best serve the nation's interests, they agreed that active civic engagement and political participation were central to republican government. Alexis de Tocqueville, one of the keenest analysts of early America, concurred: "Town meetings are to liberty what primary schools are to science; they bring it within the people's reach, they teach men how to use and how to enjoy it. A nation may establish a free government, but without municipal institutions it cannot have the spirit of liberty."[26] Throughout most of the country's history, American democracy has benefited from healthy levels of civic and political participation. Despite the concerns of Jefferson and many after him about the potential ills of industrial society, the industrial era and the process of nation-building that accompanied it sustained a strong ethic of civic engagement.

American democracy, however, has in recent decades begun to falter and show signs of losing its momentum and direction. Active participation in political life has dropped sharply since the 1960s. Harvard professor Robert Putnam has measured civic engagement on a number of different dimensions. His findings are as follows: "Americans have become perhaps 10–15 percent less likely to voice our views publicly by running for office or writing Congress or the local newspaper, 15–20 percent less interested in politics and public affairs, roughly 25 percent less likely to vote, roughly 35 percent less likely to attend public meetings, both partisan and nonpartisan, and roughly 40 percent less engaged in party politics and indeed in political and civic organizations of all sorts." "In effect," he concludes, "more than a third of America's civic infrastructure simply evaporated between the mid-1970s and the mid-1990s."[27] Putnam contends that information technology and mass media are the culprits, pointing to a direct link "between television watching and decreased civic engagement."[28] The more time spent in front of the television, the less time available for civic activities.

At least at first glance, digital technology and the information revolution it has spawned should have the potential to reverse declining engagement by enhancing social contact and cohesion. After all, the Internet makes communication easy, fast, and cheap. Some groups have in fact used the organizing capacities of the Internet to great advantage. The International Campaign to Ban Landmines relied heavily on e-mail to educate and mobilize its activists, as has, paradoxically, the antiglobalization movement. Associations and political groups are turning to Web sites and e-mail campaigns as their main instruments for disseminating information. Some of Putnam's critics contend that he exaggerates the slump in civic activity by focusing only on traditional forms of association and failing to measure these new types of engagement.[29]

The information age, however, appears to be cutting into not just the time available for civic participation, but also the quality and character of whatever social engagement remains. Americans are using the Internet to filter their information, getting only those e-newsletters and accessing only those Web sites in which they are interested. The more time people spend using the Internet, the less time they devote to the traditional media.[30] Dwindling exposure to a broad range of opinions and facts threatens to produce a more polarized and less deliberative electorate.[31]

Politics via the Internet is also coming at the expense of face-to-face contact, making more acute the fragmentation and atomization of political life. Writing a check to a candidate or sending an e-mail to a congressional office is not the same as attending a public meeting and exchanging ideas with fellow citizens. An e-mail message may communicate an idea, but it is devoid of the emotion, body language, and gesture that bring political discussion to life. As Joel Kotkin of Pepperdine University notes, "By abolishing the need for actual face-to-face contact, the Internet increases loneliness and social isolation, expanding virtual networks that lack the intimacy of relationships nurtured by physical proximity."[32] Putnam is similarly worried by what he calls "citizenship by proxy," and adds that "anonymity is fundamentally anathema to deliberation."[33]

The digital era also appears to have contributed to the displacement of civic-mindedness with a spirit of individualism and self-absorption. Daily life has become customized. Cell phones enable one to stay in constant touch, but they also crowd out deliberative time. The ability to order everything from groceries to medicine to books over the Internet is certainly convenient, but it also promotes materialism, a need for immediate gratification, and an ethic of entitlement rather than one of responsibility. As David Brooks notes, "The fear is that America will decline not because it overstretches, but because it enervates as its leading citizens decide that the pleasures of an oversized kitchen are more satisfying than the conflicts and challenges of patriotic service."[34] Even Thomas Friedman, who usually uses his columns to hail the digital age, has caught a glimpse of its darker side.

In an article entitled "Cyber-Serfdom," he warns that "there is a back-lash brewing against the proliferation of technology in our lives. . . . You are now involved in a continuous flow of interactions in which you can only partially concentrate on each. . . . Now you are always in. And when you are always in you are always on. And when you are always on, what are you most like? A computer server." "That," Friedman admits, "has become spiritually depleting."[35]

Signs abound of this growing ethic of entitlement. The sport utility vehicle (SUV) is clogging America's highways and city streets. During 2000, one out of every two cars purchased in the United States was an SUV, a minivan, or a light truck. SUVs may provide the height of comfort and horsepower to their owners. But they typically get about thirteen miles per gallon, compared with more than thirty for the average compact car, and therefore drive up energy consumption and hasten global warming. The United States contains only 4 percent of the world's population, but accounts for about 25 percent of global energy consumption; its drivers should not be purchasing cars that only make matters worse. And largely because of pressure from the automobile and energy industries, the House of Representatives in August 2001 voted down a bill that would have mandated higher fuel efficiency for SUVs.[36]

The U.S. Army, perhaps the country's premier institution of public service, in 2001 chose "An Army of One" as its main advertising slogan. It is hard to imagine a clearer statement of changing social norms and the rising appeal of individualism. The Amtrak Metroliner from New York to Washington used to provide a respite from the bustle of the city, offering time for quiet reflection or a conversation with a fellow traveler. It is now a cacophony of individuals talking at full volume into their cell phones. Amtrak, by popular demand, proceeded to designate a quiet car in which portable phones are banned.

Matters are poised to get worse, not better. Younger Americans watch more television and spend more time on the Internet than any other age cohort. They are also less engaged in civic activity and place a higher premium on wealth and material comfort than any other age group. As these individuals mature and older generations pass on, aggregate levels of civic engagement are likely to decline even further. As Putnam observes, "The biggest generational losses in engagement still lie ahead."[37]

The abatement of political and social capital in the United States stems from the impact of the digital age, not just on civic engagement, but also on the quality of governance. Americans are becoming less involved in public affairs in part because they are otherwise engaged, but also because they are losing faith in public institutions and sense that the integrity of their political system is in jeopardy. In the 1960s, three out of four Americans said they could trust the U.S. government to do what is right most of the time. By the 1990s, public opinion had reversed itself; three out of four Americans did not trust the government to do what is right.[58] David Brooks sums up the plight of American politics as follows:

> These days most of us don't want to get too involved in national politics because it seems too partisan and ugly. And as a result, most American citizens have become detached from public life and have come to look on everything that does not immediately touch them with an indifference that is laced with contempt. We have allowed our political views to be corroded with an easy pseudo-cynicism that holds that all politicians are crooks and all public endeavor is a sham. As the public opinion polls demonstrate with utmost clarity, we have lost faith in public institutions and many private ones.[39]

Although perhaps overstated, Brooks's critique will ring true with many Americans. And here too the information revolution appears to be a big part of the problem.

The media—television in particular—have replaced the town hall as the main arbiter of American politics. Gaining access to public office requires gaining access to the air waves, which in turn requires large sums of money. The digital era has only reinforced these trends, fostering an explosion of news channels, most of them broadcasting in frenzied fashion around-the-clock. Media consultants and communications directors are indispensable in crafting and honing images and messages, again adding to the costs of running for office. Courting corporate donors and filling campaign coffers have thus become central ingredients—perhaps *the* central ingredient—in winning election to public office. In the 2000 presidential election, Bush and Gore spent $187 million and $120 million respectively, with a significant portion going to television advertisements. Michael Bloomberg used $69 million of his own money in his successful bid to become mayor of New York City in 2001. Furthermore, campaign spending has been steadily rising. Estimates put total (presidential and congressional) campaign spending for the 2000 election at $3 billion, up from $2.2 billion in 1996, and $1.8 billion in 1992.[40]

The role of money in politics essentially turns into a business proposition what the founding fathers meant to be a contest of ideas and character. Putting a campaign together is less about crafting a platform and listening to constituents than it is about raising money—or having personal wealth—and hiring good pollsters and media consultants. The link between corporate capitalism and digital technology also gives major donors undue influence, jeopardizing the notion of one person, one vote, and diminishing incentives for the electorate to go to the polling station. Consider the collapse of Enron in 2001–2002. It is hard to have faith in corporate America when Enron's executives—or those of WorldCom—so blatantly misled their employees and shareholders. It is equally hard to have faith in the U.S. government when 212 of the 248 senators and representatives serving on the committees investigating Enron had received campaign contributions from the energy company or its accounting firm, Arthur Andersen.[41]

The penetration of politics by corporate money encourages and in fact rewards individuals who are adept at manipulating this system, and discourages those who seek to uphold a more traditional notion of republican government and civic responsibility. It is no accident that America's politicians are finding themselves under investigation or dodging scandals—these are the types of individuals that thrive in the current system. It is also no accident that the likes of Lee Hamilton, Sam Nunn, Nancy Kassebaum, and Dale Bumpers voluntarily left politics—these are the types of individuals who were ultimately unwilling to compromise themselves by playing the game. These are worrying trends, especially in light of James Madison's hope that America's system of government would "extract from the mass of the society the purest and noblest characters which it contains."[42]

Politicians and commentators have regularly acknowledged the damage being done to American politics by campaign finance. John McCain, as both senator and presidential candidate, has long pressed hard for reform. And authoritative figures like former Senator Bumpers have admitted that "the money factor is the number one impediment to good government."[43] After years of futile attempts to alter the system, legislation finally cleared the Senate and House in 2002. But to ensure its passage, the bill's drafters limited the scope of reform. Even its supporters admitted that the legislation will only "marginally reduce the influence of big money" and "barely dent the huge cost of campaigns."[44]

The penetration of American politics by this combination of private finance and digital technology has also affected the conduct of business in Washington itself. The number of lobby groups has grown exponentially during the past three decades. Their employees descend on Capitol Hill on a daily basis, armed with promises of both money and votes.[45] New associations regularly open offices in Washington, where they peddle influence, rather than around the country, where they once mobilized activists. Their members now make contributions instead of attend meetings. Social protest has become professionalized and bureaucratized. According to political scientist Ronald Shaiko, instead of engaging in grassroots organizing, "public interest organizations are hiring economists, Ivy League lawyers, management consultants, direct mail specialists, and communications directors."[46]

Policy think tanks have been similarly affected. The older generation of think tanks—the Council on Foreign Relations, the Brookings Institution, the Carnegie Endowment for International Peace—were established with mandates to inform public debate and provide nonpartisan analysis of issues central to public policy. In recent decades, however, partisan positioning has become widespread, pressuring these organizations to become more political, in part because of the requisites of corporate fund-raising. Washington has also seen the proliferation of organizations that bill themselves as research institutes or think tanks but that are in reality advocacy groups. Institutions like the Heritage Foundation have an explicit political agenda and are backed by donors with a direct interest in that agenda. The New Atlantic Initiative (NAI), a research program based at the American Enterprise Institute, hosted dozens of conferences on NATO enlargement in the late 1990s. But most of its participants were of a similar mind; NAI was interested in making enlargement happen, not in fostering a considered debate on the topic.

These advocacy groups are well funded and making full use of the digital age. Ideas, like votes in Congress, are up for sale. With the decline of the think tank as impartial arbiter has come a decline in the quality and integrity of public debate.

These trends have combined to give American politics a remote and plastic feel. Public form grows ever more divorced from private reality. The central messages of the 2000 Republican Convention were moderation, centrism, and compassionate conservatism. Once in office, President Bush veered sharply to the right, beholden to interest groups and conservative donors. The administration greeted with great fanfare the tax cut it passed in the spring of 2001. But most analysts dismissed its implications and exposed a legislative compromise consisting largely of smoke and mirrors.[47] Double-talk has hardly been the exclusive provenance of the Republicans. On issues ranging from health care to missile defense to humanitarian intervention, the Clinton administration's rhetoric usually bore little resemblance to reality.

Congress's behavior has been no better, earning it a reputation for anything but the deliberative body intended by its founders. The editorial board of the *New York Times*, in an essay entitled "An Ineffectual Congress," had this to say in its lead editorial on November 1, 2000, six days before the presidential election:

> The 106th Congress, with little to show for its two years of existence, has all but vanished from public discourse.... On almost every matter of importance—gun control, patients' bill of rights, energy deregulation, Social Security—Congress has done little or nothing, failing to produce a record worthy of either celebration or condemnation.... But if Congress has done a lousy job for the public at large, it is doing a fabulous job of feathering its own nest and rewarding commercial interests and favored constituencies with last-minute legislative surprises that neither the public nor most members of Congress have digested.

The lagging performance of America's institutions of governance stems not only from domestic developments, but also from the importance of transnational political mobilization. The communications revolution affords activists new opportunities to build broad coalitions that cut across national boundaries. Groups engaged in promoting goals such as safeguarding human rights, banning landmines, protecting the environment, and resisting globalization have organized effective international campaigns, relying heavily on the Internet. These new forms of participation and mobilization have been reasonably effective in achieving the desired ends, but they do circumvent the nation-state, confounding the national realm of politics. The salience of America's institutions diminishes as its citizens find transnational engagement a more effective option for pursuing their political aims.

Declining civic engagement and deteriorating governance appear to be caught in a vicious circle. As Americans turn away from public affairs, they leave more room for special interests to carry the day. An inattentive electorate also makes elected officials less accountable to voters. The quality of governance erodes as a result, only reinforcing the public's cynicism and its disengagement. In light of the strong links that exist between civic participation and numerous public goods—responsive government, social trust and cohesion, low crime, and economic efficiency—these are deeply worrisome trends.[48]

The information age and digital era are by no means the sole causes of this overall weakening of American democracy. The distorting effects of corporate money on politics can hardly be blamed on the Internet. In the run-up to the 1912 election, Theodore Roosevelt and Woodrow Wilson were already debating how to curb excessive corporate influence. So too is it likely that forces other than information technology have contributed to the sharp decline in civic engagement since the 1960s.

But the evidence strongly suggests that the digital era and the information revolution are prime sources of the deterioration taking place in the country's dominant institutions of governance. At a minimum, the political and social consequences of digital technology are tearing at the fabric of American democracy at a time when that fabric, for different reasons, has already begun to wear thin. The stresses appearing in the practice of democracy are consistent with the notion that a shift in the mode of production is taking place and that the United States is consequently entering a historical transition from one era to another. This transition is just beginning and the digital age is still in its infancy. But early indicators militate against complacency about the durability of America's current political institutions.

IF THE ADVENT and diffusion of digital technology mark the opening of a new historical era, then this change in the mode of production should affect the dominant institutions of communal identity as well as those of governance. Just as America's democratic institutions may be tested by the forward march of history, so might the nation-state find itself challenged by the social changes wrought by the digital era.

Nationalism was the handmaiden of industrial society; the end of the industrial era may therefore weaken the foundations of the nation-state.

Here too the early evidence is consistent with the claim that an epochal transition is getting under way. Again, it is too soon to make any conclusive judgments about the social consequences of the shift from an industrial to a digital economy. But by examining the logic of digital society and what limited data are available, it is possible to generate a number of plausible, exploratory propositions.

The industrial era promoted the adoption of nationalism as the dominant form of communal identity by uprooting people from the land, exposing them to the common experience of mass education, bringing them into contact with each other in cities and factories, and tying together the nation-state with railways and interstate highways. In the words of Emile Durkheim, "Social life, instead of concentrating itself in innumerable small foci that are distinct but alike, becomes general. Social relationships . . . push out beyond their original boundaries on all sides." As industrialization proceeds, he continues, "the more individuals there are who are sufficiently in contact with one another to be able mutually to act and react upon one another."[49] It was this moving and mixing of peoples that led to the industrial melting pot, integrated new immigrants into multiethnic cities, and fostered a common national identity.

The digital era appears to be reversing many of these social trends. As Joel Kotkin observes, "The rise of the digital economy is repealing the economic and social geography of contemporary America."[50] The solidarity promoted by the industrialized workplace is giving way to a social fragmentation arising from the individualized workstation. The number of Americans working from home is rising rapidly.[51] Using the Internet to work with distant colleagues that one may never meet may increase efficiency, but it does so at the expense of social connections. The trade union, the symbol of social solidarity during the industrial era, has been in a steady state of decline. Since the 1950s, unionized employees have fallen from 33 to 14 percent of the U.S. workforce.[52]

The digital era is also altering patterns of labor mobility in ways that may slow, if not reverse, the social and ethnic intermixing promoted by the industrial era. Nonindustrial firms and their employees have much more flexibility in choosing where they locate. Proximity to rivers, ports, railways, and raw materials is much less important.

"The more technology frees us from the tyranny of place," Kotkin writes, the more quality of life, weather, values, and cultural affinity figure in determining where workers locate.[53]

America's cities are struggling as labor mobility becomes a matter more of choice rather than of necessity. Industrial metropolises like St. Louis and Detroit have lost about half their populations since the 1950s. Wealthier, mostly white urbanites have been moving to the suburbs or to more rural communities in places like North Carolina or Colorado. During the 1990s, more than 40 percent of those who settled in nonmetropolitan areas were former city-dwellers. The communities benefiting from this migration may be affluent and productive, but they are also socially and racially homogeneous. Remaining in the inner city are poorer, low-skilled minorities, often separated into ethnic enclaves. Almost two-thirds of the children living in urban centers are nonwhite. And most white children remaining in the inner city are in working-class families.[54]

Chicago, New York, and San Francisco seem to be exceptions, enjoying more resilient economies and less urban flight. But even these commercial cities are losing some of their previous social and ethnic heterogeneity. In San Francisco and New York, housing prices are making many parts of the city accessible only to high-income residents, most of whom are white.[55] Middle-class blacks are also congregating in their own communities. Bowie, Maryland, for example, has become a magnet for professional blacks working in the Baltimore-Washington metropolitan area.[56]

The digital era thus appears to be coming at the expense of the industrial melting pot that helped forge the modern American nation-state. After the decades of progress facilitated by the civil rights movement, America may be heading back toward greater racial and social segregation. Anthony Walton of Bowdoin College is justified to worry about "glittering cybercities on the hill," which "learn to exist without contemplating or encountering the tragedy of the inner city."[57] And Robert Kaplan is right to wonder how American nationhood will fare as the country becomes comprised of "isolated suburban pods and enclaves of races and classes unrelated to each other."[58]

A digital economy that is less effective in promoting social solidarity may also prove less effective in integrating immigrants into a multiethnic mainstream. Immigration to the United States picked up during the 1990s, raising the percentage of foreign-born residents in the population to a level not seen since before World War II. In the early twentieth century, 90 percent of the immigrants to the United States were of European extraction. By the end of the century, most were of either Hispanic or Asian origin. Whereas Asian immigrants, like their European predecessors, tend to integrate quickly into American society, recent and forthcoming Hispanic immigrants may remain more segregated.

The 2000 census reported that almost one in five Americans at least five years old speaks a language other than English at home. Within that group, 60 percent speak Spanish, and 43 percent indicated they did not speak English "very well."[59] Hispanic children also tend to live in bilingual households longer than children of Asian immigrants.[60] In addition, a growing percentage of Latinos is attending segregated schools. In 1998, almost 37 percent of Latino students went to schools with a minority enrollment of 90 percent or higher, up from 23 percent in 1968.[61] The sheer size of the Hispanic community (more than 35 million), its concentration in the Southwest, the absence of the diffusion once engendered by the labor demands of industry, the back-and-forth flow of human traffic made possible by the proximity of their countries of origin—all these factors may combine to slow the integration of the Hispanic population into a multiethnic America.

It is not just ethnic and social integration that is at stake; the digital economy might also strengthen regional dividing lines. Since its early days, the United States has had to confront the diverging cultures and economic interests of its various regions. These differences have to some extent been diluted by the population movements that accompanied industrialization and the sense of common cause engendered by World War II and the Cold War. But they are making a comeback.

With families freer to take values and political persuasion into consideration in making decisions about where they live, people will tend to congregate with those who are like-minded. Especially if the Internet encourages Americans to filter the information to which they are exposed, cultural polarization could increase along regional lines. Robert Putnam's finding that there remain wide cultural differences between North and South, especially on matters of civic engagement, underscores the potential implications of greater regional polarization.[62] In this respect, it is worth noting how Zell Miller, a Democratic senator from Georgia, explained Al Gore's dismal performance in the South in the 2000 election. "Southerners," Miller wrote, "believed that the national Democratic Party did not share their values.... If Southern voters ever start to think you don't understand them—or even worse, much worse, if they think you look down on them—they will never vote for you."[63]

On the economic front, diverging regional interests may well take on a new form. For many U.S. regions, despite the tightening of borders that followed the terror attacks of September 2001, commerce is more frequently flowing across national boundaries than within them. Mexican workers are heading to the United States and U.S. companies are relocating to Mexico. As the Hispanic population of America's Southwest continues to rise, its economic and cultural links to Mexico will grow only stronger. El Paso and Ciudad Juárez as well as San Diego and Tijuana essentially constitute continuous metropolitan areas despite the borders dividing them. New Mexico is pursuing joint development initiatives with its neighbor and sister state, Chihuahua. In March 2002, the United States and Mexico agreed to a new system of joint border control intended to speed the flow of people and commerce while providing adequate security.[64] According to Adela de la Torre, director of the Mexican American Studies and Research Center at the University of Arizona in Tucson, "In the context of people who live on the border, there is no border. We share our lives with people who live in Mexico."[65]

America's northern border is undergoing a similar transformation. The first New York–Ontario Economic Summit took place in June 2001, chaired by New York's governor, George Pataki, and Ontario's premier, Michael Harris. As one commentator put it, "The meeting's agenda embraced what many on both sides of the Niagara and St. Lawrence rivers have been asserting for some time—the region's destiny lies with forging closer commercial ties that make the U.S.-Canadian border largely irrelevant."[66] After the terror attacks of September 2001, some proposed that the United States and Canada should have a common security perimeter, allowing for the integrated processing of immigrants and visitors as they enter either country.[67] In December, the two countries signed a pact providing for more cooperation on domestic security and border control. Portland, Seattle, and Vancouver are forming ever-stronger economic and cultural links. Robert Kaplan suggests that the growing loyalty of residents to their shared region—Cascadia—may before long overwhelm allegiance to their respective states and nations.[68] Business strategist Kenichi Ohmae joins Kaplan in questioning whether the nation-state still represents a "genuine shared community of economic interests" and defines "meaningful flows of economic activity."[69]

During the heyday of the nation-state, cultural, economic, and political boundaries all coincided. With the arrival of the digital era, communal identity and flows of commerce are in the midst of profound change, but political boundaries are remaining the same. At a minimum, this growing misfit is likely to lead to a decline in the salience of the nation-state. More likely, ongoing economic, political, and social change will call into question whether the nation-state, at least as currently conceived, will remain the world's dominant political unit.

Arthur Schlesinger, Jr., in *The Disuniting of America*, notes that the United States is "an experiment, reasonably successful for a while, in creating a common identity for people of diverse races, religions, languages, cultures. But the experiment can continue to succeed," Schlesinger warns, "only so long as Americans continue to believe in the goal. If the republic now turns away from [George] Washington's old goal of 'one people,' what is its future?—disintegration of the national community, apartheid, Balkanization, tribalization?"[70] It may seem far-fetched to imagine that a wealthy, multiethnic, democratic country like the United States could head in this direction. But Americans only need look northward to find an example of a wealthy, multiethnic, democratic country that faces the prospect of fragmentation. In the last referendum held in 1995, French-speaking Quebec came within a hair's breadth of breaking away from Canada, with 49.4 percent of voters favoring secession.

Many observers suggested that the events of September 2001 would help reverse these worrisome political and social trends. As Robert Putnam commented, "I think there is the potential that Sept. 11 will turn out to be a turning point for civic America. It's a horrible tragedy, but there could be some good coming from it if it causes us to become more connected with one another . . . and more open-minded about the role of government." America unquestionably came together after the terrorist strikes, with both civic spirit and trust in the government rising sharply. Americans of all backgrounds shared in the collective grief and anger. This outpouring of national unity was as impressive as it was sincere. But it is difficult to interpret it as anything other than a temporary reaction to exceptional circumstances. As Putnam himself admitted, "This could vanish in the blink of an eye."[71] The battle against terrorism is not well suited to reversing social trends deeply rooted in change in the underlying mode of production and its impact on political life.

The point here is not that the digital era will inevitably lead to the political fragmentation of America. The United States is a remarkably adaptive and resilient country.[72] This flexibility leaves it positioned to keep up with the fast pace of change that will be a defining characteristic of the digital age.

But the point is that serious challenges of a novel nature lie ahead. These challenges have the potential to compromise the foundations of republican democracy and the national state. Far from paving the way for a halcyon future of prosperity and stability, the digital era promises to usher in as profound a political and social transformation as that wrought by the arrival of the industrial age.

PREPARING FOR EPOCHAL CHANGE

TO VENTURE A GUESS at what the dominant political and social institutions of the digital era might look like would be too speculative an enterprise—similar to trying to sketch out the industrial era from the vantage point of 1700. Nonetheless, the observation that the end of American primacy is coinciding with the end of the era of industrial capitalism does lead to a set of insights about the future.

America will not be able to manage effectively its waning primacy and the uncertain international environment that will follow unless it also addresses the weaknesses in its domestic institutions. Fashioning a new grand strategy and crafting a new internationalism to go with it require responsive political institutions, an attentive public, and a national identity strong enough to sustain sacrifice and a sense of common purpose.

The public and private sectors should therefore work together to rekindle civic engagement and prevent the ethnic, social, and regional segregation that could ultimately threaten the integrity of the American nation-state. Although the digital age appears to have had adverse effects on civic activity, imaginative use of the Internet does have the potential to enhance political participation. Some scholars look to the "information commons" and the establishment of "deliberative domains" to encourage Internet discourse among public institutions, public interest groups, and citizens.[73] The Internet could boost access to public meetings and records.[74] Digital technology could also be used to facilitate voting and to hold virtual town halls.[75]

Civic engagement over the Internet is, however, no substitute for direct human contact and deliberation. Even as associations improve their Web sites and staff their offices in Washington, they should mobilize grassroots efforts to reclaim the integrity of the political system, mandate more ambitious campaign finance reform, and limit the adverse influence of corporate lobbying on public life. And even as new shopping malls go up, they should include space for civic activities such as community meetings, public theater, and charitable work.

Public and private efforts will also be needed to combat the social fragmentation and polarization that could accompany the digital age. Investments in the inner city will be needed to restore the economic vitality and social heterogeneity of many urban centers. The federal government and state legislatures should jointly work to reverse the trend that is sending a growing percentage of Latino children to segregated schools. A program of national service would ensure the mixing of Americans from different ethnic and social backgrounds and would help build social capital and cultivate a shared sense of allegiance to the broader national community.

The onset of the digital era has equally important implications for American foreign policy. As this century unfolds, two different types of historical cycles will together transform the global environment. Most of this book has focused on the cyclical rise and fall of great powers that takes place within a given historical era. It is the forward motion of this cycle that is reflected in the ascent of Europe and the end of America's unipolar moment. This final chapter has been about the broader historical cycles driven by progress in the mode of production and resulting in the rise and fall of different eras. It is the forward motion of this cycle that is reflected in the decline of the industrial era and the opening of the digital age.

These two cycles are concurrently reaching a critical point. American primacy is waning at the same time that an epochal transition is getting under way. The pace of change is admittedly quite different. The decline of American hegemony will play itself out over this decade and the next. The end of the industrial era and the rise of the digital age will unfold over this century and the next. Nonetheless, that these two cyclical transitions are coinciding does warrant special concern about the challenges facing the international community.

Epochal change will for two reasons magnify the turbulence that will accompany the return of a multipolar world. The first is that the transition from the industrial to the digital age will put special strain on the world's political systems. The privileged international position of the United States, the EU, and Japan stems largely from their advanced economies. But their achievements also put them at the front of history; they will be the first to feel the dislocating effects of the digital economy on their societies. If their main political and social institutions are faltering in the years ahead, these polities may well be focused on their own problems and ill placed to respond to a fluid and complicated international environment. States whose domestic institutions are in transition are also prone to attempts to export their problems through aggressive foreign policies. The French Revolution and its impact on France's political and social institutions played a large role in fueling geopolitical ambition and generating the Napoleonic Wars. World War I can be directly traced to the industrialization of Germany and the brand of nationalism that emerged from the political turmoil wrought by economic change. States whose primary domestic institutions are in the midst of transformation are often difficult actors on the international stage.

Epochal change may magnify turbulence for a second reason—trouble is likely to break out across the epochal dividing line. States at different stages of history often take each other on, in large part because they embody competing organizing principles. After the transition to the agricultural era, agrarian states and nomadic tribes regularly engaged in warfare, their struggle ending only after nomadic society proved no match against the economic and military advances produced by agrarian society. After the onset of the industrial age, those states that made the transition to republican democracy regularly found themselves in conflict with states clinging to more authoritarian forms of rule. It may well be that those states that make the transition to the digital age will find themselves at odds with those still in earlier stages of history. The September 2001 terror attacks against America were, if nothing else, a lashing out against history's leading edge by those trailing far behind.

This problem could be particularly acute due to the distance that now exists between those states at the front of history and those further back. Never before has the gap been so large. Digital technology is penetrating the most advanced countries, and then accelerating their historical progress. Americans have been busy debating how best to expand broadband Internet access to households and whether to support stem cell research. Meanwhile, many of the world's less advanced countries are still in a phase of history in which they are progressing slowly, if at all. Their citizens have been busy looking for firewood, wondering where their next meal will come from, and worrying whether they will have access to even the most primitive health care facilities. These two worlds have almost nothing in common, making it hard for them to come together to address collective challenges, be they humanitarian, environmental, or geopolitical in nature. As the digital era proceeds, this distance between the leading and lagging edges of history will only increase.

The pressures facing developing countries to catch up rapidly are a final source of potential turbulence. States rushing to make it into the digital era are likely to bypass important developmental stages, potentially exacting high costs down the road. Russia is seeking to integrate quickly into global markets. But the absence of a strong middle class could leave it without the political ballast needed to weather the vagaries of the international economy. During the 1990s, the countries of Southeast Asia benefited from their strong links to global financial markets. But as these countries moved their economies into the digital era, they found their traditional political and social institutions both unwieldy and unresponsive, ultimately contributing to the financial crisis that swept the region. The cell phone has made it to Macedonia as well as to many other developing countries in the world. But in the absence of a professional and independent press corps, its ability to disseminate rumors and stoke political passions contributed to the ethnic violence that broke out in 2001. States that rush through history may well pay a heavy price for doing so.

This is a sobering portrait of what lies ahead. At a minimum, these insights make clear that history will not be ending anytime soon. The return of a multipolar world and the unfolding of the digital era are inevitable, the product of history's evolution and its cycles, both of which are inexorable. American primacy will wane as Europe, and eventually Asia, rise. The digital age will move forward in step with unstoppable innovations in technology. Human choice matters, but history has its own vital momentum.

Where there is more room for human choice—and a great deal of it—is in preparing for the challenges that will accompany history's march. The first step in getting ready for the geopolitical and epochal transitions already unfolding is to recognize that they are taking place and to map out their causes and implications. The central goal of this book has been to do just that. It is now the task of those convinced by its warnings to get on with the difficult, but essential, duty of preparing for the end of the American era.

Notes

PREFACE

1. Andrew Sullivan, "America at War: America Wakes Up to a World of Fear," *Sunday Times* (London), September 16, 2001.

CHAPTER ONE

1. ADM 116/3099, June 22, 1912, memo by Winston Churchill, pp. 2–3. (All citations of archival documents in this chapter refer to papers held at Britain's Public Records Office, Kew. ADM, CAB, and WO stand for Admiralty, Cabinet, and War Office, respectively.)

2. J. H. Rose, A. P. Newton, and E. A. Benians, *The Cambridge History of the British Empire*, vol. 1 (Cambridge: The University Press, 1929), p. 95.

3. Foreign Office memo cited in Paul M. Kennedy, *The Rise and Fall of British Naval Mastery* (London: Macmillan, 1983), p. 219.

4. India Office Library, Curzon Papers, vol. 144, Godley to Curzon, November 10, 1899, cited ibid., p. 211.

5. CAB 38/8/14, February 24, 1905, "Our Present Minimum Military Requirements," p. 1.

6. Crowe Memorandum of January 1, 1907, cited in Henry Kissinger, *Diplomacy* (New York: Simon & Schuster, 1994), p. 193.

7. Cited in Kennedy, *The Rise and Fall of British Naval Mastery*, p. 224.

8. CAB 24/107, June 9, 1920, "British Military Liabilities," pp. 1–2.

9. CAB 4/21/1087B, March 11, 1932, "Imperial Defense Policy," p. 2; CAB 2/5, April 6, 1933, Minutes of the 258th Meeting of the Committee of Imperial Defence.

10. CAB 16/111/120, June 20, 1934, "Disarmament Conference 1932," p. 2.

11. CAB 16/111/125, July 18, 1934, "Naval Defence Requirements," p. 1.

12. Grenfell cited in Williamson Murray, *The Change in the European Balance of Power, 1938–1939* (Princeton: Princeton University Press), p. 75.

13. WO 33/1004, January 10, 1922, "The Interim Report of the Committee on National Expenditure," Doc. VII, p. 51.

14. Ironside cited in William R. Rock, *British Appeasement in the 1930s* (London: Edward Arnold, 1977), p. 46.

15. CAB 21/700, February 22, 1937, "Review of Imperial Defence," p. 12.

16. CAB 53/13, J.P. 315, September 23, 1938, "The Czechoslovak Crisis," cited in Murray, *European Balance of Power*, p. 209.

17. Martin Gilbert, *The Roots of Appeasement* (London: Weidenfeld & Nicolson, 1966), p. 186.

18. "Excerpts from Pentagon's Plan: 'Prevent the Re-Emergence of a New Rival,'" *New York Times*, March 8, 1992.

19. "Interview of the President by Wolf Blitzer, CNN Late Edition," June 20, 1999. Available at: http://clinton6.nara.gov/1999/06/1999-06-20-late-night-edition-cnn-interview.html.

20. "After Kosovo: Building a Lasting Peace," remarks delivered at the Council on Foreign Relations, New York, June 28, 1999. Available at: http://www.cfr.org/public/pubs/AlbrightRem.html.

21. Richard Haass, cited in Thom Shanker, "White House Says the U.S. Is Not a Loner, Just Choosy," *New York Times*, July 31, 2001.

22. Alan Sipress, "Bush Retreats from U.S. Role as Peace Broker," *Washington Post*, March 17, 2001.

23. David E. Sanger, "Bush Tells Seoul Talks with North Won't Resume Now," *New York Times*, March 8, 2001.

24. The United States Commission on National Security/21st Century, "New World Coming: American Security in the 21st Century." Available at: http://www.nssg.gov/Reports/NWC.pdf.

25. Tyndall Report, as cited in David Shaw, "Foreign News Shrinks in an Era of Globalization," *Los Angeles Times*, September 27, 2001.

26. Hall's Magazine Editorial Reports, cited in James F. Hoge, Jr., "Foreign News: Who Gives a Damn?" *Columbia Journalism Review*, vol. 36, no. 4 (November–December 1997), pp. 48–52.

27. Pew Center for the People and the Press, "Public and Opinion Leaders Favor Enlargement," October 7, 1997. Available at: http://208.240.91.18/natorel.htm.

28. Gerard Baker and David Buchan, "American Isolationism Put to the Test," *Financial Times*, October 15, 1999.

29. On September 14, 2001, both the Senate and the House voted on a resolution authorizing the president "to use all necessary and appropriate force" to respond to the attacks. The resolution passed 98 to 0 in the Senate and 420 to 1 in the House. In a poll conducted between September 20 and 23, 2001, 92 percent of the public supported military action against whoever was responsible for the attacks. See "Poll Finds Support for War and Fear on Economy," *New York Times*, September 25, 2001.

30. Shibley Telhami, "The Mideast Is Also Changed," *New York Times*, September 19, 2001.

31. François Heisbourg, "De l'après-guerre froide à l'hyperterrorisme," *Le Monde*, September 13, 2001.

32. Adam Clymer, "A House Divided. Senate, Too," *New York Times*, December 2, 2001.

33. Powell cited in Lawrence F. Kaplan, "Drill Sergeant," *The New Republic*, March 26, 2001. Available at: http://www.tnr.com/032601/kaplan032601.html.

34. General export figures are from U.S. Bureau of the Census, "U.S. International Trade in Goods and Services, January 1998 to December 2000." Available at: http://www.census.gov/foreign-trade/Press-Release/2000pr/Final_Revisions_2000/exh1.txt. Export figures for Canada and Mexico are from Tables 10 and 10a, U.S. Department of Commerce, Bureau of Economic Analysis, "U.S. International Transactions Account Data." Available at: http://www.bea.doc.gov/bea/international/bp_web/list.cfm?anon=127.

35. For contemporary analyses urging that Americans return to a more isolationist posture, see Eric A. Nordlinger, *Isolationism Reconfigured: American Foreign Policy for a New Century* (Princeton: Princeton University Press, 1995); and Eugene Gholz, Daryl G. Press, and Harvey M. Sapolsky, "Come Home, America: The Strategy of Restraint in the Face of Temptation," *International Security*, vol. 21, no. 4 (Spring 1997), pp. 5–48.

CHAPTER TWO

1. "The Sources of Soviet Conduct," *Foreign Affairs*, vol. 25, no. 4 (July 1947), pp. 566–582.

2. "Moscow Embassy Telegram #511," February 22, 1946, in *Containment: Documents on American Policy and Strategy, 1945–1950*, ed. Thomas H. Etzold and John Lewis Gaddis (New York: Columbia University Press, 1978), pp. 55–63.

3. "United States Objectives and Programs for National Security," NSC-68, April 14, 1950, ibid., p. 427.

4. Paper prepared by Mr. John Foster Dulles, Consultant to the Secretary of State, "Estimate of Situation," November 30, 1950, in *Foreign Relations of the United States, 1950*, vol. 6 (Washington, D.C.: Government Printing Office, 1950), p. 162.

5. "Final Report of the Joint MDAP Survey Mission to Southeast Asia," December 6, 1950, ibid., p. 166.

6. Dulles, "Estimate of Situation," p. 162.

7. Francis Fukuyama, "The End of History?" *National Interest*, no. 16 (Summer 1989), pp. 3–18; Francis Fukuyama, *The End of History and the Last Man* (New York: Free Press, 1992).

8. John J. Mearsheimer, "Back to the Future: Instability in Europe After the Cold War," *International Security*, vol. 15, no. 1 (Summer 1990), pp. 5–56; John J. Mearsheimer, "Why We Will Soon Miss the Cold War," *Atlantic Monthly*, vol. 266, no. 2 (August 1990), pp. 35–50.

9. Samuel P. Huntington, "The Clash of Civilizations?" *Foreign Affairs*, vol. 72, no. 3 (Summer 1993); Samuel P. Huntington, *The Clash of Civilizations and the Remaking of World Order* (New York: Simon & Schuster, 1996).

10. Matthew Connelly and Paul Kennedy, "Must It Be the Rest Against the West?" *Atlantic Monthly*, vol. 274, no. 6 (December 1994), pp. 61–83. Kennedy also published his views about the emerging international system in a book entitled *Preparing for the Twenty-first Century* (New York: Random House, 1993).

11. Robert D. Kaplan, "The Coming Anarchy," *Atlantic Monthly*, vol. 273, no. 2 (February 1994), pp. 44–76; Robert D. Kaplan, *The Coming Anarchy: Shattering the Dreams of the Post Cold War* (New York: Random House, 2000).

12. Thomas L. Friedman, *The Lexus and the Olive Tree* (New York: Farrar, Straus & Giroux, 1999).

13. Fukuyama, "The End of History?" p. 4.

14. Fukuyama, *The End of History and the Last Man*, p. xviii.

15. For contemporary scholarship on the democratic peace, see Michael W. Doyle, "Kant, Liberal Legacies, and Foreign Affairs," *Philosophy and Public Affairs*, vol. 12, nos. 3 and 4 (Summer and Fall 1983), pp. 205–235, pp. 323–353; Bruce M. Russett, *Grasping the Democratic Peace: Principles for a Post–Cold War World* (Princeton: Princeton University Press, 1993); *Debating the Democratic Peace*, ed. Michael E. Brown, Sean M. Lynn-Jones, and Steven E. Miller (Cambridge, Mass.: MIT Press, 1996); and *Paths to Peace: Is Democracy the Answer?* ed. Miriam Fendius Elman (Cambridge, Mass.: MIT Press, 1997).

16. Fukuyama, *The End of History and the Last Man*, p. xx.

17. Ibid., p. 276.

18. Fukuyama, "The End of History?" p. 18.

19. Francis Fukuyama, "Second Thoughts: The Last Man in a Bottle," *National Interest*, no. 56 (Summer 1999), pp. 16–33.

20. Mearsheimer, "Back to the Future," p. 142.

21. Although Mearsheimer focused exclusively on Europe as he pieced together his initial map of the post–Cold War world, he later extended his analysis to East Asia in a book entitled *The Tragedy of Great Power Politics* (New York: Norton, 2001). He adheres to the basic positions expressed in his earlier articles, foreseeing the gradual withdrawal of U.S. forces from Europe and East Asia and the return of great-power rivalry to both regions. Other realists such as Kenneth Waltz also see the economic rise of Japan and China as a precursor to geopolitical rivalry in the region. "Sooner or later, usually sooner," Waltz warns, "the international status of countries has risen in step with their material resources." Kenneth N. Waltz, "The Emerging Structure of International Politics," *International Security*, vol. 18, no. 2 (Fall 1993), p. 66. See also Aaron L. Friedberg, "Ripe for Rivalry: Prospects for Peace in a Multipolar Asia," *International Security*, vol. 18, no. 3 (Winter 1993–1994), pp. 5–33.

22. Mearsheimer, "Why We Will Soon Miss the Cold War," p. 36.

23. Mearsheimer, "Back to the Future," p. 147.

24. Mearsheimer, "Why We Will Soon Miss the Cold War," p. 35.

25. Ibid., p. 46.

26. Ibid.

27. Ibid., p. 40.

28. Ibid., p. 42.

29. Ibid., p. 50.

30. Huntington, "The Clash of Civilizations?" p. 24.

31. Huntington, *The Clash of Civilizations and the Remaking of World Order*, pp. 41–43.

32. Huntington, "The Clash of Civilizations?" p. 25.

33. Ibid., p. 31.

34. Ibid., p. 22.

35. Ibid., p. 29.

36. Ibid., p. 48.

37. Huntington, *The Clash of Civilizations and the Remaking of World Order*, p. 20.

38. Huntington, "The Clash of Civilizations?" p. 49.

39. Paul M. Kennedy, *The Rise and Fall of the Great Powers: Economic Change and*

Military Conflict from 1500 to 2000 (New York: Random House, 1987); Robert D. Kaplan, *Balkan Ghosts: A Journey Through History* (New York: St. Martin's, 1993); and Robert D. Kaplan, *The Ends of the Earth: A Journey at the Dawn of the 21st Century* (New York: Random House, 1996).

40. Connelly and Kennedy, "Must It Be the Rest Against the West?" pp. 62, 69, 79.

41. Kennedy, *Preparing for the Twenty-first Century*, p. 331.

42. Robert D. Kaplan, *The Coming Anarchy*, p. xiii.

43. Ibid., p. 24.

44. Connelly and Kennedy, "Must It Be the Rest Against the West?" p. 62.

45. Robert S. Chase, Emily B. Hill, and Paul Kennedy, "Pivotal States and U.S. Strategy," *Foreign Affairs*, vol. 75, no. 1 (January–February 1996), p. 63.

46. Kaplan, *The Coming Anarchy*, pp. 7, 19.

47. Connelly and Kennedy, "Must It Be the Rest Against the West?" p. 79.

48. Kaplan, *The Coming Anarchy*, p. 120.

49. Ibid.

50. Ibid., p. 125.

51. Friedman, *The Lexus and the Olive Tree*, pp. 7–8.

52. Ibid., p. xviii.

53. Ibid., p. 201.

54. Ibid., p. 86.

55. See, for example, Robert O. Keohane, *After Hegemony: Cooperation and Discord in the World Political Economy* (Princeton: Princeton University Press, 1984).

56. See, for example, Thomas Risse-Kappen, *Cooperation Among Democracies: The European Influence on U.S. Foreign Policy* (Princeton: Princeton University Press, 1997).

57. Joseph S. Nye, Jr., *Bound to Lead: The Changing Nature of American Power* (New York: Basic Books, 1990).

58. Friedman, *The Lexus and the Olive Tree*, pp. 196–198.

59. Ibid., p. 41.

60. Ibid.

61. Ibid., p. 212.

62. Thomas Friedman, "World War III," *New York Times,* September 13, 2001.

63. Rankings based on market capitalization as of March 28, 2002, *Financial Times Global 500 Guide,* May 8, 2002. Available at: http://specials.ft.com/spdocs/FT3BNS7BWOD.pdf.

64. Jane Perlez, "With Time Short, Albright Stays Aloft," *New York Times,* July 3, 2000.

65. World Bank, *China 2020: Development Challenges in the New Century* (Washington, D.C.: World Bank, 1997), p. 103.

66. Senate Resolution 208, November 8, 1999.

67. Henry Kissinger, "U.S. Intervention in Kosovo Is a Mistake," *Boston Globe,* March 1, 1999.

68. Cited in Edmund Andrews, "Bush Angers Europe by Eroding Pact on Warming," *New York Times,* April 1, 2001.

69. David Sanger, "Bush Flatly States U.S. Will Pull Out of Missile Treaty," *New York Times,* August 24, 2001.

70. Dana Milbank, "Bush Advocates a Wider NATO," *Washington Post,* June 16, 2001.

71. "Bush Unpopular in Europe, Seen as Unilateralist," August 15, 2001. Available at: http://people-press.org/reports/display.php3?ReportID=5. Survey conducted by the *International Herald Tribune,* the Council on Foreign Relations, and the Pew Research Center for the People and the Press. See also Adam Clymer, "Surveys Find European Public Critical of Bush Policies," *New York Times,* August 16, 2001.

72. John Kifner, "56 Islamic Nations Avoid Condemning U.S. Attacks, but Warn on Civilian Casualties," *New York Times,* October 11, 2001.

73. Laurie Goodstein, "Muslim Scholars Back Fight Against Terrorists," *New York Times,* October 12, 2001.

74. See Stephen M. Walt, *The Origins of Alliances* (Ithaca: Cornell University Press, 1987).

CHAPTER THREE

1. President Calvin Coolidge, State of the Union Address, December 4, 1928, as cited in John Kenneth Galbraith, *The Great Crash, 1929* (New York: Time Inc., 1961), p. 7.

2. Ibid., pp. 26–27, 70.

3. Cited ibid., p. 38.

4. Cited ibid., p. 73.

5. Cited ibid., p. 74.

6. Ibid., p. 80.

7. Piers Brendon, *The Dark Valley: A Panorama of the 1930s* (New York: Knopf, 2000), p. 86.

8. Charles P. Kindleberger, *The World in Depression, 1929–1939* (Berkeley: University of California Press, 1973), pp. 171–172.

9. Dietmar Rothermund, *The Global Impact of the Great Depression, 1929–1939* (London: Routledge, 1996), p. 55.

10. Cited in Brendon, *The Dark Valley,* p. 31.

11. Cited in Tatsuji Takeuchia, *War and Diplomacy in the Japanese Empire* (New York: Doubleday, 1935), p. 353.

12. Kindleberger, *The World in Depression,* p. 308.

13. Galbraith, *The Great Crash,* pp. 173–174.

14. Thomas L. Friedman, *The Lexus and the Olive Tree* (New York: Farrar, Straus & Giroux, 1999), p. 7.

15. Ibid., pp. 7–8.

16. Thomas Paine, "Rights of Man," in *Collected Writings* (New York: Literary Classics of the United States, 1995), pp. 598–599.

17. John Stuart Mill, *Principles of Political Economy: With Some of Their Applications to Social Philosophy* (Fairfield, N.J.: Augustus M. Kelley Publishers, 1976), p. 582.

18. Norman Angell, *The Great Illusion: A Study of the Relation of Military Power in Nations to Their Economic and Social Advantage* (New York: Putnam, 1910), pp. 31, 54–55. The title refers to the illusion that states can improve their well-being through war.

19. Congressman Paul Ryan, statement to U.S. House of Representatives, Committee on Banking and Financial Services, Subcommittee on Domestic and International Monetary Policy, "Margin Lending," March 21, 2000. Available at: http://commdocs.house.gov/committees/bank/hba63474.000/hba63474_0.HTM.

20. Robert J. Shiller, *Irrational Exuberance* (Princeton: Princeton University Press, 2000), p. 35.

21. Ibid., pp. xii–xiii.

22. Ibid., pp. 5–9. Note that Shiller uses his own method to calculate the average price-earnings ratio and that his values may therefore diverge from those provided by other sources.

23. New York Stock Exchange, "New York Stock Exchange Member Firms Customers' Margin Debt, January 1992 through February 2002." Available at: http://www.nyse.com/pdfs/margin0202.pdf. See also Gretchen Morgenson, "Buying on Margin Becomes a Habit," *New York Times,* March 24, 2000.

24. U.S. House of Representatives, Committee on Banking and Financial Services, Subcommittee on Domestic and International Monetary Policy, "Margin Lending," March 21, 2000. Available at: http://commdocs.house.gov/committees/bank/hba63474.000/hba63474_0.htm.

25. International Monetary Fund, *International Capital Markets: Developments, Prospects, and Key Policy Issues* (Washington, D.C.: IMF, 2000), pp. 10–11.

26. Stephan Haggard, *The Political Economy of the Asian Financial Crisis* (Washington, D.C.: Institute for International Economics, 2000), pp. 4, 6.

27. Gerard Baker and Stephen Fidler, "O'Neill Signals Hands-Off Stance on World Economy," *Financial Times,* February 15, 2001.

28. Regulations stipulate that investors can borrow no more than 50 percent of the value of the stock they are purchasing. In August 2001, new rules governing day trading were implemented, tightening equity and margin requirements in order to discourage speculation and limit risk.

29. Remarks by Chairman Alan Greenspan, December 5, 1996, Francis Boyer Lecture of the American Enterprise Institute for Public Policy Research. Available at: http://federalreserve.gov/boarddocs/speeches/1996/19961205.htm.

30. Charlie Rose Transcript no. 2713, program of June 27, 2000.

31. See Haggard, *The Political Economy of the Asian Financial Crisis,* pp. 1–13.

32. Remarks by Chairman Alan Greenspan, "Global Challenges," July 12, 2000, at the Financial Crisis Conference, Council on Foreign Relations, New York. Available at: http://federalreserve.gov/boarddocs/speeches/2000/20000712.htm.

33. Quotes from Steven Pearlstein, "Debating How to Repair Global Financial System," *Washington Post,* September 24, 2000.

34. Robert Gilpin, *The Challenge of Global Capitalism: The World Economy in the 21st Century* (Princeton: Princeton University Press, 2000), p. 161.

35. See Paul A. Papayoanou, *Power Ties: Economic Interdependence, Balancing, and War* (Ann Arbor: University of Michigan Press, 1999), p. 63.

36. On the media and their role in the spread of nationalist fervor, see Jack L. Snyder, *From Voting to Violence: Democratization and Nationalist Conflict* (New York: Norton, 2000).

37. Martin Wolf, "The Economic Failure of Islam," *Financial Times,* September 26, 2001.

38. Thomas Friedman, "Smoking or Non-Smoking?" *New York Times,* September 14, 2001.

39. See Joseph Yam, "International Capital Flows and Free Markets," remarks made at the Credit Suisse First Boston Asian Investment Conference, March 26, 1999. Available at: http://www.info.gov.hk/hkma/eng/speeches/speechs/joseph/speech_260399b.htm.

40. Karl Polanyi, *The Great Transformation: The Political and Economic Origins of Our Time* (Boston: Beacon Press, 1957).

41. Martin Wolf, "The Lure of the American Way," *Financial Times,* November 1, 2000.

42. Rothermund, *The Global Impact of the Great Depression,* p. 29.

43. Immanuel Kant, *Perpetual Peace: A Philosophical Essay* (New York: Macmillan, 1917). Originally published in 1795.

44. See chap. 2, n. 15.

45. William Jefferson Clinton, "Confronting the Challenges of a Broader World," address to the U.N. General Assembly, New York City, September 27, 1993. Available at: http://dosfan.lib.uic.edu/ERC/briefing/dispatch/1993/html/Dispatchv4n039.html.

46. For critiques of the democratic peace school, see David Spiro, "The Insignificance of the Liberal Peace"; Christopher Layne, "Kant or Cant: Myths of the Democratic Peace"; and Henry S. Farber and Joanne Gowa, "Polities and Peace," in *Debating the Democratic Peace,* ed. Michael E. Brown, Sean M. Lynn-Jones, and Steven E. Miller (Cambridge, Mass.: MIT Press, 1996).

47. Francis Fukuyama, *The End of History and the Last Man* (New York: Free Press, 1992), p. xx.

48. Ibid., p. 276.

49. On the role of German intellectuals in the evolution of nationalism, see Elie Kedourie, *Nationalism* (London: Hutchinson, 1966). Kedourie provides a summary of the views of both Herder and Fichte.

50. Fukuyama, *The End of History and the Last Man,* p. 276.

CHAPTER FOUR

1. See Robert Gilpin, *War and Change in World Politics* (New York: Cambridge University Press, 1981); and Paul M. Kennedy, *The Rise and Fall of the Great Powers: Economic Change and Military Conflict from 1500 to 2000* (New York: Random House, 1987).

2. For a concise summary of this conventional wisdom, see Antony J. Blinken, "The False Crisis over the Atlantic," *Foreign Affairs,* vol. 80, no. 3 (May–June 2001), pp. 35–48.

3. Cited in Otto Pflanze, *Bismarck and the Development of Germany,* vol. 1 (Princeton: Princeton University Press, 1990), p. 97.

4. Benjamin Disraeli, February 9, 1871, cited in J. C. G. Rohl, *From Bismarck to Hitler: The Problem of Continuity in German History* (New York: Barnes & Noble, 1970), p. 23.

5. Cited in V. R. Berghahn, *Germany and the Approach of War in 1914* (New York: St. Martin's, 1973), p. 174.

6. Cited in Fritz Fischer, *World Power or Decline: The Controversy over Germany's Aims in the First World War*, trans. Lancelot Farrar, Robert Kimber, and Rita Kimber (New York: Norton, 1974), p. 26.

7. Margaret Thatcher, *The Downing Street Years* (New York: HarperCollins, 1993), pp. 796–797. See also Robert J. Art, "Why Europe Needs the United States and NATO," *Political Science Quarterly*, vol. 111, no. 1 (Spring 1996), pp. 1–39.

8. On Roman military strategy, see Edward N. Luttwak, *The Grand Strategy of the Roman Empire from the First Century A.D. to the Third* (Baltimore: Johns Hopkins University Press, 1976).

9. Ammianus Marcellinus, *The Later Roman Empire (A.D. 354–378)* (Harmondsworth, Middlesex: Penguin Books, 1986), p. 412.

10. The capital of the Western Empire in the late fourth century moved to Milan and then in the early fifth century to Ravenna.

11. Edward Gibbon, *The History of the Decline and Fall of the Roman Empire*, with an introduction, notes, and appendices by J. B. Bury, vol. 4 (New York: AMS Press, 1974), pp. 174–175.

12. Lactantius, *On the Deaths of the Persecutors*, cited in Chris Scarre, *Chronicle of the Roman Emperors: The Reign-by-Reign Record of the Rulers of Imperial Rome* (London: Thames & Hudson, 1995), p. 196.

13. Gibbon, *The History of the Decline and Fall of the Roman Empire*, vol. 4, pp. 174–175.

14. On the causes of decline, see Gibbon, *The History of the Decline and Fall of the Roman Empire*, vols. 1–7; J. B. Bury, *History of the Later Roman Empire: From the Death of Theodosius I to the Death of Justinian (A.D. 395 to A.D. 565)* (London: Macmillan, 1923); and A. H. M. Jones, *The Later Roman Empire, 284–602: A Social, Economic and Administrative Survey* (Oxford: Blackwell, 1964). On the Byzantines, see A. A. Vasiliev, *History of the Byzantine Empire, 324–1453* (Madison: University of Wisconsin Press, 1952).

15. Gibbon, *The History of the Decline and Fall of the Roman Empire*, vol. 4, pp. 174–175.

16. William C. Wohlforth, "The Stability of a Unipolar World," *International Security*, vol. 24, no. 1 (Summer 1999), p. 8.

17. For an account of Europe's evolution emphasizing the primacy of economic motives, see Andrew Moravcsik, *The Choice for Europe: Social Purpose and State Power from Messina to Maastricht* (Ithaca: Cornell University Press, 1998).

18. European Parliament, "Principles and General Completion of the Internal Market," Fact Sheet 3.1.0. Available at: http://www.europarl.eu.int/factsheets/3_1_0_en.htm.

19. Robert Schuman, "Declaration of 10 May 1950." Available at: http://europa.eu.int/comm/dg10/publications/brochures/docu/50ans/decl_en.html#DECLARATION.

20. Jean Monnet, *Memoirs*, trans. Richard Mayne (Garden City, N.Y.: Doubleday, 1978), p. 392.

21. Treaty establishing the European Coal and Steel Community. Available at: http://www.europe.eu.int/abc/obj/treaties/en/entoc29.htm.

22. Tony Barber, "The Euro Takes Its Place in the Flow of History," *Financial Times*, August 30, 2001.

23. European Commission, *Eurobarometer: Public Opinion in the European Union*, Report no. 56, pp. 14, 38–39, 55–56. Available at: http://europa.eu.int/public_opinion/Standard_en.htm.

24. See Suzanne Kapner, "U.S. Venture Capital Sees Treasure in Europe," *New York Times*, May 30, 2001.

25. British companies made foreign acquisitions worth $337 billion; French companies, $137 billion; and U.S. companies, $136 billion. "Europe's Corporate Invasion of North America at All-Time High," KPMG Corporate Finance, January 15, 2001.

26. See Norbert Walter, "The Euro: Second to (N)one," *German Issues,* no. 23 (Washington, D.C.: American Institute for Contemporary German Studies, 2000).

27. The first pillar includes the policy areas addressed in the successive treaties leading to economic and monetary union. It contains regulations and legislation pertaining primarily to the free movement of persons, goods, services, and capital across borders. Justice and home affairs covers asylum and immigration, civil and criminal justice, and police cooperation.

28. Approval of legislation requires 62 of 87 votes. Germany, France, Italy, and the United Kingdom each have 10 votes in the Council. The smaller countries have votes in proportion to their population. Allocation of votes will change as enlargement proceeds.

29. "Britain's Role in Europe," November 23, 2001. Available at: http://www.number10.gov.uk/news.asp?NewsId=3101&SectionId=32.

30. See Ezra Suleiman, "Is Democratic Supranationalism a Danger?" in *Nationalism and Nationalities in the New Europe,* ed. Charles A. Kupchan (Ithaca: Cornell University Press, 1995).

31. Joschka Fischer, "From Confederacy to Federation—Thoughts on the Finality of European Integration," speech at Humboldt University, Berlin, May 12, 2000. Available at: http://www.auswaertiges-amt.de/www/de/infoservice/download/pdf/reden/redene/r000512b-r1008e.pdf.

32. Cited in Michael J. Sandel, *Democracy's Discontent: America in Search of a Public Philosophy* (Cambridge, Mass.: Harvard University Press, 1996), p. 15.

33. For an evaluation of the EU's need for a constitution, see Andrew Moravcsik, "Despotism in Brussels?" *Foreign Affairs,* vol. 80, no. 3 (May–June 2001), pp. 114–122. On public support for a constitution, see *Eurobarometer,* Report no. 56, pp. 46–47.

34. Fischer, "From Confederacy to Federation."

35. See Philip Stephens and Brian Groom, "Blair's Broad Horizons," *Financial Times,* May 25, 2001.

36. "Prime Minister's Speech to the Polish Stock Exchange," October 6, 2000. Available at: http://www.number-10.gov.uk/news.asp?NewsId=1341&SectionId=32.

37. Robert Graham, "Chirac Seeks EU 'Pioneer Group' on Security," *Financial Times,* August 27, 2001.

38. Suzanne Daley, "French Premier Opposes German Plan for Europe," *New York Times,* May 29, 2001.

39. See Martin Walker, "Overstretching Teutonia: Making the Best of the Fourth Reich," *World Policy Journal,* vol. 12, no. 1 (Spring 1995), p. 13.

40. PricewaterhouseCoopers, "European Pension Reform," *European Economic Outlook* (September 2000), p. 28. Available at: http://www.pwcglobal.com/gx/eng/ins-sol/spec-int/eeo/pwc_euro_pension_reform_9-00.pdf.

41. See Thomas Fuller, "Europe Wants Workers to Move," *International Herald Tribune*, February 13, 2002.

42. Fischer, "From Confederacy to Federation."

43. The Missouri Compromise of 1820 maintained a political balance between free states and slave states by simultaneously admitting Missouri as a slave state and Maine as a free state. The compromise also regulated the extension of slavery into the western territories, barring slavery from the Louisiana Purchase north of a specified latitude. See David M. Potter, *The Impending Crisis, 1848–1861* (New York: Harper & Row, 1976), pp. 53–58.

44. Fischer, "From Confederacy to Federation."

45. The government of Silvio Berlusconi later backed away from participating in the deal but indicated that Italy might join again at a later date.

46. Roger Cohen, "Storm Clouds over U.S.-Europe Relations," *New York Times*, March 26, 2001.

47. Ibid.; Roger Cohen, "A More Assertive Europe," *New York Times*, March 30, 2001.

48. Speech on the occasion of the Twentieth Anniversary of the Institute Français des Rélations Internationales, Élysée Palace, November 4, 1999. Text distributed by the French embassy in Washington, D.C.

49. "Prime Minister's Speech to the Polish Stock Exchange," October 6, 2000. Available at http://www.number-10.gov.uk/news.asp?NewsId=1341&SectionId=32.

50. "Vedrine Criticizes U.S. over International Ties," Agence France-Press, November 3, 1999. Available at http://wnc.fedworld.gov as document FBIS-WEU-1999-1103; Craig R. Whitney, "On the Ropes, Chirac Fights Back in French TV Interview," *New York Times*, December 13, 1996; and "Yeltsin 'Very Satisfied' with Talks with Jiang Zemin," ITAR-TASS, December 10, 1999. Available at: http://wnc.fedworld.gov as document FBIS-CHI-1999-2110.

51. Suzanne Daley, "French Minister Calls U.S. Policy 'Simplistic,'" *New York Times*, February 7, 2002; Alan Friedman, "Schroeder Assails EU Deficit Critics," *International Herald Tribune*, February 2, 2002; Steven Erlanger, "Europe Opens Convention to Set Future of Its Union," *New York Times*, March 1, 2002; and T. R. Reid, "EU Summit Ends with a Bang and a Whimper," *Washington Post*, March 17, 2002.

52. Daley, "French Minister Calls U.S. Policy 'Simplistic.'"

53. Edmund Andrews, "Angry Europeans to Challenge U.S. Steel Tariffs at WTO," *New York Times*, March 6, 2002.

CHAPTER FIVE

1. I. M. Destler and Steven Kull, *Misreading the Public: The Myth of a New Isolationism* (Washington, D.C.: Brookings Institution Press, 1999); Max Boot, "The Case for American Empire," *The Weekly Standard*, vol. 7, no. 5 (October 15, 2001), pp. 27–30; and Paul Johnson, "The Answer to Terrorism? Colonialism," *Wall Street Journal*, October 9, 2001.

2. See Arthur M. Schlesinger, Jr., *The Cycles of American History* (Boston: Houghton Mifflin, 1986).

3. Cited in Felix Gilbert, *To the Farewell Address: Ideas of Early American Foreign Policy* (Princeton: Princeton University Press, 1961), pp. 42–43.

4. *The Papers of Thomas Jefferson,* ed. Julian P. Boyd, vol. 8 (Princeton: Princeton University Press, 1953), p. 28; Jefferson to James Madison, August 28, 1789, ibid., vol. 15, p. 367.

5. Hamilton, *Federalist 6,* in James Madison, Alexander Hamilton, and John Jay, *The Federalist Papers* (London: Penguin Books, 1987), p. 106; Jay, *Federalist 4,* ibid., p. 97.

6. Text in Gilbert, *To the Farewell Address,* p. 145. Hamilton's thinking is discussed on pp. 130–131.

7. Hamilton, *Federalist 7,* in Madison et al., *The Federalist Papers,* p. 113.

8. "Autobiography," 1775, in *The Works of John Adams, Second President of the United States,* ed. Charles F. Adams, vol. 2 (Boston: Little, Brown, 1850–1856), p. 505.

9. Cited in Gilbert, *To the Farewell Address,* p. 145.

10. Hamilton, *Federalist 11,* in Madison et al., *The Federalist Papers,* p. 133.

11. Jefferson, Inaugural Address of 1801, cited in Jeffrey W. Legro, "Whence American Internationalism," *International Organization,* vol. 54, no. 2 (Spring 2000), p. 259.

12. Cited in Gilbert, *To the Farewell Address,* p. 43.

13. Text available ibid., p. 145.

14. On the differing cultures of America's regions, see Michael Lind, "Civil War by Other Means," *Foreign Affairs,* vol. 78, no. 5 (September–October 1999), pp. 123–142.

15. James Madison, a leading Republican and Virginia planter, actually favored commercial discrimination, particularly against Britain. In contrast to the Federalists, who favored protection to foster industrial growth, Madison called for tariffs as a temporary instrument needed to open foreign markets and expand U.S. exports of agricultural products. See Drew R. McCoy, *The Elusive Republic: Political Economy in Jeffersonian America* (Chapel Hill: University of North Carolina Press, 1980), pp. 137–145.

16. See David Hackett Fischer, *Albion's Seed: Four British Folkways in America* (New York: Oxford University Press, 1989), esp. chap. 5.

17. Alexander DeConde, *Entangling Alliance: Politics and Diplomacy Under George Washington* (Durham, N.C.: Duke University Press, 1958), p. 57.

18. For a summary of Hamilton's thinking on commercial policy and the need for a thriving manufacturing sector, see McCoy, *The Elusive Republic,* pp. 146–152.

19. DeConde, *Entangling Alliance,* p. 59.

20. At that point in time, the presidency went to the candidate receiving the most votes and the vice presidency to the runner-up.

21. Caius (a pseudonym) cited in McCoy, *The Elusive Republic,* p. 164.

22. Jefferson and Hamilton cited in Michael H. Hunt, *Ideology and U.S. Foreign Policy* (New Haven: Yale University Press, 1987), pp. 25–26.

23. Hamilton to Colonel Edward Harrington, in *The Works of Alexander Hamilton,* ed. Henry Cabot Lodge, vol. 8 (New York: Putnam, 1885–1886), pp. 259–260.

24. Despite the 1778 alliance with France, Washington announced that the United States would remain neutral when war broke out in Europe in 1793. This decision did not enjoy universal support, with James Madison arguing that the U.S. should not neglect its "duties to France." The alliance was technically in effect until 1800, when it was replaced with a commercial convention. See Walter LaFeber, *The American*

Age: United States Foreign Policy at Home and Abroad Since 1750 (New York: Norton, 1989), pp. 23–26, 44, 50.

25. On the use of U.S. force outside the Western Hemisphere, see Harry Allanson Ellsworth, *One Hundred Eighty Landings of United States Marines, 1800–1934* (Washington, D.C.: History and Museums Division Headquarters, U.S. Marine Corps, 1974); and Ellen C. Collier, "Instances of Use of United States Forces Abroad, 1798–1993" (Washington, D.C.: Congressional Research Service, Library of Congress, 1993). On the establishment and operation of overseas squadrons, see Harold Sprout and Margaret Sprout, *The Rise of American Naval Power, 1776–1918* (Annapolis, Md.: Naval Institute Press, 1990).

26. Cited in Dexter Perkins, *Hands Off: A History of the Monroe Doctrine* (Boston: Little, Brown, 1941), p. 28.

27. Cited in LaFeber, *The American Age*, p. 84.

28. Cited in Perkins, *Hands Off*, p. 79.

29. See Thomas R. Hietala, *Manifest Design: Anxious Aggrandizement in Late Jacksonian America* (Ithaca: Cornell University Press, 1985); and McCoy, *The Elusive Republic*.

30. C. Vann Woodward, "The Age of Reinterpretation," *American Historical Review*, vol. 66, no. 1 (October 1960), pp. 4, 2.

31. For a summary of the positions of Britain and France during the Civil War, see LaFeber, *The American Age*, pp. 140–145.

32. Cited in Perkins, *Hands Off*, pp. 240, 229.

33. LaFeber, *The American Age*, pp. 149–151.

34. Jackson delivered and published "The Significance of the Frontier in American History" in 1893. See Frederick Jackson Turner, *The Early Writings of Frederick Jackson Turner*, compiled by Everett E. Edwards (Madison: University of Wisconsin Press, 1938); and Frederick Jackson Turner, *The Frontier in American History* (New York: Holt, Rinehart, and Winston, 1962).

35. Walter LaFeber, *The New Empire: An Interpretation of American Expansion, 1860–1898* (Ithaca: Cornell University Press, 1963), pp. 282, 408.

36. Cited in LaFeber, *The American Age*, p. 182.

37. For a thorough study of the role that regional interests have played in shaping U.S. foreign policy from the late 1800s through the present, see Peter Trubowitz, *Defining the National Interest: Conflict and Change in American Foreign Policy* (Chicago: University of Chicago Press, 1998).

38. On this change in the names of the two main parties and for a summary of the issues that divided Whigs and Democrats, see Hietala, *Manifest Design*, pp. 3–9.

39. On these institutional shifts and their impact on policy, see Fareed Zakaria, *From Wealth to Power: The Unusual Origins of America's World Role* (Princeton: Princeton University Press, 1998); Ernest R. May, *Imperial Democracy: The Emergence of America as a Great Power* (New York: Harcourt, Brace and World, 1961); and LaFeber, *The American Age*, pp. 185–204.

40. Cited in Hunt, *Ideology and U.S. Foreign Policy*, p. 37.

41. George F. Kennan, *American Diplomacy* (Chicago: University of Chicago Press, 1984), p. 17.

42. Cited in Thomas J. Knock, *To End All Wars: Woodrow Wilson and the Quest for a New World Order* (New York: Oxford University Press, 1992), p. 96.

43. Amos Pinchot cited ibid., p. 104.

44. Cited ibid., p. 112.

45. Ibid., p. 124.

46. Thomas A. Bailey, *Woodrow Wilson and the Great Betrayal* (New York: Macmillan, 1947), pp. 1–2.

47. Cited ibid., p. 185.

48. Cited ibid., p. 184.

49. Cited in Legro, "Whence American Internationalism," p. 260.

50. Cited in Bailey, *Woodrow Wilson and the Great Betrayal,* p. 86.

51. Cited in Knock, *To End All Wars,* p. 241.

52. Bailey, *Woodrow Wilson and the Great Betrayal,* p. 32.

53. Robert A. Divine, *Second Chance: The Triumph of Internationalism During World War II* (New York: Atheneum, 1967), p. 10.

54. Cited in John A. Garraty, *Henry Cabot Lodge: A Biography* (New York: Knopf, 1968), p. 352.

55. See Bailey, *Woodrow Wilson and the Great Betrayal,* pp. 61, 115, 193.

56. Cited in Garraty, *Henry Cabot Lodge,* p. 312.

57. Cited in Bailey, *Woodrow Wilson and the Great Betrayal,* p. 42.

58. *The New Republic* cited in Knock, *To End All Wars,* p. 262; Knock quote from p. 165.

59. Hobson and Oswald Garrison Villard, cited ibid., p. 253.

60. For an overview of isolationism during the 1930s, see Thomas N. Guinsburg, "The Triumph of Isolationism," in *American Foreign Relations Reconsidered, 1890–1993,* ed. Gordon Martel (London: Routledge, 1994), pp. 90–105.

61. Cited in John Lewis Gaddis, *The United States and the Origins of the Cold War, 1941–1947* (New York: Columbia University Press, 1972), p. 24.

62. On U.S. diplomacy and war preparations between 1938 and 1941, see David Reynolds, *From Munich to Pearl Harbor: Roosevelt's America and the Origins of the Second World War* (Chicago: Ivan R. Dee, 2001).

63. Kenneth Davis, *FDR: The War President, 1940–1943* (New York: Random House, 2000), p. 270.

64. Robert Dallek, *Franklin D. Roosevelt and American Foreign Policy, 1932–1945* (New York: Oxford University Press, 1979), p. 283.

65. Ibid., p. 319.

66. Divine, *Second Chance,* pp. 48–49.

67. Ibid., p. 51.

68. John Culver and John Hyde, *American Dreamer: The Life and Times of Henry A. Wallace* (New York: Norton, 2000), p. 263.

69. Divine, *Second Chance,* p. 80.

70. Robert A. Divine, *Roosevelt and World War II* (Baltimore: Johns Hopkins Press, 1969), pp. 51–52.

71. Forrest Davis, "What Really Happened at Teheran," *Saturday Evening Post,* May 20, 1944, p. 46.

72. Cited in Daniel Yergin, *Shattered Peace: The Origins of the Cold War and the National Security State* (Boston: Houghton Mifflin, 1977), p. 45.

73. One of the principal differences between the body envisaged by Welles and the

U.N. that ultimately came into being was that France joined the other four great powers as a permanent, veto-wielding member of the Security Council.

74. Divine, *Second Chance*, pp. 142, 144, 147, 153, 130.

75. Cited in Gaddis, *The United States and the Origins of the Cold War*, p. 29.

76. Trubowitz, *Defining the National Interest*, p. 148.

77. Cited ibid., p. 98.

78. Cited in Divine, *Second Chance*, p. 143.

79. Divine, *Second Chance*, p. 63.

80. *Washington Dispatches, 1941–1945: Weekly Political Reports from the British Embassy*, ed. H. G. Nicholas (Chicago: University of Chicago Press, 1981), p. 518.

81. Senator Robert Reynolds of North Carolina cited in Divine, *Second Chance*, p. 152.

82. Cited ibid., p. 242.

83. Clark Eichelberger cited ibid., p. 35.

84. Michael Leigh, *Mobilizing Consent: Public Opinion in American Foreign Policy, 1937–1947* (Westport, Conn.: Greenwood Press, 1976), p. 124.

85. Legro, "Whence American Internationalism," p. 274.

86. Truman cited in Howard Jones, *"A New Kind of War": America's Global Strategy and the Truman Doctrine in Greece* (New York: Oxford University Press, 1989), p. 43; and Gaddis, *The United States and the Origins of the Cold War*, p. 351.

87. Survey conducted by the Gallup Poll and Potomac Associates, as reported in William G. Mayer, *The Changing American Mind: How and Why American Public Opinion Changed Between 1960 and 1988* (Ann Arbor: University of Michigan Press, 1992), p. 65.

88. The Nixon Doctrine reaffirmed America's treaty commitments and pledged to offer a nuclear shield to threatened allies. But Nixon also asserted that "in cases involving other types of aggression, we shall furnish military and economic assistance when requested in accordance with our treaty commitments. But we shall look to the nation directly threatened to assume the primary responsibility of providing the manpower for its defense." On the Nixon Doctrine, see Charles A. Kupchan, *The Persian Gulf and the West: The Dilemmas of Security* (Boston: Allen & Unwin, 1987), pp. 31–40.

CHAPTER SIX

1. As the term is used in this book, a "populist" foreign policy is one that rests on three principles. First, policy should be shaped by the interests and judgments of common Americans, not just by elites in Washington and New York. Second, foreign policy should be conducted so as to preserve America's decentralized form of democracy and the liberties of its citizens. Foreign ambition should accordingly be kept in check because of its potential to strengthen the hand of the federal government and impair domestic freedoms. In similar fashion, international institutions are suspect because they compromise American sovereignty and autonomy. Third, the United States should resort to the use of armed force only when its national interests, narrowly defined, are directly threatened. In *Special Providence: American Foreign Policy and How It Changed the World* (New York: Knopf, 2001), Walter Russell Mead distinguishes between Jeffersonian and Jacksonian schools of populism. Although current

populist thinking shares much common ground with the Jeffersonian and Jacksonian traditions, I prefer to use the generic term because of the profound differences that exist between contemporary American politics and the politics of the early decades. For example, Jefferson envisioned an agrarian America whose military strength and international ambition would remain quite limited. In that sense, his vision of the country became outmoded as America industrialized and became a major power. In similar fashion, Jackson's brand of populism was similar to, but is by no means synonymous with, contemporary populism.

2. Cited in Tim Weiner, "Mexican President Warmly Greeted in Washington," *New York Times,* August 25, 2000.

3. The term comes from Richard N. Haass, *The Reluctant Sheriff: The United States After the Cold War* (New York: Council on Foreign Relations Press, 1997).

4. See Michael R. Gordon and Bernard E. Trainor, *The Generals' War: The Inside Story of the Conflict in the Gulf* (Boston: Little, Brown, 1995), pp. 32–34.

5. Karl Mannheim, "The Problem of Generations," in *Essays on the Sociology of Knowledge,* ed. Paul Kecskemeti (London: Routledge & Kegan Paul, 1952), p. 298.

6. William G. Mayer, *The Changing American Mind: How and Why American Public Opinion Changed Between 1960 and 1988* (Ann Arbor: University of Michigan Press, 1992), chap. 7.

7. Eighty-five percent of Americans between eighteen and twenty-nine years old agreed with the statement "We should pay less attention to problems overseas and concentrate on problems here at home." This was 5 to 10 percentage points higher than for older age groups. "America's Global Role: A Nation Divided?" Princeton Survey Research/Pew, survey conducted in October 1999. Available at: http://www.publicagenda.org/issues/nation_divided_detail.cfm?issue_type=americas_global_role&list=6.

8. Elite College History Survey, Center for Survey Research and Analysis at the University of Connecticut, conducted for the American Council of Trustees and Alumni, December 1999. Available at: http://www.goacta.org; and Diane Jean Schemo, "Students, Especially 12th Graders, Do Poorly on History Tests," *New York Times,* May 10, 2002.

9. Jane Perlez, "As Diplomacy Loses Luster, Young Stars Flee State Dept.," *New York Times,* September 5, 2000. In 2001, the State Department launched a publicity campaign to reverse its recruiting woes. The campaign was an apparent success, with the number of applicants for the 2001 Foreign Service entrance exam substantially larger than for the 2000 exam. See David Stout, "Sign-Ups for Foreign Service Test Nearly Double After 10-Year Ebb," *New York Times,* August 31, 2001. Interest in careers at the State Department and the CIA also rose following the terror attacks of September 2001.

10. The Chicago Council on Foreign Relations carries out a public opinion survey every four years. The 1994 survey indicated that 98 percent of U.S. leaders and 65 percent of the public "favor an active part for the US in world affairs." The figures for 1998 were 96 percent and 61 percent respectively, indicating only a slight drop. In general, public opinion surveys show only a minor decrease in internationalism since the end of the Cold War. See *American Public Opinion and U.S. Foreign Policy 1999,* ed. John E. Reilly (Chicago: Chicago Council on Foreign Relations, 1999). Available at: http://www.ccfr.org/publications/opinion/AmPuOp99.pdf.

11. James M. Lindsay, "The New Apathy," *Foreign Affairs,* vol. 79, no. 5 (September–October 2000), pp. 2–8. The public opinion data in this paragraph are also from the Lindsay article.

12. Peter Trubowitz (University of Texas at Austin), draft paper presented at the Autonomous National University of Mexico, Mexico City, August 20, 2000.

13. Associated Press, "Stymied by Senate, Would-Be Envoy Quits," *New York Times,* September 1, 2000.

14. Alison Mitchell, "Bush and the G.O.P. Congress: Do the Candidate's Internationalist Leanings Mean Trouble?" *New York Times,* May 19, 2000.

15. Brookings Institution scholars Ivo Daalder and Michael O'Hanlon offer a damning critique of the alliance's strategy: "The allies viewed force simply as a tool of diplomacy, intended to push negotiations one way or another. They were unprepared for the possibility that they might need to directly achieve a battlefield result.... NATO's war against Serbia was a vivid reminder that when using military power, one must be prepared for things to go wrong and to escalate." Ivo H. Daalder and Michael E. O'Hanlon, *Winning Ugly: NATO's War to Save Kosovo* (Washington, D.C.: Brookings Institution Press, 2000), p. 105.

16. Remarks by the president at Memorial Day service, May 31, 1999, The White House, Office of the Press Secretary.

17. Carlotta Gall, "Serbs Stone U.S. Troops in Divided Kosovo Town," *New York Times,* February 21, 2000.

18. Jane Perlez, "Kosovo's Unquenched Violence Dividing U.S. and NATO Allies," *New York Times,* March 12, 2000.

19. Robert Byrd, "Europe's Turn to Keep the Peace," *New York Times,* March 20, 2000.

20. Michael Cooper, "Cheney Urges Rethinking Use of U.S. Ground Forces in Bosnia and Kosovo," *New York Times,* September 1, 2000.

21. Steven Lee Myers, "Bush Candidate for Defense Job Sees Overhaul," *New York Times,* January 12, 2001.

22. George W. Bush, Republican Presidential Nomination Acceptance Speech, Philadelphia, August 3, 2000. Available at: http://www.vote-smart.org/vote-smart/speeches.phtml?func=speech&speech=B000001559.

23. "The Armageddon Nominee," *Boston Globe,* April 2, 2001.

24. Steven Lee Meyers, "U.S. Signs Treaty for World Court to Try Atrocities," *New York Times,* January 1, 2001.

25. "The Armageddon Nominee," *Boston Globe.*

26. Hugo Young, "We've Lost That Allied Feeling," *Washington Post,* April 1, 2001.

27. Statement to NATO foreign ministers in Brussels, December 15, 1999, p. 4. Available at: http://www.state.gov/www/policy-remarks/1999/991215_talbott_nac.html.

28. Assistant Secretary of Defense Franklin Kramer, testimony before the Senate Foreign Relations Committee, March 9, 2000, p. 5. Available at: http://frwebgate.access.gpo.gov/cgi-bin/getdoc.cgi?dbname=106_senate_hearings&docid=f:65627.pdf.

29. Associated Press, "U.S. Defense Secretary Says NATO Could Become a Relic of History," December 5, 2000. Available at: http://www.cnn.com/2000/WORLD/europe/12/05/nato.ap/index.html.

30. "The Alliance at Risk," *Guardian,* November 24, 1999.

31. Cited in Stephen Fidler, "Between Two Camps," *Financial Times*, February 14, 2001.

32. John R. Bolton, testimony before the House International Relations Committee, November 10, 1999, p. 1. Available at: http://www.house.gov/international_relations/106/full/106first/testimony/bolton.htm.

33. Both Bush and Powell qualified their support by stipulating that planning for the EU force had to take place within NATO and strengthen NATO's capabilities. See White House, Office of the Press Secretary, "Remarks by the President and Prime Minister Blair in Joint Press Conference," Camp David, February 23, 2001. Available at: http://www.whitehouse.gov/news/releases/2001/02/20010226-1.html. For Powell's views, see U.S. Department of State, Office of the Secretary, "Press Availability with NATO Secretary General Lord Robertson," Brussels, Belgium, February 27, 2001. Available at: http://www.state.gov/secretary/rm/2001/index.cfm?docid=1000.

34. John Vinocur, "America's 'We'll Call If We Need You' War," *International Herald Tribune*, October 3, 2001.

35. The Pew Global Attitudes Project, survey released on December 14, 2001. Available at: http://www.people-press.org.

36. Steven Erlanger, "German Joins Europe's Cry that the U.S. Won't Consult," *New York Times*, February 13, 2002; Suzanne Daley, "Many in Europe Voice Worry U.S. Will Not Consult Them," *New York Times*, January 31, 2002; and Steven Erlanger, "Protest, and Friends Too, Await Bush in Europe," *New York Times*, May 22, 2002.

37. Andrew Sullivan, "America at War: America Wakes Up to a World of Fear," *Sunday Times* (London), September 16, 2001; and Marshall Wittman, panel discussion at the New America Foundation, "21st Century Infamy: The Terrorism of September 11th and Implications for American Foreign Policy," September 13, 2001.

38. Tom Segev, *One Palestine, Complete: Jews and Arabs Under the British Mandate*, trans. Haim Watzman (New York: Metropolitan Books, 2000), pp. 495, 460.

39. Martha Crenshaw, "The Effectiveness of Terrorism in the Algerian War," in *Terrorism in Context*, ed. Martha Crenshaw (University Park, Pa.: Penn State University Press, 1995), pp. 512–513.

40. Alistair Horne, *A Savage War of Peace: Algeria, 1954–1962* (New York: Viking, 1977), p. 444.

41. Crenshaw, "The Effectiveness of Terrorism in the Algerian War," p. 480.

42. Thomas Friedman, "A Memo from Osama," *New York Times*, June 26, 2001.

43. Discussion on "International Correspondents," CNN, October 6, 2001.

44. Alan Sipress and Lee Hockstader, "Sharon Speech Riles U.S.," *Washington Post*, October 6, 2001.

45. See Elaine Sciolino and Eric Schmitt, "U.S. Rethinks Its Role in Saudi Arabia," *New York Times*, March 10, 2002; and Shibley Telhami, "Shrinking Our Presence in Saudi Arabia," *New York Times*, January 29, 2002.

46. Richard Morin and Claudia Deane, "Poll: Americans' Trust in Government Grows," *Washington Post*, September 28, 2001.

47. "Presidential Debate I," October 3, 2000, Boston, Massachusetts. Available at: http://www.foreignpolicy2000.org/debate/candidate/candidate.html.

48. Cited in Steven Mufson and John Harris, "Novice Became Confident Diplomat on World Stage," *Washington Post*, January 15, 2001.

49. Sebastian Mallaby, "The Man Without a Bumper Sticker," *Washington Post,* January 15, 2001.

50. "U.S. Urges Bin Laden to Form Nation It Can Attack," *The Onion,* October 3, 2001.

51. See Peter Trubowitz, *Defining the National Interest: Conflict and Change in American Foreign Policy* (Chicago: University of Chicago Press, 1998), pp. 171–234.

52. The "South Region," as defined by the Bureau of the Census, includes Alabama, Arkansas, Delaware, Florida, Georgia, Kentucky, Louisiana, Maryland, Mississippi, North Carolina, Oklahoma, South Carolina, Tennessee, Texas, Virginia, West Virginia, and Washington, D.C. Population data from U.S. Census Bureau, "Resident Populations of the 50 States, the District of Columbia, and Puerto Rico," *Census 2000.* Available at: http://blue.census.gov/population/cen2000/phc-t2/tab01.pdf. Recruitment data from Office of the Assistant Secretary of Defense for Force Management Policy, "AC Enlisted Accessions by Geography," *Population Representation in the Military Services.* Available at: http://dticaw.dtic.mil/prhome/poprep98/html/2-geography. html.

53. The figures used in this calculation include active, reserve, and guard facilities and exclude sites under ten acres in size or under $10 million in value. Data from Department of Defense, Office of the Deputy Undersecretary for Defense (Installations & Environment), "Base Structure Report (A Summary of DoD's Real Property Inventory), Fiscal Year 2001 Baseline." Available at: http://www.acq.osd.mil/installation/irm/irm_library/bsr2001.pdf; and U.S. Census Bureau, "Land Area, Population, and Density for States and Counties," *Census 1990.* Available at: http://www.census.gov/population/censusdata/90den_stco.txt.

54. Department of Defense, Washington Headquarters Services, Directorate for Information Operations and Reports, "Prime Contract Awards by Region and State, Fiscal Years 2000, 1999, and 1998," Table I-1. Available at: http://web1.whs.osd.mil/peidhome/geostats/p06/fy2000/po6tab1.htm.

55. Peter D. Feaver and Richard H. Kohn, "The Gap: Soldiers, Civilians, and Their Mutual Misunderstanding," *National Interest,* no. 61 (Fall 2000), pp. 29–37. See also the Triangle Institute for Strategic Studies, "Project on the Gap Between the Military and Civilian Society," Digest of Findings and Studies Presented at the Conference on the Military and Civilian Society, October 28–29, 1999. Available at: http://www.unc.edu/depts/tiss/RESEARCH/CIVMIL.htm.

56. Walter Russell Mead, "The Jacksonian Tradition and American Foreign Policy," *National Interest,* no. 58 (Winter 1999–2000), pp. 5–29.

57. The Department of Defense reports that members of the military tend to come from backgrounds that are "somewhat lower in socioeconomic status than the U.S. average . . . with the top quartile of the population underrepresented." Parents of recruits are also underrepresented in the "high-status professions." See Office of the Assistant Secretary of Defense (Force Management Policy), "Population Representation in the Military Services," November 2000. Available at: http://dticaw.dtic.mil/prhome/poprep99/index.html.

58. Timothy Egan, "Plan to Expand U.S. Powers Alarming Some in Colorado," *New York Times,* October 3, 2001.

59. The Senate resolution authorizing air strikes passed by a vote of 58 to 41. The regional breakdown was as follows. Northeast: Yes—14, No—4. South: Yes—17, No—

14, Mountain West: Yes—5, No—11. The House resolution blocking the administration from sending ground troops to Yugoslavia without congressional approval passed by a vote of 249 to 180. The regional breakdown was as follows. Northeast: Yes—35, No—51. South: Yes—84, No—59, Mountain West: Yes—20, No—3. The House resolution supporting air strikes produced a tie vote of 213 to 213. The regional breakdown was as follows. Northeast: Yes—64, No—21. South: Yes—67, No—75. Mountain West: Yes—5, No—19. The Midwest and Pacific West generally voted for the war in the Senate and against it in the House, with the Midwest exhibiting stronger opposition and the Pacific West more closely divided.

60. The northern region includes the Northeast and what the Census Bureau calls the North Central—more commonly referred to as the Midwest. The South and West cover all other states, including the Mountain and Pacific West. U.S. Census Bureau, Census 2000, "Ranking Tables for States: 1990 and 2000." Available at: http://www.census.gov/population/www/cen2000/phc-t2.html. Population estimates from U.S. Census Bureau, Census 1990, "Projections of the Total Populations of States: 1995–2025." Available at: http://www.census.gov/population/projections/state/stpjpop.txt.

61. U.S. Census Bureau, Census 1990, "Projections of the Resident Population by Race, Hispanic Origin, and Nativity: Middle Series, 2050–2070." Available at: http://www.census.gov/population/projections/nation/summary/np-t5-g.pdf. U.S. Census Bureau, Census 1990, "Projections of the Resident Population by Race, Hispanic Origin, and Nativity: Middle Series, 2075–2100." Available at: http://www.census.gov/population/projections/nation/summary/np-t5-h.pdf.

62. U.S. Census Bureau, Census 1990, "Projected State Populations, by Race, Sex, and Hispanic Origin: 1995–2025." Available at: http://www.census.gov/population/projections/state/stpjrace.txt.

63. On the political impact of Americans of Central European descent on the debate over NATO expansion, see Dick Kirschten, "Ethnics Resurging," *National Journal*, vol. 27, no. 8 (February 25, 1995), pp. 478–484. On the general influence of diasporas and ethnic groups on U.S. foreign policy, see Tony Smith, *Foreign Attachments: The Power of Ethnic Groups in the Making of American Foreign Policy* (Cambridge, Mass.: Harvard University Press, 2000).

64. See Rodolfo O. de la Garza and Harry P. Pachon, *Latinos and U.S. Foreign Policy: Representing the "Homeland"?* (Lanham, Md.: Rowman & Littlefield, 2000), pp. 13, 24–25.

65. Ernest Gellner, *Nations and Nationalism* (Ithaca: Cornell University Press, 1983).

66. Mayer, *The Changing American Mind*, p. 211.

67. Lind, "Civil War by Other Means," p. 139. See also Joel Kotkin, *The New Geography: How the Digital Revolution Is Reshaping the American Landscape* (New York: Random House, 2000).

CHAPTER SEVEN

1. For his role in contributing to my thinking on these issues, I am indebted to G. John Ikenberry and his book *After Victory: Institutions, Strategic Restraint, and the Rebuilding of Order After Major Wars* (Princeton: Princeton University Press, 2001).

2. Felix Gilbert, *To the Farewell Address: Ideas of Early American Foreign Policy* (Princeton: Princeton University Press, 1961), pp. 7, 14.

3. Ibid., pp. 14–15.

4. See Daniel H. Deudney, "The Philadelphian System: Sovereignty, Arms Control, and Balance of Power in the American States-Union, Circa 1787–1861," *International Organization*, vol. 49, no. 2 (Spring 1995), pp. 191–228.

5. Jay, *Federalist 5*, in James Madison, Alexander Hamilton, and John Jay, *The Federalist Papers* (London: Penguin Books, 1987), pp. 101, 102, 103; Jay, *Federalist 4*, ibid., p. 100.

6. Hamilton, *Federalist 7*, ibid., p. 111.

7. Jay, *Federalist 5*, ibid., p. 101; Jay, *Federalist 4*, ibid., p. 100; Hamilton, *Federalist 7*, ibid., p. 113; Hamilton, *Federalist 11*, ibid., p. 129.

8. Hamilton, *Federalist 51*, ibid., p. 320.

9. Cited in Thomas R. Hietala, *Manifest Design: Anxious Aggrandizement in Late Jacksonian America* (Ithaca: Cornell University Press, 1985), p. 184.

10. Deudney, "The Philadelphian System," pp. 217–218.

11. Cited in Michael H. Hunt, *Ideology and U.S. Foreign Policy* (New Haven: Yale University Press, 1987), p. 30.

12. Deudney, "The Philadelphian System," pp. 214–216.

13. Robert Stewart Castlereagh, *Correspondence, Dispatches, and Other Papers of Viscount Castlereagh*, 3d series, vol. 11 (London: H. Colburn, 1850), p. 105.

14. Official communication to the Russian ambassador in London, January 19, 1805, cited in René Albrecht-Carrié, *The Concert of Europe* (New York: Walker, 1968), p. 28.

15. Cited ibid., p. 142.

16. Cited in Bruce Cronin, *Community Under Anarchy: Transnational Identity and the Evolution of Cooperation* (New York: Columbia University Press, 1999), p. 56.

17. Cited ibid., p. 60.

18. Cited in Albrecht-Carrié, *The Concert of Europe*, p. 50.

19. Cited ibid., p. 37.

20. Cited in Cronin, *Community Under Anarchy*, p. 58.

21. Concert protocol of November 15, 1818, cited ibid., p. 60; Castlereagh cited in Charles K. Webster, *The Foreign Policy of Castlereagh, 1812–1815: Britain and the Reconstruction of Europe* (London: G. Bell, 1931), p. 480; Castlereagh, *Correspondence, Dispatches, and Other Papers of Viscount Castlereagh*, p. 105; and Metternich cited in Jacques Droz, *Europe Between the Revolutions, 1815–1848* (New York: Harper & Row, 1967), p. 17.

22. See Charles A. Kupchan, "After Pax Americana: Benign Power, Regional Integration, and the Sources of a Stable Mulipolarity," *International Security*, vol. 23, no. 2 (Fall 1998), pp. 42–79.

23. Cited in Gregory F. Treverton, *America, Germany, and the Future of Europe* (Princeton: Princeton University Press, 1992), p. 104.

24. Speech at the University of Louvain, Belgium, February 1, 1996, cited in "Kohl Issues New Warning to Britain over EU Reform," Agence France-Presse, February 2, 1996.

25. Hamilton, *Federalist 11*, in Madison et al., *The Federalist Papers*, p. 133. Here Hamilton makes allusion to the writings of l'Abbé Guillaume Thomas François Raynal, particularly his *Recherches Philosophiques sur les Américains*.

26. Cited in William Drozdiak, "Even Allies Resent U.S. Dominance: America Accused of Bullying World," *Washington Post,* November 4, 1997.

27. Lionel M. Gelber, *The Rise of Anglo-American Friendship: A Study in World Politics, 1898–1906* (London: Oxford University Press, 1938), p. 411.

28. For optimistic views of China's future, see Robert S. Ross, "Beijing as a Conservative Power," *Foreign Affairs,* vol. 76, no. 2 (March–April 1997), pp. 33–44; and Nicholas Berry, "China Is Not an Imperialist Power," *Strategic Review,* vol. 24, no. 1 (Winter 2001), pp. 4–10. For pessimistic views, see Richard Bernstein and Ross H. Munro, "The Coming Conflict with China," *Foreign Affairs,* vol. 76, no. 2 (March–April 1997), pp. 18–32; and Constantine Menges, "China: Myths and Reality," *Washington Times,* April 12, 2001.

29. Data for Chinese and U.S. GDP from International Monetary Fund, "The World Economic Outlook (WEO) Database, December 2001." Available at: http://www.imf.org/external/pubs/ft/weo/2001/03/data/index.htm. Data on California's economy from California Technology, Trade & Commerce Agency, "California Gross State Product." Available at: http://134.186.44.154/ersi/oer/GSP.html#GSP.

30. International Institute for Strategic Studies, *The Military Balance, 2001–2002* (London: International Institute for Strategic Studies, 2001), pp. 25, 194. Estimates of Chinese military spending vary according to which expenditures are included in the defense budget and what adjustments are made to take purchasing-power parity into consideration. See Bates Gill and Michael O'Hanlon, "China's Hollow Military," *National Interest,* no. 56 (Summer 1999), pp. 56–57.

31. The United States imported $100 billion worth of goods and services from China in 2000, while exporting to China $16 billion. U.S. Census Bureau, Foreign Trade Division, "Trade with China: 2000." Available at: http://www.census.gov/foreign-trade/balance/c5700.html.

32. Doug Struck, "Koreans' Anger About Textbook Surprises Japan," *International Herald Tribune,* May 19–20, 2001.

33. Doug Struck, "Japan's Neighbors Cool to Koizumi," *Washington Post,* August 25, 2001.

34. *Zhongguo Qingnian Bao* (China Youth Daily), February 15, 1997, cited in Kokubun Ryosei, "Japan-China Relations After the Cold War: Switching from the '1972 Framework,'" *Japan Echo,* vol. 28, no. 2 (April 2001), p. 9.

35. Joseph S. Nye, *Peace in Parts: Integration and Conflict in Regional Organization* (Boston: Little, Brown, 1971).

36. Economic Cooperation Bureau, Japan Ministry of Foreign Affairs, ODA Hakusho 1999 Joukan (ODA White Paper Volume I), pp. 150–151.

37. The average annual per capita income for the region is $4,000. Low-income countries are generally defined as those with per capita incomes below $785. See the World Bank Group, "Latin America and the Caribbean." Available at: http://lnweb18.worldbank.org/External/lac/lac.nsf/694dc25670b0e319852567d6006a9c9e/e0c627bbe9bc8361852567edoo51fbf5?OpenDocument.

38. The World Bank Group, "Regional Brief: Sub-Saharan Africa." Available at: http://www.WorldBank.org/afr/overview.pdf.

39. Carol Lancaster, *Aid to Africa: So Much to Do, So Little Done* (Chicago: University of Chicago Press, 1999), p. 20.

40. Ibid., p. 2.

41. Gene B. Sperling, "Toward Universal Education," *Foreign Affairs*, vol. 80, no. 5 (September–October 2001), pp. 7–13.

42. Amartya Sen, *Development as Freedom* (New York: Knopf, 1999), p. 42.

43. Some of the most innovative programs are using the Internet to put communities proposing projects into direct contact with potential donors in the public and private sectors, keeping overhead costs to a minimum.

44. Lancaster, *Aid to Africa*, pp. 233–238.

45. See Richard N. Gardner, "The One Percent Solution," *Foreign Affairs*, vol. 79, no. 4 (July–August 2000), p. 8; and Joseph Kahn, "White House Adds Billions to an Increase in Foreign Aid," *New York Times*, March 20, 2002.

46. Lael Brainard, "Terrorism and Textiles," *New York Times*, December 27, 2001.

47. See John Cassidy, "Helping Hands: How Foreign Aid Could Benefit Everybody," *New Yorker*, March 18, 2002, pp. 60–66. See also "Does Aid Help?" *Washington Post*, February 9, 2002.

48. Lancaster, *Aid to Africa*, p. 3.

49. See Clifford A. Kupchan, "Devolution Drives Russian Reform," *Washington Quarterly*, vol. 23, no. 2 (Spring 2000), pp. 67–77.

50. For discussion of Islam and political development, see John L. Esposito and John O. Voll, *Islam and Democracy* (New York: Oxford University Press, 1998); and Bernard Lewis, "Islam and Democracy: A Historical Overview"; Robin B. Wright, "Islam and Liberal Democracy: Two Visions of Reformation"; Abdou Filali-Ansary, "Islam and Democracy: The Challenge of Secularization"; Mohamed Elhachmi Hamdi, "The Limits of the Western Model"; and Laith Kubba, "Recognizing Pluralism," in *Journal of Democracy*, vol. 7, no. 2 (April 1996).

51. Jesse Helms, "Saving the U.N.: A Challenge to the Next Secretary-General," *Foreign Affairs*, vol. 75, no. 5 (September–October 1996), p. 2.

52. Senate Hearing 105-724, "Is a U.N. Criminal Court in the U.S. National Interest?" July 23, 1998 (Washington, D.C.: Government Printing Office, 1998), p. 4.

53. Ikenberry, *After Victory*, p. 54.

54. Intergovernmental Panel on Climate Change, "The Regional Impacts of Climate Change: An Assessment of Vulnerability." Available at: http://www.grida.no/climate/ipcc/regional/index.htm.

55. For discussion of the merits of multilateralism and the conditions under which it should be pursued, see Joseph S. Nye, Jr., *The Paradox of American Power: Why the World's Only Superpower Can't Go It Alone* (New York: Oxford University Press, 2002).

56. U.S. Department of Transportation, Office of the Assistant Secretary for Aviation and International Affairs, "U.S. International Air Passenger and Freight Statistics, June 2000," released February 2001, p. 5. Available at: http://ostpxweb.ost.dot.gov/aviation/international-series.

57. For other suggestions on how to promote the socializing role of international institutions, see Joseph S. Nye, Jr., "Globalization's Democratic Deficit: How to Make International Institutions More Accountable," *Foreign Affairs*, vol. 80, no. 4 (July–August 2001), pp. 2–6.

58. Cited in Cronin, *Community Under Anarchy*, pp. 61, 56.

CHAPTER EIGHT

1. Cited in Drew R. McCoy, *The Elusive Republic: Political Economy in Jeffersonian America* (Chapel Hill: University of North Carolina Press, 1980), p. 12.

2. Cited in Michael J. Sandel, *Democracy's Discontent: America in Search of a Public Philosophy* (Cambridge, Mass.: Harvard University Press, 1996), p. 147.

3. Cited ibid., p. 126.

4. Cited ibid., p. 146.

5. Cited in McCoy, *The Elusive Republic*, p. 102.

6. Cited in Sandel, *Democracy's Discontent*, p. 163.

7. Cited ibid., pp. 176–177.

8. Cited ibid., p. 179.

9. Thomas R. Hietala, *Manifest Design: Anxious Aggrandizement in Late Jacksonian America* (Ithaca: Cornell University Press, 1985), pp. 102–104.

10. Cited in Sandel, *Democracy's Discontent*, p. 216.

11. Cited ibid., p. 218.

12. Stephen Jay Gould, *Time's Arrow, Time's Cycle: Myth and Metaphor in the Discovery of Geological Time* (Cambridge, Mass.: Harvard University Press, 1988), p. 51.

13. This conceptualization of historical change represents a synthesis of several different intellectual traditions. The works most influential in its formulation include the following. On the importance of modes of production in shaping political and social institutions: Talcott Parsons, *The Evolution of Societies* (Englewood Cliffs, N.J.: Prentice-Hall, 1977); Emile Durkheim, *The Division of Labor in Society* (New York: Free Press, 1984); Karl Marx, *Capital: A Critical Analysis of Capitalist Production*, trans. Samuel Moore and Edward Aveling (London: Allen & Unwin, 1971); and Ernest Gellner, *Nations and Nationalism* (Ithaca: Cornell University Press, 1983). On the cyclical and evolutionary nature of history: Gould, *Time's Arrow, Time's Cycle;* George Modelski, *Long Cycles in World Politics* (Seattle: University of Washington Press, 1987); Robert Gilpin, *War and Change in World Politics* (New York: Cambridge University Press, 1981). On the feedback effect of social change on technology and innovation: William H. McNeill, *The Rise of the West: A History of the Human Community* (Chicago: University of Chicago Press, 1963); and William H. McNeill, *The Pursuit of Power: Technology, Armed Force, and Society Since A.D. 1000* (Chicago: University of Chicago Press, 1982). For a thoughtful overview of much of this literature, see Stephen K. Sanderson, *Social Transformations: A General Theory of Historical Development* (Cambridge, Mass.: Blackwell, 1995). See also Jared Diamond, *Guns, Germs, and Steel: The Fates of Human Societies* (New York: Norton, 1999).

14. Figures 3 and 4 are schematic in nature and not intended to assign precise dates to each historical era. Rather, each era gradually shades into the next, with some parts of the world advancing much more quickly than others. It is also important to note that this identification of historical eras and their dimensions by no means enjoys a scholarly consensus; these are topics of ongoing debate among historians, anthropologists, sociologists, and specialists from other fields. The purpose of this section is to lay out a general logic of historical change, not to offer a more definitive account of an issue that remains complex and contested.

15. This summary draws on the overview of historical change in Sanderson, *Social Transformations*.

16. See Edward Gibbon, *The History of the Decline and Fall of the Roman Empire*, with introduction, notes, and appendices by J. B. Bury, vol. 2 (New York: AMS Press, 1974), pp. 311–317.

17. See Benedict Anderson, *Imagined Communities: Reflections on the Origin and Spread of Nationalism* (New York: Verso, 1991).

18. Some historians and sociologists see the rise of commercial capitalism as marking the end of the agrarian era. See, for example, Sanderson, *Social Transformations*, chap. 5. Although commercialism did spread during the 1500s and 1600s, it was not until the industrial revolution that the dominant political and social institutions of agrarian society gave way to new forms. This book thus takes the eighteenth century to be the key historical switching point.

19. B. R. Mitchell, *International Historical Statistics: Europe, 1750–1993* (London: Macmillan, 1998), p. 934; and David S. Landes, *The Unbound Prometheus: Technological Change and Industrial Development in Western Europe from 1750 to the Present* (New York: Cambridge University Press, 1969), pp. 187–188.

20. Needless to say, the industrial mode of production initially gave rise to many different types of states, including those with authoritarian governments and socialist economies. Most of these states, however, did not fare well during the course of the twentieth century, ultimately moving toward democracy and capitalism. For further discussion of the impact of industrial capitalism on political and social institutions, see Ralf Dahrendorf, *Class and Class Conflict in Industrial Society* (Stanford: Stanford University Press, 1959); Clark Kerr et al., *Industrialism and Industrial Man: The Problems of Labor and Management in Economic Growth* (Cambridge, Mass.: Harvard University Press, 1960); Anthony Giddens, *Sociology: A Brief but Critical Introduction* (New York: Harcourt Brace Jovanovich, 1982); and F. A. Hayek, *The Fatal Conceit: The Errors of Socialism* (Chicago: University of Chicago Press, 1988).

21. Gellner, *Nations and Nationalism*, p. 52.

22. As of 1998, farmworkers made up roughly 2 percent of the U.S. workforce and agricultural output represented roughly 1 percent of domestic product. Information on the U.S. workforce from Bureau of Labor Statistics, "Employees on Nonfarm Payrolls by Major Industry Division, Annual Averages, 1947–2000." Available at: http://www.bls.gov/opub/rtaw/pdf/table12.pdf. GDP figures from Bureau of Economic Analysis, "Gross Domestic Product by Industry in Current Dollars, 1947–99." Available at: http://www.bea.doc.gov/bea/dn2/gpo.htm. Number of farmworkers in the workforce from U.S. Bureau of Labor Statistics, "Agricultural Production." Available at: http://stats.bls.gov/oco/cg/cgs001.htm.

23. Using a narrower definition, in 1999 the service and financial sectors accounted for roughly 40 percent of GDP (21.5 percent from services, and 19.4 percent from finance, insurance, and real estate). If government, retail trade, and wholesale trade are included in the service sector, which they often are, the service sector and financial sector account for almost 70 percent of domestic product. It is difficult to estimate the percentage of overall economic output that could be considered produced by the digital sector of the economy. The manufacturing of computers, for example, is still counted as industrial output under current accounting procedures. The U.S. gov-

ernment is in the midst of revising these accounting procedures, a sign of the changing nature of the economy. For data, see Bureau of Economic Analysis, "Gross Domestic Product by Industry in Current Dollars, 1994–2000." Available at: http://
www.bea.doc.gov/bea/dn2/gpoc.htm#1994-2000.

24. U.S. Department of Commerce, "The Emerging Internet Economy II," June
1999, pp. 25–35. Available at: http://www.esa.doc.gov/esa/pdf/ED2report.pdf. Department of Commerce, "The Emerging Digital Economy," pp. 17, 28, 3–4. Available
at: http://www.esa.doc.gov/508/esa/pdf/EmergingDig.pdf.

25. The UCLA Internet Report, "Surveying the Digital Future," October 2000.
Available at: http://www.ccp.ucla.edu.

26. Cited in Sandel, *Democracy's Discontent*, p. 27.

27. Robert D. Putnam, *Bowling Alone: The Collapse and Revival of American Community* (New York: Simon & Schuster, 2000), pp. 46, 43.

28. Ibid., p. 238.

29. Critics point out that volunteering and charitable giving have not fallen off
and that political participation via the Internet has replaced more traditional forms of
participation. For assessments of the contending positions, see William A. Galston and
Peter Levine, "America's Civic Condition: A Glance at the Evidence," in *Community
Works: The Revival of Civil Society in America*, ed. E. J. Dionne, Jr. (Washington, D.C.:
Brookings Institution Press, 1998), pp. 30–36; and D. W. Miller, "Perhaps We Bowl
Alone, but Does It Really Matter?" *Chronicle of Higher Education*, July 16, 1999, pp.
A16–17.

30. Norman Nie and Lutz Erbring, "Internet and Society, A Preliminary Report,"
February, 17, 2000. Available at: http://www.stanford.edu/group/siqss/Press_
Release/Preliminary_Report.pdf.

31. See Cass Sunstein, *republic.com* (Princeton: Princeton University Press, 2001).

32. Joel Kotkin, *The New Geography: How the Digital Landscape Is Reshaping the
American Landscape* (New York: Random House, 2000), p. 169.

33. Putnam, *Bowling Alone*, pp. 342–343.

34. David Brooks, *Bobos in Paradise: The New Upper Class and How They Got
There* (New York: Simon & Schuster, 2000), p. 271.

35. Thomas Friedman, "Cyber-Serfdom," *New York Times*, January 30, 2001.

36. Data from David Leonhardt and Barbara Whitaker, "Higher Fuel Prices Do
Little to Alter Motorists' Habits," *New York Times*, October 10, 2000. See also Dianne
Feinstein and Olympia Snowe, "The Low Cost of Lowering Auto Emissions," *New
York Times*, August 1, 2001.

37. Putnam, *Bowling Alone*, p. 357, and chap. 14. See also Ted Halstead, "A Politics
for Generation X," *Atlantic Monthly*, vol. 284, no. 2 (August 1999), pp. 33–42.

38. Harris Poll data as analyzed in Putnam, *Bowling Alone*, p. 47.

39. Brooks, *Bobos in Paradise*, p. 271.

40. Federal Election Commission Candidate Summary Reports for the Bush and
Gore campaigns available at: http://herndon1.sdrdc.com/cgi-bin/cancomsrs/?_00
+P00003335 and http://herndon1.sdrdc.com/cgi-bin/cancomsrs/?_00+P80000912.
Television advertising expense statistics for the two campaigns available from the
Brennan Center for Justice, "Political Television Advertising for 2000 Campaign
(June 1–November 7)." Available at: http://www.brennancenter.org/cmagpdf/cmag
2000_wrapup.pdg.pdf. Estimates of total expenses for all 2000 federal elections from

Center for Responsive Politics, "Campaign Finance Reform." Available at: http://www.opensecrets.org/news/campaignfinance/index.asp. For Bloomberg's spending, see Michael Cooper, "At $92.60 a Vote, Bloomberg Shatters an Election Record," *New York Times,* December 4, 2001.

41. Don Van Natta, Jr., "Enron or Andersen Made Donations to Almost All Their Congressional Investigators," *New York Times,* January 25, 2002.

42. Cited in Sandel, *Democracy's Discontent,* p. 131.

43. Fox News, Fox Special Report with Brit Hume, "Interview with Dale Bumpers," July 20, 2001.

44. Albert R. Hunt, "Don't Stop at McCain-Feingold," *Wall Street Journal,* February 21, 2002.

45. See John B. Judis, *The Paradox of American Democracy: Elites, Special Interests, and the Betrayal of the Public Trust* (New York: Pantheon, 2000), chap. 5.

46. Cited in Putnam, *Bowling Alone,* p. 159.

47. See, for example, Paul Krugman, *Fuzzy Math: The Essential Guide to the Bush Tax Cut* (New York: Norton, 2001).

48. On the role that civic engagement plays in promoting societal health, see Putnam, *Bowling Alone,* chaps. 16–22.

49. Durkheim, *The Division of Labor in Society,* p. 201.

50. Kotkin, *The New Geography,* p. 3.

51. See D'Vera Cohn and Sarah Cohen, "Census Sees Vast Change in Language, Employment," *Washington Post,* August 6, 2001.

52. Putnam, *Bowling Alone,* p. 81.

53. Kotkin, *The New Geography,* p. 7.

54. Ibid., pp. 45, 64, 70.

55. Evelyn Nieves, "Blacks, Hit by Housing Costs, Leave San Francisco Behind," *New York Times,* August 2, 2001.

56. Nurith C. Aizenmen, "In Bowie, Race Is on the Agenda," *Washington Post,* April 9, 2001.

57. Anthony Walton, "Technology Versus African-Americans," *Atlantic Monthly,* vol. 283, no. 1 (January 1999), p. 18.

58. Robert D. Kaplan, *An Empire Wilderness: Travels into America's Future* (New York: Random House, 1998), p. 63.

59. Eric Schmitt, "Census Data Show a Sharp Increase in Living Standard," *New York Times,* August 6, 2001. See also Cohn and Cohen, "Census Sees Vast Change in Language, Employment."

60. Janny Scott, "Rethinking Segregation Beyond Black and White," *New York Times,* July 29, 2001. For a contrasting view, see Gregory Rodriquez, "Still, E Pluribus Unum," *San Diego Union-Tribune,* July 18, 1999.

61. Harvard Graduate School of Education, "School Segregation on the Rise Despite Growing Diversity Among School-Aged Children," July 19, 2001. Available at: http://www.gse.harvard.edu/news/features/orfield07172001.html.

62. See Putnam, *Bowling Alone,* map on p. 293.

63. Zell Miller, "The Democratic Party's Southern Problem," *New York Times,* June 4, 2001.

64. Kevin Sullivan, "U.S., Mexico Set Plan for a 'Smart Border,'" *Washington Post,* March 23, 2002.

65. Reed Karaim, "On Both Sides Now, the Costly Consequences of Vigilance," *Washington Post,* March 10, 2002.

66. Stephen Flynn, "Rethinking the U.S.-Canadian Border," *Buffalo News,* July 1, 2001.

67. Richard Holbrooke, interview on Fox News, Special Report with Brit Hume, October 19, 2001.

68. Kaplan, *An Empire Wilderness,* pp. 322–328. See also Joel Garreau, *The Nine Nations of North America* (Boston: Houghton Mifflin, 1981).

69. Kenichi Ohmae, "The Rise of the Region State," *Foreign Affairs,* vol. 72, no. 2 (Spring 1993), p. 78.

70. Arthur M. Schlesinger, Jr., *The Disuniting of America* (New York: Norton, 1992), p. 118.

71. Cited in Richard Morin and Claudia Deane, "Poll: Americans' Trust in Government Grows," *Washington Post,* September 28, 2001.

72. On the sources of this resilience, see John A. Hall and Charles Lindholm, *Is America Breaking Apart?* (Princeton: Princeton University Press, 1999).

73. See Sunstein, *republic.com,* pp. 170–172; and David Bollier, *Silent Theft: The Private Plunder of Our Common Wealth* (New York: Routledge, 2002).

74. James H. Snider, "E-Democracy as Deterrence: Public Policy Implications of a Deterrence Model of Democratic Accountability," paper presented at the 2001 Annual Meeting of the American Political Science Association. Available from: Snider@newamerica.net.

75. For a balanced evaluation of the ability of digital technology to strengthen participatory democracy, see Benjamin R. Barber, "Three Scenarios for the Future of Technology and Strong Democracy," *Political Science Quarterly,* vol. 113, no. 4 (Winter 1998–1999), pp. 573–589. See also Benjamin R. Barber, "Civil Society: Getting Beyond the Rhetoric—A Framework for Political Understanding," in *Civic Engagement in the Atlantic Community,* ed. Josef Janning, Charles Kupchan, and Dirk Rumberg (Gütersloh: Bertelsmann Foundation, 1999).

Select Bibliography

Adams, Charles F. *The Works of John Adams, Second President of the United States.* Boston: Little, Brown, 1850–1856.

Albecht-Carrié, René. *The Concert of Europe.* New York: Walker, 1969.

Anderson, Benedict. *Imagined Communities: Reflections on the Origin and Spread of Nationalism.* New York: Verso, 1991.

Angell, Norman. *The Great Illusion: A Study of the Relation of Military Power in Nations to Their Economic and Social Advantage.* New York: Putnam, 1910.

Art, Robert J. "Why Europe Needs the United States and NATO." *Political Science Quarterly,* vol. 111, no. 1 (Spring 1996), pp. 1–39.

Bailey, Thomas A. *Woodrow Wilson and the Great Betrayal.* New York: Macmillan, 1947.

Barber, Benjamin R. "Three Scenarios for the Future of Technology and Strong Democracy." *Political Science Quarterly,* vol. 113, no. 4 (Winter 1998–1999), pp. 573–589.

Berghahn, V. R. *Germany and the Approach of War in 1914.* New York: St. Martin's, 1973.

Bernstein, Richard, and Ross H. Munro. "The Coming Conflict with China." *Foreign Affairs,* vol. 76, no. 2 (March–April 1997), pp. 18–32.

Berry, Nicholas. "China Is Not an Imperialist Power." *Strategic Review,* vol. 24, no. 1 (Winter 2001), pp. 4–10.

Blinken, Antony J. "The False Crisis over the Atlantic." *Foreign Affairs,* vol. 80, no. 3 (May–June 2001), pp. 35–48.

Bollier, David. *Silent Theft: The Private Plunder of Our Common Wealth.* New York: Routledge, 2002.

Boyd, Julian P., ed. *The Papers of Thomas Jefferson.* Princeton: Princeton University Press, 1953.

Brendon, Piers. *The Dark Valley: A Panorama of the 1930s.* New York: Knopf, 2000.

Brooks, David. *Bobos in Paradise: The New Upper Class and How They Got There.* New York: Simon & Schuster, 2000.

Brown, Michael E., Sean M. Lynn-Jones, and Steven E. Miller, eds. *Debating the Democratic Peace.* Cambridge, Mass.: MIT Press, 1996.

Bury, J. B. *History of the Later Roman Empire: From the Death of Theodosius I to the Death of Justinian (A.D. 395 to A.D. 565)*. London: Macmillan, 1923.

Castlereagh, Robert Stewart. *Correspondence, Dispatches, and Other Papers of Viscount Castlereagh*. London: H. Colburn, 1850.

Chace, Robert S., Emily B. Hill, and Paul Kennedy. "Pivotal States and U.S. Strategy." *Foreign Affairs*, vol. 75, no. 1 (January–February 1996), pp. 33–51.

Connelly, Matthew, and Paul Kennedy. "Must It Be the Rest Against the West?" *Atlantic Monthly*, vol. 274, no. 6 (December 1994), pp. 61–83.

Crenshaw, Martha, ed. *Terrorism in Context*. University Park, Pa.: Penn State University Press, 1995.

Cronin, Bruce. *Community Under Anarchy: Transnational Identity and the Evolution of Cooperation*. New York: Columbia University Press, 1999.

Culver, John, and John Hyde. *American Dreamer: The Life and Times of Henry A. Wallace*. New York: Norton, 2000.

Daalder, Ivo H., and Michael E. O'Hanlon. *Winning Ugly: NATO's War to Save Kosovo*. Washington, D.C.: Brookings Institution Press, 2000.

Dahrendorf, Ralf. *Class and Class Conflict in Industrial Society*. Stanford, Calif.: Stanford University Press, 1959.

Dallek, Robert. *Franklin D. Roosevelt and American Foreign Policy, 1932–1945*. New York: Oxford University Press, 1979.

Davis, Kenneth. *FDR: The War President, 1940–1943*. New York: Random House, 2000.

DeConde, Alexander. *Entangling Alliance: Politics and Diplomacy Under George Washington*. Durham, N.C.: Duke University Press, 1958.

de la Garza, Rodolfo O., and Harry P. Pachon, eds. *Latinos and U.S. Foreign Policy: Representing the "Homeland"?* Lanham, Md.: Rowman & Littlefield, 2000.

Destler, I. M., and Steven Kull. *Misreading the Public: The Myth of a New Isolationism*. Washington, D.C.: Brookings Institution Press, 1999.

Deudney, Daniel H. "The Philadelphian System: Sovereignty, Arms Control, and Balance of Power in the American States-Union, Circa 1787–1861." *International Organization*, vol. 49, no. 2 (Spring 1995), pp. 191–228.

Diamond, Jared. *Guns, Germs, and Steel: The Fate of Human Societies*. New York: Norton, 1999.

Dionne, E. J., Jr. *Community Works: The Revival of Civil Society in America*. Washington, D.C.: Brookings Institution Press, 1998.

Divine, Robert A. *Roosevelt and World War II*. Baltimore: Johns Hopkins Press, 1969.
———. *Second Chance: The Triumph of Internationalism in America During World War II*. New York: Atheneum, 1967.

Doyle, Michael W. "Kant, Liberal Legacies, and Foreign Affairs." *Philosophy and Public Affairs*, vol. 12, nos. 3 and 4 (Summer and Fall 1983), pp. 205–235, pp. 323–353.

Droz, Jacques. *Europe Between the Revolutions, 1815–1848*. New York: Harper & Row, 1967.

Durkheim, Emile. *The Division of Labor in Society*. Translated by W. D. Halls. New York: Free Press, 1984.

Ellsworth, Harry Allanson. *One Hundred Eighty Landings of United States Marines, 1800–1934*. Washington, D.C.: History and Museums Division Headquarters, U.S. Marine Corps, 1974.

Elman, Miriam Fendius, ed. *Paths to Peace: Is Democracy the Answer?* Cambridge, Mass.: MIT Press, 1997.

Esposito, John L., and John O. Voll. *Islam and Democracy*. New York: Oxford University Press, 1998.

Etzold, Thomas H., and John Lewis Gaddis, eds. *Containment: Documents on American Policy and Strategy, 1945–1950*. New York: Columbia University Press, 1978.

Feaver, Peter D., and Richard H. Kohn. "The Gap: Soldiers, Civilians, and Their Mutual Misunderstanding." *National Interest*, no. 61 (Fall 2000), pp. 29–37.

Fischer, David Hackett. *Albion's Seed: Four British Folkways in America*. New York: Oxford University Press, 1989.

Fischer, Fritz. *World Power or Decline: The Controversy over Germany's Aims in the First World War*. Translated by Lancelot Farrar, Robert Kimber, and Rita Kimber. New York: Norton, 1974.

Friedberg, Aaron L. "Ripe for Rivalry: Prospects for Peace in a Multipolar Asia." *International Security*, vol. 18, no. 3 (Winter 1993–1994), pp. 5–33.

Friedman, Thomas L. *The Lexus and the Olive Tree*. New York: Farrar, Straus & Giroux, 1999.

Fukuyama, Francis. "The End of History?" *National Interest*, no. 16 (Summer 1989), pp. 3–18.

———. *The End of History and the Last Man*. New York: Free Press, 1992.

———. "Second Thoughts: The Last Man in a Bottle." *National Interest*, no. 56 (Summer 1999), pp. 16–33.

Gaddis, John Lewis. *The United States and the Origins of the Cold War, 1941–1947*. New York: Columbia University Press, 1972.

Galbraith, John Kenneth. *The Great Crash, 1929*. New York: Time Inc., 1961.

Gardner, Richard N. "The One Percent Solution." *Foreign Affairs*, vol. 79, no. 4 (July–August 2000), pp. 2–11.

Garraty, John A. *Henry Cabot Lodge: A Biography*. New York: Knopf, 1968.

Garreau, Joel. *The Nine Nations of North America*. Boston: Houghton Mifflin, 1981.

Gelber, Lionel M. *The Rise of Anglo-American Friendship: A Study in World Politics, 1898–1906*. London: Oxford University Press, 1938.

Gellner, Ernest. *Nations and Nationalism*. Ithaca: Cornell University Press, 1983.

Gholz, Eugene, Daryl G. Press, and Harvey M. Sapolsky. "Come Home, America: The Strategy of Restraint in the Face of Temptation." *International Security*, vol. 21, no. 4 (Spring 1997), pp. 5–48.

Gibbon, Edward. *The History of the Decline and Fall of the Roman Empire*. 7 vols. Edited with an introduction, notes, and appendices by J. B. Bury. 1909. Reprint, New York: AMS Press, 1974.

Giddens, Anthony. *Sociology: A Brief but Critical Introduction*. New York: Harcourt Brace Jovanovich, 1982.

Gilbert, Felix. *To the Farewell Address: Ideas of Early American Foreign Policy*. Princeton: Princeton University Press, 1961.

Gilbert, Martin. *The Roots of Appeasement*. London: Weidenfeld & Nicolson, 1966.

Gill, Bates, and Michael O'Hanlon. "China's Hollow Military." *National Interest*, no. 56 (Summer 1999), pp. 55–62.

Gilpin, Robert. *The Challenge of Global Capitalism: The World Economy in the 21st Century*. Princeton: Princeton University Press, 2000.

————. *War and Change in World Politics.* New York: Cambridge University Press, 1981.

Gordon, Michael R., and Bernard E. Trainor. *The Generals' War: The Inside Story of the Conflict in the Gulf.* Boston: Little, Brown, 1995.

Gould, Stephen Jay. *Time's Arrow, Time's Cycle: Myth and Metaphor in the Discovery of Geological Time.* Cambridge, Mass.: Harvard University Press, 1988.

Haass, Richard N. *The Reluctant Sheriff: The United States After the Cold War.* New York: Council on Foreign Relations Press, 1997.

Haggard, Stephan. *The Political Economy of the Asian Financial Crisis.* Washington, D.C.: Institute for International Economics, 2000.

Hall, John A., and Charles Lindholm. *Is America Breaking Apart?* Princeton: Princeton University Press, 1999.

Halstead, Ted. "A Politics for Generation X." *Atlantic Monthly,* vol. 284, no. 2 (August 1999), pp. 33–42.

Hayek, F. A. *The Fatal Conceit: The Errors of Socialism.* Chicago: University of Chicago Press, 1988.

Helms, Jesse. "Saving the U.N.: A Challenge to the Next Secretary-General." *Foreign Affairs,* vol. 75, no. 5 (September–October 1996), pp. 2–7.

Hietala, Thomas R. *Manifest Design: Anxious Aggrandizement in Late Jacksonian America.* Ithaca: Cornell University Press, 1985.

Horne, Alistair. *A Savage War of Peace: Algeria, 1954–1962.* New York: Viking Press, 1977.

Hunt, Michael H. *Ideology and U.S. Foreign Policy.* New Haven: Yale University Press, 1987.

Huntington, Samuel P. "The Clash of Civilizations?" *Foreign Affairs,* vol. 72, no. 3 (Summer 1993), pp. 22–49.

————. *The Clash of Civilizations and the Remaking of World Order.* New York: Simon & Schuster, 1996.

Ikenberry, G. John. *After Victory: Institutions, Strategic Restraint, and the Rebuilding of Order After Major Wars.* Princeton: Princeton University Press, 2001.

Janning, Josef, Charles Kupchan, and Dirk Rumberg, eds. *Civic Engagement in the Atlantic Community.* Gütersloh: Bertelsmann Foundation, 1999.

Jones, H. M. *The Later Roman Empire, 284–602: A Social, Economic and Administrative Survey.* Oxford: Blackwell, 1964.

Jones, Howard. *"A New Kind of War": America's Global Strategy and the Truman Doctrine in Greece.* New York: Oxford University Press, 1989.

Judis, John B. *The Paradox of American Democracy: Elites, Special Interests, and the Betrayal of the Public Trust.* New York: Pantheon, 2000.

Kant, Immanuel. *Perpetual Peace: A Philosophical Essay.* New York: Macmillan, 1917.

Kaplan, Robert D. *Balkan Ghosts: A Journey Through History.* New York: St. Martin's, 1993.

————. "The Coming Anarchy." *Atlantic Monthly,* vol. 273, no. 2 (February 1994), pp. 44–76.

————. *The Coming Anarchy: Shattering the Dreams of the Post Cold War.* New York: Random House, 2000.

————. *An Empire Wilderness: Travels into America's Future.* New York: Random House, 1998.

————. *The Ends of the Earth: A Journey at the Dawn of the 21st Century.* New York: Random House, 1996.

Kecskemeti, Paul, ed. *Essays on the Sociology of Knowledge.* London: Routledge & Kegan Paul, 1952.

Kedourie, Elie. *Nationalism.* London: Hutchinson, 1966.

Kennan, George Frost. *American Diplomacy.* Chicago: University of Chicago Press, 1984.

————. "The Sources of Soviet Conduct." *Foreign Affairs,* vol. 25, no. 4 (July 1947), pp. 566–582.

Kennedy, Paul M. *Preparing for the Twenty-first Century.* New York: Random House, 1993.

————. *The Rise and Fall of British Naval Mastery.* London: Macmillan, 1983.

————. *The Rise and Fall of the Great Powers: Economic Change and Military Conflict from 1500 to 2000.* New York: Random House, 1987.

Keohane, Robert O. *After Hegemony: Cooperation and Discord in the World Political Economy.* Princeton: Princeton University Press, 1984.

Kerr, Clark, John T. Dunlop, Frederick H. Harbison, and Charles A. Myers. *Industrialism and Industrial Man: The Problems of Labor and Management in Economic Growth.* Cambridge, Mass.: Harvard University Press, 1960.

Kindleberger, Charles P. *The World in Depression, 1929–1939.* Berkeley: University of California Press, 1973.

Kirschten, Dick. "Ethnics Resurging." *National Journal,* vol. 27, no. 8 (February 25, 1995), pp. 478–484.

Kissinger, Henry. *Diplomacy.* New York: Simon & Schuster, 1994.

Knock, Thomas J. *To End All Wars: Woodrow Wilson and the Quest for a New World Order.* New York: Oxford University Press, 1992.

Kotkin, Joel. *The New Geography: How the Digital Revolution Is Reshaping the American Landscape.* New York: Random House, 2000.

Krugman, Paul. *Fuzzy Math: The Essential Guide to the Bush Tax Cut.* New York: Norton, 2001.

Kupchan, Charles A. "After Pax Americana: Benign Power, Regional Integration, and the Sources of a Stable Multipolarity." *International Security,* vol. 23, no. 2 (Fall 1998), pp. 42–79.

————. *The Persian Gulf and the West: The Dilemmas of Security.* Boston: Allen & Unwin, 1987.

————. *The Vulnerability of Empire.* Ithaca: Cornell University Press, 1994.

————, ed. *Nationalism and Nationalities in the New Europe.* Ithaca: Cornell University Press, 1995.

Kupchan, Clifford A. "Devolution Drives Russian Reform." *Washington Quarterly,* vol. 23, no. 2 (Spring 2000), pp. 67–77.

LaFeber, Walter. *The American Age: United States Foreign Policy at Home and Abroad Since 1750.* New York: Norton, 1989.

————. *The New Empire: An Interpretation of American Expansion, 1860–1898.* Ithaca: Cornell University Press, 1963.

Lancaster, Carol. *Aid to Africa: So Much to Do, So Little Done.* Chicago: University of Chicago Press, 1999.

Landes, David S. *The Unbound Prometheus: Technological Change and Industrial*

Development in Western Europe from 1750 to the Present. New York: Cambridge University Press, 1969.

Legro, Jeffrey W. "Whence American Internationalism." *International Organization,* vol. 54, no. 2 (Spring 2000), pp. 253–289.

Leigh, Michael. *Mobilizing Consent: Public Opinion in American Foreign Policy, 1937–1947.* Westport, Conn.: Greenwood Press, 1976.

Lind, Michael. "Civil War by Other Means." *Foreign Affairs,* vol. 78, no. 5 (September–October 1999), pp. 123–142.

Lindsay, James M. "The New Apathy." *Foreign Affairs,* vol. 79, no. 5 (September–October 2000), pp. 2–8.

Lodge, Henry Cabot, ed. *The Works of Alexander Hamilton.* New York: Putnam, 1885–1886.

Luttwak, Edward N. *The Grand Strategy of the Roman Empire from the First Century A.D. to the Third.* Baltimore: Johns Hopkins University Press, 1976.

Madison, James, Alexander Hamilton, and John Jay. *The Federalist Papers.* Edited by Isaac Kramnick. London: Penguin Books, 1987.

Mannheim, Karl. "The Problem of Generations." In *Essays on the Sociology of Knowledge,* edited by Paul Kecskemeti. London: Routledge & Kegan Paul, 1952.

Marcellinus, Ammianus. *The Later Roman Empire, 284–602: A Social, Economic and Administrative Survery.* Harmondsworth, Middlesex: Penguin Books, 1986.

Martel, Gordon, ed. *American Foreign Relations Reconsidered, 1890–1993.* London: Routledge, 1994.

Marx, Karl. *Capital: A Critical Analysis of Capitalist Production.* Translated by Samuel Moore and Edward Aveling. London: Allen & Unwin, 1971.

May, Ernest R. *Imperial Democracy: The Emergence of America as a Great Power.* New York: Harcourt, Brace and World, 1961.

Mayer, William G. *The Changing American Mind: How and Why American Public Opinion Changed Between 1960 and 1988.* Ann Arbor: University of Michigan Press, 1992.

McCoy, Drew R. *The Elusive Republic: Political Economy in Jeffersonian America.* Chapel Hill: University of North Carolina Press, 1980.

McNeill, William H. *The Pursuit of Power: Technology, Armed Force, and Society Since A.D. 1000.* Chicago: University of Chicago Press, 1982.

———. *The Rise of the West: A History of the Human Community.* Chicago: University of Chicago Press, 1963.

Mead, Walter Russell. "The Jacksonian Tradition and American Foreign Policy." *National Interest,* no. 58 (Winter 1999–2000), pp. 5–29.

———. *Special Providence: American Foreign Policy and How It Changed the World.* New York: Knopf, 2001.

Mearsheimer, John J. "Back to the Future: Instability in Europe After the Cold War." *International Security,* vol. 15, no. 1 (Summer 1990), pp. 5–56.

———. *The Tragedy of Great Power Politics.* New York: Norton, 2001.

———. "Why We Will Soon Miss the Cold War." *Atlantic Monthly,* vol. 266, no. 2 (August 1990), pp. 35–50.

Mill, John Stuart. *Principles of Political Economy: With Some of Their Applications to Social Philosophy.* Fairfield, N.J.: Augustus M. Kelly Publishers, 1976.

Mitchell, B. R. *International Historical Statistics: Europe, 1750–1993*. London: Macmillan, 1998.

Modelski, George. *Long Cycles in World Politics*. Seattle: University of Washington Press, 1987.

Monnet, Jean. *Memoirs*. Translated by Richard Mayne. Garden City, N.Y.: Doubleday, 1978.

Moravcsik, Andrew. *The Choice for Europe: Social Purpose and State Power from Messina to Maastricht*. Ithaca: Cornell University Press, 1998.

————. "Despotism in Brussels?" *Foreign Affairs*, vol. 80, no. 3 (May–June 2001), pp. 114–122.

Murray, Williamson. *The Change in the European Balance of Power, 1938–1939: The Path to Ruin*. Princeton: Princeton University Press, 1984.

Nicholas, H. G., ed. *Washington Dispatches 1941–1945: Weekly Political Reports from the British Embassy*. Chicago: University of Chicago Press, 1981.

Nordlinger, Eric A. *Isolationism Reconfigured: American Foreign Policy for a New Century*. Princeton: Princeton University Press, 1995.

Nye, Joseph S., Jr. *Bound to Lead: The Changing Nature of American Power*. New York: Basic Books, 1990.

————. "Globalization's Democratic Deficit: How to Make International Institutions More Accountable." *Foreign Affairs*, vol. 80, no. 4 (July–August 2001), pp. 2–6.

————. *The Paradox of American Power: Why the World's Only Superpower Can't Go It Alone*. New York: Oxford University Press, 2002.

————. *Peace in Parts: Integration and Conflict in Regional Organization*. Boston: Little, Brown, 1971.

Ohmae, Kenichi. "The Rise of the Region State." *Foreign Affairs*, vol. 72, no. 2 (Spring 1993), pp. 78–87.

Paine, Thomas. *Collected Writings*. New York: Literary Classics of the United States, 1995.

Papayoanou, Paul A. *Power Ties: Economic Interdependence, Balancing, and War*. Ann Arbor: University of Michigan Press, 1999.

Parsons, Talcott. *The Evolution of Societies*. Englewood Cliffs, N.J.: Prentice-Hall, 1977.

Perkins, Dexter. *Hands Off: A History of the Monroe Doctrine*. Boston: Little, Brown, 1941.

Pflanze, Otto. *Bismarck and the Development of Germany*. Princeton: Princeton University Press, 1990.

Polanyi, Karl. *The Great Transformation: The Political and Economic Origins of Our Time*. Boston: Beacon Press, 1957.

Potter, David M. *The Impending Crisis, 1848–1861*. New York: Harper & Row, 1976.

Putnam, Robert D. *Bowling Alone: The Collapse and Revival of American Community*. New York: Simon & Schuster, 2000.

Reilly, John E., ed. *American Public Opinion and U.S. Foreign Policy 1999*. Chicago: Chicago Council on Foreign Relations, 1999.

Reynolds, David. *From Munich to Pearl Harbor: Roosevelt's America and the Origins of the Second World War*. Chicago: Ivan R. Dee, 2001.

Risse-Kappen, Thomas. *Cooperation Among Democracies: The European Influence on U.S. Foreign Policy*. Princeton: Princeton University Press, 1997.

Rock, William R. *British Appeasement in the 1930s*. London: Edward Arnold, 1977.

Rohl, J. C. G. *From Bismarck to Hitler: The Problem of Continuity in German History*. New York: Barnes & Noble, 1970.

Rose, J. H., A. P. Newton, and E. A. Benians. *The Cambridge History of the British Empire*. Cambridge: The University Press, 1929.

Ross, Robert S. "Beijing as a Conservative Power." *Foreign Affairs*, vol. 76, no. 2 (March–April 1997), pp. 33–44.

Rothermund, Dietmar. *The Global Impact of the Great Depression, 1929–1939*. London: Routledge, 1996.

Russett, Bruce M. *Grasping the Democratic Peace: Principles for a Post–Cold War World*. Princeton: Princeton University Press, 1993.

Sandel, Michael J. *Democracy's Discontent: America in Search of a Public Philosophy*. Cambridge, Mass.: Harvard University Press, 1996.

Sanderson, Stephen K. *Social Transformations: A General Theory of Historical Development*. Cambridge, Mass.: Blackwell, 1995.

Scarre, Chris. *Chronicle of the Roman Emperors: The Reign-by-Reign Record of the Rulers of Imperial Rome*. London: Thames & Hudson, 1995.

Schlesinger, Arthur M., Jr. *The Cycles of American History*. Boston: Houghton Mifflin, 1986.

————. *The Disuniting of America*. New York: Norton, 1992.

Segev, Tom. *One Palestine, Complete: Jews and Arabs Under the British Mandate*. Translated by Haim Watzman. New York: Metropolitan Books, 2000.

Sen, Amartya. *Development as Freedom*. New York: Knopf, 1999.

Shiller, Robert J. *Irrational Exuberance*. Princeton: Princeton University Press, 2000.

Smith, Tony. *Foreign Attachments: The Power of Ethnic Groups in the Making of American Foreign Policy*. Cambridge, Mass.: Harvard University Press, 2000.

Snyder, Jack L. *From Voting to Violence: Democratization and Nationalist Conflict*. New York: Norton, 2000.

Sperling, Gene B. "Toward Universal Education." *Foreign Affairs*, vol. 80, no. 5 (September–October, 2001), pp. 7–13.

Sprout, Harold, and Margaret Sprout. *The Rise of American Naval Power, 1776–1918*. Annapolis, Md.: Naval Institute Press, 1990.

Sunstein, Cass. *republic.com*. Princeton: Princeton University Press, 2001.

Takeuchi, Tatsuji. *War and Diplomacy in the Japanese Empire*. Garden City, N.Y.: Doubleday, 1935.

Thatcher, Margaret. *The Downing Street Years*. New York: HarperCollins, 1993.

Treverton, Gregory F. *America, Germany, and the Future of Europe*. Princeton: Princeton University Press, 1992.

Trubowitz, Peter. *Defining the National Interest: Conflict and Change in American Foreign Policy*. Chicago: University of Chicago Press, 1998.

Turner, Frederick Jackson. *The Early Writings of Frederick Jackson Turner*. Compiled by Everett E. Edwards. Madison: University of Wisconsin Press, 1938.

————. *The Frontier in American History*. New York: Holt, Rhinehart & Winston, 1962.

Vasiliev, A. A. *History of the Byzantine Empire, 324–1453*. Madison: University of Wisconsin Press, 1952.

Walker, Martin. "Overstretching Teutonia: Making the Best of the Fourth Reich." *World Policy Journal,* vol. 12, no. 1 (Spring 1995), pp. 1–18.

Walt, Stephen M. *The Origins of Alliances.* Ithaca: Cornell University Press, 1987.

Walton, Anthony. "Technology Versus African-Americans." *Atlantic Monthly,* vol. 283, no. 1 (January 1999), pp. 14–18.

Waltz, Kenneth N. "The Emerging Structure of International Politics." *International Security,* vol. 18, no. 2 (Fall 1993), pp. 44–79.

Webster, Charles K. *The Foreign Policy of Castlereagh, 1812–1815: Britain and the Reconstruction of Europe.* London: G. Bell, 1931.

Wohlforth, William C. "The Stability of a Unipolar World." *International Security,* vol. 24, no. 1 (Summer 1999), pp. 5–41.

Woodward, C. Vann. "The Age of Reinterpretation." *American Historical Review,* vol. 66, no. 1 (October 1960), pp. 1–19.

Yergin, Daniel. *Shattered Peace: The Origins of the Cold War and the National Security State.* Boston: Houghton Mifflin, 1977.

Zakaria, Fareed. *From Wealth to Power: The Unusual Origins of America's World Role.* Princeton: Princeton University Press, 1998.

Index